ARMIES AND POLITICS

By the same author

Time to Change Course
New Theories of Revolution
An Introduction to Neo-Colonialism
Africa, the Way Ahead
Africa, the Lion Awakes
Africa, the Roots of Revolt
Under the Red Duster
Editor: Ho Chi Minh, Selected Articles and Speeches

ARMIES AND POLITICS

by

Jack Woddis

INTERNATIONAL PUBLISHERS, New York

First published by Lawrence & Wishart 1977

Copyright © Jack Woddis 1977

First American edition published by I.P.N.Y., 1978

Library of Congress Cataloging in Publication Data

Woddis, Jack.
  Armies and politics.

  Includes index.
    1. Sociology, Military. 2. Coups d'état.
  3. Social conflict. 4. Social classes. I. Title.
U21.5.W58   301.5'93   77–11724
ISBN 0–7178–0495–X

Printed in Great Britain

Contents

1 Coups – Right, Left and Centre   7
2 The Army and Political Power   16
3 Can the Army Act Independently of Classes?   38
4 External and Internal Factors   48
5 Coups and Conspiracies   56
6 Why Progressive Military Coups Take Place   66
7 Officers and Social Class   78
8 Sudan – Coup and Counter-coup   100
9 Why Reactionary Coups Succeed   123
10 The Indonesian Catastrophe   131
11 Chile – Why the Coup Succeeded   154
12 Portugal – An Army Won and Lost   214
13 Western Europe – Aligning the Army with the People   248
14 Lessons for Britain – and Warnings from Northern Ireland   275
   Index   303

Acknowledgements are due to numerous individuals who assisted me with information, drew my attention to particular sources, and provided me with many stimulating ideas. I was particularly aided by a large body of translators, far too numerous to mention by name, who translated texts from Spanish, Portuguese, Italian, French, German and Arabic. Several people were very helpful, too, in making suggestions on democratic reforms in the British Armed Forces, which contributed considerably to my thoughts in the final chapter.

To all these individuals, who can in no way be held responsible for any shortcomings in the book, I am truly grateful.

JACK WODDIS

London,
1 March 1977

I

Coups – Right, Left and Centre

In Colombia there is an old joke or saying which has an Army
officer asking a retiring brother officer: 'And what do you intend
to do now, after you retire?' And the other cocks a surprised brow
and replies, '*Pues claro, hombre, conspirar!*'[*][1]

Military plots, *coups d'état*, assassinations have become so commonplace
in the last decade, especially in the Third World,[2] that news of a coup
and a forcible change of government in Africa, Asia or Latin America
becomes increasingly less and less of a shock as one president is toppled
after another and yet one more government bites the dust.

But while the immediate impact may be less each time, the
questioning and the probing into the cause of this phenomenon increases;
and to this understandable desire to comprehend the causes of these
sudden political convulsions in the Third World is now added a new
interest or anxiety and concern, namely the political role of the armed
forces in developed capitalist countries, not only in those European
countries whose industrial achievements lag behind – such as Spain,
Greece and Portugal – but in the advanced capitalist countries, too, in
Great Britain, France, Italy and in others.

Since the Second World War it is undoubtedly the Third World that
has been the main scene of military coups, of open military intervention
in political life, the establishment of military governments or the
installation of military presidents, sometimes accompanied by the
dissolution of political parties and heavy restrictions on the democratic
activity of civilian society (as in Uganda), at other times buttressed by a
single party political system (as in Zaire under General Mobutu).

One has only to look at the factual evidence to appreciate immediately
the extent of this problem. Eliezer Be'eri[3] enumerates thirty-seven coups
and coup attempts by Arab army officers between the years 1936 and
1967. Another calculation provides a total of eighty-three coups and
attempted coups in the Middle East between the years 1945 and 1972.[4]
The form that these coups took was varied, and so were their targets.

* 'Conspire, of course, man!'

Some were against civilian governments, others against existing military rulers. Some replaced military regimes by new military dictatorships, others paved the way for military-civilian or purely civilian rule. In some cases the new government which assumed power was worse than the one it replaced; in others it was an improvement, even substantially so.

In Africa, an analysis made in 1968[5] showed thirty-two coups and attempted coups in the short period between 1963 and September 1968. Since then there have been a number of other coups and attempted coups in Africa, including the overthrow of President Modibo Keita in Mali (19 November 1968); the military overthrow of the monarchy in Libya (September 1969); the military coup in Somalia (21 October 1969); the seizure of power from President Obote of Uganda by Major-General Idi Amin (25 January 1971); an abortive coup in Sierra Leone (23 March 1971); the coup and counter-coup in the Sudan in July 1971 (following the earlier coup in 1969); the military coup against the Busia government in Ghana (13 January 1972); the assumption of power in Malagasy by a new government headed by Major-General Ramanantsoa (19 May 1972; though this was an action backed by strikes and mass demonstrations in the capital and not just limited to activity by the military); the assassination of Sheikh Abeid Karume in Zanzibar (April 1972); an attempted military coup to restore Dr Busia in Ghana (14 July 1972); a military coup in Dahomey (26 October 1972); one in Ruanda (5 July 1973); the overthrow of the Emperor and his system in Ethiopia in 1974; and so on. These additional coups would give a grand total of some fifty coups, successful and unsuccessful, on the African continent in a space of little over a decade.

Writing in Le Monde (5 August 1970), Philippe Decraene pointed out that, in the ten years since the French-speaking African territories had gained their independence, only seven out of the seventeen African statesmen who had led their countries to independence before or in 1960 were then still in power. Perhaps even more significant for our study, eight of the ten new presidents were by then army officers, while in the remaining two territories affected, namely in Gabon and Dahomey, where the governments were officially civilian, the army was playing a major role.

As in the case of the Arab countries, the coups in Africa have varied considerably as to their aims and their character, some paving the way for positive political developments, others turning back the political clock.

In South and South-East Asia there have also been a number of coups and coup attempts in recent years, including two in Pakistan (Ayub Khan and later Yayha Khan), several attempts in Sri Lanka, a coup in Burma, one in Thailand, several in Bangla-Desh, and one in Indonesia in September 1965, in the course of which some 500,000 people were massacred. As a result of this last coup all the top posts in the government and state apparatus were occupied by the military who took the positions of President, eighteen ministers, eleven of the twenty security generals, twenty-three out of fifty-seven chief directors of government departments, and one third of the members of parliament. Understandably it was said in Indonesia following the coup: 'Once we were governed by one hundred Ministers, now we are governed by one hundred Generals.'

For the whole of Asia (excluding the Middle East), Gavin Kennedy's count provides forty-two coups and attempted coups for the period 1945 to 1972.[6]

In Latin America the military coup has been such a marked feature in a number of countries over many years that to many people in Europe who do not know why this happens it appears almost a way of life, even often a subject to be laughed at, though it is in no sense a joke for the people concerned.

The military coup in Bolivia in 1964 was listed as the 180th coup in Bolivia's 139 years of history. Since then Bolivia has experienced two further coups, followed by two unsuccessful attempts which ended in the overthrow of the government of General Torres. His successor, too, has been the target of a number of military attempts to remove him. In Honduras, in the 125 years prior to 1950, the government changed hands 115 times, mostly as a result of coups. The last thirty years have not changed the general pattern in Latin America, a count of seventeen countries there showing sixty-eight coups for the period 1943 to 1963.

In the last few years military governments in Latin America, such as of Brazil (since the coup of 1964) and of Argentina (up to the time of Peron's return in 1973 and then again subsequently, especially after Peron's death), have played a dominant role. The year 1973 witnessed two major counter-revolutionary coups – one in Uruguay carried out by the existing President in order to stifle the growing clamour of discontent and crush the organised opposition, especially grouped around the Frente Amplio (Broad Front); and the other, the savage military-fascist coup in Chile against President Allende and the Popular Unity Government. Latin America, in recent years, has been the scene also of the assumption of power by military governments of a different type, as in Peru, Panama and Ecuador, where, in all three cases and in varying degree, policies have been adopted aimed at weakening the positions of US imperialism and the major foreign monopolies, and of initiating some progressive social and economic reforms. Subsequent developments, however, have demonstrated the impermanency of these changes.

The clearly established prevalence of military coups and military governments in the Third World, especially in the last thirty years, should not lead us into thinking that the direct or indirect political intervention of the military into politics is a phenomenon confined to these countries. The lessons of the twentieth century in the United States and especially in Europe should be sufficient not to lead us into such a false assumption, based largely as it is on the mythical impartiality of the State and its armed forces in the Western world. It is true that direct military intervention in Europe has not in this century been so frequent nor generally so overtly decisive in political affairs as in the countries of the Third World. But this to a considerable extent arose in the first half of this century from the strength of capitalism and its State in the major capitalist countries, and in the resultant relative stability of the social system over this whole period. It is noticeable that where capitalism was weaker or where the stability of the system had begun to break down, open political intervention by the armed forces took place, even in some of the strongest capitalist states. In more recent years several new factors have emerged. The strength of the working-class and democratic movement in a number of West European countries, the world relationship of political forces, and the subsequent changes within the armed forces themselves, have made direct political intervention by the armed forces a more hazardous operation. Not that it is to be entirely ruled out; but ruling circles in the major European capitalist centres, as well as the top military echelon, have now to face new restraints on their actions.

The deep crisis which overtook capitalist Europe after the October 1917 revolution in Russia and following the ending of the Second World War saw a sharp turn towards repressive regimes in a number of countries in which the role of the military was considerably pronounced. It is not without significance that military coups or the installation of military or military-civilian governments took place mainly in the less developed capitalist countries — Marshal Mannerheim's military dictatorship in Finland, Pilsudski's in Poland, and Admiral Horthy's in Hungary, to be followed in 1926 by the fascist coup in Portugal which military collaboration made possible. Later military-fascist regimes in Spain under Franco and in Greece after the 1967 coup are further illustrations of the direct political role of the military in less developed capitalist countries of Europe.

The example of Italy and the advent of fascism in 1922 is also instructive here. Italy at that time was certainly a more developed capitalist country than post-1918 Finland, Poland or Hungary, but she was still relatively undeveloped compared with Germany, Britain or France. Furthermore, the post-1918 years in Italy were years of mass discontent, marked by a growing wave of revolutionary feeling as evidenced particularly by the occupation of the factories. These mass actions of the working people rendered unstable Italy's political system. Under these conditions, the military stepped on to the political scene and played a major role in assisting the setting up of fascist terror gangs to suppress the workers and peasants.

The army authorities supplied arms. Professional officers trained the bands and directed operations. The General Staff issued a circular (20 October 1920) instructing Divisional Commanders to support the Fascist organisations.[7]

The American journalist, Edgar Mowrer, wrote:

From the army the Fascists received sympathy, assistance and war material. Officers in uniform took part in punitive expeditions. The Fascists were allowed to turn national barracks into their private arsenals.[8]

When the final stages of preparation for the fascist take-over were complete in 1922, it was the combined action of the King, the Government and the army chiefs which hammered the last nail into the coffin. The mythical 'March on Rome' allegedly led by Mussolini was in fact organised by six army generals, and on the very eve of the 'March' the Italian Commander-in-Chief addressed a mass rally of the fascists. Declaring martial law, the Government handed over control to the military who, in their turn, permitted the fascists to occupy railways, postal and telegraphic offices and other public buildings. This done, the King announced that he had refused to sign the martial law decree, martial law was withdrawn, the Government resigned and Mussolini and his fascists took over.

Thus the armed forces in Italy played a major role in enabling the fascist take-over. The combination of political reaction, the army and other sections of the state proved too strong for the workers. This experience was not lost on the young Communist Party, and later strategies and tactics worked out by Gramsci and Togliatti and developed further by the present leadership of the Italian Communist Party have, as we shall examine later, taken fully into account the role of the armed forces in modern society.

In Germany, the military has openly and emphatically intervened in political life twice in the last sixty years, each time to assist the ruling capitalist class to maintain its power in the face of a growing challenge, primarily from the working class. Thus once again the myth of the neutral and impartial character of the armed forces stands exposed. It may appear, in normal political times, that, the army is outside politics, but when the political system is being seriously challenged and faces a major crisis, military intervention, on a larger or lesser scale, is usually resorted to by the rulers, *providing that they think such a drastic step has become necessary and providing that they believe that the existing circumstances make it possible for such a measure to succeed.*

Thus, after the overthrow of the old German state in November 1918 it was the combination of the role of the right-wing Social Democratic leaders and the active intervention of the most reactionary monarchist officers at the head of the counter-revolutionary Freikorps that led to the murder of Karl Liebknecht and Rosa Luxemburg and the defeat of the 1918 revolution. Giving evidence in a libel case in Munich in November 1925, General Groener, who had been Chief of the German General Staff at the time of the November Revolution, stated that an alliance had been established in 1918 between the Social Democrat President of Germany, Ebert, and the reactionary General Staff:

On November 10, 1918, I had a telephone conversation with Ebert, and we concluded an alliance to fight Bolshevism and Sovietism and restore law and order. . . . Every day between 11 p.m. and 1 a.m. the staff of the High Command talked to Ebert on a special secret telephone. . . .[9]

Thus, with the direct aid of reactionary army officers the workers were suppressed and the 1918 revolution aborted. In all the counter-revolutionary actions of the 1920s – the Kapp putsch in 1920 and the ensuing terror in the Ruhr against the workers who had defended the republic, the Horsing terror in Saxony in 1921, the military overthrow of the elected Zeigner Government in Saxony in 1923 – Germany's reactionary military officers played a key role in maintaining the rule of the big German bankers and industrialists.

As with 1918 and the ensuing years, so in the period leading up to Germany's second period of crisis and political challenge, in the late

1920s and early 1930s, the military intervened to prop up capitalism and crush democracy and the workers' movement. The emergence of fascism in Germany and its assumption of power in 1933 had a variety of reasons which it is not the purpose of this study to analyse. Suffice it to point to the post-Versailles crisis of German capitalism, the incredible inflation, the mass unemployment, the failure, in fact refusal, of the right-wing Social Democrat leaders to organise the working people to stop Germany's drift to the right, first under the Brüning dictatorship and then under that of von Papen, and the refusal of the Social Democrat leaders to form a united front with the Communists to oppose fascism, a failure to which sectarian tactics by the Communists themselves partly contributed.

Under these conditions the main thrust of German big business, which was to hoist fascism into power, was carried forward. The fascist movement led by Hitler, with the aid of unparalleled national and social demagogy, effected by a combination of mysticism appealing to the people's deepest and most primitive instincts, and radical slogans reminiscent of those of socialism itself, won a mass base for itself among wide strata of the people, including among backward workers. This success would not have been possible without its accompanying terror against the most militant sections of the workers and without its anti-semitic outrages. The latter performed the double service of providing a diversion and, at the same time, enabling the fascist stormtroops to become 'blooded' so that in their new brutalised role they were ready to undertake violent attacks against all opponents – workers, democrats, intellectuals.

Essential to bring the fascists to power was also financial backing and, on the part of the State institutions, as least their benign behaviour if not direct connivance. In all this the armed forces occupied a key position, for it they had stood as a force to defend democracy against the fascist assault the outcome could have been different. But the German armed forces, officered by some of the most conservative, bigoted, hide-bound, anti-working class and anti-democratic elements in German society, had no interest in standing on the side of democracy and the workers and against fascism and the big industrialists, bankers and landlords. Quite apart from the role of individual officers or ex-officers in the 1920 Kapp putsch and the counter-revolutionary Freikorps, the armed forces, as a State institution, were to play a decisive role in bringing fascism to power in Germany. Hitler himself recounted in his autobiography, how he first came into contact with the National Socialist Party (then in its first form as the 'German Labour Party' in 1919) under orders from Army headquarters.

Having played a key role in paving the way for the installation of the Nazis in power in 1933, the German officer class as well as the army as an institution became a decisive factor in the maintenance of Hitler's terror regime at home as well as in the prosecution of his aggressive and barbarous wars against the people of Europe, starting with the savage intervention against the Spanish Republic in 1936 and culminating in the massive onslaught against the Soviet Union in 1941. All subsequent evidence demonstrates beyond all doubt that, whatever opposition may have been expressed by a minority of the officers as Hitler's gamble became increasingly exposed and as defeat came ever nearer, the leaders of the German army and above all its General Staff remained to the very end firm supporters of the fascist regime.

In the last two decades, in Europe as well as in the Third World, the role of the military in politics has become very pronounced. We have already indicated the extent to which the armed forces have carried out coups in the Third World, and installed military governments. The heavy weight of the Pentagon in American politics, its links with big business and especially the modern arms industry, its considerable influence in the universities[10] is so well known as not to warrant detailed treatment here. The political tension in the French army at the time of the ending of the Algerian war in 1960, the bringing in of the army as a force of political intimidation during the 1968 French general strike, the 1967 colonel's coup in Greece and the later disastrous attempt of the fascist-inclined Greek officers to overthrow President Makarios in Cyprus, the constant warnings of dangerous collaboration between Italian fascists and certain high-ranking officers in the Italian armed forces, the repressive role of the British army in Northern Ireland since 1970, and, in sharp contrast, the radical participation of the Armed Forces Movement in Portugal's post-Caetano democratic revolution – all these are sufficient to indicate how important the armed forces have become in the evolution of political developments in Europe today.

NOTES

1 Quoted from V. L. Fluharty, *Dance of the Millions: Military Rule and Social Revolution in Colombia*, Pittsburg, 1957, p. 308.
2 The term 'Third World' used in this book refers to the non-socialist countries of Asia, Africa, the Middle East and Latin America (as well as some scattered islands lying

midway between the continents). These are termed 'Third' in contrast to the socialist countries on the one hand, and the industrialised, advanced capitalist and imperialist countries on the other. The reason for placing the 'Third World' countries in a different category is that while they are certainly not yet socialist and cannot be counted as part of the socialist world, neither are they imperialist but in fact are themselves victims of imperialist exploitation to a varying degree, in one form or another. Moreover, the peoples of the 'Third World' and in some cases their governments are increasingly striving to take their countries out of the imperialist orbit, thus creating the possibility of socialist development.

This categorisation has nothing in common with the theories of those who, embracing the idea of a 'Third Way', believe that it is possible to evolve some new form of social organisation and political system which is neither capitalist nor socialist. Neither is it meant to include the unscientific concept put forward by the Chinese Communist leaders that there is a 'First World' comprising 'two super-powers', the United States and the Soviet Union, a 'Second World' comprising other capitalist countries, and a 'Third World' of Asia, Africa and Latin America which, in addition to its majority of non-socialist countries, also includes socialist states such as China.

3 Eliezer Be'eri, *Army Officers in Arab Politics and Society*, London, 1970, p. 243.
4 Gavin Kennedy, *The Military in the Third World*, London, 1974, Appendix A.
5 See Jack Woddis, 'Military Coups in Africa', *Marxism Today*, December 1968.
6 op. cit.
7 R. P. Dutt, *Fascism and Social Revolution*, London, 1934, p. 102.
8 E. A. Mowrer, *Immortal Italy*, New York, 1922, p. 144.
9 See Dutt, op. cit., p. 112.
10 See Jack Woddis, *New Theories of Revolution*, London, 1972, pp. 325–30.

2

The Army and Political Power

To understand the role of the armed forces in the total system of political power one must first consider the nature of political power itself. What is political power? And what are its main pillars? Moreover, do the different instruments of political power possess permanently the same degree of importance relative to one another, or do they, at different phases of class conflict, become of greater or lesser significance according to the nature and stage of the conflict itself?

These are fundamental questions which require prior examination if we are fully to comprehend the particular and changing role of the armed forces in the total political systems of which they are part. Additionally, it is essential to consider these questions because, on the one hand reformists, liberals and conservatives tend to argue as if political power rested solely or almost entirely with parliament and government, while some of ultra-left views, on the other hand, tend to dismiss parliament and parliamentary government as virtually irrelevant, and to see political power in the somewhat simplified form of an armed institution ready to repress and shoot down anyone who challenges it. Lenin wrote in *Letters on Tactics*, in April 1917:

For we have always known and repeatedly pointed out, the bourgeoisie maintains itself in power *not* only by force but also by virtue of the lack of class consciousness and organisation, the routinism and downtrodden state of the masses.[1]

On another occasion he expressed the view that *political power is the ability to compel by force if necessary*. These definitions of Lenin's certainly embrace the idea of force or coercion as an element of political power, but they go beyond this. Machiavelli argued that State political power rested on a combination of 'coercion and consent'.[2] Machiavelli's concept, which contains certain elements of Lenin's, was taken up by Gramsci, and has recently been drawn on by Enrico Berlinguer when discussing the lessons of the coup against the Allende Government in Chile.[3]

Taken together, these different formulations help us to understand the nature of political power. Although in each case the conception may contain a different emphasis, all of them contain a certain common kernel, namely that 'force' or 'coercion' or 'compulsion' is an essential element of political power but that 'consent' or acceptance by a substantial part of the population, even when gained by deception, is also essential.

Basically that power rests on the fact that the ownership of the means of production, distribution and exchange (i.e. of the factories, land, shops and banks) is in the hands of private capitalists, mainly powerful ones. It is this economic basis that gives rise to the political power being in the hands of the most powerful monopolies. How does this power operate in an advanced capitalist country such as Britain?

There are three main pillars of power at the disposal of the monopoly capitalists. These three pillars are inter-related, and it is their combination that makes it possible for the ruling class to maintain its domination of our society.

First, there is power over people's minds, the power of ideas which partly by people's force of habit in their thoughts and actions, and partly by deception (which today, with the power of the mass media, has become a major weapon), wins or seduces the majority into accepting the *status quo*. It is this power which enables the rulers to gain the 'consent', the acceptance, of the ruled, which is a reality even when gained by duplicity.

Secondly, there is power exercised through parliament and government, and through the State, which in a bourgeois-democratic country such as Britain is, constitutionally, subject to the authority of parliament and government. Of special signficance is the power of the ruling class over the State institutions of coercion – the legal apparatus, the police, prisons and armed forces. Other parts of the State, the ministries, government departments, and upper echelons of the Civil Service, perform a certain supporting role in the functioning of the coercive side of the State (e.g. the immigration authorities, customs and taxation departments, etc.), but equally play a role in securing the people's acceptance of measures which are often very much against their real interests.

Thirdly, there is economic power, the private ownership of the commanding heights of the economy by the big banks, big industrial monopolies, and big landlords and property companies. This economic power naturally gives these forces the opportunity to influence the main pattern of economic policy in the country; but economic power does not exercise a purely economic function. It plays a role, too, in the exercise of coercion in the sense that pressures and sanctions (dismissals of individual militants, mass redundancies, lock-outs or threats of closure) can be used to compel workers to accept wages and conditions which probably they would otherwise not accept. (The fear of eviction can play the same role in relation to tenants and landlords.) Economic power also enables the monopolies to establish media power (commercial radio and television, films, newspapers and journals), which assist them to win the 'consent' of a majority of people, aided by a combination of deception, demagogy and distortion. Economic power and the wealth derived therefrom also enables the big monopolies to establish and maintain political parties and other subsidiary political and research bodies, which again play a part in the total system of political power.

In the same way, the coercive arms of the State are themselves part of the ideological strength of the ruling class.[4] People's awareness that the army, police and the law are not really on their side, are not really at their disposal or ready to act in their defence, can become a serious inhibiting factor for many of them, a form of weakening their resistance so that they come to accept the *status quo*. On the other hand, among more conservative sections of the population uncritical acceptance of the myth of the impartiality of the State, and a consequent belief that the existing 'law and order' must be maintained, renders them consenting supporters of the existing system, even to the point of becoming more ready to support a right-wing backlash.

All three pillars of power in capitalist Britain are therefore interconnected, each one reinforcing the other, and each playing an additional role beyond its own main function. Under 'normal' conditions of bourgeois democracy, as in Britain, the ruling class maintains its domination of society *mainly* by its ability to persuade a majority to accept the existing system. Yet, at all times, bourgeois democracy in Britain is based on the rule of the big bourgeoisie itself, despite the democratic gains secured by the working people after centuries of struggle.

Thus, even in the outwardly most democratic systems of capitalist democracy, State power and particularly its coercive aspects are ever present to back up capitalist domination; and when the ability of the rulers to maintain the people's acceptance begins to falter, they increasingly seek to make more pronounced use of coercive measures, although whether they can use these measures or not is, of course, another matter.

If State political power rests on a combination of coercion and 'consent', with different pillars of power functioning interchangeably in each sphere, then clearly the relation of class forces at any given stage influences the extent to which greater reliance is placed by the ruling class on coercion or 'consent'.

In Russia, in 1917, as Gramsci has stressed, the main problem of the revolution was to overthrow the State power of a small ruling class whose domination was based mainly on repression, and where it had not been able to build up a system of firm, extensive alliances with other classes. Thus the problem was to shatter, with a violent, powerful blow, the system of coercion of an isolated, small class.

In Western Europe, however, argued Gramsci, the situation was, in the main, very different:

In Russia the State was everything, civil society was primordial and gelatinous; in the West, there was a proper relation between State and civil society, and when the State trembled a sturdy structure of civil society was at once revealed. The State was only an outer ditch, behind which there stood a powerful system of fortresses and earthworks: more or less numerous from one State to the next, it goes without saying – but this precisely necessitated an accurate reconnaisance of each individual country.[5]

As regards Italy, Gramsci pointed out that these 'fortresses' include a strong Church (with its own schools, papers, banks, etc.) and a diversified educational and cultural system through which the ruling class provides itself with intermediate personnel who help it to maintain its power by widespread consent. As a result, the ruling class in a country such as Italy is not detached and isolated, and does not rule simply by force, but has managed to build around itself a system of alliances, including at the economic and social level, by means of concessions, welfare, and so on, and at the political and moral level, winning wide sections of intellectuals and even sections of the working class to accept a capitalist and conservative outlook.

Gramsci's main concern was to find a valid strategy for revolutionary change in Italy. This required, among other things, finding a way to win over the millions of Catholic belief.[6] Conditions in Britain are, of course, very different. Not only do we not have any equivalent of a Christian Democrat Party, or an influence, in political terms, of religion on the scale of that in Italy; we also have a mass Labour Party, based on a united trade union organisation which now embraces 11 million wage and salary workers. Such a Party does not exist in Italy where the Socialist Party and the Social Democrat Party are both relatively small.[7] For a change to socialism to succeed in Britain, therefore, the task is somewhat different, requiring above all the winning of the majority of trade unionists for socialism and, through that process, defeating the right-wing hold in the Labour Party as well.

Nevertheless, Gramsci's conception of revolutionary advance in Italy, the validity of which is being borne out by the gains of the Italian Communist Party and other left and democratic forces, is not without significance for other West European countries.

One can say that by and large the countries of Western Europe, despite their variations, present a fairly common pattern, with the political power of the monopoly capitalists largely depending on their being able to maintain this system of alliances, this bloc of social, political, cultural and moral forces. This whole system requires, for its continued operation, the economic possibilities to make concessions when necessary, combined with a continued ability to exercise intellectual domination. Therefore, to end the rule of monopoly capitalism in Western Europe one cannot tackle the State in isolation. The whole question of the State, its character, its transformation, its very behaviour, is closely bound up with the shifting relationship of class and political forces, with the system of alliances, with the ability or otherwise of the ruling class to continue to make concessions and maintain its intellectual hold on decisive sections of the people.

If, as we have argued, the people's acceptance of the existing system is one of the pillars of political power, then the working class, if it is to challenge and defeat that power, needs to organise its own mass consent to revolutionary change. This means that it must build its own system of alliances with other classes and social strata. It must win allies away from monopoly capitalism in order to isolate and weaken it, to add forces to its own side and to prevent the ruling class using such strata for counter-revolutionary purposes. It must develop its own intellectual challenge to capitalism and secure its own intellectual leadership in society.

No State power rests solely on coercion. Even the most repressive fascist State requires an ideological base, although this is founded on demagogic slogans, on extreme chauvinism, racialism, anti-semitism, and anti-communism.

In a bourgeois democratic country such as Britain, the political parties play a major role in winning the people's 'consent'. The Tory party represents the interests of big capital, but millions of small producers, farmers, shop-keepers, professional and technical people, and even many workers, support it and vote for it. Yet the Tory party does not act in the interests of the millions who vote for it, and this provides the possibility of the organised working class movement detaching many of these millions over to its side: and that is vital if the ruling class is to be defeated.

Apart from the capitalist parties such as the Tories and Liberals, the workers have also built up their parties, the Labour Party and the Communist Party. Within the Labour Party, the right-wing leaders play an important part in the system of capitalist class rule in Britain. It has been their role over the years to confuse and divide the movement, to limit its activities, especially in the political field, to sap the confidence of the working class in its own strength and capacity to struggle, in its ability to win victories and manage society. It has persuaded the movement that it should work for reforms within the system, not to work to bring about a revolutionary change of the system itself.

Recent years, and especially the big struggles of the early 1970s, have shown that a weakening of the grip of the right-wing leaders unleashes the enormous potential power of the working class movement to such an extent that it begins to challenge the ability of the ruling class to carry on as hitherto.

This brings us back to Lenin's formulation that political power is the ability to compel by force if necessary. This formulation contains three essential ideas. First, that compulsion or coercion is not necessarily the permanent nor the main direct form of maintaining and exercising political power. Secondly, that the ruling class turns to the use of force when this has become necessary. Thirdly, that when faced with this necessity, the ruling class, if it is to retain its political power, has to be in a position to place its main reliance on coercion and have the means to do this.

This third point is of immense importance. The Marxist concept that the State is 'a machine for the oppression of one class by another'[8] has sometimes been used in a literal, exaggerated or distorted way as though the various parts of the State, and especially the powers of coercion, are really monolithic, material instruments, ready to be picked up and used by the ruling class whenever it deems it necessary. Yet, we should remember that Engels defined the coercive departments of the State as bodies of 'armed *people*' – and people are not a 'machine' nor inanimate 'instruments' at the ready disposal of those who may want to use them.

At the same time, of course, one should not ignore the fact that the armed forces, just like other State institutions, are not just composed of 'people' in an abstract sense. The people concerned are themselves of different class composition, and with different political ties or sentiments; and the top posts are overwhelmingly in the hands of ruling class representatives, sons (and a few daughters) of rich businessmen, landowners and top professionals, educated in public schools and Oxbridge. It is these top State officials who take the decisions and so influence largely the way the State institutions operate in their normal daily affairs. The armed forces themselves have their own internal forms of 'law and order', through which the officers exercise a quasi-dictatorial role; and it is the practice, in consequence, for the troops to obey the voice of command. But what happens under 'normal' conditions in no way determines how State institutions will act under quite different circumstances, when the character and scale of class and social conflict can affect not only the rank-and-file personnel of State institutions, including the army, but also the middle echelon and even some at the topmost pinnacle, even if only temporarily and for limited aims.

When Lenin refers to 'the ability' of the ruling class to make use of its powers of coercion it is precisely this aspect to which he is drawing our attention. Clearly, the converse of Lenin's point – namely, the *in*ability of the ruling class in some situations to make use of its own forces of coercion at a moment of crisis – is of very considerable importance, and especially for those concerned with the tactics of revolutionary struggle.

Professor Crane Brinton has written that 'it is almost safe to say that no government is likely to be overthrown until it loses the ability to make adequate use of its military and police powers'.[9] Making basically the same point, and in a much more emphatic manner, Le Bon has argued that 'It is obvious that revolutions have never taken place, and will never take place, save with the aid of an important faction of the army.'[10] (The situation has been different in many Third World countries where, in the course of the national liberation struggle, it has been necessary for the indigenous people to create their own armed forces and confront the foreign troops of the imperialists.)

The propositions of Crane Brinton and Le Bon were confirmed by the events in Portugal on 25 April 1974, when, largely through the action of the Armed Forces Movement, it became possible to overthrow fascism which had clearly lost its 'ability to compel by force if necessary'.

Dr George Rudé has noted that it would seem to be 'almost a truism that the key factor in determining the outcome of popular rebellion and disturbance is the loyalty or disaffection of the armed forces at the government's disposal'.[11] Continuing his argument, Dr Rudé discusses the general propositions regarding the ability or otherwise of a ruling class to use the army to defend its system at a moment of crisis, and here, it seems to me, he puts his finger on the key issue.

'Such assertions,' he writes, 'are true enough as far as they go; yet they are not the whole truth and they even tend, when presented in such baldly military terms, to beg the further and more important question of why the army refuses to obey or why the government loses control of its means of defence. *Essentially, this is a social and political rather than a military question* (italics added). For if a magistrate condones riots or soldiers fraternise with or refuse to fire on rebels, it is because the ties of class or political affiliation are at that moment stronger than allegiance to the established order of government.'

This emphasises the danger of a mechanical use of terms such as the State being an 'instrument', 'a machine', or 'a weapon'. Even more, it is politically hazardous to allow one's political thinking about the State and questions of political power to be influenced or dominated by conceptions arising from a strict verbal meaning of these terms. Armed forces are an instrument only in a very particular sense. They certainly include instruments, weapons, machines, such as guns and ammunition and so on, with which they are equipped. But whether or not the ruling class is able to rely unconditionally on this institution depends in the last resort not on the equipment or firing power of the armed forces, important as this may be, but on whether the armed forces are prepared to use their weapons against the rulers' oponents. In other words, it depends on social and political factors. This is why it is misleading to try and reduce everything to the slogan 'political power grows out of the barrel of a gun'. Political power grows out of the total political alignment of forces including the strength and organization of the people. It is this which, in the last resort, determines if, when and *in what direction* the guns are going to be used.

This was confirmed only too clearly in Portugal on 25 April 1974, when the democratic struggle of the Portuguese people, alongside the military resistance and success of the people of Guinea-Bissau, Mozambique and Angola, became such a powerful combination that opinions in the armed forces were decisively changed, thus opening the way to the formation of the Armed Forces Movement and the victory of 25 April. The more recent setbacks suffered by the Armed Forces Movement and its virtual demise in no way invalidate this argument; on the contrary, they confirm it, since it has been mainly political factors which has produced a certain turn-around inside the Portuguese army.

The political factors which determine the behaviour of the armed forces are basically of two kinds. Firstly, there are the forces operating outside the army, primarily the political relationship of class forces. This largely determines the possibility and the degree of necessity for the ruling class to use the armed forces for open political aims. It helps to determine, too, whether there is an alternative open to the ruling class of seeking a solution not involving the use of the armed forces, by making concessions to its class opponents.

A clear example of the latter was the crisis in 1972 over the Pentonville 5, whom the British Government had to release in face of the massive protest of the whole Labour Movement and the threat of a general strike called by the General Council of the TUC to secure the release of the arrested dockers. Theoretically, the Government could have defied the Labour Movement and called on the armed forces to break the projected strike; but in the given circumstances, in the light of the then existing relationship of forces, it deemed it wiser not to risk a further escalation of the class confrontation by using its full State power, even though the armed forces displayed no signs of inner contradiction or division at that given time, and in that limited sense, therefore, presented themselves as 'an instrument' ready for use. The Government, despite its having the armed forces, the law, prisons, police, and mass media at its disposal, had to retreat; although it has to be borne in mind that in this particular conflict there was no question of a change of political power involved, only the release of five men from prison resulting in a heavy blow against the Industrial Relations Act. So the Government, in this instance, organised a tactical withdrawal while keeping its political power and domination intact, but a little bruised.

Yet, one should not ignore the immense potential power of the British working class revealed in those conflicts and its possibility, if united and with a clear political vision, of making a challenge to the big monopolies not just for immediate demands but for a change of political power.

The Government faced similar problems with the UCS and other factory occupations, and the 1972 miners' strike. Again, the ruling class had all the State institutions available to it, but the relation of forces at the time obliged it to seek other ways of overcoming the problems involved, even at the cost of big concessions.

But circumstances operating outside the armed forces are only one factor determining whether the ruling class possesses 'the ability to compel by force'. There are also factors operating inside the State institutions themselves, though these, in the last resort, are produced and precipitated by the surrounding circumstances, by the clash of classes, by ideological influences, by the economic and other crises of society and by the general strains in its entire fabric.

After all, the individuals who comprise the armed forces are in no sense completely isolated and immured from the surrounding great movements and shifts of public opinion. Influenced as they may be by the nature of their training, by the views projected by the most reactionary members of the top brass, by their class and social ties, by the purposes they are expected to fulfil, and by the fact of being part of a specialised, hierarchical institution, barracked and housed apart from the general population, they are nevertheless subject to other counter-influences. Their relatives and friends, in the midst of swirling changes taking place in civilian life, may themselves be progressively influenced to an extent by these developments. Some of this may rub off on officers and other ranks by letters, by personal contact and so on. Men in the armed forces read papers, journals and books, listen to radio, watch television, talk with one another. Despite the reactionary character of much of what they read, hear or see on their TV screens, the sight of a workers' demonstration with its slogans on the screen, even the occasional broadcast by a Communist on the radio, may have some influence on their thinking.

In countries where armed forces have been used against guerrilla forces, as in Peru, Uruguay, Bolivia, the experience of this fighting was, in fact, an important factor in producing a radical wing of the officer corps. In the case of Peru, where it was combined with special training for officers in social, economic and political matters, in the expectation that such instruction would assist them in acting to prop up the establishment, it had a somewhat contrary effect. This has happened, too, in those countries where the officers have been obliged to study Marxist writings and the works of guerrilla leaders such as Che Guevara, in the hope that this knowledge would make them more effective counter-insurgency operators. Once again, the result was often quite different.

Thus, as political situations mature, processes get under way inside the armed forces, and these processes sometimes reach a stage which makes it impossible for the ruling class to use the army against the people. In such cases things may develop to a situation, as in the Sudan in 1964, when the army officers showed reluctance to act against the people or intervene against the general strike which was a prime cause of the downfall of

General Abboud. Or, it may reach a more advanced stage, as in Portugal in 1974, when the majority of the armed forces, including a decisive section of the middle officers and a few at the top, took a key part in toppling Caetano's fascist regime.

Both in the Sudan and in Portugal, up to the time of the downfall of the old regime, the armed forces were formally speaking at the disposal of the rulers. The 'instrument', the 'machine', was there. The equipment was available. The men were armed. They were trained and led by capable officers. But neither the soldiers nor the officers were 'instruments' or 'machines'. They were thinking individuals, subject, even if in different ways, to the selfsame influences and political considerations that affect the thinking and behaviour of those not in uniform. And when the civilian population in both cases showed in no uncertain terms that it wanted to do away with the old system, when similar influences had worked their way into the armed forces, and when the most reactionary officers realised that they could no longer obtain obedience to their command if they tried to uphold the government of the day, then the 'machine' of the institutionalised force was no longer available to the rulers. It was politics that had the last word.

These experiences (and there are a number of others) indicate clearly what attitude a revolutionary movement should take towards the armed forces. Some people on the left adopt a crude, over-simplified approach, and regard the army as one monolithic and reactionary organisation, as the enemy which must be confronted and destroyed. Such barren anti-militarism, even if accompanied by reference to Marx and Lenin on the need to 'smash the State' of the ruling class, is not a Marxist position, nor can it lead to revolutionary success.

Already, at the end of the nineteenth century, Engels was noting how technological advances in the army and its growth in size had rendered the old-style street fighting of 1848 of limited value *unless accompanied by other factors*. Yet, even up to 1848, he stressed that the main aim of street fighting was not to win outright military victory but to make the troops 'yield to moral influences. . . . If they succeed in this, the troops fail to respond, or the commanding officers lose their heads, and the insurrection wins. . . . Even in the classic time of street fighting, therefore, the barricade produced more of a moral than a material effect. It was a means of shaking the steadfastness of the military.'[12]

With changes after 1848, Engels argued that conditions had become far more unfavourable for civilian fighters and far more favourable for the military. This disadvantageous situation, wrote Engels, had to be 'compensated by other factors', the principal one of which was 'the masses themselves'. But in order for the masses to understand what had to be done, 'long, persistent work' was needed. This work was required in order to bring mass pressure to bear on the whole of society, including the State and especially the armed forces, in order to make the army yield to 'moral influences' and 'shake its steadfastness'.

Today, in the advanced capitalist countries in Western Europe, this has become a major question, both in the struggle to end reactionary and fascist regimes and in defence of democratic government. Experiences since the commencement of this century underline the necessity for the working class and democratic movement to influence the army, to win for it democratic rights and better conditions of service, promotion and pay, and to establish a situation in which troops yield to 'moral influences' and begin to act as a defender of the nation, and of people's rights and aspirations, and cease being used internally as a tool of big business and reaction to suppress the people. In other words, the strategy to be followed – and this is being done, with increasing success, in Italy, France and Spain[13] – is not that of trying to 'smash' the army of the ruling class, but of transforming it in order to deprive the monopolies of their possibilities of using the army to 'compel by force'.

The fact that even the army reared by Portuguese fascism could be won away from the monopolies at the moment of crisis and side with the people's anti-fascist revolution, justifies the correctness of this approach – and this is notwithstanding the difficulties that subsequently arose when the political balance in the armed forces shifted away from the left.

Neutralising, or winning part or even a majority of the army also helps the working class to win allies in civilian life. The middle strata are very much influenced by the attitude of the armed forces.[14] The officers play a particular role here because of their class and social links with such strata. But in addition, the army, as an institution, has considerable prestige among wide sections. The working class, too, is not unmindful of army behaviour, and the soldiers, after all, in Western Europe, are mainly workers. All this affects the total politics of the country.

The issue, therefore, is not the people versus the army, but whether the army will stand with the majority of people against the small minority who own the banks, land and industries, control the mass media and wield State power – or will it continue to act as the defender of privilege and reaction. It is in the interests of the people, and in the interests of the army itself, that it undergo a democratic transformation and become an institution for progress that assists the democratic transformation of society as a whole.

There is one final word of warning here. I have argued that the progressive forces in the army, even the majority of the armed forces when the changes have gone that deep, can and must play an important role in helping to change society.

But there are certain limitations to this if one is considering, for example, the armies in Western Europe. The army personnel is of mixed class and social origin, with officers coming from upper and middle class families. All army personnel are tied to civilian life by a thousand strands. They reflect all the political tendencies in civilian life. The officers include individuals with ambitions and, sometimes, with Bonapartist hopes and strivings. As an institution, the army is autocratic, hierarchical, and at best paternal. It is used to instruct and command. Even when officers accept democracy it is often a kind of 'autocratic democracy', a democracy under their guidance and control. The army, therefore, cannot fulfil the role of a political party, nor can it act as a leader of the people. It has a role to play, but not as the commander of the revolution. If it tries to act as if it were, there can be acute dangers, as we have seen only too well in Portugal, not to mention Third World countries such as Egypt, Syria and Peru.

Since the State, both in its coercive and non-coercive aspects, is a key pillar in the system of political power, those concerned with ending capitalism and constructing socialism must be concerned, too, with the question of the State and, above all, what must be done with it.

A revolution involves a change of class power. A socialist revolution requires a change of power from the hands of the big monopolies into the hands of the working class and its allies.

On more than one occasion Lenin emphasised the well-known formula of Marx regarding the necessity to 'smash the State' of the bourgeoisie. Lenin even employs such drastic terms as 'smash the old machinery of State to atoms', and 'leave not a stone of it standing'. It would, I believe, be misleading to try and apply such ideas mechanically, especially in conditions of Britain or other advanced capitalist countries. In a certain sense one can argue that there is a certain ambiguity in Lenin's remarks on this question if one simply puts side by side his various observations at different times and in connection with varying circumstances. For example, notwithstanding his urgent calls to 'smash the State', in his last years he more than once felt obliged to point out that, in fact, one of the things which the Bolsheviks failed to do was to 'smash the State'. This whole question clearly merits at least some discussion.

Writing in April 1917,[15] Lenin noted — 'The world-wide experience of bourgeois and landowner governments has evolved *two* methods of keeping the people in subjection. The first is violence' — and here he cites Russia where the tsars 'demonstrated to the Russian people the maximum of what can and cannot be done in the way of these hangmen's practices'.

But he then goes on to point to 'another method, best developed by the English and French bourgeoisie, who learnt their lesson in a series of great revolutions and revolutionary movements of the masses'. This other method, he explains, is 'the method of deception, flattery, fine phrases, numberless promises, petty sops and concessions of the unessential while retaining the essential'.

There is, possibly, too much of a sweeping contrast between the two methods described here. After all, the tsars did not rely *only* on the hangman. The peasants, the vast majority of the people, even when they began to turn against the landlords in 1905, still had faith in the tsar, the 'little Father', and were, in large part, also influenced in their thinking by the priests; thus confirming, once again, that all forms of political power rely on a certain measure of 'consent' as well as on the powers of 'coercion'. Similarly, modification needs to be made as well regarding Lenin's definition of the second method utilised in Britain, France and other West European countries; for here, too, alongside the deception and concessions through which the big capitalists secure the 'consent' of the people, there is also reliance on the use of the State's coercive powers.

Yet, broadly speaking, Lenin was absolutely correct to point to the essence of the difference in the two instances — tsarist Russia relying *mainly* on force, Western Europe *mainly* on deception and concession. It is not illogical, therefore, to argue that if, as Lenin pointed out, there were two rather different methods of bourgeois rule, then there could be generally speaking, two different methods of ending that rule.

Careful reading of Lenin's writings up to the October revolution, and in the first years after it, indicates that Lenin tended to link the question of 'smashing the State' with the question of the political party of the working class winning to its side not only the majority of wage workers, but also the majority of all working people, including peasants and other small producers, artisans and traders. Lenin's conclusion, emphasised on more than one occasion, was that under conditions of capitalism the rulers had such great power to maintain their intellectual hold over the mass of the petty-bourgeoisie and even over substantial sections of workers, that it was impossible to win a majority.

First, he argued, the working class had to 'smash the 'State'; only after that was accomplished could the working class, with the aid of State power, win a majority. Thus, in December 1919, he wrote:

. . . the proletariat must first overthrow the bourgeoisie and win *for itself* state power, and then use the state power . . . as an instrument of its class for the purpose of winning the sympathy of the majority of the working people.[16]

Again:

. . . state power in the hands of one class, the proletariat, can and must become an instrument for winning to the side of the proletariat the non-proletarian working masses, an instrument for winning those masses from the bourgeoisie and from the petty-bourgeois parties.[17]

And again:

. . . the proletariat cannot achieve victory if it does not win the majority of the population over to its side. But to limit that winning to polling a majority of votes in an election *under the rule of the bourgeoisie*, or to make it the condition for it, is crass supidity, or else sheer deception of the workers.[18]

And then he adds:

In order to win the majority of the population to its side the proletariat must, in the first place, overthrow the bourgeoisie and seize state power; secondly it must introduce Soviet power and completely smash the old state apparatus. . . .[19]

Lenin explains that the 'solid majority of the population' is made up not only of the proletariat or 'that section of the proletariat which realises its revolutionary aims and is capable of fighting for their realisation', but also of a 'mass of toilers' who do not realise that they are 'proletarians', who are 'half-proletarian and half petty-bourgeois', who have no faith in their own strength nor that of the proletariat, and who do not realise 'that it is possible to secure the satisfaction of their essential needs by expropriating the exploiters'.

These sections of the working population, avers Lenin, are 'allies for the vanguard of the proletariat'; moreover, all these toilers, together with the proletariat 'form a solid majority of the population.' But once again Lenin comes back to his essential point:

. . . the proletariat can win these allies only with the aid of an instrument like state power, that is to say, only after it has overthrown the bourgeoisie and has destroyed the bourgeois state apparatus.[20]

The final point worth noting here is Lenin's argument as to why he considered the working class, even if a minority of the population, is able to break the power of the capitalists.

The strength of the proletariat in any capitalist country is far greater than the proportion it represents of the total population. That is because the proletariat economically dominates the centre and nerve of the entire economic system of capitalism, and also because the proletariat expresses economically and politically the real interests of the overwhelming majority of the working people under capitalism.

Therefore, the proletariat, even when it constitutes a minority of the population (or when the class-conscious and really revolutionary vanguard of the proletariat constitutes a minority of the population), is capable of winning to its side numerous allies from a mass of semi-proletarians and petty bourgeoisie who never declare in advance in favour of the rule of the proletariat, who do not understand the conditions and aims of that rule, and only by their subsequent experience become convinced that the proletarian dictatorship is inevitable, proper and legitimate.[21]

The argument is clear enough. Under conditions of capitalism it is not possible to win a majority for socialism. Therefore the working class, even if a minority, must first take power. This involves a violent smashing of the existing State machine. Only *after* power has been seized, the State smashed, and proletarian power established, will it be possible for the working class, with the aid of their new State, to win a majority to its side.[22]

One has only to ponder this approach for a short while to realise that it really has no relevance at all to the strategies for socialism worked out by the Communist Parties in the advanced capitalist countries. There is not, to my knowledge, a single programme or Congress document of any Communist Party in Western Europe (whatever different views they may hold on other matters) which today bases itself on the conception of the taking of power by a minority as the only way to win the support of the majority. Surely, therefore, if Lenin's view on the 'smashing of the State' was so linked with his belief that without this it was not possible to win a majority to the side of the working class, one is justified in querying at least one aspect of the idea of 'smashing the State'.

It should be remembered that these concepts of Lenin up to 1919 were put forward under the impact of the harsh nature of the struggle in Russia, the harsh realities of the class structure of Russia (a small working class in a sea of peasants), the impact of the imperialist war (with the consequent militarisation even of the advanced capitalist States, accompanied by a vast growth of the bureaucracy), and the experience of the two Russian revolutions of 1917.

Yet all this notwithstanding, Lenin did not entirely shut his eyes to other possibilities, and even gave a clue as to an alternative way. In one of his references to the need for the working class to 'smash the bourgeois State machine' and then use it to satisfy the needs of the people in order to 'gain the sympathy and support of the majority of the toiling non-proletarian masses',[23] Lenin remarks, in passing: 'The contrary would be a rare exception in history (and even in such an exception the bourgeoisie can resort to civil war, as was shown in the case of Finland.')

The question is: Has the 'rare exception' today become a more realistic alternative road in Western Europe, where Lenin had already noted an important difference in the form of ruling class power as compared with tsarist Russia, as Gramsci (as we noted above) was to do later?

What gives added weight to this whole matter, and, to a considerable degree, adds strength to the argument that the 'rare exception' has today passed the stage of being exceptional and has now become the real alternative for the people in Western Europe,[24] is the fact that after 1919 Lenin, who in his last years gave much thought to developments in Europe, returned to this question of winning the majority. Under the impact of the defeat of the armed uprisings in Germany in March, 1921, Lenin apparently revised his views.[25]

At the Third Congress of the Communist International (CI) in 1921 an intense debate took place. There was fierce discussion both before the Congress and during the Congress itself. The issue was the question of 'winning a majority'. Analysing the reasons for the German defeats in 1921, Lenin declared that to be succesful in achieving a revolutionary change it was necessary for the Communists 'to have the majority behind them all over the country, and not just in one small district.'[26] Taking up his theme in the actual preparations for the Third Congress of the CI, Lenin took issue with Radek, Zinoviev and others who wanted to delete from the draft thesis the reference to the need to win a majority of the working class. Lenin insisted that winning a majority of the workers was 'the basis of everything', and added:

The tactics of the Communist International should be based on a steady and systematic drive to win a majority of the working class, *first and foremost within the old trade unions*. Then we shall win for certain, whatever the course of events.

At the Congress itself Lenin developed his ideas still further and emphasised that 'what is essential to *win* and retain power is not only the majority of the working class . . . but also the majority of the working and exploited rural population'[27] – which meant, in practice, an absolute majority of the population.

This is clearly a fundamental modification of his former views. Lenin recognised the new situation developing in the world, and also the characteristics of Western Europe which differed in important aspects from those of pre-revolutionary Russia. This, again, should justify one querying whether the term 'smash the State machine' is adequate to embrace today's problems and possibilities.

The concept of 'smashing the State' was also very much identified with the concept of the *armed* overthrow of the capitalist system, with the *armed* 'seizure of power', with the likelihood of heavy civil war. In other words, 'smashing the State' was regarded as an essential part of a clash of class forces in which *military struggle* was an essential element. The strategy being followed by a number of Communist Parties today, in the advanced capitalist countries, envisages a revolutionary transformation of society *without armed insurrection*, *without civil war*. Surely this has an important bearing on one's approach to the State institutions, including the armed forces? Can one argue that 'smashing the State' is an appropriate slogan for a strategy based on a change of political power without an armed insurrection?

But there are additional reasons why it seems to me that the term is inappropriate.

Firstly, even in the classic formulae about 'smashing the state' one finds the phrase 'the proletariat cannot simply lay hold of the ready-made state machine and use it for its own purposes'.[28] The capitalist State must be replaced 'by a new one'. Talking in terms of 'smashing' the State can, I believe, serve to hide the essence of the question, which is that the working class needs a new State, a qualitatively different State suited to the aims of building socialism.

Secondly, Lenin himself drew attention to parts of the State which did not require 'smashing'. These included certain non-coercive parts of the State, such as banking, statistics, and accounting:

This apparatus must not, and should not, be smashed. It must be wrested from the control of the capitalists; the capitalists and the wires they pull must be *cut off*, *lopped off, chopped away from* this apparatus. . . .[29] It is not enough to 'remove' the capitalists; we must (after removing the undesirable and incorrigible 'resisters') employ them *in the service of the new state*. This applies both to the capitalists and to the upper sections of the bourgeois intellectuals, office employees, etc.[30]

Thirdly, the non-coercive sides of the State in Britain today are far more comprehensive, more diverse, and have a far larger personnel than the State in old Russia. Our State institutions embrace extensive economic functions and the nationalised industries, as well as education, the health services, social services, and so on. In essence what is required in these State sectors is a democratic transformation and forms of democratic control, not any 'smashing' of such bodies which, under socialism, can really serve the people's interests once the essential democratic changes have been made.

Fourthly, the personnel employed in the various departments of the British State today bear no comparison with those employed in the tsarist State of 1917. In a certain sense quantity has produced a new quality. The needs of a modern State like that of Britain requires such an expansion of personnel that, in addition to the top ruling class personnel, the State has had to employ immense numbers from the lower middle class and even from the working class, compared with earlier States which relied so much for its personnel on those coming from a higher strata of society. One has only to think of the average State employee in a Chekhov story or as depicted by Gogol to get the real flavour of the difference.

The vast majority of the hundreds of thousands employed in our State and in local Government, too, are in trade unions affiliated to the TUC through which they are linked with the industrial working class. Their members take part in strikes and other protest actions, often alongside other trade unionists. Radical political tendencies are making themselves felt in the civil service unions and in the National Association of Local Government Officers (NALGO) and the National Union of Public Employees (NUPE).

There is no reason why a solid majority of the State personnel, apart from those at the top, cannot be won to ally their fortunes with the industrial working class, with other white-collar sections, and with the broad anti-monopoly alliance for a radical new Britain and, through that experience, won for socialism, too. Such a possibility of winning the majority of the personnel of the State never existed in Russia in Lenin's time.

Fifthly, in most West European countries the working class and democratic movement in proportion to the population as a whole is a much larger and more weighty factor in political life, constitutes a far greater force in the economy and potentially represents a massive power which can attract to its side the overwhelming majority of the population. In Britain, in fact, the wage-earning class and its families already constitute a majority.

Sixthly, the coercive sides of the State are beginning to be influenced by the big political developments of our time. We have already noted the role played by the Armed Forces Movement in overthrowing the fascist regime in Portugal. As we shall see later, significant changes are taking place in the armed forces of France, Italy and Spain under the impact of powerful political movements affecting wide strata of the population in those countries.

In Britain, of course, the same tendencies are not yet apparent. Apart from the fact that we have a professional army, which makes things more complex, the political movement in the country as a whole has not yet reached the stage that it has in France or Italy, and it is therefore not surprising that substantial changes in the outlook of the personnel of the army and other coercive departments of the State are not yet in evidence. This confirms once again that it is above all political developments in a given country, the thinking and actions of the civilian population, that are prime causes of changes in the attitude and behaviour of the armed forces. Because the political struggle in Britain is at a different stage from that of France or Italy we have a dangerous situation in which authoritarian trends are being more and more asserted. In this situation the coercive sides of the State could become still more remote from the people. This is an additional reason why the struggle must be waged for the democratic transformation of all departments of the State.

There is a seventh and final reason why our approach to the State cannot be a mechanical repetition of what Lenin considered appropriate for Russia in 1917. We live in an epoch of big world changes. The favourable balance of world forces makes the question of direct military intervention by the imperialists in support of counter-revolution much more difficult. This danger should never, of course, be ignored; but in Western Europe, for example, with big progressive developments taking place in the same epoch in a number of countries, the possibility of direct interference by the imperialists becomes all the more hazardous for them. This, too, it seems to me, must have an important influence on the possibilities of taking the State away from the monopolies in a new way.

NOTES

1 Lenin, *Collected Works*, Vol. 24, pp. 46–7.
2 Niccoló Machiavelli, *The Prince*.
3 Enrico Berlinguer, 'Reflections after the Events in Chile', *Marxism Today*, February 1974.

4 See, for example, Alan Hunt, 'Law, State and Class Struggle', *Marxism Today*, June 1976.

5 Antonio Gramsci, *Selections from Prison Notebooks*, London, 1971, p. 238.

6 Today, this includes many outside the ranks of Christian Democrat supporters.

7 In the 1976 general elections in Italy the Socialist Party received 10·2 per cent of the votes for Parliament, and the Social Democrats 3·1 per cent, compared with 33·8 per cent for the Communist Party.

8 Lenin, 'The State: Speech made to Students of Sverdlov University', 11 July 1919, *Collected Works*, Vol. 29, p. 480.

9 Crane Brinton, *The Anatomy of Revolution*, New York, 1960.

10 G. Le Bon, *The Psychology of Revolution*, New York, 1913.

11 George Rude, *The Crowd in History, 1730–1848*, New York, 1964, p. 266.

12 Engels, *Introduction to the Class Struggles in France, 1848–1850*, by Karl Marx (written and published in 1850); Introduction by Engels written in 1895: Marx and Engels, *Selected Works*, Vol. 1, pp. 120–1 (Moscow/London, 1950).

13 The same general position holds good for Portugal, too, despite setbacks; and in Greece, too, communists are working in the same direction.

14 The reverse is also true, and this is an additional and very important reason why the working class needs to establish an alliance with the middle strata.

15 Lenin, *Collected Works*, Vol. 24, p. 63.

16 Lenin, 'The Elections to the Constituent Assembly', *Collected Works*, Vol. 30, p. 263.

17 ibid., p. 262.

18 ibid., p. 265.

19 ibid., p. 265.

20 ibid., p. 274.

21 ibid., p. 274.

22 Of course, in the conditions prevailing in Russia in 1917 – with not only the class conscious vanguard of the working class constituting a minority of the total population but even the entire working class being so, with the mass of millions-strong peasants not having yet been won for socialism, with a capitalist class too weak and inexperienced to maintain its rule, with Russia in deep crisis arising from the first world war, and with revolutionary change posed as the only way out of the crisis and the war – Lenin and the Bolsheviks were absolutely correct to lead the advanced sections of the workers and peasants to take political power and then use that power to win over the overwhelming majority of the people. Conditions in Britain, and indeed in other West European countries, in 1976 are completely different from those in Russia in 1917, or in 1919 when Lenin was drawing his conclusions (cited above) regarding the need to 'smash the State' in order to win a majority.

23 ibid., p. 273.

24 The same arguments hold good for other advanced capitalist countries; the Japanese Communist Party, for example, envisages this alternative road as the way to socialism in Japan, on the basis of a democratic majority.

25 Those who may fear being labelled 'revisionist' because they find some idea of Lenin's no longer valid should take courage from Lenin who never hesitated to revise Lenin if experience showed this was necessary.

26 Lenin, *Collected Works*, Vol. 42, p. 323.

27 Lenin, *Collected Works*, Vol. 32, p. 476.

28 Lenin, 'Can the Bolsheviks Retain State Power?', *Collected Works*, Vol. 26, p.102.
29 ibid., p. 106.
30 ibid., p. 109.

3

Can the Army Act Independently of Classes?

In examining the role of the armed forces in the countries of the Third World a number of scholars have referred to the writings of Marx and Engels on the State, drawing particular attention to their comments on the exceptional autonomous role played by the armed forces at certain periods. It seems to me, however, that some writers, in referring to those special circumstances, have reached somewhat extravagant conclusions which require examination.

Marx, Engels and Lenin always stressed the class nature of the State, which they defined as 'a machine for the oppression of one class by another, a machine for holding in obedience to one class other, subordinated classes'.[1] The emergence of the State, however, was an historic process during the course of which the State itself underwent modifications. The State arose when classes first appeared in society. But, stressed Engels, it was not only a product of class society, but a manifestation that class antagonisms could not be reconciled by society. As a result the 'armed people' were replaced by an armed 'public power', a power arising out of society 'but placing itself above it, and increasingly separating itself from it'.[2] This public power, noted Engels, 'consists not merely of armed people but also of material adjuncts, prisons and institutions of coercion of all kinds'. Within the State, stressed Lenin, 'a standing army and police are the chief instruments of state power'.[3]

Engels' explanation as to how the State first arose is so crucial for our argument here that it is necessary to quote him at some length.

[The State] is a product of society at a certain stage of development; it is the admission that this society has become entangled in an insoluble contradiction with itself, that it is cleft into irreconcilable antagonisms which it is powerless to dispel. But in order that these antagonisms, classes with conflicting economic interests, might not consume themselves and society in sterile struggle, a power seemingly standing above society became necessary for the purpose of moderating the conflict, of keeping it within the bounds of 'order'; and this power, arisen out of society, but placing itself above it, and increasingly alienating itself from it, is the State. . . . As the State arose from the need to hold class antagonisms in check, but as it arose, at the same time, in the midst of the conflict of these classes, it is, as a rule, the state of the most powerful, economically dominant class, and thus acquires new means of holding down and exploiting the oppressed class. Thus, the state of antiquity was above all the state of the slave owners for the purpose of holding down the slaves, as the feudal state was the organ of the nobility for holding down the peasant serfs and bondsmen, and the modern representative state is an instrument of exploitation of wage labour by capital. By the way of exception, however, periods occur in which the warring classes balance each other so nearly that the state power, as ostensible mediator, acquires, for the moment, a certain degree of independence of both. Such was the absolute monarchy of the seventeenth and eighteenth centuries, which held the balance between the nobility and the class of burghers; such was the Bonapartism of the First, and still more of the Second French Empire, which played off the proletariat against the bourgeoisie and the bourgeoisie against the proletariat. The latest performance of this kind, in which ruler and ruled appear equally ridiculous, is the new German Empire of the Bismarck nation: here capitalists and workers are balanced against each other and equally cheated for the benefit of the impoverished Prussian cabbage junkers.[4]

As the above quotation makes clear, the State *arose* in the first place from the need to 'hold classes in check' when class antagonisms had become irreconcilable, but, in the process of time, the State *became* an instrument of class domination and oppression. The State, including the army, is therefore not neutral as far as social classes are concerned. Although, in Engels' words, it is a power 'separating itself' from society and *seemingly* standing above society', it is not at all separate from the classes which make up that society. On the contrary it is a special apparatus of men created by the ruling classes to maintain their political power and thereby their ownership of the means of production by which they are able to continue their system of exploitation, whether of slaves, feudal serfs and bondsmen, or of wage earners.

At the same time, both Marx and Engels drew attention to certain circumstances in which the armed forces could assume a kind of autonomous position of their own. They said this was possible when society was in a stage of transition, at the junction of two epochs, with a relative equilibrium between the main contending classes and the consequent inability of either of these warring classes to act as a force capable of exercising political power.

Since it is these references in particular which have given rise to attempts by some writers to draw analogies with the role of military governments in a number of Third World countries, it is necessary to consider more fully what Marx and Engels referred to and what they actually said.

Commenting on the Second Empire in France in his *Outlines of 'The Civil War in France'*, Marx wrote that the State power had become 'independent of society itself', and that it had begun to suppress 'even the interests of the ruling classes'.[5]

Bonaparte, noted Marx, was compelled to create 'an artificial caste, for which the maintenance of his regime becomes a bread-and-butter question'.[6] In commenting on this, Dr G. Mirsky writes:

This machine has already gained self-contained motion and even the economically dominating class can pose a certain threat to it; the corporative interests of the military bureaucratic apparatus do not tolerate a division of power; only a monopoly of power can guarantee to this caste the solidity of its position, the stability of its privileges, and ensure its 'daily bread'.[7]

Engels has also noted the temporary independence of the State power in France in the nineteenth century, and the ability of the army to act as a provisional arbiter due to the relative equilibrium of the main contending classes. He has further commented on this same possibility in other contexts. Writing in 1855 on the military uprisings in Spain, he noted:

As a consequence of the long, unceasing wars against Napoleon, the various (Spanish) armies and their commanders acquired substantial political power and this, at first, endowed them with a praetorian character. From the revolutionary period there still remained in the army many energetic men; the enlistment of guerrilla fighters in the regular army even strengthened this element. Thus, soldiers and subalterns were still permeated with the revolutionary tradition, while their officers clung to their praetorian pretensions.[8]

Engels then comes to this conclusion:

Since all the parties have employed the army as a tool, it should occasion no surprise if it takes the government into its own hands for a time.

In Britain, where the theories of the impartiality of the State as a neutral 'umpire' standing above classes have assumed considerable force in the thinking of the people, the role of the army in internal politics is usually overlooked. Generally it is seen only as a defence against an external enemy. It is as well to recall Engels' remarks about the decisive role which the army can play.

In politics there are only two decisive powers, the organised force of the State, the Army, and the unorganised, elemental force of the popular masses.[9]

Today, in developed capitalist countries, the people's 'unorganised, elemental force', even though it displays its power at moments of crisis and upheaval, is very much underpinned by a highly *organised* working class which, in Britain for example, has become overwhelmingly the decisive class in society, not only numerically and organisationally, but also from the point of view of its actual economic role as well as of its potential political role.

The examples given above of the temporarily independent role played by the army in France, Germany and Spain should not lead one to conclude that the army can become entirely separated from class forces in society. It is, after all, composed of people who come from definite strata and classes in society. This is true of the countries of the Third World as much as it is of other countries. Mirsky has argued:

The army in the developing countries is not simply a 'copy of society', not simply the arithmetic sum of a definite number of peasants by birth, petty bourgeois, etc. All these people acquire a new quality, fuse into a new organism. The army acquires the traits of a corporation with its own interests.[10]

It becomes a 'self-contained mechanism', with the 'exclusiveness of a caste', and, as Mirsky rightly perceives, 'the proud consciousness of belonging to this "select" profession can turn into a superiority complex with respect to "civilians"'. Such a separate, relatively well-organised body can often be tempted to take things into its own hands, as it were, to 'end corruption', to 'save the nation', or to 'restore law and order'. Quite clearly it has been so tempted in the past one hundred years in Latin America, and, more recently, in the last few decades in Africa, Asia and the Middle East. Even in Europe such 'temptations' have not always been resisted by the military.

The question naturally arises: if the armed forces can, on occasions, apparently take on an independent role, and, in Mirsky's words, 'acquire the traits of a corporation with its own interests', can it then pursue a policy separate from the interests of the main classes in society? The answer basically must be: 'No.'

First, in a society based on the private ownership of the means of production, the armed forces have been created as an instrument to maintain that society, based on its domination by the class – slave, feudal or capitalist – owning those means of production.

Second, once the army has taken direct power into its own hands, it either continues to act as an instrument of the particular class dominating society and owning the means of production, or it breaks with it. Either way, it has to take up the practical affairs of government, to adopt economic policies, to pursue a particular course as regards the interests of the workers, farmers or peasants, landlords, capitalists and middle strata, and to take an attitude towards other countries, imperialist, socialist and Third World.

In other words, after taking full power into its hands, the military either pursues a policy which is basically the same as that followed by its predecessors – in which case the class essence of its position quickly becomes clear; or, it makes modifications, or even drastic changes, in one direction or another, in the interests of this class or that. Its apparent role as an arbiter between contending classes in such conditions can be only a very temporary phenomenon. Once it begins to act as the new government it gradually commences to reflect class interests. Its leading personnel, may, as an élite force, use their new power to join the class of bureaucratic capitalists – but this only confirms that the army cannot really act independently of classes.

It is not without significance that in relation to the exceptions cited by Marx and Engels in which the army appeared to be acting for a time independently of the main warring classes in society, both writers indicated that, even while playing this apparent role as an autonomous arbiter, the army definitely furthered the interests of specific classes. Thus in the long quotation above from *The Origin of the Family, Private Property and the State*, Engels, referring to Germany under Bismarck, points out that while the capitalists and workers were balanced against each other, they were 'equally cheated [by Bismarck and the State] for the benefit of the impoverished Prussian cabbage junkers'.

Similarly, in relation to France under the second Bonaparte, who used the army to play off the workers against the capitalists and vice versa, and who, in the words of Marx, had utilised the State power to flout 'even the interests of the dominating classes', Marx nevertheless made some important qualifications in his analysis. Thus he wrote:

Only under the second Bonaparte does the state seem to have made itself completely independent. As against civil society, the state machine has consolidated its position so thoroughly that the chief of the Society of December 10 suffices for its head, an adventurer blown in from abroad, raised on the shield by a drunken soldiery, which he has bought with liquor and sausages, and which he must continually ply with sausage anew. . . . And yet the state power is not suspended in mid air. Bonaparte represents a class, and the most numerous class of French society at that, the *small-holding (Parzellen) peasants*. . . . Just as the Bourbons were the dynasty of big landed property and just as the Orleans were the dynasty of money, so the Bonapartes are the dynasty of the peasants.[11]

Moreover, as Mirsky notes, even while playing this role as an arbiter between the two major contending classes, and acting on behalf of the peasants, Bonaparte's army was 'objectively a bourgeois one and at a decisive moment defended the interests of the bourgeoisie'.[12]

It seems to me important to evaluate fully the arguments of Marx and Engels since, as I have already remarked, some scholars dealing with the role of the military in the Third World have utilised these exceptions provided by the founders of scientific socialism to argue as if Third World armies constitute a new classless factor in society. In reality these armies can be considered, to an extent, to be led by a section of the bourgeoisie or by 'the petty-bourgeoisie in uniform'. And this petty-bourgeoisie, under the impact of world developments, and influenced by internal class pressures and social problems, either becomes part of the bureaucratic bourgeoisie, as, for example, in Indonesia, or alternatively, as in Somalia, consciously allies itself with the workers and peasants and seeks a radical transformation of society. In a number of cases the situation is more complex, and the class character of the policy pursued by the military government is not so easy to determine. This is especially so if the military leaders seek to weaken the power of the former reaction and yet, at the same time, hold the workers in check, as for example, has been the case, to an extent, in Ghana since the overthrow of the Busia civilian regime, and was also the case in Egypt immediately following the overthrow of Farouk.

It must, of course, be understood that what we are concerned with here are not necessarily the motives of the ruling group of officers. The results of what they are striving to accomplish are never exactly what they intended; often, they are quite different. Neither must we allow ourselves to form conclusions on the basis of what the officers may proclaim as their objectives. They may declare their intention to abolish poverty, introduce freedom, end corruption, modernise the country, even to bring in measures of socialism. Yet the results of what they do may strengthen capitalism, place new fetters on the people, involve new forms of corruption, create a growing gap between rich and poor, and increase the dependence of the country's economy on the big international monopolies. It is not always easy to discern whether the ruling group of officers who have newly assumed power are genuine radicals who, even while pursuing unhelpful policies, are sincerely trying to safeguard the people's interests and build a strong, independent national economy; or whether they are a bunch of cynical rogues making liberal use of today's radical catch-words in order to mislead the people while busily filling their own pockets. The final test is the objective result of what they are doing – although a mature revolutionary party will naturally take a different attitude towards honest, if mistaken, officers, than it will towards demagogic villains.

Yet, despite the complexities of the situation in so many countries and the need to examine each specific case with some caution, it is necessary to assert that notwithstanding the apparent and temporary autonomous position of the military, and quite independently of the belief the officers themselves may have in their playing a fully independent role, once they have taken power and have to exercise the functions of government they cannot pursue a classless policy or govern in the interests of no class. If they make no changes whatsoever, or merely marginal ones, then objectively they serve the class interests of those that were furthered by the political or military representatives they have displaced. If, on the other hand, they proceed to introduce important changes in the economy and in social and political life, such changes must bear some relationship to the different classes in society.

Whether the rule of the armed forces is aimed at expanding democracy in order to facilitate the assumption of political power by the workers and peasants and the construction of socialism (I am not referring here to the habit of some military and political leaders in the Third World of making declarations about 'socialism' without providing a scientific definition, and without any genuine intention of introducing it), or whether military rule represents a shift between different sections of the bourgeoisie and petty-bourgeoisie, or a shift from feudalism to capitalism, it is quite clearly connected with class interests of one kind or another.

This is so even if what the army does in the field of policy has results which it never intended or was not even aware of. It may think it is simply 'modernising' society, providing it with more industry, a better educational system, social services and so on, but the society which it helps to create cannot be a society separate from or devoid of class content.

In most cases the military-bureaucratic caste will pursue a policy which promotes the development of capitalism thus ensuring, whatever the original intentions of the military leaders, the country's continuing subordination to imperialism. Men make their own history, but they do it within an inherited set of circumstances and under conditions controlled, in the last resort, by the relation of class forces within the given country and in the world as a whole.

The army of the former Cuban dictator, Batista, provides an interesting example. Because of the class structure of Cuba, and the fact that the land was not under the control of feudal landlords, but dominated by large capitalist plantations, mainly owned by US monopolies, Cuba's army in the 1950s could not be based on the traditional Latin American pillar of the landed oligarchy. Batista's army was largely his own personal instrument; but he himself was a puppet of the United States. Thus his army was maintained by the US whose interests it existed to serve. As a result, it was, writes Wood,[13] 'politically and socially isolated, since it possessed no real roots in class needs' (i.e. in the needs of domestic classes).

The middle strata did not trust it, even the bourgeoisie did not regard it as an adequate instrument for their class purposes. Its venal behaviour as a whole resulted in its general alienation from most sections of the population.

Following Batista's own corrupt example, the army officers were mainly preoccupied with amassing huge private fortunes for themselves and leading a life of opulence and pleasure. They were usually involved in every money-making racket, in smuggling, the drug traffic, prostitution, gambling, and bribery. 'As uncouth *parvenus* who acquired riches through a lucky strike', comments Andreski,[14] 'they were lazy and dissolute. Having risen through treachery, they felt neither loyalty to their chief nor to each other, whilst the possession of big funds in foreign banks undermined their will to undergo dangers for the sake of retaining power.'

Increasingly this army became isolated from the overwhelming majority of the population, including sections of the ruling class.

Yet, by its regime of terror and repression, Batista's State, including the army and the police, maintained the capitalist system, provided the conditions for the local bourgeoisie to continue their exploitation of the working people, and made it possible for the US monopolies to carry on their robbery and domination of Cuba. Batista's army was not essentially a direct instrument of the local bourgeoisie, but the policy it pursued served their class interests, as well as those of United States imperialism.

At the present time, when the struggle of the people of the Third World to create new social structures that will overcome poverty and backwardness is so intertwined with their fight against imperialism, the army in these developing countries often fulfils the dual function of serving the external interests of foreign imperialism as well as those of the internal capitalists. Sometimes, in carrying out its role as a servant of external imperialism, the army becomes very much cut off from the decisive classes in the society, and appears to have an independent existence. Such puppet armies, however, still serve specific and definable class interests, even though the interests in question may be those of the big external monopolies.

The Greek colonels' junta provides a rather similar example to that of Batista. In coming to power the Papadopoulos regime not only faced the opposition of the workers and peasants, but found ranged against itself the monarchy, the bourgeois circles led by the conservative Karamanlis, and sections of the bourgeoisie led by the liberal Papandreou. The colonels' coup was prompted and backed by NATO, and especially the United States. In a sense, this was its main class base. But, in pursuing his reactionary, anti-democratic policy, Papadopoulos also preserved Greek capitalism, even though the Greek capitalist political parties were opposed to his regime and were banned by it.

In the present epoch world factors play a much more important role than they did at the time Marx and Engels were analysing the role of armies in nineteenth-century France and Germany. The twentieth century saw the evolution of capitalism from its phase of free competition to the phase of monopoly, of imperialism. Monopoly capital spread its tentacles to the four corners of the globe, and the Third World countries became direct victims of this system of imperialist exploitation. The October Revolution in 1917, and the emergence of thirteen more socialist states after the Second World War, tore a huge gap in the imperialist world system. The evolution of the Third World today takes place at a time when the major contradiction is that between the two systems, capitalism and socialism.

It is in the midst of such a changing world, a world which is heeling over towards socialism notwithstanding all the difficulties still to be faced, that the military in the developing countries plays out its role. The power of the armed forces in these countries to act, even for a short time, as an independent arbiter, is no longer conditioned solely by the interplay and balance of internal class forces. World relationships, too, have to be taken into account, and often these constitute a decisive element in determining the actions and policies of the military leaders.

In the advanced capitalist countries, too, the military leaders face new problems. Their ability to act as if they were outside of politics becomes an increasingly unconvincing performance. For them it has never really been a question of 'keeping out of politics'. Their traditional role has been, in most cases, that of upholding capitalism. But such an automatic response is no longer inevitable. More and more they are being faced with the question of choice; open intervention to preserve the system, or the wiser and more patriotic course of allowing the people the freedom to decide on radical change. For army officers and soldiers the latter is surely the more sensible and more attractive path for the army to follow.

NOTES

1 Lenin, 'The State', speech made to students of Sverdlov University, 11 July 1919, *Collected Works*, Vol. 29, p. 480.

2 Engels, *The Origin of the Family, Private Property and the State*, in Marx and Engels, *Selected Works*, 1949 edition (Moscow), pp. 244, 247, 289.

3 Lenin, *State and Revolution*, *Collected Works*, Vol. 25, p. 389.

4 Engels, op cit., pp. 289–90.

5 Marx, *On the Paris Commune*, Moscow, 1971, pp. 150–1.

6 Marx, *The Eighteenth Brumaire of Louis Bonaparte*, in *Marx/Engels, Selected Works in One Volume*, p. 175.

7 Mirsky, 'The Political Role of the Army in Asian and African Countries' in *The Army and Society*, Moscow, 1969, p. 74.

8 Engels, 'The European Armies', in *Marx-Engels, Werke*, Berlin, 1961–3, Vol. 11, pp. 479–80.

9 Engels, *The Role of Force in History*, London, 1968, p. 62.

10 Mirsky, op. cit., p. 76.

11 Marx, *The Eighteenth Brumaire of Louis Bonaparte, Selected Works*, Vol. 1, op. cit., p. 302.

12 Mirsky, op. cit., p. 75.

13 Dennis B. Wood, 'The Long Revolution: Class Relations and Political Conflict in Cuba, 1868–1968', *Science and Society*, Spring 1970, p. 7.

14 Stanislav Andreski, *Parasitism and Subversion*, London, 1966, pp. 247–8.

4

External and Internal Factors

No two coups are the same, nor are the situations in which they take place identical. Each coup has its own characteristics, motivations, objectives and class character, as well as its own specific relationship to external factors. Conditions, institutions, class structure and class relationships, traditions and political frameworks vary considerably from country to country. The social and class composition of the armed forces, of the ordinary soldiers and of the officer caste, a composition moreover which is not static, also has its distinctive features. Methods of training and sources of arms supply play their part as well.

At the same time, however, there are common features which must be taken into account. The actions of military officers in the last two decades have taken place in a stage of world history in which the forces of progress, of socialism, national liberation and the international working class are becoming stronger, while the forces of reaction, of feudalism and imperialism, are becoming weaker. Imperialism has been forced into a number of retreats and, despite its capacity to hit back and cause immense damage, cannot in the long run subdue the continuing struggle, including that in the Third World, to abolish the remnants of feudalism and to end imperialist domination and exploitation.

This process, however, is not that of a simple direct forward march. It proceeds under complex conditions; the developing countries are beset by numerous and weighty internal problems and external pressures. They suffer constant setbacks and even serious defeats as in Indonesia, Brazil, Ghana, Uganda, Sudan, Uruguay and, perhaps most serious of all, in Chile.

Imperialism still wields considerable power. In many countries in the Third World it has support from domestic reaction, and the forces of internal progress are not yet strong enough to counter the blows against them. Nor is the world anti-imperialist movement yet powerful enough to prevent a number of these defeats from taking place. This arises not only because of the divisions in the ranks of the anti-imperialists but because the total balance of world forces is not yet decisive enough to ensure success in all cases to those opposed to imperialism.

While it is true that in an overall sense the forces of world progress are now strong enough to make it impossible for imperialism any longer to do as it wishes, it would be wrong to interpret this as meaning that imperialism is in the midst of a headlong retreat. World progress in support of the heroic people of Indochina was strong enough to help compel US imperialism eventually to end its open aggression against the people of Vietnam, Laos and Cambodia, but it did not have sufficient power to prevent the initial aggression from taking place, nor to save the people of Indochina from ten years of barbarous attack in which millions died and incalculable damage was done. World progress was strong enough to help the Cuban people safeguard their revolution, but it was powerless to stop the subsequent landing of US marines in the Dominican Republic and the brutal crushing of the people's struggle there to re-establish democratic government. Further, it was unable to do anything decisive to prevent Bordaberry's coup in Uruguay, nor could it stop the US economic offensive against the Chilean Popular Unity Government, let alone prevent the final *coup de grâce* by Pinochet and his thugs. The favourable international relation of forces has contributed towards the advances made in Iraq, Syria and the Democratic Republic of Yemen; but it was unable to stop the counter-coup in Sudan in July 1971 with its attendant slaughter of the Communist leaders, nor has it been able so far to compel Israel to end its ten years of occupation of the Arab lands it seized during the June 1967 war.

In other words, we live at a time in which the world forces of progress – the socialist countries, the national liberation movements, and the international working class – are increasingly deciding the trend of world developments, yet the tide does not flow continuously and irresistibly in a single direction, without temporary halts or retreats, some of them of a very serious nature. It would, of course, be wrong not to understand the historic, global trend towards progress taking place in this epoch; but it would be equally incorrect to overestimate the stage reached, to lapse into a state of complacent euphoria, to fail to take all necessary precautions against reactionary moves or to fall into a state of acute shock and demoralisation each time there is a setback or heavy loss, including a reactionary coup, because it was assumed, in a somewhat simplified fashion, that mankind was on the move and progress could no longer be halted.

Only the most favourable conjunction of internal and external factors can provide the best chances of a victory for progress. Of key importance here is the unity and strength of the internal forces of revolution. Where the movements are weak, or divided, or make serious mistakes, or, despite considerable advances, are unable to mobilise decisive internal support, they can be defeated by internal reaction backed by external imperialism, notwithstanding all the present strength of the world anti-imperialist camp. Even where the internal forces of progress are more united and have powerful local backing they may be faced with acute difficulties if the power of the international movement against imperialism is not in a position to bring its weight to bear in a decisive way at the decisive time.

There are sufficient examples from history to illustrate this. The Russian Revolution of October 1917 took place at a time when all the basic conflicts in Russian society – between workers and employers, between peasants and landlords, between the oppressed peoples in the 'prisonhouse of nations' and Russian imperialism, between revolutionary democracy and the ruling autocracy, between the people's yearning for peace and the Kerensky government's attempt to continue the war – had reached their most acute stage. The Russian Communists were able to unite these various streams, with that of the soldiers who wanted to end Russian participation in the imperialist slaughter, into a powerful revolutionary current directed against the whole capitalist edifice of that society.

These favourable internal factors enabled the Russian Revolution to succeed and defend itself because the external factors were also favourable. The peoples of the other countries involved in the war were weary of the fighting, the sacrifice, the endless slaughter. There was growing unrest in the armies of both camps, as well as at home in the rear. The Russian Revolution which had been preceded by the Easter Uprising in Ireland in 1916 was followed by revolution in Germany in 1918, Hungary in 1919, the French naval mutiny in the Black Sea in 1919, mass desertions from the Italian army and the occupation of the factories in 1920 and in Britain the 'revolt on the Clyde', the formation of 'councils of action', and the 'Hands off Russia' campaign. Although the imperialists intervened in Russia, sending in the armies of fourteen countries, the resistance of the Russian working people and their new Red Army, combined with the world-wide movement of solidarity with the Revolution, forced the interventionists to call off their attack and the Revolution triumphed.

Spain from 1936 to 1939 provides a different example. There the initial fascist coup failed to achieve its immediate objective of overthrowing the Republic. The internal relation of forces, the readiness of the majority of Spanish workers to fight and die to defend their democratic achievements, the willingness of the peasants and sections of the urban middle strata to support them, and the loyalty to the Republic displayed by a substantial part of the army itself, provided a basis to rally the majority of Spanish people to defeat the fascists. If matters had been left solely to the internal forces, the Republic could probably have been saved, fascism defeated, and a new advanced form of democracy established opening up prospects of a broad-based democratic transition to socialism.

But though the internal relations of forces were favourable, the external relations were not. The Soviet Union sent arms, food and materials, and volunteers. The Communist Parties throughout the world and other democratic forces provided personnel for the International Brigades, collected funds and medical aid for Spain and gave whatever support they could. But fascist Germany and Italy sent in thousands of well-equipped troops, aircraft, tanks and warships; and the hypocritical policy of 'non-intervention', initiated by France and Britain, resulted in the Spanish Republic being denied its legal right to obtain arms and other assistance. Only the Soviet Union and Mexico respected Spain's moral and legal right to receive help, and acted on that basis.

The examples of the revolutionary struggles in Russia and Spain, each in a different way, illustrate the importance of the external relation of forces when internal conflicts take place. But just as the internal process of revolution even in favourable conditions runs up against difficulties if the external factors are unfavourable, so, conversely, even when the external factors are favourable (and this can include the geographical proximity of an ally, especially a powerful one) the revolution finds it difficult to advance in a given country if its own forces are insufficiently strong.

This is borne out by the contrasting examples of Vietnam and Egypt. The populations of these two countries are roughly the same; their industrial strength somewhat similar, with Egypt in some ways more industrially developed. Both countries faced external aggression. Both were supplied with large quantities of modern military equipment by the Soviet Union and other socialist countries. Vietnam faced the direct onslaught of US imperialism which employed over 500,000 troops, a large air-fleet, naval craft, and all the most savage and sophisticated weapons of war. Egypt in the 1967 Six-Day war faced a heavily armed attack from Israel. The Vietnamese fought continuously for over ten years, and despite the most appalling loss of life and destruction to which they were subjected, they emerged triumphant. The Egyptians, notwithstanding all their military equipment, collapsed in 1967 in six short days, their aircraft left to be destroyed on the airfields, their tanks and artillery abandoned as officers and troops fled the enemy.

The external relations of forces in each case were basically similar, yet the internal situations were vastly different. In the case of Vietnam, the people were united under revolutionary leadership and their armed forces (this went for the armed forces of the Democratic Republic in the North as well as for those of the National Liberation Front in the South) were imbued with the political understanding that they were fighting for a new and just social order.

In Egypt, despite the progress since the overthrow of Farouk in 1952, there was still a considerable capitalist class, owning factories and land, and utilising state positions for economic advancement, speculation and corruption; and the armed forces in 1967 very much reflected that situation. There was a wide gap separating the officers from the peasant soldiers, a gap arising from social backgrounds as well as from the quite contrasting economic, social and political perspectives that each saw before them. Political understanding and morale were low, and links between the armed forces and the civilian population weak.

The examples cited here of Russia, Spain, Vietnam and Egypt are not all directly related to the question of coups, but they illustrate that political processes, including those that have reached a very acute stage of conflict, are hastened or held back by a combination of external and internal factors. At the same time, they show that even a favourable external relationship of forces, including military aid, cannot act as a substitute for the growth of the internal forces of revolution. These principles are very relevant to any serious consideration of military coups.

In considering the question of coups today and examining why they often succeed it is essential to bear in mind the totality of forces at work, both the international interplay of class relations and the internal relationship – for what the military might do in a given situation is very much determined by all these circumstances which influence the thinking of both officers and soldiers and consequently their behaviour.

In Britain we have had civilian governments and parliamentary procedures for so long that the question of a military coup, with the country being governed openly and directly by a military establishment, as is so often the case in countries of the Third World, has for long appeared as a quite unbelievable situation, certainly not as the norm. Yet, as Eliezer Be'eri points out:

A State in which the elected representatives of all or most of the people determine the laws, in which the administrative apparatus is responsible to a separate legislative body and the military leaders are subject to the authority of these legislative and executive arms of government – such a State is a relatively new phenomenon in history, very rare prior to the nineteenth century.[1]

Of course, one should not overstate the position. It is correct, as Be'eri points out, that civilian governments were not always the normal form of rule in Europe. Historically a separation of functions between military and political authority only came about over a long period of time. The head of State came to power either by militarily defeating internal rivals or by vanquishing an external enemy; or he inherited power from such a military victory and conquest, and had often to lead his armies into battle to defend his power. Under feudalism, the monarchy and the barons were military leaders as well as being large landowners and exploiters of serf labour; and, at the same time, they constituted the governing political authority. The evolution of the army as a separate weapon of the State took place in Europe over a considerable period, taking final shape with the decline of feudalism and the rise of capitalism.

But it would be incorrect to conclude that, because of the changes that have taken place in Europe over the centuries, the dangers of a military government can no longer arise in our continent. We have, after all, seen a military government installed in Greece as recently as 1967. Even if this is an exception in recent years, Europe has in no way been immune to the dangers of weighty military pressure and even open intervention in politics and government. In Britain we had the Curragh mutiny in 1914, when British army officers openly acted to thwart a modest reform intended to solve the Irish crisis at that time. Neither should one ignore the role played by military officers, even by the top leadership itself, in paving the way for fascism in Italy, Germany[2] and Spain. In more recent times, too, reactionary French officers tried to organise a coup in France in the dying days of the Algerian war; in Italy there has been an open identification of leading military personnel with the fascist MSI party, as well as a NATO-inspired plot to organise a military coup. In the United States, while the Pentagon does not directly hold the reins of government, it undoubtedly wields considerable influence over the government's policies.

The important thing, after all, is that the modern army in the advanced capitalist countries of Europe and the United States has been built up as a key component of the whole power structure of State monopoly capitalism. Through their economic links with big business, and because of their social and ideological identification with the status quo, the high-ranking officers who control the armed forces, conceive their role and that of the officers and men under them as that of defenders of the system.

It does not seem worth labouring the point that high-ranking officers in these countries [advanced capitalist countries] have constituted a deeply conservative and even reactionary element in the state system and in society generally, and that their social origin, class situation and professional interest have led them to view the character and content of 'democratic' politics with distaste, suspicion and often hostility. . . . [It] is not sufficient to speak of military conservatism in general terms. For that conservatism has long assumed a much more specific character, in the sense that it encompasses an often explicit acceptance, not simply of 'existing institutions', or of particular 'values', but of a quite specific existing economic and social system and a corresponding opposition to any meaningful alternative to that system.[3]

For top officers this identification with the system has often become cemented through their direct alliance with major monopolies, especially those connected with the arms industry, such as chemicals, electronics, aircraft and the space industry as well as general weaponry (tanks, artillery, etc.). This is outstandingly true of the United States. It is well-known that many of the high-ranking officers who arrived in Europe with the US armies in 1944–5 were leading representatives of major US firms who had come to size up their future business prospects and secure an early foothold for that purpose. Emphasising the tie-up between the military and the monopolies in the United States, Professor Huntington has written:

Few developments more dramatically symbolised the new status of the military in the postwar decade than the close association which they developed with the business élite of American society . . . Professional officers and businessmen revealed a new mutual respect. Retired generals and admirals in unprecedented numbers went into the executive staffs of American corporations; new organisations arose bridging the gap between corporate management and military leadership. For the military officers, business represented the epitome of the American way of life.[4]

The industrial-military complex is equally true of Britain, even though not generally so well-known.

NOTES

1 Be'eri, op. cit., p. 275.
2 See above, pp. 11–14.
3 Ralph Miliband, *The State in Capitalist Society*, London, 1969 (paperback 1973), pp. 116–17.
4 S. P. Huntington, *The Soldier and the State*, 1957, pp. 361–2 (cited in Miliband, op. cit.).

5

Coups and Conspiracies

Some people argue as if all coups can be explained solely in terms of imperialist conspiracies, of plots and assassinations organised directly by the Central Intelligence Agency and the intelligence services of other imperialist states.

It is true, of course, that the CIA and other agencies are actively engaged in plotting the downfall of progressive regimes in Europe as well as in the Third World. A number of coups, in fact, can be clearly and directly laid at their door, such as the coup against Mossadeq in Iran, Arbenz in Guatemala, Bosch in Dominica, Jagan in Guyana, Sihanouk in Cambodia, and the coup against Allende and his Popular Unity Government in Chile. The 1967 colonels' coup in Greece was also initiated by the CIA, as was the 1974 coup against Makarios. Undoubtedly there are many other coups for which the CIA was responsible,[1] quite apart from those already in blue-print stage or being otherwise considered. When the full story of this 'Murder Incorporated' comes to light it will no doubt be demonstrated that its ramifications have been far greater than has been generally appreciated.

Yet to see only the plotters, to rivet our gaze solely on the intelligence agent and his actions, would limit our understanding of what lies behind the plots. We would be neglecting the significance of the circumstances surrounding a given coup, what had created the situation in which the coup was considered necessary, what factors facilitated the success of the coup, what were the objectives of the coup, which classes or strata in society benefited from it, and so on.

If, for example, we consider the question of the political intervention of the military in the Third World where the vast majority of coups have taken place in recent decades and where most of the military or military/civilian governments exist, we shall see that while foreign intelligence agents play a vital part their possibilities of doing so and the manner of their operations is very much linked to all the surrounding circumstances. If CIA initiatives produce success for the United States in one case and fail lamentably in another this is not because the intelligence operators worked harder, more cunningly and with greater determination in 'Operation A' than they did in 'Operation B', but primarily because other factors – political, social, economic – were more favourable for the success of the coup in one given set of circumstances and at one particular time than they were in the other.

In this period of neo-colonialism, in which the imperialist states seek to establish governments in the Third World which will collaborate with them, the actual planting of agents, or their open purchase, is only part of the game. An equally important aim is to support or create *allies*, to nourish the social forces on which governments friendly to the imperialists can be based. This is true also of the most reactionary military coups, in which imperialism makes use of existing situations, of current crises, internal conflicts and rivalries, the personal and social ambitions of individuals and groups, the interplay of class and social forces, in order to ensure the advance of its own interests.

As Be'eri puts it:

Generally it is true that foreign agents can operate and exert influence when there are local people who are interested in co-operating with the force in whose service they are acting.[2]

Ruth First makes the same point:

Local allies, not agents, are the key.[3]

At the same time, as she herself correctly notes:

. . . even though no dollars need pass hands, and no secret codes pass between intelligence operators, the West has its own ways of influencing events before and after a *coup d'état*, to spur its occurrence and secure its survival.[4]

As she explains, the basic structures of African states and societies, for example, are such that they contain the seeds of coups within themselves. And, as she adds:

It is precisely because foreign powers and bodies like the CIA understand this well, that their interventions, even very indirect ones, are so effective.[5]

It is, of course, certainly true that the CIA has been 'effective' in many Third World countries in having been able to organise a number of military coups, but a price has also been paid through the extent to which the hand of the CIA has become known, thus bringing the United States and its agencies into world wide disrepute. This exposure of CIA operations arises partly from the habit US officials have of bragging openly about the coups which the CIA have pulled off, as for example in the case of John Puerefoy, the US Ambassador in Guatemala at the time of the coup against Arbenz, in 1954.[6] More recent exposures (*The Pentagon Papers*, *The CIA and the Cult of Intelligence*, *Inside the Company – CIA Diary*),[7] in the latter two cases by former CIA employees themselves, have thrown still more light on the method of operations followed by the CIA, and the extent of their activities.

What is striking about these revelations is the picture they provide of a strange combination of crude thuggery and the sophisticated manipulation of individuals. Brutal assassinations, the open purchase of individuals and organisations, and clumsy forgeries rub shoulders with the delicate selection and influencing of key personnel in foreign states. Reporting on the activities of the CIA in the Congo in the early 1960s, Marchetti and Marks[8] write:

Clandestine Service operators regularly bought and sold Congolese politicians, and the agency supplied money and arms to the supporters of Cyril Adoula and Joseph Mobutu. By 1964, the CIA had imported its own mercenaries into the Congo, and the agency's B-26 bombers, flown by Cuban exile pilots – many of whom were Bay of Pigs veterans – were carrying out regular missions against insurgent groups.

Hedrick Smith has described the CIA's involvement in the assassination of President Diem of South Vietnam, when his failures and political isolation had rendered him expendable, in the following terms:

For weeks – and with the White House informed every step of the way – the American mission in Saigon maintained secret contacts with the plotting generals through one of the Central Intelligence Agency's most experienced and versatile operatives, an Indochina veteran, Lieut.-Col Lucien Conein. He first landed in Vietnam in 1944 by parachute for the Office of Strategic Services, the wartime forerunner of the CIA.

So trusted by the Vietnamese generals was Colonel Conein that he was in their midst at Vietnamese General Staff headquarters as they launched the coup. Indeed, on Oct. 25, a week earlier, in a cable to McGeorge Bundy, the President's special assistant for national security, Ambassador Lodge had occasion to describe Colonel Conein of the CIA – referring to the agency, in code terminology, as CAS – as the indispensable man:

'CAS has been punctilious in carrying out my instructions. I have personally approved each meeting between General Don [one of three main plotters] and Conein who has carried out my orders in each instance explicitly. . . .

'Conein, as you know, is a friend of some 18 years' standing with General Don, and General Don has expressed extreme reluctance to deal with anyone else. I do not believe the involvement of another American in close contact with the generals would be productive.'

So closely did the CIA work with the generals, official documents reveal, that it provided them with vital intelligence about the arms and encampments of pro-Diem military forces after Mr Lodge had authorized CIA participation in tactical planning of the coup.[9]

And so, through a CIA operative, acting in collaboration with South Vietnamese officers who had been 'won over' and/or bought, the US State Department (for, after all, the US Ambassador in Saigon was directly involved and obviously acting on the instructions of his government) coolly plotted the assassination of one of its allies who had become expendable.

This well illustrates the extent to which bodies such as the CIA are directly responsible for a number of military coups. Equally, it shows that to achieve such an objective the CIA had to work through individuals in the country concerned who, for one reason or another – ideological sympathy, cash, desire for power – were prepared to act as allies to the United States.

How the CIA functions, how its different arms of operations assist one another, how it strives in country after country to influence and, if necessary, overthrow governments, has been partly revealed by Agee, by Marchetti and Marks, and by the notorious Minutes of the Bissell Meeting.[10] As these minutes reveal, the report given by Richard Bissell was mainly devoted to the subject of what in CIA terminology is known as 'covert intelligence'. This, according to Bissell, covers two categories of covert operations, firstly espionage and the obtaining of information; and secondly, attempting 'to influence the internal affairs of other nations, sometimes called "intervention" by covert means'. Expounding his thesis at some length, Bissell shows the nature of the connection between the two categories and the way in which the collection of intelligence information provides the basis on which the US is able to take the appropriate action to influence internal developments. As Bissell puts it:

. . . the underdeveloped world presents greater opportunities for covert intelligence collection, simply because governments are much less highly oriented; there is less security consciousness; and there is apt to be more actual or potential diffusion of power among parties, localities, organisations and individuals outside of the central governments. The primary purpose of espionage in these areas is to provide Washington with a timely knowledge of the internal power balance. . . . Why is this relevant? Changes in the balance of power are extremely difficult to discern except through frequent contact with power elements. Again and again we have been surprised at *coups* within the military; often we have failed to talk to the junior officers or non-coms who are involved in the *coups*. The same problem applies to labour leaders, and others. Frequently we don't know of power relationships, because power balances are murky and sometimes not well known even to the principal actors. Only by knowing the principal actors well do you have a chance of careful prediction. There is real scope for action in this area; the technique is essentially that of 'penetration', including 'penetrations' of the sort which horrify classicists of covert operations. . . . Many of the 'penetrations' don't take the form of 'hiring' but of establishing a close or friendly relationship (which may or may not be furthered by the provision of money from time to time).

In some countries the CIA representative has served as a close counselor (and in at least one case a drinking companion) of the chief of state. These are situations, of course, in which the tasks of intelligence collection and political action overlap to the point of being almost indistinguishable.[11]

Bissell outlined eight categories of covert action: (1) political advice and counsel; (2) subsidies to an individual; (3) finance and 'technical assistance' to political parties; (4) support to organisations, including trade unions, and co-operatives, as well as to business firms, etc.; (5) covert propaganda; (6) 'private' training of individuals and exhange of persons; (7) economic operations; (8) paramilitary political operations designed to overthrow a regime (as in the case of the Bay of Pigs), or to support a regime (as in Laos).

It can well be imagined how the large-scale use of these various methods of intervention can, and has in fact, caused serious damage to the independent functioning of governments in many parts of the world. Among the countries in which intervention, successful in some cases and unsuccessful in others, has taken place through the covert operations of the CIA, Marchetti and Marks mention Indonesia, Tibet, Congo (Zaire), Philippines, China, Burma, Korea, Cuba, Laos, Vietnam, Guatemala, Peru, Bolivia and Iran. Many more could be added to the list. In fact, there cannot be many countries where the CIA has not intervened in one form or another, either to remove or to support an existing government.

Bissell sums up his, and presumably the State Department's and CIA's views (although these do not always coincide in detail)[12] in these words:

The essence of such intervention in the internal power balance is the identification of allies who can be rendered more effective, more powerful, and perhaps wiser through covert assistance. Typically these allies know the source of their assistance but neither they nor the United States could afford to admit its existence. *Agents for fairly minor and low sensitivity interventions, for instance some covert propaganda and certain economic activities, can be recruited simply with money. But for the larger and more sensitive interventions, the allies must have their own motivation.* On the whole the

Agency has been remarkably successful in finding individuals and instrumentalities with which and through which it could work in this fashion. Implied in the requirement for a pre-existing motivation is the corollary that an attempt to induce the local ally to follow a course of action he does not believe in will at least destroy his effectiveness and may destroy the whole operation (italics added).[13]

Bissell expresses in his report the realisation of the ruling circles in the United States that their role in world affairs, and the particular role of the CIA itself, has made the use of Americans in foreign countries for CIA work a hazardous undertaking. Accordingly, he recommends an increasing utilisation of nationals of each of the countries concerned in place of US citizens. Such people, he explains, after a period of 'indoctrination and training' should be 'encouraged to develop a second loyalty, more or less comparable to that of the American staff'.[14] The desirability of doing this, he stresses, increases as 'we shift our attention to Latin America, Asia and Africa where the conduct of US nationals is easily subject to scrutiny and is likely to be increasingly circumscribed'.

Part of this process is that of what is known in CIA circles as 'building assets'. This involves the winning over or buying up of potential allies or agents prior to their actual use in a scheduled operation, often years earlier. Direct CIA operators have to be 'adept at convincing people that working for the agency is in their interest'. This work of 'convincing people' is carried out in various forms, including 'appeals to patriotism and anti-communism', often 'reinforced with flattery, or sweetened with money and power', or even obtained by the use of 'blackmail and coercion'. Recruitment of agents and allies on these lines is carried on over a long period so that, in the given country, the CIA will have built up 'a network of agents in that country's government, military forces, press, labour unions, and other important groups; *thus there is, in effect, a standing force in scores of countries ready to serve the CIA when the need arises*'[15] (italics added). Within this process of 'building assets', special attention is paid by the CIA to both army and police in the given country.

The scale of operations of the intelligence agencies is massive; and this is not surprising considering the stakes involved at this very acute stage of world history. The official figures for the CIA alone are 16,500 employees at a cost of 750 million dollars a year (not including the Directors' Special Contingency Fund). But, as Marchetti and Marks point out, these figures do not reflect the 'tens of thousands who serve under contract (mercenaries, agents, consultants, etc.) or who work for the agency's proprietory companies'.[16] These authors estimate the CIA staff to be 'two or three times as large as it appears to be'. Similarly, the CIA's annual budget is far higher than the authorised 750 million dollars a year. In fact, as noted by Marchetti and Marks, 'the CIA's chief of planning and programming reverently observed a few years ago that the director does not operate a mere *multimillion*-dollar agency but actually runs a *multibillion*-dollar conglomerate . . .'.[17]

But that does not yet complete the story, for the CIA is not the only intelligence agency available to the rulers of the United States. The table below gives a fuller picture, although one must remember that these are official figures only and, from what we have seen of the CIA above, reflect only a part of the total numbers involved.

SIZE AND COST OF US INTELLIGENCE COMMUNITY (*approximate*)

Organization	Personnel	Annual budget
Central Intelligence Agency	16,500	$750,000,000
National Security Agency*	24,000	$1,200,000,000
Defence Intelligence Agency*	5,000	$200,000,000
Army Intelligence*	35,000	$700,000,000
Naval Intelligence*	15,000	$600,000,000
Air Force Intelligence* (Including the National Reconnaissance Office)	56,000	$2,700,000,000
State Department (Bureau of Intelligence and Research)	350	$8,000,000
Federal Bureau of Investigation (Internal Security Division)	800	$40,000,000
Atomic Energy Commission (Division of Intelligence)	300	$20,000,000
Treasury Department	300	$10,000,000
Total	153,250	$6,228,000,000

* Department of Defense agency.
[*Source*: Marchetti and Marks, op. cit., p. 80.]

As Marchetti and Marks comment:

Clearly, the CIA is not the hub, nor is its Director the head, of the vast US intelligence community. The sometimes glamorous, incorrigibly clandestine agency is merely a part of a much larger interdependent federation dominated by the Pentagon. And although the Director of Central Intelligence is nominally designated by each President in turn as the government's chief intelligence adviser, he is in fact overshadowed in the realities of Washington's politics by both the Secretary of Defense and the President's own Assistant for National Security Affairs, as well as by several lesser figures, such as the Chariman of the Joint Chiefs of Staff. . . . The CIA's primary task is not to coordinate the efforts of US intelligence or even to produce finished national intelligence for the policy-makers. *Its job is, for better or worse, to conduct the government's covert foreign policy*[18] (italics added).

It is on the basis of such devious methods of approach that imperialist intelligence agencies influence military and political figures in the countries in which they operate and foster traitors with 'a second loyalty' to the CIA.[19] The agencies of British, French, German and Japanese imperialisms have not been so exposed and written-up as has the CIA; and there are, moreover, aspects and methods of their activities which differ from those of the United States. But in broad general lines the kind of approach outlined by Bissell governs the activities of all the imperialist intelligence agencies.

It is this general approach, too, which governs most coups in which imperialism has a hand. Imperialist intervention, while it employs many paid agents, relies largely on its utilisation of existing situations and internal crises (some of which it creates or aggravates, but most of which arise from other internal factors). To make the most fruitful use of such developments, imperialism has to be well acquainted with the main social forces, with the realities of class relations and their ebb and flow, and with the personal ambitions and motivations of the key personnel in the State and in the general political life of the particular country.

In other words, to advance its own ends, imperialism seeks out those social forces and individuals whose short-term or longer-term interests will place them on its side, even if only temporarily; or, if necessary in the given circumstances, it seeks out and promotes those who may not be committed to supporting imperialism directly but who have not taken up a consistent and clear anti-imperialist position, and who, it is therefore hoped, will stand in the way of the most firm anti-imperialist forces in the country.

At a time when the main contradiction in the world is that between socialism and capitalism, a major preoccupation of the imperialists is to keep the developing countries 'with the West'. This is not only a question of maintaining valuable sources of profit, of rich raw materials, cheap land and cheap labour, and monopoly controlled markets. It also involves keeping a grip on strategic areas, including small islands, whose wealth may not be great but whose geographical situation is crucial for holding on to profitable territories in the area, or for providing an important base for attack on national liberation movements, or against the socialist countries.

It is with all these considerations in mind that imperialism strives to influence the leading personnel in the military establishments of the developing countries. Most of these considerations also apply equally to the activities of imperialist agencies operating in the developed capitalist countries.

The ability to succeed in such ventures, and their motivation, are related to what Bissell has termed 'the internal power balance'. Where the internal balance of power is heavily weighted against those who seek to carry out a coup, all the accumulated experience and expertise of the coup organisers is unlikely to avail. No army or group of military leaders acts in a vacuum. This is a truism that the CIA and other intelligence agencies well understand, even if some students of coups appear to think that one can explain the political role of the military in terms of what the army leaders themselves aim to achieve.

NOTES

1 See, for more details: Norodom Sihanouk and Wilfred Burchett, *My War with the CIA*, London, 1973; Philip Agee, *Inside the Company – CIA Diary*, London, 1975; Neil Sheehan, etc., *The Pentagon Papers*, New York, 1971; Victor Marchetti and John D. Marks, *The CIA and the Cult of Intelligence*, London, 1974.

2 Be'eri, op. cit., p. 272.

3 First, *The Barrel of a Gun*, London, 1970, p. 417.

4 ibid., p. 414.

5 ibid.

6 This is in marked contrast to the more stiff upper-lipped silence of British intelligence operators who no doubt have many coups to their 'credit'. Ironically, it was the British military intelligence services which helped to train both the OSS (Office of Strategic Services) as well as its follower, the CIA.

7 See above, note 1.

8 Marchetti and Marks, op. cit., p. 31.

9 *The Pentagon Papers* (Neil Sheehan, Hedrick Smith, E. W. Kenworthy and Fox Butterfield), New York, 1971, p. 159.

10 Richard Bissell was a senior officer of the CIA's Clandestine Services, of which he became head in 1958 on the recommendation of Allen Dulles, CIA Chief. He planned the ill-fated Bay of Pigs invasion of Cuba in April 1961. He was succeeded by Richard Helms in February 1962. On 8 January 1968 the Intelligence and Foreign Policy Group of the Council of Foreign Affairs, a United States institution whose members include Allen Dulles and which receives funds from the CIA, held a private meeting

which was addressed by Bissell. The minutes of this meeting were 'liberated' from the files of David Truman, Dean of Columbia College, during a student strike there in 1968, and subsequently published by the Africa Research Group. Ruth First (*The Barrel of a Gun*) utilised this document, with citations, when writing her book in 1969, which was published in 1970. Inexplicably, Marchetti and Marks, referring to the same document, provide a different date, college and individual as the source of the information. Thus they allege it was captured in 1971, that it was found during a student occupation at the Harvard University Centre for International Affairs, Cambridge, Massachusetts, and that it was taken from the files of William Harris. Marchetti and Marks have some explaining to do, for clearly Ruth First could not have quoted from a document in 1969 if it was not revealed until 1971!

11 Marchetti and Marks, op. cit., Appendix, p. 386.

12 A certain myth has developed as to the virtual independence of the CIA from control by the United States government and its bodies. Marchetti and Marks (the former worked for the CIA for fourteen years, and the latter was a State Department employee for four years) challenge this view. Though they agree that the actual operations of the CIA are not always subject to control, yet: 'Every major CIA proposal for covert action – including subsidies for foreign political leaders, political parties or publications, interference in elections, major propaganda activities, and paramilitary operations – still must be approved by the President or the 40 Committee' (p. 326), a body headed, at the moment of writing, by Secretary of State Kissinger. '. . . It is the President and Kissinger who ultimately determine how the CIA operates . . . both men believe in the need for the United States to use clandestine methods and "dirty tricks" in dealing with other countries, and the current level and types of such operations obviously coincide with their views of how America's secret foreign policy should be carried out' (p. 333).

13 ibid., p. 389.

14 ibid., pp. 390–1.

15 ibid., p. 37. The all-embracing character of these operations is well brought out by Philip Agee in his detailed account of the activities of the CIA in Uruguay (see *Inside the Company*, op. cit.), as well as by Sihanouk and Burchett (op. cit.).

16 ibid., p. 58.

17 ibid., p. 62.

18 ibid., p. 104.

19 Marchetti and Marks (p. 252) explain that one of the training methods used in the CIA is designed to show how well the trainee is suited 'for convincing a foreign official he should become a traitor to his country; for manipulating that official, often against his will; and for "terminating" the agent when he has outlived his usefulness to the CIA'.

6

Why Progressive Military Coups Take Place

Understandably, since military coups have been associated mainly with the Third World, generalised theories about the causes and characteristics of coups in the last decade or so have been developed largely in relation to these countries, even though some of the conclusions in this regard have a relevance to advanced capitalist countries, too.

Writing specifically about the 1952 action of the Egyptian military officers which overthrew King Farouk, Aharon Cohen has put forward the following related set of circumstances to explain why military coups take place:

When the old rulers are no longer able to hold on to power, the middle classes too weak to seize it, and the working class not yet matured for this task, officers fill the vacuum which has been formed.[1]

Ruth First has made much the same point:

Coups d'état occur because governments are too weak to rule, but radical forces too weak to take power.[2]

These definitions can be taken as a starting point, but they require further discussion. Obviously not all coups take place for the same reason, nor are they of the same character. Mirsky[3] provides four main reasons for military coups in the developing countries:

(1) The presence in the country of extensive, mainly nationalistic, dissatisfaction with an insufficiently independent or openly pro-Western political ruling élite, which does not want to and is unable to carry out the necessary social reforms, in the absence of a strong and organised civilian opposition to the regime. This factor was chief in Egypt and Iraq.[4]

(2) A long drawn out inner political crisis, due to the inability of the civilian government to solve internal problems and lead the country out of a dead end.

(3) Dissatisfaction of the educated élite with an inert and archaic despotic regime (for example, in Yemen).

(4) The inefficiency of the civilian government, combined with corrupt

administration, the apathy and disappointment of the masses, and the fear of the privileged élite that the left forces may gain ground and bring about a people's revolution [e.g. Ayub Khan in Pakistan, Abboud in the Sudan, and Gursel in Turkey; i.e. a coup to preempt a revolution].

To these four main reasons of Mirsky, who strangely omits all mention of right-wing coups against anti-imperialist governments, it is necessary to add three more:

(1) Coups to overthrow progressive governments [e.g. against Ben Bella in Algeria, Arbenz in Guatemala, Sukarno in Indonesia, Nkrumah in Ghana, Modibo Keita in Mali, Obote in Uganda, Allende and Popular Unity in Chile; one could even include here such moderately liberal governments as that of Mossadeq in Iran, Goulart in Brazil, and General Torres in Bolivia].

(2) Coups in which 'tribalism' or ethnic factors are important [e.g. the young officers' coup in Nigeria in 1966, followed by Ironsi's coup, leading to General Gowon's coup, and culminating in the Nigeria-Biafra war].

(3) Coups in which imperialist conflicts are fought out by proxy [e.g. Tshombe (Anglo-Belgian) versus Mobutu (United States) in Congo (Kinshasa) – now Zaire].

It should be observed that the last two categories often intertwine, especially as the imperialists utilise 'tribal' and ethnic conflicts for their own purposes.

Dealing specifically with coups in Africa, Ruth First has argued:

The heat of the political crisis in new states is generated largely by the struggle over the spoils between competing layers of the power élite.[5]

It seems to me that this view places too much emphasis on what is happening at the top, where the actual shift of control takes place, and not enough on what has happened down below to necessitate a change of rule. After all, if, as both Aharon Cohen and Ruth First have rightly pointed out, one of the main factors opening the way to military coups is the inability of the former rulers to solve the country's problems and to maintain their rule, the question is immediately posed: Why is this so? Who or what has made their position so weak?

In examining this question it is necessary to make a clear distinction between:

(a) Coups of a progressive character (e.g. Egypt in 1952, Iraq in 1958, Burma in 1962, Peru in 1968, Somalia in 1969, etc.).
(b) Reactionary coups which pre-empt a possible progressive civilian change of government (e.g. Pakistan – both Ayub Khan and Yayha Khan).

(c) Coups of a clearly reactionary character aimed at removing a progressive government (e.g. overthrow of Nkrumah, Sukarno, etc.).

As regards the first group, there has developed in military circles what has been termed the 'theory of the natural course'. An early proponent of this theory was Kemal Atatürk:

Every time the Turkish nation wished to take a step forward, it cast its eyes on the army. . . . When I speak of the army, I speak of the intelligentsia of the Turkish nation – the true masters of the country.[6]

Of course, it is natural for army officers to see themselves, or to present themselves, in the most favourable light. Even the most reactionary officers, carrying out right-wing coups, have tended to depict themselves as the most sincere and disinterested patriots whose sole concern is the welfare of their people.

The limitations of progressive coups and progressive military governments will be examined later, but at this point it is necessary to observe that in such coups the officers who declare for a progressive course and who claim that they are the only force that can bring about the necessary changes, seldom link themselves with the advanced working class and revolutionary forces in their country prior to carrying through their coup; and subsequently, after they are installed in government, they usually reveal an ambivalent attitude towards the working class and democratic movement towards which they display suspicion, fear, contempt and even open hostility.

There are, of course, exceptions to this pattern, as for example in Somalia where the military-led regime is making strenuous and genuine efforts to organise the workers and peasants, help raise their political understanding and assist in the formation of a political movement through which the people can express their views and demands. In some other cases, such as Peru,[7] Iraq and Algeria, all three instances where the governments came into being as a result of a coup, and where progressive steps have been taken against both domestic reaction and foreign imperialism, the working people have new opportunities for democratic activity, yet still under some degree of restraint.

The role of the Armed Forces Movement in Portugal is obviously of great significance here, especially as the Portuguese working class, its trade unions and other mass social organisations, and its political parties, including the Communist Party, now have opportunities to carry on their democratic activity after fifty years of fascist repression. The relationship established between the Portuguese Armed Forces Movement and the working class and people since the overthrow of the Caetano fascist regime is quite a new feature in modern Europe which we shall examine in more detail later.

In considering why progressive coups take place in the Third World, perhaps the use of the term 'progressive' should first be explained. In relation to internal democracy, to the power and participation of the workers and peasants, such regimes have obvious shortcomings. Even among the most progressive there remain attitudes of paternalism, if not reserve, towards the working people. The 'progressive' character of these regimes, however, is not determined by such considerations but by their total role and policy in relation to internal feudalism and external imperialism, although even here there are sometimes ambiguities in their position.

In their steps to weaken feudalism, economically, politically and ideologically; in their measures to reconstruct the economy, provide education for wider strata of the population, establish some degree of social services; and in their endeavours to restrict and cut back imperialism's grip on the country's economic life, these military rulers are helping to drag their countries out of the past. In acting thus they are playing a progressive role, even though their outlook, formed and moulded by their class and social position, prevents them giving full scope to the democratic initiative of the people, and especially to the workers and peasants.

Their basic attitude towards the democratic activities of the working people is also revealed in their concept of the relative roles played by the military and the people in the actual coup itself. Military leaders in a number of Arab countries, for example, have claimed that the armed forces are the only available force, and the force best equipped, to carry through the kind of fundamental political, economic and social changes which have become necessary. Gamal Abdul Nasser, for example, in his *Philosophy of the Revolution*,[8] attempted to justify the army's action in these words:

. . . the state of affairs . . . singled out the army as the force to do the job [i.e. carry through revolutionary changes – Author]. The situation demanded the existence of a force set in one cohesive framework, far removed from the conflict between individuals and classes, and drawn from the heart of the people: a force composed of men able to trust each other, a force with enough material strength at its disposal to guarantee swift and decisive action. These conditions could be met only by the army. . . .

General Kassem, too, put forward somewhat the same explanation to justify the army's action and assumption of power through the overthrow of the regime of Nuri Said in 1958. The army, he claimed, 'would not have launched this revolution had our brothers outside the army been able to wrong their rights by force of peace. But they had been overcome and were enfeebled.'[9] Kingsley Martin once likewise asserted that: 'In Arab countries the only force then able to to carry out the necessary revolution is the army. . . .'[10] In essence, these views, accepting the necessity for revolutionary change in the Middle East, but advancing the thesis that the army is the only force which can carry through such a transformation, ignore or even eliminate entirely the role of the people as the makers of history, and especially the particular role of the working class in helping to provide both the ideology and the organised cohesiveness which the revolution requires. In the belief of those who hold to such a theory, *The Communist Manifesto* has been supplanted by (Nasser's) *The Philosophy of the Revolution.*'[11]

In fact, however, neither in Egypt nor in Iraq was the army or rather the group of progressive officers which led the armed action the sole force of the revolution. It is even arguable whether they were the main historic agent. Both in Egypt and in Iraq there had been decades of struggle and sacrifice by the mass of the people; and especially in Iraq, in the period leading up to the overthrow of Nuri Said, massive popular actions had already shaken up the old regime and paved the way for its demise in which the death blow was struck by the progressive officers. Despite Kassem's claim that the people's movement was 'enfeebled', it grew particularly in the two years leading up to the July 1958 revolution.

The Iraqi people's movement had, in fact, developed over many years; and a major factor had been the Communist Party.

From the time of the first national revolution in modern Iraq in 1920 right up to the overthrow of Nuri Said in July 1958 Iraq was constantly shaken by the people's resistance. One highlight was the national revolt of 1948 which compelled the British Labour Government to abandon its attempt to force the Portsmouth Treaty on the Iraqi people. The Iraqi puppet government of the time exacted a terrible revenge on the people. Thousands were thrown into prison, and the Communist leaders were hanged, including its general secretary. In the 1950s the struggle mounted again, especially after the Anglo-French attack on Egypt in 1956. The people rose in open revolt. Strikes and demonstrations took place in many parts of the country, including a giant demonstration of 200,000 in Mosul. Scores of demonstrators were killed and hundreds arrested.[12] Despite Nuri Said's attempt to drown the revolt in blood, the struggle continued and in early 1957 a National Unity Front was established, uniting the Communist Party, the Ba'ath Socialist Party, the National Congress Party and representatives of many different sections of the people. In May and June 1958 the struggle was already reaching new heights. Significantly, the Communist illegal newspaper, *Itihad Al-Shab* wrote at the end of May 1958: 'The rule of the traitors is collapsing. Let us prepare ourselves for the awaited moment.'

The army could not remain unaffected by these stormy developments. Most of the officers came from student circles known for their anti-imperialist and revolutionary sympathies, while the soldiers were peasants. The powerful protest actions of the Iraqi people galvanised the army, weakened the regime and encouraged the radical officers to act.

The army responded to the rising movement of resistance. In their common interests the army and the people joined forces. It is the strength of this united movement which guaranteed the success of the revolution and the establishment of the new Republic of Iraq.[13]

This is a different assessment than that given by General Kassem, but it is one that takes account of the way in which the revolution actually developed instead of relying on a kind of military mythology.

In Egypt, Nasser similarly attempted to explain the dominant role played by the military by depicting the people as a passive, backward and almost inert mass.

The leaders accomplished their mission. [i.e. the overthrow of the Farouk regime – Author.] They stormed the strongholds of oppression, dethroned the despot and stood, awaiting the holy march in close orderly ranks to the great goal.

They awaited long, however. The masses did come, but how different is fiction from facts. The masses did come. But they came struggling in scattered groups. The Holy March to the Great Goal was halted, and the picture in those days looked dark, dastardly and foreboding. It was then that I realised with an embittered heart torn with grief that the vanguard's mission did not end at that hour. It has just begun.[14]

There is an element of truth in this description. The Egyptian people were 'struggling in scattered groups'. Their ranks has been repeatedly divided by their own internecine disputes, as well as by the intrigues of Western trained security organs. But Nasser and his colleagues were not acting in a situation of complete political vacuum. The Egyptian people's struggle for liberation, even if marked by grave difficulties and beset by constant setbacks, in no sense began only in 1952. If the people were at first cautious about the officers that is not at all surprising. One should never forget that the overthrow of Farouk, important and progressive an act as it was, was accompanied in its opening phase by harsh repression against the Egyptian working class, the militant trade unions and the Communists.

The Egyptian people's struggle had been an essential factor in the overthrow of Farouk, whose regime had already been rendered unpopular and weak as a result of the constant efforts of the people against it. This is a further point lacking in Nasser's analysis. Whatever may have been the intelligent understanding and judgment of men such as Nasser, Khalid Muhiaddin and other young officers who helped to create the Free Officers' movement which overthrew Farouk, its very creation was a result of the political convulsions Egypt was experiencing in the 1940s and 1950s.

It was the National Committee of Workers and Students which led the demonstrations of 21 February 1945, forcing the imperialists to pull their troops out of the towns and limit their positions to the Canal Zone. Following that, it was the workers who waged big strikes during the battle for the evacuation of the Canal Zone itself. The years 1951–2 saw considerable activity once again by the Egyptian workers, against the occupation of the Canal Zone by British troops, against the Treaty of 1936 and the planned Middle East Defence Pact, and in favour of establishing a general confederation of workers for the whole of Egypt. The conference to establish such a united trade union body was due to take place on 27 January 1952 – but the night before, Farouk staged a coup and arrested the militant trade union leaders and many members.

Concerned at the growing mass movement which had forced the Farouk regime to abrogate the 1936 treaty and to refuse to join the Middle East Defence Pact put forward by the United States and Britain, and alarmed in particular at the increased role played by the organised workers, imperialism sought to turn the movement back. The coup of 23 July 1952, which overthrew Farouk, was a progressive step, and opened a new possibility in Egypt. But, at the same time, a number of those who participated in this coup, as well as some of the forces who welcomed it, regarded it as a 'pre-emptive coup' which could forestall the possibility of the people themselves overthrowing the Farouk regime.

This other face of the Neguib regime was quickly revealed. On 11–13 August 1952, the police and the army opened fire on 30,000 striking workers at the Misr textile factories in Kafr-el-Dawar, killing 12 and wounding scores of others. On 7 September, two of the strike leaders, Mustapha Khamis and Mohammed Bakry, were hanged in Alexandria.

The Trades Union Congress, which was to have set up a united trade union federation for the whole of Egypt, and which was prevented in January 1952 by the Farouk regime, suffered the same fate at the hands of the new military government of Neguib. Called for 14 September, the founding congress was banned. Anti-labour legislation was adopted. Trade union leaders, such as Ahmed Taha Ahmed, elected general secretary of the preparatory committee for the Conferation of Trade Unions of Egypt, were sent to jail, along with Communists and other anti-imperialists.

After all this, it is misrepresenting history for Nasser to assert that the military officers had to assume control of Egypt because the masses were divided and inert. As Peter Mansfield (a well-informed commentator on Egyptian politics, even though a somewhat ardent admirer of Nasser) has pointed out:

There was a left wing of the Wafd which, unlike the rest of the party, was genuinely interested in radical social reform. In 1945 a Workers' Committee of National Liberation had been formed in Cairo under communist influence and, about the same time, a National Committee of Workers and Students with supporters in the trade unions, universities, and secondary schools.[15]

Yet, admits Mansfield, 'the Free Officers made very little attempt to contact any civilian elements that might have been interested in the regeneration of Egypt'.[16] This, of course, is an understatement. It was not so much a question of the Free Officers failing to contact other anti-imperialist forces. In fact, as indicated above, the officers swiftly moved against these forces, and especially the working class, in order to ensure their own undivided control of the government and State.

There is no doubt plenty of room for research and debate as to what was achieved by Egypt under Nasser, after the removal of Neguib in 1954. Certainly important economic and social advances were made, the power of Egyptian private capital and landlordism was weakened through by no means eliminated, the grip of foreign capital was largely broken, and Egypt enabled to play an important role against imperialism on the world scene. But the difficulties into which Egypt lapsed so quickly after Nasser's death in 1970 and once Sadat had taken control are in no sense divorced from the limitations of military leadership and from the dual character of the Free Officers' regime which was evidenced from the very beginning.

Officers may claim that their assumption of power is essential because there is no other force available or capable of making the changes which society demands; and such claims may be justified in some cases, as, for example, in Somalia, or Libya. The genuineness of such claims, however, should be assessed in relation to the attitude of a military government towards the other anti-imperialist forces in the country, and especially the organised workers and their political parties and trade unions. In the case of Iraq and Egypt, as we have seen, the military were in no sense filling a political vacuum. Once power was in their hands they used it not only for progressive economic and social change, but also to maintain such important transformations under their own control and to limit the scope of any independent, democratic initiative by the masses and, especially, by the working class.

The examples of Egypt and Iraq bring us back to the propositions put forward by Cohen and First and cited at the beginning of this chapter, and the conditions which give rise to military coups. Here we have been considering progressive coups, but the thesis advanced separately by Cohen and First has just as much relevance to coups of a reactionary character, although in the latter case the intervention, direct or indirect, of external forces, can act as a counter to the working class and radical forces even where they are mature and well-organised, as they were, for example, in Chile and Sudan.

If, as Cohen and First rightly argue, a major cause of a coup is the enfeeblement of the old regime, then undoubtedly the causes of that growing weakness must demand our attention. Especially significant are the actions of the working people in their endeavour to win a better life for themselves. There is little doubt that in Nigeria, for example, the extensive general strikes of 1963 and 1964[17] largely undermined the basis of the Federal Government of Balewa, leading to the electoral crisis of 1965 and so to the military coup of 1966 which destroyed the old regime. The actions of the workers and especially that of the one million who joined the 1964 general strike, tore apart the fabric of Nigerian society and produced a situation in which the old rulers could no longer carry on.

The young officers struck *after* the mass actions of the workers had already weakened the regime, almost certainly beyond repair. But the action of the officers was not consciously and organisationally linked by them with the mass movement. Hence they were easily removed by General Ironsi who, in turn, was overthrown by General Gowon. In the Sudan, too, Nimeiry's May 1969 coup came *after* the regime had already been severely weakened by mounting mass struggles led by the Communist Party. In this case there were some links between the officers organising the coup and the Communist Party, which helped to consolidate the regime established after the coup; but, as we shall examine later, these links, as far as the dominant group of officers was concerned, were not based on mutual confidence, nor really on common objectives once the coup had succeeded. Thus there ensued the later crisis and Nimeiry's savage turn against the Communist Party.

The examples of Egypt, Iraq, Nigeria and Sudan indicate that, in some respects, a pre-coup situation often contains certain of the features specified by Lenin as the essentials of a revolutionary situation.[18] Sometimes, of course, a coup is attempted precisely because the country is in the midst of a revolutionary situation. This was to an extent the case with the Kornilov coup in July 1917 in Russia, and even more so with the obvious moves for a new coup which were taking place in October 1917 to forestall the revolution itself.

The features which a coup and a revolutionary situation share in common are the inability of the ruling circles to carry on ruling in the old way, and a growing mass discontent of the people towards the regime, often manifested in a major political crisis affecting wide sections of the people. In a pre-coup situation, however, the crisis of the ruling class may not yet be so profound, and thus a shift can take place within the structure of the ruling class itself, with power passing from one group to another but without any real threat to the existing social system despite changes in the political framework (e.g. Greece in 1967).

Additionally, there is the question of the mass movement. In a revolutionary situation, even though the mass of people may no longer be prepared to go on living in the old way, and even though there may be a section of the people prepared to sacrifice their lives to bring about a change, the movement as a whole may not be yet strong enough to assert itself decisively, especially if there is no strongly organised revolutionary force or party able to lead the people to victory. In that event, there can be two possible outcomes – a progressive military intervention by radical officers, backed by popular sympathy and support; or a reactionary military coup designed to pre-empt and head off the gathering revolutionary storm or to crush it altogether.

New military governments are emerging in a number of Third World countries at an historic turning point in world history, when imperialism is suffering heavy blows and socialism and national liberation are advancing. It is a time, too, of internal political turmoil and change. The old basis of society is no longer acceptable – not to the workers, not to the peasants, not to the intelligentsia of these countries, nor to some sections of its capitalist class. Nor is it acceptable to many of the military officers who are linked sometimes with different sections of the indigenous capitalist class – with entrepreneurs, the village rich, the local manufacturers – or with the petty-bourgeoisie, or even with sections of workers or peasants. These officers cannot remain uninfluenced by the social forces and political upheavals which surround them. Patriotic, modern, radical officers appear on the scene. They strike and topple the existing backward regimes.

Often, though not always, the way has been prepared for them by years of struggle by other social forces, by struggles largely conducted by workers and peasants, struggles, moreover, which have successively weakened the regime, and have sometimes boiled up on the virtual eve of the coup.

NOTES

1 Cohen, *Ha'olam ha'aravi shel yameynu*, Merhavia, 1958, p. 261 (cited in Be'eri, op. cit., p. 8).
2 First, op. cit., p. 452.
3 Mirsky, op. cit., p. 83.
4 This is arguable in these two cited cases, especially in the case of Iraq which, at the time of the overthrow of Nuri Said, had one of the best organised revolutionary movements in the entire Arab world (see below for further comment on this point).
5 First, op. cit., p. 429.
6 Quoted by G. S. Harris, 'The role of the military in Turkish politics', *Middle East Journal*, Vol. 19, 1965, p. 56.
7 More recently there has been a turn to the right.
8 Cited in Be'eri, op. cit., p. 4.
9 ibid., pp. 4–5.
10 *New Statesman*, 16 February 1962.
11 Be'eri, op. cit., p. 7.
12 See Idris Cox, 'Factors Behind the Revolt in Iraq', *World News*, 26 July 1958.
13 Ahmed Bakir, 'How Iraq Unity Was Brought About', *World News*, 26 July 1958.
14 *The Philosophy of The Revolution*, op. cit.
15 Peter Mansfield, *Nasser*, London, 1969, p. 66.
16 ibid., p. 67.
17 See Woddis, *New Theories of Revolution*, London, 1972, pp. 152–7.
18 Lenin (*'Left-Wing' Communism – An Infantile Disorder*) defines a revolutionary situation in the following terms: '. . . it is not enough for the exploited and oppressed masses to realise the impossibility of living in the old way, and demand changes; for a revolution to take place, it is essential that the exploiters should not be able to live and

rule in the old way. It is only when the *'lower classes' do not want* to live in the old way and the 'upper classes' *cannot carry on in the old way* that the revolution can triumph. This truth can be expressed in other words: revolution is impossible without a nation-wide crisis (affecting both the exploited and the exploiters). It follows that, for a revolution to take place, it is essential, first, that a majority of the workers (or at least a majority of the class-conscious, thinking, and politically active workers) should fully realise that revolution is necessary, and that they should be prepared to die for it; second, that the ruling classes should be going through a governmental crisis, which draws even the most backward masses into politics . . . weakens the government, and makes it possible for the revolutionaries to rapidly overthrow it' (*Collected Works*, Vol. 31, London, 1966, pp. 84–5).

7

Officers and Social Class

In considering the role of armies in politics, and in particular that of the officers, it is necessary to make a distinction between progressive military interventions and reactionary coups. Officers who act to end a reactionary regime and establish a progressive government, even when they come from the same class or social strata as those who seize power in order to establish a tyranny, are quite clearly motivated by different aims. As we have noted above, the term 'progressive' in this context has a particular meaning. Broadly speaking, it refers to those regimes that take a stand against imperialism and internal feudalism, and strive to bring about radical, modernising changes in the economic and social structure. It does not necessarily follow that such army-led anti-imperialist governments provide full scope for the development of internal democracy, nor that they are assisting their countries to march towards socialism, although frequently the latter is a declared aim and one, in fact, which in some few cases is genuinely worked for.

How far these progressive officers can succeed in their professed socialist aims, however, is often limited by their attitude towards the people's democratic participation. One need only consider the experiences following the establishment of military governments in Egypt (1952), Iraq (1958), Sudan (1969) and Libya (1969), to see straightaway that despite the firm anti-imperialist speeches of such military rulers, and often their significant anti-imperialist actions, the democratic rights of the working people remained limited.

Are Marxists against progressive military coups? In general, Marxists are opposed to such actions. A basic change of power must be an affair of the masses, not of small élite groups or conspiracies. A revolution, as Lenin remarked, signifies a change of class power; and this requires the movement of millions of people, not the intrigues of a handful of plotters. But too rigid a clinging to such formulas without examining the concrete circumstances in each particular case can sometimes lead to wrong conclusions.

Although we have hitherto used the term 'coup' to denote both right-wing military putsches as well as progressive interventions by the military, there are important differences between the two kinds of action. It was for this reason that Lenin sharply differed from those Marxists who denounced James Connolly for his participation in the Easter 1916 Rising in Ireland. These critics called Connolly a 'putschist'. In Connolly's defence, Lenin wrote:

The term 'putsch', in its scientific sense, may be employed only when the attempt at insurrection has revealed nothing but a circle of conspirators or stupid maniacs and has aroused no sympathy among the masses.[1]

For Lenin, it will be noted, what was decisive was not the limited extent to which the people might have *initially* participated in the action but their attitude and relation to it once it had taken place. Lenin, of course, was dealing here not with a military coup but with an armed action by civilians; but is there not a certain sense in which Lenin's remarks on Easter 1916 have a relevance here?

For a serious political party this is a very important matter. It can sometimes happen that while mass struggles have been developing, and while the revolutionary forces are oriented to a further advance of these struggles as the main way to carry through revolutionary change, a group of radical and patriotic officers can initiate its own attack on the unpopular regime and even topple it. The revolutionary movement may not have favoured such a military step as the way forward, but once it has taken place an attitude towards the progressive military group has to be taken, an attitude both to the coup itself and to the new government which is subsequently established.

The Sudanese Communist Party, for example, has had to face this problem more than once.

In assessing the role of progressive military interventions one has to take into account not only their success in eliminating a former reactionary regime, but also the extent to which they have been able subsequently to introduce important radical changes. In some cases military governments which have been established as a result of a coup, backed often by popular support, have introduced significant reforms, as in Egypt under Gamal Abdul Nasser, or in Peru under General Velasco Alvarado, or in Somalia under Mohammed Siyad Barre. Measures of land reform have been introduced, foreign enterprises nationalised, state industry built up, educational and other social reforms begun, closer relations established with socialist countries, and an anti-imperialist position taken up in external relations.

This new progressive role being played by some military leaders in the Third World is partly to be explained by the changing class composition of the officer corps. The class character of the officer caste is not always easy to determine. As Morris Janowicz has noted,[2] 'no profession resists enquiry into its social origins as stubbornly as does the military'.

Consequently, class characterisations of officers in Third World countries are often apt to be rather vague. In the Middle East, for example, officers have often been referred to as 'intellectuals in uniform', but from which basic class these 'intellectuals' have originated is usually left undefined. The Soviet scholar, G. Mirsky, has referred to officers in some Third World countries as being 'the best educated section of the intelligentsia, always better equipped than others with progressive ideas', and ready to 'struggle for the modernisation of their backward countries.'[3] Four years later, writing in *Literturnaya Gazetta*, 2 August 1967, he stressed a quite different tendency as a marked characteristic of a number of these officers.

The ideological outlook of the military leaders is bourgeois in respect of its background and remains today the principal support of neo-colonialism. They . . . have no taste for large-scale social changes. They also lack the necessary qualifications for leadership of a state.[4]

Neither of these sweeping and opposed generalisations really help to define the problem. As Be'eri rightly comments, 'the intelligentsia is not an independent class', nor does it possess or display a 'class-disinteredness'. Developing his argument, Be'eri writes:

The French intelligentsia in the eighteenth century mostly ranged itself by the side of the rising revolutionary bourgeois class, as did the Russian in the nineteenth. The Arab intelligentsia in the twentieth century is much more split in its orientation. One reason is the great variety in its strata of origin. The French and Russian intellectuals of two hundred and one hundred years ago were in major part descendants of the bourgeoisie and the petty nobility. The Arab intellectuals of the last two generations come from various levels with conflicting interests – sons of the bourgeoisie and estate owners, sons of professional men, wealthy villagers and others. And despite the great importance of the intellectual born of the ruling class who goes over to the oppressed class and provides it with ideological ammunition, this is not the only image of the intellectual. Many intellectuals remain attached to their class of origin, serving it in their own manner, yet none the less faithfully and effectively. It would only be a mistake to regard all intellectuals or so-called intellectuals as automatically aligned with the forces of progress.

The intelligentsia as such is neither progressive nor reactionary. At times it serves as the all-important forum of ideas within every progressive movement and organises its forces. But it fulfils the same functions in reactionary groups as well.[5]

Dealing specifically with Africa, Tigani Babiker[6] has drawn attention to the fact that, in contrast to developed capitalist countries, or even Latin America, the majority of officers in African armies are drawn from the educated petty-bourgeoisie and even from the educated sons of workers and peasants.

In this respect [he comments], they form part of the African intelligentsia. The old generation of officers, normally holding the higher ranks, were directly trained by colonial instructors or in the military colleges of the West. They are in general not only oriented, by virtue of their training and education, towards Western norms and ideals, but form also, by virtue of their rank, part of the bureaucratic bourgeoisie, with a stake in the preservation of the capitalist path of development. The majority of the younger generation of officers, however, have, in all probability, participated, at least in their schooldays, in the anti-imperialist struggles. Therefore, they are more likely to be imbued with hatred for imperialism, to be connected with the younger people at present leading the revolutionary struggle and to be more amenable to revolutionary ideas.

This point should naturally be taken with some reservations. It is true that a number of these younger officers have been influenced by anti-imperialist ideas, and some by more radical and even socialist ideas concerning the future development of their own country. But past struggles and experiences, together with generation links with the modern radicals in their society, are not the only influences working on them. They frequently have instructors from Western military establishments; sometimes they, too, like the older officers, are sent abroad for further training – to Sandhurst, Fort Bragg, Fort Gulick (Panama), or St Cyr – where they are subject to very sophisticated and pervasive brain-washing. Apart, also, from the direct ideological influences pressing on them from all sides, and which arise from the society of which they are part, there is the fact of their own social origins and class connections.

It is precisely because these officers come from a variety of classes and social strata, are subject to different and even counterposed concepts and policy-alternatives, are pushed and pulled by contending class forces, and seek in this complex and ever-changing society to safeguard their own position, protect their group interest, and serve an ill-defined and vaguely understood national aspiration, that the path they follow is so often tortuous. Understandably some officers side with reaction, some with progress, and others, just as frequently, move from one camp to the other, and even back again to their first allegiance.

As regards Latin American, a number of scholars have noted the changed class composition of the officer caste. In these countries the traditional ruling circles in the nineteenth century (and even into the twentieth) were based on the trinity of the army, the church and landowning oligarchy. These three forces were largely intertwined; and the officers were mainly drawn from the landowning oligarchy. The economic and social changes of the past few decades, however, have modified the class structure of these countries, and this has had its impact on the composition of the armed forces, especially on its officer sections.

Representatives of the middle class came to renew the composition of the senior officers. This explains why younger men have come to take command posts, men with modern thinking. . . . The number of representatives of the land-owning oligarchy is dwindling in the Latin American armies, and there have appeared many who are connected with the working sections of the population and the intelligentsia.[7]

Virtually the same point is made by Lieuwen,[8] who explains that as a consequence of the economic and social transformations of the twentieth century, '. . . there began to appear in the lower echelons of the officer corps representatives of the rising urban middle groups. The sons of industrialists, bureaucrats, and urban professional men began to acquire the educational background and the modern, progressive outlook that made them superior cadets in the military academies. . . . The military representatives of these new urban groups . . . had no ties with either the landed oligarchy or the church hierarchy.'

It is hard, notes Vega,[9] to generalise about the Latin American armies, since the situation varies so much from one country to another. Yet, as a general trend, one cannot ignore the evolution over recent years of a technically trained officer-corps, of a body of men equipped with a new, modern education in many fields and with a subsequent change in their attitude to society:

. . . For several decades it was only the military schools that trained engineers and technicians in Brazil. The creation of a national steel industry in Cordoba was initiated by the Argentine army. For a long time the only complete communications networks in the continent – telephone, telegraph and radio – were those of the armed forces, and the army was frequently the main or the only organisation involved in exploration, cartography and surveying. . . . The role of the new officer was not as brilliant as that of the general who was an expert in rebellion or court flattery, but he foreshadowed a figure whose importance was to grow as the complexity of social and economic problems made parades before powerless government officers superfluous and increased the importance of technical knowledge in the service of the state.[10]

Mere technical qualifications, however, important as they were, were not in themselves sufficient to bring about a change in political attitudes on the part of the officers. The acquiring of technical expertise has been taking place in a period of great crisis in Latin America, which has witnessed a growth in the people's activity to end the domination of their continent by the United States, to secure national control over natural resources, to abolish poverty and backwardness, and win the democratic freedoms that would facilitate the pursuit of these economic and social goals. All this has also had its impact on the armed forces, with a die-hard core, selected, trained, and backed up by US imperialism to impose ever more barbarous regimes on the people, and a progressive trend, supported by the people's struggle, constantly emerging, despite temporary setbacks and even serious defeats.

In this situation, the armed forces of Latin America have often come to see themselves as engines of social change rather than as the mere servants of the landed oligarchy, the local businessmen and the big foreign companies. This is so even when the social changes introduced by the army have served these same class interests which they previously upheld in a more subordinate role. National strivings, however, find their reflection in these armies, and so there has developed a kind of military populism which sometimes takes on quite radical attitudes, notably towards US interests and the landed oligarchy. Ironically, the attempt by the ruling circles to provide the officers with an education which gives them a fuller appreciation of society, in the hope that this would make them better defenders of the existing system, often produces quite different results.

In some Latin American countries, the military staff colleges . . . have Marxists teaching social science subjects. As a result, a young officer is caught between the stern anti-communism of his usually religious upbringing, and the Marxist teaching he receives in the universities and staff colleges. His natural tendency, then, is to become non-Communist in the formal sense, but highly nationalistic, even xenophobic, and leftist in social and economic orientation.[11]

Vega, too, has noted, in the case of Peru, the impact on the officers of the special education they receive to fit them for their new role in society. 'The Centre for Advanced Military Studies (CAEM)', he notes, '. . . is rapidly becoming a centre for the study of social and economic problems.'[12] Consequently, 'The army, and more particularly the CAEM, is accused of being influenced by extremist doctrines and of infiltration by communist sympathisers.'

Generalisations of this character, of course, can often give rise to exaggerated conclusions, even though the essence of these class changes in the composition of the officer corps in Latin America noted by these commentators is valid. Despite these changes, however, Lieuwen, in making an overall assessment, finds that 'the conclusion is inescapable that, on balance, the armed forces have represented a static or reactionary social force in Latin American politics since 1930'.[3] Military regimes which really promoted reform were, in his opinion, 'the exception; political intervention by the armed forces was more often than not a conservative holding action, even to the point of dissolving popular political parties by force'.

Such an assessment was probably true when Lieuwen wrote in 1960 – significantly just after the revolutionary overthrow of Batista in Cuba. It is still true that most military interventions in Latin America continue to be regressive. But one can no longer consider the armed forces in Latin America as a 'static' social force. In several important instances – Colonel Francisco Caamano Deno and the popular role of the Armed Forces in the Dominican Republic, in 1965; General Juan Velasco Alvarado's anti-imperialist Government in Peru, 1968–75; the partially progressive and anti-imperialist stance of the military government that took over in Ecuador in February 1972; the anti-imperialist government of General Omar Torrijos in Panama, arising from the army take-over in 1968; even the short-lived regime of General Torres in Bolivia 1970–1 – the general thrust of the military forces has been against imperialism and, to a certain extent, against the internal oligarchy.

In Bolivia the Communist Party has noted the way in which the armed forces have become 'a necessary reflection of the concrete historical situation to which they belong. . . . Despite pressures, distortions and the penetration of imperialist ideological principles, the armed forces, like the entire superstructure, reflect the realities of the society in which they live – its contradictions, trends, limitations, and possibilities'.[14] Pointing to the changes that took place within the armed forces in the 1960s, with the emergence of 'democratic, nationalist annd even anti-imperialist trends', it notes that the army, officered by men mainly from the urban middle strata, with the rank and file drawn from workers and peasants, could not remain immune 'to the impact of political struggle, let alone to the impact of the social crisis. While the army is indoctrinated chiefly in training centres controlled by imperialism,[15] it is also influenced by the ideas of progressive and revolutionary forces.'

Mistakes by the progressive movement, however, as well as weaknesses and errors of the Torres Government itself, led to the defeat of the patriotic-minded officers led by General Torres in 1971 and the re-installation of a repressive regime. Yet, the emergence in the army of a progressive trend among the officers indicated 'the appearance on the political scene of a new potential ally of the people's forces. . . . It suggested that the more clear-thinking officers concerned over the country's destiny had come out of the morass of ideological and political prejudices imposed on them in US military training centres and had drawn nearer an understanding of the causes of the country's backward and dependent condition.'[16]

Failure to recognise the changed political attitude of many of the officers, and to take instead a leftist 'anti-militarist' stand – which was done by some left groups; or, on the other hand, an exaggerated view of the contradictions in the armed forces, which led to calls to isolate *all* the officers and set up a 'people's army' under the NCOs (the Association of Sergeants and NCOs took such an unrealistic and dogmatic position),[17] contributed to the downfall of the Torres Government.

In other cases also, where reaction has temporarily assumed the dominant position – as in Chile, Uruguay, Argentina and even Brazil – it would be utterly wrong to regard the situation inside the armed forces as an expression of a 'static' social force. In Chile, as we shall examine in more detail later, the coup against the Popular Unity Government was prefaced by a coup *inside* the armed forces in order to break the power of General Prats and his progressive army colleagues.[18] In Uruguay, the dictatorship of Bordaberry was imposed in the face of strong opposition from sections of the armed forces. There is also differentiation evident in the armies of Brazil and Argentina, and no doubt in other Latin American armies, too.

In other words, the new and significant factor inside the armies of Latin America is that the former stable or static situation is drawing to a close; new, progressive tendencies are beginning to assert themselves, even though in somewhat muted fashion in many cases, To a large degree these new tendencies are associated with the changes in the social and class composition of the officer corps.

For many countries in the Middle East, Halpern[19] considers that the same transformations are taking place, with the army officer corps becoming, in his view, 'the instrument of the new middle class', that is to say graduates, technicians, teachers, officers, managers and so on. Continuing his argument, Halpern writes:

As the army officer corps came to represent the interests and views of the new middle class, it became the most powerful instrument of that class.

Halpern carries his argument beyond this, however, presenting the officers of the Arab world as 'the principal revolutionary and potentially stabilising force' in the transformations taking place. Be'eri agrees that many Arab officers are linked with such strata of the new middle class, and that 'the officer corps does not represent the class which was the direct successor of colonial rule in the Arab countries: the large landlords and their intellectual hangers-on'.[20] Yet, he argues with considerable justification, Halpern's assessment is too simplified and too generalised – and not only because 'social background is no indicator of ideology' when dealing with individual officers.

As Be'eri points out, 'The Arab officer corps is not a single uniform group. It is not only the representative of the salaried middle class. Many officers have family and social ties with capitalists and businessmen and these are not discriminated against by the new regime. The officers permit and even encourage the former proprietors to share in the management of their enterprises after nationalisation or to serve as capitalists in enterprises conducted under joint public and private ownership. . . .'[21]

Many officers, he adds, are also closely tied to well-to-do farmers, and this is the source of one of the dilemmas of the officers, a basis, in fact, of an as yet unresolved contradiction in most Arab countries.

Like office workers and intellectuals generally in the Arab world, many officers are of rural origin, the sons and brothers of village notables of all kinds. . . . In contrast to the large urban absentee landlords, many of these wealthy notables live in the village itself; they are the village strongmen who exploit the hired agricultural labourers and the tenants directly, sometimes in the harshest fashion. The interests of this class conflict with those of the large landowners, competing with them for the acquisition of the lot of a small fellah who has gone into bankruptcy or has become a labourer. But the interests of these wealthy villagers conflict no less with the aspirations and demands of the poor villagers, the masses of small fellaheen and tenants, and the propertyless agricultural workers. The well-to-do farmers are prepared to agree to the nationalisation of industrial enterprises, transport, irrigation, even to the expropriation of lands from large estates, especially when part of the expropriated land become theirs. However, where their own possessions are concerned, they firmly defend the sanctity of private property. . . . Furthermore, the position of the well-to-do farmers has grown stronger. The agrarian reforms which were introduced by the officers' governments eliminated the economic power and political influence of those who were above them in the village; and all the agrarian reforms have thus far stopped at a rather high ceiling of land ownership without adversely affecting the class of well-to-do farmers. . . . Their share in political power is not especially large, their intiative and activity in the dynamics of the economic changes are limited, but the interests of this class are protected and it constitutes one of the foundations of the military dictatorship.[22]

Thus, in a number of Arab states the regimes established by the military leaders include in their social base both the rich villagers (or *kulaks*) as well as the urban petty-bourgeoisie, technocrats, intellectuals and parts of the State bureaucracy, factory managers and sections of private capitalists.

Because of its class position, social origin, outlook, education, training and social and political relations, this new generation of officers tends to favour modernisation and is therefore drawn, in various degrees and forms, to pursuing policies against backwardness and feudalism as well as against imperialist restrictions and influences. The anti-imperialist direction of their policies, in many cases, is not necessarily an initial motivation of their actions, but any serious attempt to slough off the inherited backwardness and outworn institutions and practices which predated the assumption of power by such officers can result in pushing them into anti-imperialist positions.

This is not inevitable. Very often officers from the same generation, and from the same class origins, are found to be at the head of reactionary coups, to prevent or halt a radical re-fashioning of society, or sometimes even to overturn modest reforms. It is important to distinguish between class and social *origins* on the one hand, and class *function* on the other. It would be wrong to think that the petty-bourgeois origin of many officers automatically means that the political power and the State which they establish is that of the petty-bourgeoisie. In both their military and civilian spheres, the new States established in the Third World countries provide enormous scope for individuals in the upper echelons of the State apparatus, irrespective of their class origin, to utilise their State positions to become part of the new bourgeoisie. They can accumulate wealth through commissions on contracts given to foreign firms, and through other forms of corruption; they are often offered large bribes by imperialist agencies, including the ubiquitous CIA; they are able to acquire farms, to speculate in urban landed property, to enter trade.

It is necessary to recognise this because many specialists on Third World countries tend to equate the class and social *origins* of the leaders of the new States with their new class position, and with the class interests which they serve. The 'humble origins' of Batista did not prevent him becoming a millionaire puppet of the United States monopolies; nor could one explain the different role pursued by the leaders of Egypt today with that pursued under Nasser in terms of the different social origin of the present day rulers; in fact, most of them were in leading positions in Nasser's day, although they have in the recent period been joined by other social forces.[23]

Even radical officers have their limitations. Their ideology tends to be that of petty-bourgeois 'socialism', and is not based on a scientific outlook. Naturally they are not entirely divorced from Marxist ideas, and are influenced by the world advance of socialism and national liberation. They live, after all, in the period of the ending of colonialism and the decline of imperialism. But their aims are not as a rule those of placing the workers and peasants in power, which is essential if these countries are to build socialism; even the fulfilment of the national democratic phase of the revolution is held back if the working people are denied the possibility of full democratic participation in the process of change.

The aims of the radical officers are complex. While they have aspirations, often Utopian, of building a new, progressive society, they do not usually see that it is the working people who must be allowed and encouraged to be the main creators of that society. The views of the officers are confused by their current ties and ideological links with the social classes and strata from which they have sprung. Their aims are directed (and this is so even if it is not always consciously thought out or even intended in precise terms) to protecting the interests of the classes with which they are most closely connected.

Sometimes they may be unaware that this is what they are doing. They are striving, in their own terms, to build a new, modern and radical society. But they do it on the basis of a vision blinkered by their class origins, position and experience. They have to come to terms with various 'realities', to contend with different class pressures, to overcome immense economic shortcomings and face the most backward and complex social conditions and institutions. The people are largely illiterate, often heavily influenced by pre-capitalist superstitions and obscurantist prejudices. In trying to cut their way through this morass of problems, the radical officers, with all the limitations of their own ideology, frequently find their anti-imperialist positions weakened by the contradictory processes in which they are caught up.

Their attitude towards democracy is at worst negative, at best paternal. Trained to issue orders, to carry through the line of command, to instruct rather than to listen, their whole outlook presses against any disposition to discuss with others or to accept democratic, collective decisions. In particular, their whole training and social upbringing makes them hostile to the idea of accepting the will of those whom they have been taught to regard as socially beneath them.

The military, writes Santos, are 'accustomed . . . to the blind obedience of their inferiors, the dry voices of command, of the narrow horizon of their profession, which rarely encompasses the element of humanism'.[24]

As a result, the officers, even when progressive, tend (and this is not always intentional) to hold back the people's movement, to render it passive; and sometimes they move over to curtail it or actually repress it. Thus even 'progressive' military regimes are characterised by frequent misunderstandings, tensions and open conflicts between themselves and the more revolutionary movements of the working class, including Communist Parties.[25] Because of their class character, progressive officer regimes are an expression of contradictory processes.

To a certain extent their position is analogous with that of the national bourgeoisie. That is to say, they face two great class and social forces. On the one hand they stand against imperialism and feudalism; on the other, they face their own working people, especially the peasantry and the working class, including its most revolutionary detachment. They rely on the support of the working people to overcome the resistance of domestic and external reaction – but the support has to be on the radical officers' terms, not one of acceptance of the working people's hegemony and leadership.

In their desire to maintain their dominance, and in their determination to follow policies which restrict the power of the people, the position of the radical officers *vis-à-vis* imperialism and its internal allies tends to vacillate. Objectively, by their reserved and basically dominating attitude to their own working class, they play into the hands of imperialism. Thus the victory of the radical officers in Egypt in 1952 was accompanied by the hanging of strike leaders and the imprisonment of the Communists and trade union leaders; the victory of Kassem in Iraq in 1958 was followed by persecution of the Communists and eventually their terrible repression, endangering the whole course of the Iraqi

revolution which was placed in jeopardy once again when the later
military regimes under the Ba'athists followed the same path of fanatical
anti-communism until the unity agreement of July 1973. In the Sudan,
too, the hopes of the May 1969 Revolution were destroyed when
Nimeiry and his army colleagues began to repress the popular
movement both before and after the events of July 1971.

All experience shows that, at best, radical military regimes can play an
objectively progressive role at a certain stage of national development;
but this can be only a temporary phase, short or long. If military leaders
do not deliberately pave the way for democratic civilian rule, with
deeper and more fundamental social and economic programmes, they
will inevitably come into conflict with the rising social forces or become
the victims of a pre-emptive coup by more right-wing military elements
who seek to prevent the assumption of power by the more progressive
forces of the nation, and to swing the regime back decisively into the
camp of imperialism and domestic reaction.

Somalia provides an interesting example of an exception to the general
rule. In a recent perceptive study,[26] Basil Davidson has described how an
alliance of radical army officers and former students came together to
map out a road for revolutionary change in Somalia, culminating in the
bloodless 'coup' of 21 October 1969. Since then, and increasingly from
year to year, important democratic changes have been initiated,
although the army still holds decisive power. Yet it would be wrong to
regard the military leaders in Somalia as exercising power on their own
behalf or on behalf of any élite or privileged class or strata. On the
contrary, they are clearly and consciously striving to build up
democracy from the grassroots, to create new democratic structures for
this purpose, and to encourage the people – in the main peasants,
nomads, a small working class, intellectuals and small traders, craftsmen
and businesses – to start thinking and deciding for themselves.

This process has now led to the formation of a revolutionary party, the
Somali Revolutionary Socialist Party, based on scientific socialism and
accompanied by the organisation of lectures, discussions and
publications popularising the ideas of Marx and Lenin and other
contributions to scientific socialism. True, the secretary-general of the
new party, formed in June 1976, is General Mohammed Siyad Barre,
who led the action which overthrew the old regime in October 1969 and
subsequently became President of the Supreme Revolutionary
Council;[27] and other officers occupy key posts in Government and State.
But it would be wrong to assess this development in too simplistic a

fashion. All the evidence available tends to confirm that the military leaders of Somalia, whatever reservations one may have in general about the role of such regimes, are making a determined effort to involve the people in politics and, what is perhaps of even greater significance, to provide them with the democratic possibilities for doing so.

It is significant that the newspaper, *Stella d'Ottobre*, organ of the regime, in articles published on 31 July and 1 August 1972, examined 'The role of the Army in the political life of the developing countries', analysing in particular the possibility of the armed forces playing a progressive role in political development. It drew the important conclusion that 'the progressive orientation of a military regime depends on the development of democracy and on the broader and broader participation of the masses in economic, social and cultural reconstruction'. This has undoubtedly been the mainspring of the Somali military leaders' policies and actions.

In his important and invaluable book, *The Somalian Revolution*, Luigi Pestalozza[28] traces in considerable detail the whole course of the revolutionary process in Somalia from October 1969 up to July 1972, when President Siyad made his important speech at Camp Hallane proclaiming that 'our scientific socialism founded by Marx and Engels is Marxism-Leninism and not some abstract utopia'.

There were, of course, specific features in the Somali situation which help to explain the role of the armed forces. On the one hand, the failure of the previous political parties, including the Somali Youth League (which had led the anti-colonial struggle in the period before independence) to bring a new life to the people after independence had been won, coupled with the smallness of the working class, the nomadic character of much of the population, and the general social backwardness of the country which delayed the emergency of a cogent political force capable of replacing the corrupt and ineffective regime that was in power in October 1969; and on the other hand, the existence of an importance force of politically minded, progressive intellectuals, many of them trained in the Soviet Union and imbued with socialist ideas, who had social, personal and political links with sections of the officer corps. In general, the class structure of Somalia reflected the backward, neo-colonial type of the economy; there was a small working class and a very weak, dependent bourgeoisie. *Stella d'Ottobre* has asserted that 'no particular class structure has so far developed in Somalia'. Hence a major aim of the Revolution was 'to put down a budding capitalist bourgeois system allied to the neo-colonialist camp'.

October 1969 was the first step in the Revolution. But not everyone in the leading circles of the army had the same viewpoint. There were some who were prepared to sanction changes, but who desired to effect them in a way which would not block the path to the emergence of a new, bureaucratic bourgeoisie as one of the consequences of modernisation. Those who hoped for such an outcome and who had a pro-Western orientation, attempted to organise a counter-revolutionary coup in May 1971, but were quickly put down, and so the way was open for the more radical officers to accelerate the revolution. Perhaps the most important point about the left-wing officers led by Siyad Barre was that they grasped, from the beginning, that to take the country to socialism and to block the way to the rise of bourgeoisie, the political education and democratic activity of the working people was absolutely essential. It is this which has animated the major mobilisation and education campaigns in Somalia – the crash programmes and *iska wah ugabso* (voluntary labour), the nation-wide campaign against illiteracy,[29] the works councils and trade unions, the organisation of women and young people, the initiation of self-assistance schemes to eliminate shanty towns, dig wells, build roads, start State farms; and then, from January 1972, the Campaign for Socialism and the work of the Guidance Centres, bodies for political education which paved the way for the creation of the Somali Revolutionary Socialist Party in June 1976.

Describing the work of the Guidance Centres, Pestalozza considers them as 'perhaps the most significant factor' throughout the Campaign for Socialism.

Places of promotion and gathering points for social activities of every type, provided with large premises for meetings and assemblies, with cultural and sports facilities, school rooms and other rooms to house outside workers or students, these Centres arose precisely as structures of a new, democratic life, as meeting points and poles of development of a basic democracy. . . . They were to be the central points for the people's district and village councils, for the workers' councils, the mass organisations being formed, and the student, women's and union organisations; and with their birth, which indicated an organic moment of cohesion of the most energetic revolutionary forces, there was also to be the ousting of the local worthies in favour of the new cadres of political direction. . . . Lastly it was to be from these Guidance Centres that the propaganda action would be able to spread more effectively among all the popular masses. . . . In short, real instruments of revolutionary propulsion.[30]

There was no question of introducing merely the *forms* of democracy; nor was it regarded by the military leaders as simply a question of granting people democratic rights. Democracy, the political education of the people, the activity of the people, was, right from the outset but ever more clearly, seen as the essential condition for the progress of the revolution, as the way to block the path to capitalism and to open up the road to socialism. It is this understanding that enables one to consider the regime in Somalia as being very different to the majority of military governments in the Third World, different even to other progressive ones.

Stella d'Ottobre has written that 'the democratisation of political power is the only system to interrupt capitalistic development and to develop national productive forces, enabling the people to participate in the political and economic running of the nation'.[31] For an underdeveloped country to emerge from its state of economic dependence, it must carry through its anti-imperialist revolution, end dependence on world capitalism and overthrow 'the capitalist system installed or in the process of being installed'. To achieve this, 'the revolution must have a popular democratic content, such as that of our Revolution'. The democratisation of political power is defined as 'removing from the exploiting class all political and economic instruments and putting them in the hands of the workers'. This involves the nationalisation of foreign banks and foreign companies, the building of a State sector of the economy, and the development of co-operatives (bearing in mind also the nomadic character of sectors of Somalia's peasantry).[32]

Pestalozza argues that this shows that the Somali leaders have rejected the 'non-capitalist path' along the lines of the 'Egyptian model'. In his view, they consider that the non-capitalist path 'brings with it the formation of a stratum of technicians, officials, managers, materially and intellectually privileged compared with the great mass of the people, and who therefore appear as a *new class* or rather as a new exploiting national bourgeoisie, *insofar as the people are not organised to be the principal actors of independence and of economic and social development*'[33] (italics added).

It might seem strange that military leaders with the outlook of Siyad Barre should have considered it necessary to wait seven years before establishing the Somali Revolutionary Socialist Party; and some would no doubt argue that 'civilians' should have been allowed an earlier opportunity to have free play for their political aims, and not have to be under the thumb of the 'military'. But one cannot really argue this matter out in simple terms of 'civilians' or 'military'. Debating this matter back in 1973, Pestalozza, who spent considerable time in Somalia discussing these developments with people at different levels of society, considers that to pose 'civilian' against 'soldiers' is a 'false alternative', because in Somalia 'the Army is certainly not a purely military institution, but has definitely become transformed into a people's avantgarde working democratically in civil life; while it is not at all certain that civilians, just because they do not wear a uniform, automatically offer guarantees of being democratic and of political maturity. Indeed, and this is the second aspect of the problem, only inasmuch as one is certain of having adequate cadres for a party that is really going to represent a factor of great democracy and therefore be an effective instrument of the conscious participation of the masses, does its creation have any substantial revolutionary justification.'[34]

Already, at the time of the October 1969 coup, the Somali army contained a substantial progressive element. Apart from the fact that, following on independence, hundreds of young students were trained in the socialist countries, especially the Soviet Union, many others received their education in Italy where they came into contact with the strong working class and democratic movement. Some even joined the Communist Party while in Italy, took part in political activity and took their new knowledge and their experiences with them when they returned to Somalia. A number of them significantly occupy important posts in Somalia today.

In the mid sixties, when the Somali Government began to feel that it was not receiving sufficient backing from the West, it turned to the Soviet Union; one of the consequences of this new relationship was that numbers of officer cadets and NCOs were sent for training in Soviet academies. At the same time, there was a growing resentment by the officers at their being thrown into frontier wars, without adequate preparation, while at home a corrupt government daily demonstrated its incapacity and dishonesty.[35] Resentment over their own plight, awareness of the still more desperate plight of the people, and anger over the corrupt politicians who ruled the country, combined to instil in the army a desire for 'a profound change of course in Somalia. . . . Thus the army transformed or formed its character'.[36] The progressive, anti-imperialist component in the Army became the decisive factor in the Revolution that began in October 1969. 'Supported by the bonds established with the socialist countries, with the Arab upsurge, with the African liberation movement, it had matured above all in contact with Somali life, reacting against the failure of the national renaissance.'[37]

Because of the character and outlook of the leading forces in the action of 21 October 1969, and because of their aims, their military overthrow of the civilian regime cannot be written off just as a military coup. Admittedly, as Pestalozza points out, 'technically 21 October 1969 was a *coup d'état*, it was not the consequence of an organised mass movement, which might well have been impossible in pre-revolutionary Somalia. It is, however, a fact that once in power the Army did not limit itself to representing generically the country's needs, but made itself the representative of those areas and those social strata which were the victims of the neo-colonialist policy. . . . In these terms the Army made itself the people's vanguard, and linked itself with progressive social groups and classes. . . .'[38] In this fashion, the military leaders in Somalia, from the very beginning, acted quite differently to almost every other anti-imperialist military government. One has only to consider the behaviour of Nasser or Kassem to note the contrast.

What is even more significant is that as the years have gone by, Siyad Barre and his colleagues have drawn ever closer to the people, whose democratic activity they have constantly encouraged and helped. Furthermore, the army itself has been increasingly transformed, involved in popular civil activities, and provided with political training, so that it has emerged more and more as a people's army. Thus, in the big voluntary labour and self-assistance campaigns the army performed productive work, helping to build roads, schools, and hospitals, dig canals, and even carry on educational work among the people, many of whom were illiterate. Significantly, the slogan for the 1 May demonstrations in 1970 was 'Workers and armed forces, mainstays of the revolutionary era'.

The years 1970–71 were tense ones for the army. The open assertion of the intention of following the road of scientific socialism and the changes already being made alerted the conservative elements in the army to try to turn back the clock. The eventual clash came in May 1971. The counter-revolutionary plot of the Defence Minister, Gaveire, was defeated, and General Samantar replaced him. It was, significantly enough, between winter 1970 and the spring of 1971, that changes were introduced to do away with the category of 'limited career' officers; henceforth, anyone, even an NCO or ordinary soldier, was given the chance to reach the highest ranks on the basis of exceptional merit, assessed 'for proven fidelity to the Revolution and to socialist principles', in the words of General Samantar. From then on the political factor became a key factor in the assessment of officers. Courses, seminars, and weekly lessons on economic, historical and political themes, on the working class movement, socialism, the Revolution, the national liberation struggle, 'always from a Marxist standpoint',[39] became a decisive part of the ideological training of the army personnel.

Certainly the experience of Somalia needs to be followed closely, for here, apparently, there is an army controlling the government but which nevertheless is working to put ever more power in the hands of the working people. Basil Davidson on the basis of a later visit to Somalia than that of Pestalozza, ends his study with well-considered questioning in which he expresses some very relevant reservations:

A reasonable scepticism will still ask if a regime originating in a military take-over, especially in a country with no existing democratic structure of a modern kind, can really develop such methods, aims, and purposes? The evidence suggests that this one has; and it suggests this at all the crucial points where one may at present test such evidence. Which is not to say – but need one really make this point? – that the road ahead will not still remain a hard one. No doubt there are moments when a visitor can find himself wondering if the habits of military command, which are always liable to include the habits of 'military justice', may not become ingrained in the habits of this revolution. . . . Or the visitor may wonder, on quite another plane, if trends in the direction of bureaucratic sclerosis, that seem 'natural and inherent' to all great processes of transformation of structure are now sufficiently perceived, and, being perceived, will be sufficiently guarded against. . . .

Davidson's conclusion is that this dangerous trend to bureaucracy and conformism is not what is happening now; on the contrary, a 'process of independent and constructive change, a process of widening participation, a process of genuine democratisation' is taking place. 'All the same, history's warnings on this subject are sharp and painful in relation to revolutionary parties, especially in countries with a very weak or small working class; and these warnings are certainly there to be remembered.' In the case of army-led regimes, even the most radical, there must always be that reservation.

Marxists do not believe in any abstract or vulgar anti-militarism which writes off the armed forces as being simply a pawn of reaction and imperialism. As Lenin noted:

The armed forces cannot and should not be neutral. Not to drag them into politics is the slogan of the hypocritical servants of the bourgeoisie and of tsarism, who in fact have always dragged the forces into reactionary politics.[40]

Any serious revolutionary Party must take account of the role of the armed forces. To ignore them is impossible. To regard all soldiers and officers as a single, monolithic reactionary mass is blind sectarianism, and runs against all experience. At the same time one should not have illusions on this matter. As an institution, the army in capitalist countries, or as a body inherited from colonialism in Third World countries, is not a revolutionary force. Individuals may emerge who have radical and even revolutionary views; whole sections of the army, including parts of the officer corps, may come over to the side of progress – and this may happen more often in the future as the world relationship of forces continues to change in favour of national liberation, democracy and socialism, and as internal pressures for progressive change build up and' have their impact within the army.

Revolutionaries, if they are to succeed in their aims, need to develop a policy to hasten this process, and influence the future actions of the armed forces. But if the revolutionary process is to be carried forward to socialism, neither the army as an institution, nor officers in their personal capacity, can in general be relied upon to act as the necessary vanguard for carrying out such a transition. Military leaders who emerge in the course of a people's struggle and out of the creation of a people's army – as with Fidel Castro and his comrades in Cuba, or Samora Machel and the armies of Frelimo in Mozambique, or Agostino Neto and the MPLA in Angola – are quite another matter, for they have been closely bound with a revolutionary party. Military forces of the establishment, however, present a different problem. Work must be undertaken to neutralise them, or win them, or at least substantial sections of them, for the revolution. But to lead the struggle to ultimate success the most advanced classes in society must build their own revolutionary organisations into which they can draw the most progressive officers and soldiers.

NOTES

1 V. I. Lenin, 'The Irish Rebellion of 1916', see 'The Discussion on Self-Determination Summed Up', July 1916, *Collected Works*, Vol. 22, pp. 354–5.

2 Morris Janowicz, *The Professional Soldier*, New York, 1960, p. 80.

3 See Mirsky, 'Creative Marxism and Problems of the National Liberation Revolution': *Mirovaya Ekonomika; Mazhdunarodnyye Otnosheniya*, No. 5, 1963 (translated in *Mizan Newsletter*, London, April 1964); cited in Be'eri, op. cit., p. 359.

4 Cited in Be'eri, op. cit., p. 359.

5 ibid., pp. 355–6.

6 Tigani Babiker, 'Military Coups d'Etat in Africa'; see *Africa: National and Social Revolution* (papers read at Cairo Seminar, 24–9 October 1966), Prague, 1967, pp. 149–50.

7 A. Shulgovsky, 'The Role of the Army in Latin America's Political Life', in *The Army and Society*, Moscow, 1969, p. 98.

8 Edwin Lieuwen, *Arms and Politics in Latin America*, New York, 1960, p. 126.

9 Luis Mercier Vega, *Roads to Power in Latin America*, London, 1969, p. 48.

10 ibid.

11 Norman A. Bailey, 'The Role of Military Forces in Latin America', *Military Review*, p. 71, Kansas, February 1971.

12 Vega, op. cit.

13 Lieuwen, op. cit., p. 145.

14 Programme Theses of the Communist Party of Bolivia: Unidad, No. 409, 1971 (Supplement): see *Information Bulletin*, Nos. 18–19, Prague, 1971.

15 It has been calculated (1974) that the total number of Latin Americans who passed through US military schools in the nearly thirty years since the end of the Second World War up to 1974 was over 70,000 (Richard Gott: 'U.S. School for Latin America's Super-Soldiers', *The Guardian*, 16 April 1974).

16 L. Padilla, 'The Political Events in Bolivia', *Political Affairs*, New York, December 1971.

17 This leftist view, incidentally, was not shared by the Communist Party which strove, as its programme indicated, to ensure 'that the armed forces take the people's side and serve their interests'.

18 So afraid was General Pinochet and his military junta of the influence of General Prats that their agents sought him out and killed him in his exile in Argentina.

19 Manfred Halpern, *The Politics of Social Change in the Middle East and North Africa*, Princeton, 1963, p. 253.

20 Be'eri, op. cit., p. 465.

21 ibid., p. 466.

22 ibid., pp. 466–7.

23 See 'Political Report of the Egyptian Communist Party', July 1975, *Marxism Today*, December 1975.

24 Eduardo Santos, 'Latin American Realities'; cited in Lieuwen, op. cit., p. 143.

25 Note the varied experiences of the Communists in Egypt, Syria, Iraq, Sudan and Algeria, precisely on this question. To some extent, the same problems faced the Communist Party in Peru under the anti-imperialist military government of General Velasco Alvarado.

26 Basil Davidson, 'Notes on the Revolution in Somalia', *Socialist Register 1975*, London, 1976.

27 This body has now been dissolved. General Siyad Barre is President of the Republic and Chairman of the Council of Ministers.

28 Luigi Pestalozza, *The Somalian Revolution*, Editions Afrique Asie-Amerique Latine, Paris, 1974 (English edition).

29 Describing the literacy campaign, following the introduction of the national written language, Pestalozza writes: 'This is really and truly a question of mobilising the masses . . . a mobilisation that cannot be understood, and would never certainly have come about, without the background of solid faith in the revolutionary society that is being built, and without the political will of its socialist direction' (op. cit., Introduction to the English edition, p. 18).

30 Pestalozza, op. cit., pp. 212–13.

31 4 May 1971.

32 Important measures have also been introduced to help the continuation of small businesses, traders, craftsmen (see Pestalozza, pp. 210–11).

33 Pestalozza, op. cit., p. 121.

34 ibid., p. 247.

35 A significant fact, cited by Pestalozza, is that Siyad Barre as early as 1966, when he was Deputy Commander of the Army, gave an interview to the Italian Communist newspaper, *Unità*, in which he gave some indications of the way many of the officers were beginning to think.

36 Pestalozza, op. cit., p. 53.

37 ibid.

38 ibid., pp. 54–5.

39 According to Pestalozza, op. cit., p. 128. He provides in his notes (p. 316) a remarkable list of the subjects being taught in the Somali army in 1972 for the purpose of 'politicising' the soldiers, NCOs and officers, and 'to train – at all levels, from the ordinary ranker to the highest officer – a revolutionary army in the service of the fight for socialism'.

40 Lenin, 'The Armed Forces and the Revolution', *Collected Works*, Vol. 10, p. 56.

8

Sudan – Coup and Counter-coup

As we noted earlier, the Sudanese Communist Party has, on more that one occasion, been confronted with the problem of how to react to proposals from radical army officers that they should back a military coup to overthrow an unpopular regime. They faced this dilemma in 1964, in 1969 and again in 1971.

In 1964 Sudan was still ruled by a reactionary military junta under General Abboud. As the struggle against the unpopular regime mounted, discussion developed as to how to overthrow it. Some thought there should be an armed uprising by the people, others that there should be a general strike, backed by other mass actions. In both cases the likely response from the different sections of the army was of major importance. The Communist Party, which, in 1961, had posed the question of the general strike as the main way to remove the military junta, debated again the question in the crisis period of 1964. It naturally enough took account of the strength and opinions of the radical element among the army officers, expressed in a Free Officers' Organisation with its own secretly circulated journal, *The Voice of the Armed Forces*. This movement itself was not all of one mind in the crisis of October 1964, some favouring the replacement of Abboud by a civilian government, others believing that an honest radical military regime was preferable. The Communist Party considered that neither an armed people's uprising, nor a radical military coup, was the answer, but reaffirmed its belief in the use of the general strike and other popular actions, together with support from sections of the army, including the Free Officers, as the way forward.

By the end of October 1964, the protest movement had become so extensive that the call for a general strike received a nation-wide response, especially in the main centres. If the working people had been confronted with a resolute regime, backed by a united military force, the going would have been heavy. But the mass movement had enormous repercussions on the armed forces in which there had been gathering various storms of discontent, producing a variety of political trends.

Thus, at the moment of greatest crisis, the army, a key component of the State, a 'weapon' at the disposal of the ruling class, was no longer at the disposal of the regime. 'At the height of the crisis, the army itself fell apart.'[1] The refusal of the officers to stand by the regime, and the preparations by sections of them to stage their own revolt, sealed Abboud's fate. Yet the Free Officers, acting on their own, could never have toppled Abboud. It was the mass movement that was decisive – and, in the last resort, it was the mass movement that produced the crisis within the armed forces.

In explaining the political demise of the military junta at the end of October 1964, the *Daily Telegraph* wrote:

The effectiveness of the general strike in Khartoum/Omdurman surprised foreign observers. The capital was paralysed for four days. It was the strike weapon that compelled the generals to give way in negotiations with the National Front and swallow the insult of exclusion from the new National Government.

When in November 1964, the new civilian government faced the threat of a fresh counter-coup by reactionary forces in the army, once again it was strike action, backed by other mass activities, together with an even more pronounced stand by the young officers' movement, that proved to be the winning combination.

The *Financial Times* commented:

The Khartoum students, Communist politicians and trade union leaders have shown that an unpopular military dictatorship can be broken. The key to the fall of Abboud was the railway strike which threatened to cut off the capital from its vital oil supplies. . . . It could happen elsewhere'. [2 December, 1964]

Yet, if the mass movement, and especially that of the organised workers, was decisive, the role of the young officers was also key: what enabled an effective unison of these two forces which, as we have noted, Engels called 'the two decisive powers' in modern society, was the correct leadership of the Communist Party which had for years paid close attention to the role of the armed forces in politics and had striven to influence the radical young officers and win them to the side of the revolution.

As Ruth First has noted:

The street barricades and the general strike, the emergence of a militant leadership, drew the Sudanese in the towns and on the Gezira into direct action of the sort that shakes Cabinets, but does not necessarily dislodge armies. It was the splits in the army command and in the officer corps at several levels that toppled an already shaky junta.[2]

Thus once again life confirms Lenin's point that the '"disorganisation" of the army',[3] the winning of vital sections over to the side of the regime's opponents, the creation of hesitancy or neutrality among other components of the army, including in both categories members of the officer corps as well as privates and NCOs, is necessary for the successful prosecution of the revolution.

The overthrow of Abboud, however, did not produce a revolutionary government. The uprising of 21 October was, according to the Sudanese Communist Party, 'a national democratic revolution by virtue of its historical tasks and the social forces that accomplished it . . . [But] the government brought into being as a result of the revolution [was] a transitional national [government] and not a national democratic government.'[4]

The relation of class forces was such that the civilian government which replaced the military junta was too weak to stand against political reaction. By 1965 reaction was back in the saddle, this time in civilian garb.

Dissatisfaction with the regime grew, and by 1969 Sudan was once again facing a major crisis. Once again the Communist Party had to consider what action was necessary in order to change the regime. On more than one occasion the Party leadership was approached by sections of the Free Officers' organisation, requesting Party backing for a military coup. Each request was turned down, the Party arguing that the decisive question in a revolution is mass action, but that the activities of the people and their organisations had not yet reached the stage which would enable them to overthrow the regime.

The radical officers, however, decided nevertheless to go ahead. These officers were not of all one political trend, however. Among the senior officers, there were still some reactionary forces left over from the Abboud regime, although many of these had been removed. But the junior radical officers 'included Nationalist, Arab Socialist and Communist officers'.[5] The Sudanese Communist Party described the army in these words:

The majority of the soldiers and the NCOs come from among the toiling masses and are, therefore, against imperialism and have a vested interest in leading our country along a progressive path. . . . Most of the officers are educated petty-bourgeoisie.[6]

For the Communist Party the question of a military coup posed a number of fundamental questions. First, what was the character of the situation? Had the revolutionary process matured to a decisive stage? Secondly, what should be the main form of action? Action by the masses, supported by progressive officers and soldiers? Or a military action, backed by the people? Thirdly, which class and political trend should lead the revolution? Should it be the working class and the Communist Party, or should it be the petty bourgeoisie in uniform, namely the Free Officers' Movement?

All three questions were linked, and it was on the basis of a full consideration of all the factors involved here, as well as estimating the total relationship of forces inside the country at the time as well as externally, that the Sudanese Communist Party expressed its strong reservations to the Free Officers.

When the officers and soldiers struck on 25 May 1969, and overthrew the old regime, the Communist Party and all major progressive organisations backed them. The Sudanese Federation of Workers' Trade Unions, in which Communists played a leading role and whose General Secretary was Shafie Ahmed El Sheikh (later to be one of the martyred leaders of Nimeiry's counter-coup of July 1971) supported the 25 May coup 'from its very first days because of the basis of the objectives that it had declared regarding the emancipation of the country at a time when the movement could only retain power with such support'.[7]

In an article published in the Sudanese press, Shafie set out the Sudanese trade union movement's attitude to 25 May 1969 and the Government then set up:

Our country has been bestowed with a progressive government arising from a revolution sparked off by free soldiers and officers of our armed forces, with the support of the experience of the struggle of all the revolutionary forces of our people during the last few years who have been the witnesses of a sharp struggle between reaction and the Right-wing pro-colonialist forces on the one hand, and the revolutionary forces aspiring for emancipation and development on the other hand. The Sudanese trade union movement is one of these revolutionary forces. During the first week of the revolution we clearly set out our attitude in organising the historic demonstration which marked the beginning of the close cooperation between the mass of the people and the new revolutionary government.[8]

The Sudanese Communist Party, the Federation of Workers' Trade Unions and other progressive organisations, whatever may have been their view of the military action before it took place, decided, once the officers and soldiers had struck and had made clear their intention to pursue anti-imperialist policies, to support the new regime since it provided new opportunities for progressive advance. At the same time, the Communist Party insisted on maintaining its own organisation, reserving its independent political position, advancing its own proposals and demands, backing the progressive actions of the new government, and yet not hesitating to criticise the military leaders and their policies whenever it regarded this as necessary.

Right from the start there were problems for the Communists, notwithstanding the general character of the new government. Although Communists participated in the Government, including Joseph Garang, Minister for the South, a key post, the party was not allowed to nominate its own Ministers, who were selected by Nimeiry. Even more significant, the Communist Party, though allowed a certain freedom of action, was denied the *legal* right to exist and had to carry on its work under severe handicaps. At the same time there were moves to impose dissolution upon the Communist Party in the form of establishing a one-party system, evidently modelled on the pattern in Egypt with the Arab Socialist Union as the sole legal party. These matters were fiercely debated inside the Communist Party in which there emerged a group who favoured the liquidation of the Communist Party and virtual capitulation to Nimeiry.

The whole situation was thoroughly discussed at a special Party Conference in August 1970, when the delegates adopted an important, long resolution on 'The Present Political Situation and the Tactics of the Sudanese Communist Party'. Central to the analysis made by the Central Committee and accepted by the overwhelming majority of the delegates was the character of the revolution, the stage it had reached, and the particular role of the armed forces.

The resolution defined the tasks facing the Party and the revolution in the Sudan as two-fold – first, national tasks connected with the consolidation of the country's political independence and the achievement of economic independence; second, democratic tasks, summed up in the removal of all social and production relations hindering progress and holding back the creative activity of the people. The combination of these two sets of tasks were seen as comprising the national democratic revolution. The enemies of this revolution were characterised as the old and new imperialists, together with local support from those 'classes, sections and elements whose interests lie in backwardness and dependency'.[9] The social forces in fulfilling the national democratic phase of the revolution were defined as 'the working class, peasantry, revolutionary intellectuals and the national bourgeoisie'.

In making this analysis, the Communist Party did not ignore the fact that in life the two stages of the national democratic revolution and the socialist revolution might interpenetrate, yet at the same time that it was essential to distinguish between the two stages and formulate tactics for the national democratic stage on the basis of its being a distinct phase.

Naturally, therefore, the Party hotly contested the view that it should end its separate existence as a political party of the working class and dissolve itself in a wider National Democratic Front which would establish a one-party system. It set out its views as follows:

The one-party system at the national democratic stage of the revolution in our country with all its national, tribal, socio-political characteristics as well as its class differences, does not provide a tool capable of the unification of these classes in favour of the fulfilment of the current tasks of the revolution. The adoption of any one party to play this role would only result in the scattering of the forces of the revolution and the consequent failure to implement the tasks of the stage fully and precisely. The National Democratic Front, therefore, constitutes the organisational and political alliance of the working class, the peasantry, revolutionary intellectuals, national bourgeoisie, revolutionary officers and soldiers – an alliance based on a national democratic programme expressing the common interest and commitment of these classes. In order that this alliance should stand on a firm basis, the *independence* of its various components *must be safeguarded*.

The analysis made at the special Conference did not confine itself to explaining why a single party system was inappropriate and, in fact, politically incorrect. It also raised the question of the leadership of the National Democratic Front, emphasising that this role could only be satisfactorily fulfilled by the working class which, of all the social forces, stood out as the 'most anti-imperialist, most systematic and most democratic . . . it has the least ties with the influences of backwardness. . . . By virtue of its very structure, its position in the modern industrial sector . . . and its organisational ability, the working class is the most suited for leadership of the National Democratic Front towards the successful implementation of the tasks of the democratic revolution leading to socialism.' This leadership role, it stressed, 'cannot be jumped to or imposed merely on the strength of historic conclusions'. It could only be won by its leadership in activity and by its winning an understanding from other social forces of its particular capacity for leadership.

Analysing the new phase of the national democratic revolution following on the action of the armed forces of 25 May 1969, the resolution of the special Party conference described the new regime as an expression of the 'progressive, anti-imperialist petty-bourgeoisie who are, in fact, one of the classes interested in achieving the aims of the national democratic revolution'.

As if foreseeing the problems that were to arise in the next two years, the resolution pointed to certain specific features of the new situation. The change of regime had taken place at a time when the mass movement, in the opinion of the Communist Party, was '*not* on the upswing'. Secondly, the change of power took place by means of violence and through the action of 'progressive elements of the regular army'. Thirdly, the new ruling authority maintained 'allied relations with the working class, *up to a point*' (italics added).

In an interesting commentary on Lenin's definition of a revolutionary situation,[10] the resolution warns against confusing revolutionary crisis with general discontent. In this connection it stresses that the August 1968 strike was no proof of a revolutionary crisis, 'nor even of its approach'. In fact, after the strike the activity of sections of working people actually declined. Neither, asserts the resolution, can the success of the military operation in overthrowing the former regime 'stand as proof of the revolutionary crisis either'. Other factors – 'diverse and intricate political, technical and military factors' – were involved.

The resolution then comes to grips with the key question of its attitude to military actions in terms which have the greatest validity for the events which developed subsequently.

After quoting from Lenin's well-known essay on 'Marxism and Insurrection':

To be successful, insurrection must rely not upon conspiracy and not upon a party, but upon the advanced *class*. This is the first point. Insurrection must rely upon a *revolutionary upsurge of the people*. That is the second point. Insurrection must rely upon that *turning-point* in the history of the growing revolution when the activity of the advanced ranks of the people is at its height, and when the *vacillations* in the ranks of the enemy and in *the ranks of the weak, half-hearted and irresolute friends of the revolution* are strongest. That is the third point.[11]

– the resolution declares:

This is the class attitude of all communist parties who cannot force other political groups to accept this view. The communist parties themselves, however, have to be committed to it. This is what the Political Bureau of our Party did when the Free Officers suggested the preparation for a military coup. What is basic in the Political Bureau's decision is that the military operation should become the climax of a general revolutionary upsurge among the masses.

It is because of this clear attitude that the Sudanese Communist Party refused to be part of the military action of 25 May 1969. It should be understood that the Communist Party was not concerned solely about whether or not the action succeeded. It was preoccupied with additional political consequences. 'If the Party leadership had slackened for a single moment' in its task of explaining 'the Marxist attitude towards the question of overthrowing a political system', then the result would have been 'the spread of a coup-mentality as a means, not only of retaining State power, but also of solving the contradictions within the system, or between it and the revolutionary mass movement'.

How correct the Communist Party was to express these anxieties all subsequent events showed. The lessons are not to be confined to Sudan, since the 'coup-mentality', i.e. the tendency for army officers to consider that they must hold the reins of power, give direction to the masses and take all major decisions, with the people, and especially the working class, remaining as passive supporters of the ruling military group, has been an acute problem in practically all anti-imperialist military regimes.[12]

The Sudanese Communist Party, notwithstanding its reservations about the military action of 25 May, did not adopt a sectarian bystander's position.

The fact that *we stuck to this Marxist attitude* towards the overthrow of any political power by means of military coups *did not prevent us from evaluating, politically* what happened on 25 May and its effects on the life of our country. We realised that a new regime, progressive and anti-imperialist, had assumed power. We, therefore, decided to support, defend and develop it.

In the view of the Sudanese Communist Party, the military action of 25 May had resulted in State power coming into the hands of 'the progressive petty bourgeoisie', thus creating 'an intermediary stage' in the development of the revolution. This necessitated the Party combining its support for the new Government against imperialism and domestic reaction with mass work, in order to ensure the active participation of the people in the achievement of the National Democratic Front and its programme, the latter being the basis of any joint action between the Party and the new regime. The Party did not see itself simply as a support organisation. It would certainly support all progressive actions of the Government and the military leaders, but it would not hesitate to encourage 'active struggle against any negative steps that deprive the revolutionary masses of the tools necessary for' carrying out the democratic programme.

Drawing attention to the dangers of anti-communism and divisions being created among the forces of the revolution, the resolution stated that 'some of the ideas of revolutionary democrats coming from the Arab world have a negative influence on the progress of the revolution in our country. This negative element is aggravated by the fact that these revolutionary democrats are incapable of achieving *all* the objectives of the national democratic revolution. Furthermore, a comprehensive theory is held by them, rationalising the freezing of the revolution at a certain point. The Sudanese Communist Party has to struggle on the ideological and practical levels against this negative influence. At the same time, however, it has to take a positive stand, on the political level, in alliance with them against imperialism and for progress.'

Turning its attention to the armed forces themselves, the resolution estimated that despite the entry into the army after 1948 of students who had been profoundly influenced by the current anti-imperialist struggles and who constituted the basis of the radical armed forces movement, the army was 'still over-burdened with rightist and conservative elements'. In consequence, 'the alliance of the mass movement and the armed forces means in fact its alliance with the anti-imperialist and progressive elements inside the Armed Forces'. It added that to ensure success for the democratic revolution it was essential to carry through the 'complete democratisation' of the armed forces; and it put forward a six-point set of proposals to this end.[13]

The six points, it will be noted, included 'purging the armed forces of *all* rightist elements'. As events unfolded, however, it was soon clear that the military regime of 25 May was set on a turn to the right, not *away* from the right.

As 1970 drew to a close the situation became extremely tense. On 16 November Nimeiry, President of the Revolutionary Command Council (the body established by the army after the May 1969 coup to 'guide' the country), and simultaneously Prime Minister, announced the removal of three leading members of the Free Officers Organisation, Lt. Col Babiker El Nur, Major Farouk Osman Hamadalla and Major Hashim Mohammed El Atta. The announcement further made clear the intention of Nimeiry to carry through a purge of left-wing personnel in the Armed Forces and the Civil Service. It was also made known that Abdel Khalig Mahgoub, general secretary of the Communist Party, had been arrested, and that thirteen officers had been dismissed from the army.

It was alleged that the removed and dismissed officers had joined with Abdel Khalig Mahgoub to carry on 'subversive activities inside the armed forces and among trade unionists'. The central committee of the Sudanese Communist Party countered with a statement[14] describing Nimeiry's action as 'a continuation of the methods of putsch', aimed at 'the liquidation of the left-trend and especially the Communist Party, the liquidation of the group of Free Officers in the Armed Forces, and at effecting changes in the leadership of the democratic organisation by expelling the Communists and seasoned democratic elements under the charge of sabotage so as to transform these organisations into mere appendages of the state power and its future national organisation, depriving them of their identity and their popular democratic features'. The statement further warned that these measures were a prelude to concentrating all powers in the hand of the president and the 'liquidation of the revolution' itself.

This was fully borne out by the events which followed. On 12 February 1971, Nimeiry issued a declaration accusing the Communists of treason and of trying to seize power for themselves. At the same time 84 leading Communists were arrested, and the Youth Federation and the Sudan Women's Association were banned. In addition, all the Trade Unions were compelled to re-register in accordance with a new restrictive law. It was clear that Nimeiry was proceeding towards a show-down with the Communists and the mass organisations. His aims were clearly to crush the Communist Party, remove the militant leaderships of the main organisations of the people, and remove the left-inclined officers from the army. He went so far as to announce in his broadcast: 'You must destroy anyone who claims there is a Sudanese Communist Party. Destroy this alleged Party.'

In answering Nimeiry, the Sudanese Communist Party once again demonstrated its attitude towards the role of the armed forces and towards attempts at coups:

The President of Revolutionary Command Council's speech describes us as treacherous and says we aim to crush under foot all moral values in order to reach our goal of power. What a lie! How power can blind people! But this accusation comes from the President of the RCC. Let him just think back to the 24 May 1969, when he had discussions with a delegation of our Party and when we explained our point of view.[15] We asked him to tell his colleagues that the Communist Party would not let them down, we would not leave them to become victims of the counter-revolution but would protect their rear.[16] At the same time, we asked for zero hour to be delayed until the various groupings in the Free Officers and others should establish firm unity, and until our national movement could make progress in creating a real broad, democratic unity of the people so that what was going to happen would not be a mere coup that could freeze the revolution and so make it an easy prey for counter-coups and attacks by different sections of the army. . . . Some of your members know full well the great efforts made that night mainly by our general secretary, Mahgoub, to protect your rear on the eve of the 25 May.[17]

Disclaiming Nimeiry's accusation that the Party wanted to establish a monopoly of political power for itself, the statement asserted:

From the first we refused the idea of having just one faction of the revolutionary movement taking power alone. Since then we have said that revolutionary democracy and the granting of more civil liberties to our people is imperative for the development of our revolution. We look and still look to the armed forces as one of the elements of the state apparatus that has its definite role in protecting the country and its sovereignty, but we oppose political auctioneering by officers and we are against trying to provoke such a thing by clashes between the different revolutionary forces. . . . The regime has come to the end of the road in trying to freeze the revolution under the banner of attacking the Communist Party and following a middle path; but our people know that all its life the Communist Party has been the main support for the development of the Sudanese revolution, for protecting the present regime against all reactionary and imperialist conspiracies. . . . The Sudanese Communist Party holds that the only way out of this dilemma is through the struggle to unify all the democratic forces and establish a Government of a national democratic front, which is the only organ that can carry out successfully at this stage the tasks of the revolution and save it from a rightist relapse.

This warning and urgent appeal from the Communists was not heeded by Nimeiry. He was against a genuine democratic understanding with the Communist Party and other democratic forces. The only kind of front that he would tolerate was one completely under his domination, with the Free Officers reduced to nothing, the mass organisations turned into passive supporters of the State, and political movements and parties merged into a single political organisation under the absolute control of sections of the national and petty bourgeoisie. The issues behind this conflict were those of the revolution itself. Was the democratic revolution to continue its advance and open the way to socialism? Or was it to be halted and Sudan's compass pointer fixed in the direction of capitalism, so that Sudan would become dependent on the imperialist powers?

This big issue was fought out in the tragic days of July 1971. Once again the Communist Party had to face the question of how to act in face of the steps taken by progressive officers against an unpopular regime. It is important to consider what happened in July 1971 since it has been argued that the Communist Party itself was responsible for the action of the Free Officers in 19 July, and that by initiating such action it acted in an adventurist fashion.

As has been explained above, on two previous occasions, in 1964 and again in May 1969, the Party has been faced with the question of its reaction to a progressive 'coup'. On both occasions, the Party leadership, and especially its general secretary, Abdel Khalig Mahgoub, had opposed the proposals and explained why, in its view, the immediate and longer-term interests of the revolution required a further development of the mass movement which, it emphasised, must be the decisive agent of change. It seems highly unlikely, in the light of the past attitude of the Communist Party and of its general secretary,[18] that in July 1971 it should have abandoned its previous principled position. It is true that in May 1971, owing to the reactionary policy then being pursued by Nimeiry, the Sudanese Communist Party called for the overthrow of the Government, but this in no way justifies allegations that this means the Party was preparing a *military coup* with the aid of officers sympathetic to its general aims.

Some interesting light on the attitude of the Communist Party towards 19 July 1971, is provided by the position taken up at the time by Shafie Ahmed El Sheikh, who was general secretary of the Sudanese Federation of Workers' Trade Unions (SFWTU) and a leading member of the Communist Party at the time. He was shot after the counter-coup. The 19 July military action was led by Major Hashim Mohammed El Atta who issued the first statement concerning the coup. One of his first steps was to contact the Sudanese Federation of Workers' Trade Unions and a meeting subsequently took place. A delegation of the International Confederation of Arab Trade Unions which visited Khartoum in August 1971 has provided the following account, as told to them by Hag Abdel Rahman, Assistant Secretary of the Sudanese Federation, and reported in the Egyptian daily paper, *Al Ahram* on 13 August 1971:

During this meeting Hashim El Atta asked the workers' movement to organise demonstrations of support for the *coup d'état*. I spoke on behalf of the trade union movement regarding the independence of the working class, our commitment to the aims of the 25 May revolution, and of the necessity of maintaining the autonomy of the trade union movement. Shafie uttered a few words of thanks for the invitation to the meeting. But at the end of the meeting we stated that we did not have the right to involve the workers in demonstrations and that the question would have to be submitted to the representatives of the trade unions.

After this meeting we convened the SFWTU's Executive Committee and put Hashim El Atta's request to them. It was decided that each organisation publish a statement. The trade union councils would be convened so that the question could be put before them and a decision taken. During the meeting of the trades councils on 21 July, the organisation of a demonstration was unanimously approved for the following day.

On 21 July we received a letter from Hashim El Atta asking the trade union centre to propose four of its members so that a workers' representative could be chosen from amongst them as a minister. The SFWTU Executive Committee rejected this request considering that it was for the Executive Committee to appoint its representative and chose Shafie Ahmed El Sheikh unanimously.

This description seems utterly genuine. Moreover, it corresponds to reports from Khartoum which described how Shafie Ahmed El Sheikh, when invited at first to visit Hashim El Atta, had been rather reluctant. Furthermore, that when eventually persuaded by his colleagues to go he had again turned back when armed soldiers had stopped him at the gates of the building where he was to meet Hashim El Atta. It was only after further persuasion that he took part in the meeting. This obvious reluctance, and the difference of approach on the question of choosing a Minister from the Federation, seem to indicate that there was no prior participation by the top Party leadership in preparing the coup.

The Party, however, was faced with a difficult problem. It did not initiate the coup, but once it had taken place it had to decide what to do. As a serious political party it could not quietly fold its arms, reiterate its opposition to coups in principle, and then wait to see what would happen next. Moreover, the immediate response of the people to 19 July, the huge demonstration in Khartoum on 22 July organised by the SFWTU, showed that the action of the progressive officers had aroused clear sympathy among the people which, as Lenin argued in his comments on the Easter 1916 Rising, was a test as to whether one was dealing with a 'putsch'. Moreover, the declarations of Hashim El Atta and his colleagues immediately after Nimeiry's overthrow included a programme of deep-going democratic reform, legalising the Communist Party and making possible the formation of a national democratic front giving full and equal rights to all participating bodies.

The Sudanese Communist Party has set out at some length its assessment of 19 July[19]:

Within the current of the Sudanese revolution, the 19th of July [1971] represented a revolutionary change of political power carried out by the National Democratic Front, and more precisely by the two sides of Sudanese democratic revolutionary forces, Democrats and Marxists. Within the armed forces they were represented by the Free Officers' Organisation and the Movement of Democratic Soldiers. It transferred power to the National Democratic Front as a whole, and not into the hands of any single section of it. For the first time it was made clear that the Free Officers' Organisation, which carried out the military operation, was one of the organisations of the National Democratic Front, in contrast to the traditional posture of leaders of military coups who speak in the name of the armed forces as a whole which they consider as a vanguard in relation to the popular movement, and who confuse the functions of the armed forces as part of the apparatus of the State and an instrument of repression, with the role of the progressives within the Armed Forces.

The statements and declarations (of the leaders of 19th July) made it clear that the basis of power was the rule by the Front at all levels in the Sudanese Republic, and this was also given shape in the Republican orders issued (by the new regime).

The men of 19th July enunciated very clearly also at constitutional level, the principles of the new democratic system. They began to consult the democratic organisations and the progressive forces about the formation of the Government and the instruments of power. They gave the democratic nationalist forces the right to organise their political parties. They cancelled the legislation and edicts which hampered their liberties, they dissolved the espionage system, terror and the police State.

They opened the door for the popular struggle to achieve the tasks of the democratic revolution. They raised the flag of the rule of law and the independence of the legislature. They laid out landmarks to achieve political rights through democracy as a system of government, with a parliamentary system, an executive apparatus and the right of the masses to elect or reject their representatives. They adopted democracy in the relations of agricultural production in order to liberate the overwhelming majority of the population, and in order that the labourers should take part in the administration of production. They thus provided an opportunity for ending the conflict between political democracy and economic democracy. They also made democracy a condition and a means to unify the two parts of the country, the North and the South, and to solve the problem of the South.

They raised the flag of independence and national sovereignty, and asserted its role in the movement for Arab and African revolutionary unity, as well as its role in the anti-imperialist front and its relationship to the socialist countries and the Soviet Union in particular.

In the light of such a comprehensively favourable assessment of the attitude and policy of the leaders of the 19 July action, it is understandable that the Sudanese Communist Party should have declared its support for the overthrow of the Nimeiry regime and proceeded to win popular support for the new government. The Sudanese Communists considered that in the light of what had taken place they could not remain detached and wash their hands of the whole affair. As they saw it, the 19th of July opened up a new phase of battle and the Party had to decide on which side it stood.

Furthermore, the Party was concerned not only with the immediate democratic policy initiated by Hashim El Atta and his colleagues. It was also struggling for a vital principle, namely to assert the right and the necessity for the working class and its political party not to subordinate itself to the national bourgeoisie and petty bourgeoisie, in or out of uniform, even though it recognised the importance of the Party and the working class establishing alliances with all social classes and strata that could contribute to the fight against imperialism and feudalism.

The 19th July revealed an essential and important truth, which is that there is an alternative (potential and objective with live revolutionary cadres) to the dictatorship of the petty bourgeoisie or one of its sections. *It thus dealt a strong blow at the theories which consider this dictatorship a historical necessity, with the working class and the revolutionary movement living or co-existing in its shadow, in submission and humility.* This is the reason why the military regime of the petty bourgeoisie – and more precisely the Arab nationalists – follow a path which leads to the liquidation of the revolution. The Sudanese experience has shown that to concur with such a path, under the threat or fear of counter-revolution, only leads to that section of the petty-bourgeoisie which has monopolised power itself becoming counter-revolutionary, either by oppressing the revolution or liquidating it, or by its political and economic policies and its submissiveness to the influence of neo-colonialism.

The 19th of July has pointed out the progressive alternative. It has also shown the necessity for vigilance to protect it not only from imperialism but also from Arab right-wing forces[20] (italics added).

As is known 19 July was followed by a speedy counter-coup and the rapid defeat of the democratic possibilities which had been opened up by the union of the people's forces with the Free Officers' Organisation that had overthrown Nimeiry. This defeat does not in itself necessarily invalidate the correctness of the stand taken by the Sudanese Communist Party. After all, the Paris Commune was defeated, but no revolutionary today would condemn it on that score. Marx had expressed prior to the Commune his anxieties about any such action being taken by the working people of Paris. But once the Paris people rose and 'stormed heaven', Marx rallied to their support. 'How could they submit!' he declared, in explaining his support for their historic uprising.

The Russian Revolution of 1905 was defeated; so was the 1916 Easter Rising in Ireland; and so was the attack on the Moncada Barracks, led by Fidel Castro in July 1953. No one would seriously argue that these struggles were unjustified because they failed. A revolutionary movement does not demand, and cannot expect a guarantee or certainty of victory when it initiates or supports armed action. Naturally it strives to avoid reckless actions, and not to be dragged into hopeless ventures. But sometimes an action has to be taken even when defeat is a virtual certainty: and such a necessity can arise when those taking action consciously sacrifice themselves in the knowledge, or at least hope, that what they have undertaken will serve in the long run to inspire the masses to take up their cause. Thus it was that James Connolly, on the very day of the Easter Rising, clearly indicated that he had no hope of victory.

'We are going out to be slaughtered,' he told William O'Brien as he passed down the stairs of Liberty Hall. 'Is there no chance of success?' asked O'Brien. 'None whatever.'[21]

Yet, despite this knowledge, Connolly persisted in the Rising. He was painfully aware of the terrible impact of the 1914–18 War on the Irish people who had been deluded into supporting British imperialism.

'It would be almost impossible,' he wrote[22], 'to name a single class or section of the population not partially affected by this social, political and moral leprosy.' Even the working class, he noted, had succumbed to this 'foul disease'. This, above all, he found 'horrible and shameful to the last degree'. The sense of degradation wrought on the Irish people had, he believed, sunk so deep into their hearts that 'no agency less powerful than the red tide of war on Irish soil will ever be able to enable the Irish race to recover its self-respect, or establish its national dignity'.

As Connolly saw it, the function of the Easter Rising was to restore to the Irish people their self-respect and their national dignity. The success or failure of the Rising was, in a certain sense, irrelevant to this purpose.

The decisive thing was that the Rising should take place, that a section of the Irish people should, in the most emphatic way possible, by armed action, challenge British oppression. The sacrifice of Connolly, Pearse and others was a terrible and tragic loss; but their deaths and the defeat of Easter did not add up to total defeat. On the contrary, the sacrifice of the heroes of Easter 1916 aroused the people, and within two years the Republic was declared, the Irish people were involved in battle with Britain, and by 1920 the British rulers had to concede independence to the 26 counties in the South (although they still managed to retain six counties in the North). Lenin's defence of Connolly's action in 1916 was thus justified. The Rising, notwithstanding its defeat, aroused the sympathy of the people, and their subsequent actions forced British imperialism into a substantial retreat.

In the same way, the Sudanese Communist Party, notwithstanding the defeat of 19 July, regards what took place as a justifiable phase of struggle on the basis of which it hope to build for future success. It attributes the defeat largely to the intervention by Libya and Egypt, while not neglecting its own lack of vigilance and determination in those few critical days. According to the Sudanese Communist Party, no less than three 'adventurist and dubious' *coups d'état* were planned during the period February to July 1971, three coups 'which struggled to race each other to power within the army'.[23] One motive of Hashim El Atta and his colleagues among the Free Officers in initiating their military action of 19 July was to avert one of these 'adventurist and dubious coups'.

Explaining its attitude towards the Free Officers' Organisation and their action of 19 July, the Central Committee declares:

It [the Government] accuses your movement of being planned by the Communist Party and alleges you to have moved according to its orders. For this we do not claim the honour, and we do not refute the accusation; while you know, and so does your gallant organisation, that the plan and timing of the zero hour was fixed by your will and decision, and this fact will always stand to your credit. And when you moved, because of reasons which forced you, to fix the zero hour (and to you alone belongs the right to decide on the means and reasons) we never abandoned you and never wasted a moment in questioning you as to why you were in a hurry; but we responded to you with all our strength, consolidating your action and supporting you by our suggestions and directing your attention to loopholes. In this respect, we do not deny any accusation to avoid any punishment or condemnation. . . . And even if July 19th met with defeat, yet our popular movement has the potentialities and fundamental abilities to rise and compensate for the loss, and to complete what was not completed.[24]

It has been necessary to examine at some length the events that took place in the Sudan, not least because the policy and actions of the Sudanese Communist Party have been subject to considerable discussion. In some cases, there has been a too ready acceptance of the distorted versions offered by the Nimeiry regime as well as by those renegades who favoured the winding up of the Communist Party in 1970 and who, in a number of cases, have since found themselves a comfortable niche working for the Nimeiry regime itself.

No comprehensive analysis of the reasons for the defeat of the Sudanese revolutionary movement in July 1971 has yet been made by the Sudanese Communist Party but some elements of such an assessment have appeared in a Central Committee statement issued in November 1971.[25] It is interesting to examine briefly the main points of this analysis, especially since arguments have been put forward, mainly outside Sudan, attributing the defeat to the incorrectness of the original action of 19 July which overthrew the Nimeiry regime. Such critics have tended to brand the action of 19 July as leftist, sectarian and adventurist. The Central Committee of the Sudanese Communist Party, on the other hand, considers the initial action fully justified. The mistakes, in its view, lie not in the overthrow of Nimeiry which was carried through relatively easily, but in the failure to defend the new regime.

Negligence in the protection of the revolution is a crime for which history will not pardon the revolutionaries unless they learn from it lessons for their future struggles, and the mastery of the fundamental principle of revolutionary struggle that it is not enough to seize power, it is just as important to defend it not only in its early stage but continuously and at any cost. Had it not been for carelessness and negligence in this aspect, the counter-revolution and the bloody counter-attack would not have succeeded. We are aware that practical precautions had to be taken in several fields. . . . But carelessness and negligence were not born on 19 July, they had been inherited from the period which followed the 16th November coup and perhaps even from much further back.[26]

The Sudanese Communist Party not only defends the action of the Free Officers in initiating 'the uprising on 19 July'. It also defends its own support of the military action. Its stand, it believes, 'will remain among the prominent landmarks in the history of our struggle'.[27]

Analysing the reasons for the defeat, the central committee argues that the initial action had overwhelming support and that in the first four days there was no force within the country capable on its own of withstanding the military operation of the Free Officers backed by the people. The mistake, it believes, lay in a lack of vigilance, a certain complacency, a failure to persist fully with the uprising, and, perhaps, decisively, neglect of the danger from outside, namely the intervention from Egypt and Libya, Sudan's two partners in the Tripartite Union.

Emphasising the 'success of the rising of the Free Officers and Soldiers', the support it received from 'the democratic movement', the 'public acclaim' with which it was welcomed, and the 'profound impression' which it made 'among nationalist circles', the central committee refers to 'the causes and factors, that have now become clear, which caused the Free Officers and Soldiers not to persist in their military readiness to change the regime'. Unfortunately the document does not specify what these 'causes and factors' were which led the officers and soldiers 'not to persist'. This becomes more difficult to comprehend when one takes into account the growing popular support for the overthrow of Nimeiry expressed most dramatically in the huge demonstration in Khartoum on 22 July, the fourth day of the action.

The central committee document itself argues that 'during those four days there was not within the country any force capable on its own of changing this early course, had it not been for the outside manoeuvres and instigation on the part of the Tripartite States, and in particular on the part of Egypt and Libya, and the co-operation of British intelligence with them'.

Among the acts of outside intervention it cites the role of the Egyptian Military College at Jebel Awliya,[28] the role of the Egyptian air base at Wadi Saidna,[29] and the role of the Egyptian military attaché; and kidnapping the plane carrying Babiker Al Nur[30] back to Sudan from Britain where he had been at the time of the 19 July overthrow of Nimeiry. Accompanying Babiker Al Nur in the plane was Farouk Osman Hamadallah. These two were the outstanding leaders of the Free Officers' movement, and their capture was a very heavy political, military and psychological blow to the uprising.

The Sudanese Communist Party central committee document also alleges that after consulting with Sudan's War Minister, Khalid Hassan Abbas, who had gone to Egypt, Sadat then flew to Libya to arrange for Egyptian paratroops and planes to transport Sudanese troops from the Suez Canal, where they were doing front-line duty, back to Sudan to help overturn the new regime.

Outside intervention, and moves towards further intervention, were undoubtedly factors bringing about the defeat of the uprising. The actual intervention, and equally if not more, the threats of still more decisive intervention, made their intended impact on the Sudanese.

armed forces, causing sections of them to fall away from the Free Officers and Soldiers' movement and rally around Nimeiry.

The comparative ease with which Nimeiry and his collaborators were freed from captivity has surprised many observers. The central committee attributes this largely to the fact that the 19 July leaders 'took a lenient attitude towards elements of the previous regime, and especially towards the Revolutionary Council'.[31]

But the major weakness which the document considers to have been the cause of defeat was the failure to take 'the measures needed to safeguard the regime and the initial victories'. The key measure here would have been the 'arming of the revolutionary sections of the people which, during their long experience, had learned the importance of protecting their operations and their activities'. The ease and speed with which the initial uprising succeeded, and the wide support which it clearly enjoyed, made the leaders and the revolutionary movement in general over-confident. As a result vigilance was neglected, the danger from Egypt and Libya and their collusion with British intelligence[32] was underrated, one might say virtually ignored, Nimeiry and his arrested supporters were left in conditions in which they could easily be snatched back, and the revolutionary sections of the people were left unarmed.

The revolutionary movement, sums up the document, neglected 'the most important principles for the defence of the revolution – the safeguarding of the initial victories without mercy and at all costs'. The central committee statement claims that it, in effect, warned against this danger in its letter No. 11 after the victory of 19 July in the sense that it called for the defence of the revolution without mercy and at all costs as the foremost task, especially in order to prevent the mass movement being exposed 'to the danger of adventurism and to (other) coups in the regular army'.[33]

In a certain sense what the Sudanese communists are saying here is what Marx and Lenin said about insurrection. It is a serious matter, one shouldn't treat it lightly, and, to succeed one must press home the offensive once it has been started.

It is too early to reach any definite views about the events in the Sudan in 1971. There is certainly plenty of room for discussing whether the Free Officers should have begun their action on 19 July. The question of the Communist Party's participation is, in a sense, a separate question. It is difficult to believe, on the basis of past behaviour, that the Party was the organiser of the military action; but once the action had begun it is difficult to see how the Party could have stayed on the touchlines.

As for the defeat of the uprising and the success of the counter-coup, here too there are a number of questions that must still be considered as open. The defeat of 19 July was not a typical counter-revolutionary coup, although it is doubtful whether any such coup can be regarded as 'typical', so various are the circumstances and facets of each one. Sudan was different, however, in that it was not a coup against a progressive government which had existed for some time, had some achievements to its credit but also had fallen down in many ways; it was a counter-coup against an armed uprising which had had no time to establish and consolidate itself. Therefore many of the factors present in, for example, Indonesia, were not present.

One thing, however, does emerge from the Sudanese experience. The organised political movement of the working class (provided that such a movement does exist) must treat with reservation any action initiated by the progressive sections of the army. It should not act in any purist, isolationist or hostile spirit, but neither should it fail to weigh up carefully the consequences of activities undertaken by radical officers. As a general rule[34] the progressive military faction must not become the *determining* factor in the policy to be pursued by the working class, even when the working class finds it necessary to respond positively. At all times the working class movement must make its own assessments and decide on that basis, although naturally enough it will take full account of the aims and activities of the progressive officers as part of its analysis. If the situation in the country necessitates the armed overthrow of a reactionary regime and the armed defence of the new State – and this need often arises in the Third World – then the political and military mobilisation of the people is vital, both for the toppling of the old regime and for the defence of the new one; and for this to be done, the advanced political forces in the country must themselves take a decisive part, alongside whatever radical sections of the armed forces are prepared to throw their weight on the side of progress.

NOTES

1 First, op. cit., p. 256.
2 ibid., p. 257.
3 Lenin, *Collected Works*, Vol. 28, p. 284.
4 *Draft Programme of the Sudanese Communist Party* (see *Information Bulletin*, No. 5, Prague, 1966).
5 Joan Shaw, 'Crisis in the Sudan', *Marxism Today*, April 1971, p. 103.

6 'The Present Political Situation and the Tactics of the Sudanese Communist Party', Resolution adopted by Special Party National Conference, August 1970.

7 *Shafie Ahmed El Sheikh, Son of the Sudanese People and International Trade Unions Leader*, World Federation of Trade Unions, Prague, undated, p. 15.

8 ibid., p. 16.

9 Text of Resolution adopted by the Sudanese Communist Party National Conference, August 1970.

10 See above, pp. 76–7.

11 Lenin, *Collected Works*, Vol. 27, pp. 22–3.

12 As a factor, it has not been absent in the complex situation in Portugal following the overthrow of Caetano.

13 The six points were: '(1) Reorganisation of the Free Officers in such a way as to include all the democratic and progressive elements who should play a prominent role within this institution. (2) Purging the armed forces of *all* rightist elements. (3) Dissemination of revolutionary democratic consciousness amongst the forces and strengthening its ties with the mass movement. (4) Raising the standards of the soldiers and NCOs by changing the regulations in such a way as to create stronger links with the aims and aspirations of the Democratic Revolution. (5) Conscription from the organised democratic forces. (6) Struggling against the tendency to give officers more privileges, as this would only strengthen the rightist trends and constitute a serious obstacle to the development of the democratic revolution.'

14 'To the Masses of the Sudanese People', 16 November 1970.

15 i.e. regarding the officers' plans to overthrow the then existing regime by a military coup.

16 i.e. presumably win the civilian masses to their side.

17 Statement of Sudanese Communist Party, 12 February 1971.

18 Shortly before the 19 July 1971 action by the Free Officers, Abdel Khalig Mahgoub escaped from prison. He was arrested after the counter-coup of the same month, and hanged after a short, farcical 'trial'.

19 'Landmarks on Our Road Since the Bloodbath of 22 July 1971', Central Committee statement, November 1971.

20 ibid.

21 C. Desmond Greaves, *The Life and Times of James Connolly*, London, 1961, p. 410.

22 ibid., pp. 395–6.

23 'In Memory of Our Independence Anniversary', Central Committee, Sudanese Communist Party, December 1971.

24 ibid.

25 'Landmarks on Our Road Since the Bloodbath of 22 July, 1971', op. cit.

26 ibid.

27 ibid.

28 In the Sudan.

29 In the Sudan, fifteen miles north of Khartoum.

30 The new regime set up on 19 July had named him as President.

31 This was the body set up by Nimeiry, with the support of the Free Officers, after the overthrow of the old regime in May 1969.

32 There have been suggestions that the big British monopoly, Lonrho, was also involved. See for example, *Lonrho, Portrait of a Multinational*, by S. Cronje, M. Ling and G. Cronje, London, 1976, pp. 178–93.

33 There had been at least two other coups being prepared against Nimeiry by more right-wing groups prior to 19 July. This was an additional reason why the Free Officers' leaders decided to strike first.

34 There can be exceptions, such as in Somalia.

9

Why Reactionary Coups Succeed

Not all reactionary coups succeed, but naturally enough those that fail generally have less impact and therefore there is less awareness of them. People are more conscious of those that succeed in their objectives, especially if there has been a great deal of popular support for the toppled regime both in the country concerned and further afield. The more progressive the regime, the greater is the shock at its overthrow; and the first reaction of those most politically concerned is to ask: Why did it succeed?

Each coup has its own specific circumstances and takes place within a given relationship of forces; and the reasons for its success or failure need particular examination. Yet the capacity of the armed forces to act as a powerful counter-revolutionary force has been proved time and again in history. After all, as Engels pointed out, the army is one of the two 'decisive forces' in modern society. If the other decisive force, the people's movement, is strong enough and politically alert, it may be possible to check and defeat a coup. This happened in Spain in 1936, where the initial attempt to overthrow the legally elected Popular Front Government failed; it was only after nearly three years of warfare and intervention by fascist Germany and Italy, aided by the Anglo-French blockade in the guise of 'non-intervention', that the Spanish Republic succumbed.

Against a few successes – the defeat of the Kornilov coup by the Russian workers in 1917,[1] the Spanish people's initial check to Franco in 1936, the blocking of a counter-revolutionary coup by the Chilean people in 1969[2] – we have to record a long and sad list of reactionary coups that gained their objective. All experience shows that the weapon of the military coup (or a civilian coup, backed by the armed forces), is not easy to counter. After all, the coup has the great advantage of the element of surprise. It is a sudden physical blow struck at the most decisive obstacles (both personnel and institutions) to the assumption of power by those behind the coup. Even if the coup is expected, in a general sense, and this is sometimes the case, for example, on the eve of elections in Latin American countries, the precise timing, place and form of the coup remain as a rule unknown to all except the narrow circle of actual conspirators.

Moreover, the very nature of a reactionary coup, the sudden, heavy blow against not only government and leaders but against wide sections of the progressive movement in the particular country, with trade union and political officials at all levels, journalists, intellectuals, students, lawyers and other public figures all gathered up by its abrupt and brutal sweep, can paralyse a movement at least momentarily and, more often, for a considerable time. If, as Marx said, the defensive is the defeat of every uprising, then one can add that for intended coup victims to wait passively for the final counter-revolutionary blow guarantees their defeat. Yet defeat is sometimes difficult to avoid. If the relationship of forces on the eve of a foreseen coup is unfavourable for effective counter-measures against it, whatever political awareness of the progressive movement and however strong its desire to stop the coup, it may be impossible in a few days or even weeks to effect the necessary political changes and preparations, both political and material, to prevent such a coup taking place, still less to defeat it once it has begun.

It is important to realise this, otherwise there is a tendency to assess political processes solely in terms of subjective factors, so embracing an outlook of voluntarism. Objective factors, concrete situations, precise relationships of class forces are then ignored – the revolutionary movement alone, by its desire, capacity, determination and will, is expected to enjoy continuing success in leading forward the whole people to change society. The corollary of this is that every setback and defeat of the revolution becomes the fault of the revolutionary vanguard without whose mistakes there would have been no defeat. Such an outlook is, of course, entirely unscientific. Naturally enough, the mistakes and weaknesses of the revolutionary vanguard need to be soberly and penetratingly assessed, but they have to be seen in the wider scope of the strengths and weaknesses of the revolutionary movement as a whole, and in the context of the total relationship of forces in the given country.

A coup cannot be avoided or, if begun, defeated solely by vigilance, material preparations and physical counter-measures, although such precautions should never be forgotten. Of decisive importance is political preparation, the conducting of political work in such a fashion that conditions are not allowed to develop to a stage in which it becomes possible, and in some cases relatively easy, to initiate a coup. This involves important questions of working-class unity, winning allies for the working class, rural population, urban petty-bourgeoisie, intellectuals, professional and technical personnel, or of neutralising classes and strata which otherwise might *actively* support the coup. It also involves the question of the relation of parties to governments, and of parties and governments to the people and their organisations. It poses questions of methods of work, of avoiding sectarianism and ensuring that potential allies are not pushed, by mistaken tactics, into the arms of the other side. Conversely, it requires the avoidance of opportunism and tailing behind events, of failing to organise the necessary struggles to advance the movement. Posed, too, are questions of policy, of the way in which specific major economic, social and political questions are tackled, and the extent to which the democratic rights of the people are extended and their political training and understanding advanced so that they can play an ever-increasing role in the political life of the country.

In the developing countries the armed forces, in a certain sense, are a more decisive factor even than they are in the advanced capitalist countries. In most of the Third World countries the army is usually the most highly organised force in society, often virtually the only organised institution apart from the police which, in some instances, plays a somewhat similar role. In Asia and Africa, prior to the post-1945 tide of national liberation, the colonial governments were themselves an open display of coercion and violence, with the armed forces and the armed police in constant action to suppress the people, and with only the most limited civilian involvement in government (in many cases none at all).

It was such armies, drafted mainly for the purpose of internal suppression, recruited mainly from peasantry and hill-tribes in the belief that they would prove to be more obedient and pliable than the town workers,[3] and officered by men, many of whom received their training and military education at imperialist military colleges such as Sandhurst St Cyr, or Fort Bragg, which were inherited by the new governments when the countries of Asia and Africa began to win their independence. The inherited character of these armies and their officers is a factor which should be taken into account when assessing the role of the military in these countries and the frequency of military coups.

The army in many African countries [writes Gavin Kennedy][4] is equipped, trained and motivated for intervention. The civilian government deploys the military essentially for an internal security role, but the military is able to transform its subordinate role into a dominant one. By kinship and peer-group affiliation it is aware of the prizes flowing from command of the state. By observation of the behaviour and living standards of the European it has acquired, like everybody else with ambition, an envy for living standards commensurate with its conceptions of its special role. It can only look with paternalistic dispproval on the struggle between political factions for power. . . . The army which intervenes with relatively clean hands may campaign against corruption, . . . (but) In an atmosphere where status and prestige are bound up with power and wealth, the scarcity of income among the pious is in conflict with the aspirations of the ambitious; either they succumb to the opportunities or they slide down the social scale. There is another route that does not involve corruption directly, and that is to develop political ambitions exercisable on the basis of support from the corrupted within the military hierarchy. Thus rising political fortune may be a substitute for direct graft; the status of office, with the perks and privileges that this provides, may compensate for abstaining from the lower ranks' opportunities to graft. In these ways the army itself becomes as corrupted as the previous administration.

Thus the army, 'equipped, trained and motivated for intervention' is ever at hand to strike the decisive blow. This ability to organise a coup is aided in Third World countries by the fact that 'the number of men required to carry out a coup is surprisingly small – it certainly does not need the unanimity of the armed forces, a company or a battalion may be sufficient'.[5] Often a couple of hundred soldiers and officers are sufficient to seize the president in his palace, occupy the radio station and announce the overthrow of the regime. This usually takes place when a government has failed to fulfil the people's aspirations and has lost some of its popularity. The coup occasions, therefore, no opposition from the people, merely passivity, some curiosity and not infrequently misplaced jubilation in the streets.

This reaction, regrettable when it takes place as a result of the overthrow of a moderately progressive government, is all too inevitable in many Third World countries as a result of their evolution following the achievement of national independence. Often the national party which helped to lead the country to independence ceases to function subsequently as a political party. Its leaders enter government, they become concerned with Ministries, with various State institutions, with Parliament. From being liberation leaders who previously organised the people, shared their anxieties and struggles and even went to prison in the common cause of independence, they have now, all too often, become 'politicians' or sometimes bureaucrats. The Party ceases to act like a political party; it becomes a subordinate arm of the new State, and functions like a civil service.

The immense and complex economic and social problems which these countries face, and which are made more difficult by continuing imperialist pressures, remain unsolved. The people's expectations accordingly remain unfulfilled, the leaders become alienated from the ordinary workers and peasants who contrast their difficult life with the corruption and opulence displayed by the top circles of society.

The political education of the people is ignored; the new governments and leaders frequently fail to encourage, or even refuse to allow the people's democratic participation in running the country. Systems of 'guided democracy', whether civilian or military, eventually weaken the very basis of the 'guide', for paternalism cripples the democratic initiative of the people, isolating the 'guide' who thus becomes a comparatively easy target for a military coup, with no organised, awakened or committed mass movement ready to act against it.

Even in a number of the most advanced states that emerged in Africa and Asia in the 1950s and 1960s a number of these weaknesses emerged, undermined the basis of the regime and so paved the way to a reactionary coup.

But such weaknesses do not alone explain the success of coups. They certainly do not explain why coups are mounted. It should be remembered that reactionary coups in developing countries take place to serve the class interests of those forces which are opposed to the progressive character of the political, economic and social changes being made in the particular country, or which feel that they are threatened by the imminence of such progressive changes. The causes of a coup are one thing; the reasons why it may have succeeded are another.

Thus the *causes* for the February 1966 coup in Ghana were undoubtedly the radical nature of the reforms introduced under Nkrumah's leadership, the further changes which were envisaged by him, and the role which he was helping Ghana to play in Africa as a whole and on a world scene. But the coup succeeded largely due to Nkrumah's mistakes. At the same time, one has to take into account the objective difficulties which he and his party faced, as well as the subjective weaknesses of the movement in Ghana at that time.

Understandably enough, coups and the threat of coups in Third World countries have raised the question as to whether there can be an alternative to the official army, especially in the former colonies where the armies have been trained, structured, moulded and ideologically prepared for an anti-people's role, with inherited officers largely wedded to such conceptions. The fact that, after independence has been won, imperialist influence still weighs heavily in military matters – Western instructors, Western military hardware requiring Western training experts, officers sent to Western military colleges – makes the problem a very pressing one.

It is not only that a colonial-type army has been inherited; the character of the army is largely perpetuated by the continuing military links with the imperialist countries. Officers who have received their military training in Western academies, have in fact been specifically selected for such instruction by the former colonial power as being individuals of a sufficiently conservative outlook, or sufficiently opportunist, ambitious and corrupt, as to provide a reasonable guarantee that they would use their positions to act against any far-reaching progressive changes in their country.

The same motivation lies behind the choice which the United States makes when it selects army personnel from the Third World to be trained in US military academies, particularly for counter-insurgency techniques.

The question of transforming the armed forces into a progressive institution presents considerable difficulties. The very steps taken to provide an alternative military leadership to that of the Western trained officers, or to bring a different understanding to peasant soldiers with a 'colonial' or traditionalist outlook, can itself be the very final act which leads the reactionary officers to act and oust the progressive government. Nkrumah's decision to train officers in the Soviet Union led to the break with the British General Alexander who, under Nkrumah, had been responsible for the armed forces; and it may well have been that Nkrumah's determination to press ahead with this training was an important factor in deciding the Western trained officers of his army to remove him. Yet for Nkrumah to press ahead with such a training programme was entirely justified. The weakness was that this step was not sufficiently combined with the removal of the most reactionary officers together with economic and political measures that would have rallied the people closer to the Government, and created their readiness to struggle to uphold it. The continuous mobilisation of the people, on the basis of a correct economic and political policy, could have helped to create political conditions in the country in which the officers would have found less scope for their coup.

To turn away from Western military links as regards officer and troop training and the provision of military supplies is certainly one of the ways by which developing countries can begin to weaken the hold of imperialism. But as the experience in several countries demonstrates only too well, if these measures are not accompanied by other anti-imperialist steps and are not underpinned by deep-going democratic changes which release the people's initiative and win them solidly over to the side of their government, then all the military supplies and training from socialist countries can give no certainty that the government of the country in question will not turn to the right, and even use the arms provided by the socialist countries against the people.

Another alternative way of surmounting the problem of the inherited colonial-type army is the idea of a people's militia, or a people's army. Countries which have won their independence through armed struggle, such as China, Vietnam, Laos, Kampuchea, Cuba, Mozambique, Angola, Guinea-Bissau, or South Yemen, have, in the course of such struggle, created their own liberation armies linked to the political movement of which they are an essential component.

Most countries in the Third World, however, have to cope with what one might term the 'official army'. In Guinea, in face of repeated attempts at anti-Government coups, as well as a number of Portuguese-backed raids across the frontier from Guinea-Bissau when it was still under colonial rule, special detachments of a people's armed forces were set up. Significantly, it is these troops which are said to have been the force primarily responsible for defeating the Portuguese sea-invasion in 1971. In Tanzania, too, after Amin's coup in neighbouring Uganda, steps were taken towards the creation of a people's militia.

Yet this solution, too, presents considerable difficulties. The hierarchy of the official army is jealous of its position and is not likely to remain idle while an alternative armed force is being created over which it has no control. It clearly sees this as a threat to its own position and, just as in the case of moves to end military reliance on the West, is liable to regard steps to create a people's militia as a signal that the time has come for it to act and remove the progressive government before the latter can create its own independent force to safeguard its security.

The third solution, and that which is a realistic alternative only where there is an organised revolutionary movement, is to work to influence the official army politically. An army's past and the historic circumstances in which it was formed and trained, as well as the functions it has hitherto performed, are no reason for thinking that the soldiers and officers who make up this army are immune from change and are not susceptible to political influence. The experience of Iraq, Sudan, Egypt, and Portugal over the past thirty years indicates only too clearly that armies can be influenced by political movements and developments, particularly where there is a revolutionary civilian organisation which deliberately sets to work to change the outlook of the men in uniform and to win them, or a decisive section of them, over to the side of the people. Some failures in this work in no way invalidates the principle; they simply underline the hard nature of the problem and the need for more effective work.

These three solutions to the question: how can the armed forces be prevented from staging a counter-revolutionary coup – a purge and change of key officer personnel, the creation of a people's militia, a change in the political outlook and loyalty of the officer corps and of the armed forces as a whole – are not necessarily alternatives. In fact, in many situations what is required is a pressing ahead on all three of these fronts, together with the necessary economic and social measures to tackle the country's problems, and the necessary political measures to increase the democratic political activity and initiative of the people so that their organised and mobilised weight comes fully into play.

NOTES

1 The success of the Bolsheviks in defeating General Kornilov's counter-revolutionary coup in the summer of 1917 has been noted above.
2 See below for more details and assessment.
3 See Jack Woddis, *New Theories of Revolution*, London, 1972, pp. 60–1.
4 Gavin Kennedy, *The Military in the Third World*, London, 1974, pp. 56–8.
5 ibid., p. 24.

10

The Indonesian Catastrophe

At the end of 1965, following an attempted coup by officers claiming to be radical, a group of right-wing generals seized power, ended the regime of President Sukarno, altered the anti-imperialist direction of Indonesia's policy and ruthlessly swept away all democratic rights. This violent coup was immediately followed by one of the worst waves of counter-revolutionary terror ever known. The only parallels that spring to mind are the appalling slaughter that followed the ending of the Paris Commune, the mass killings after the Mannerheim coup in Finland in 1918, the slaughter in China after Chiang Kai-shek's coup in 1927, the terror under Hitler, and the brutal executions and massacres carried out by Franco's forces during and after the Spanish Civil War, and the mass killings after Pinochet's coup in Chile. No one knows how many died in Indonesia. For weeks the slaughter went on, streams were choked by mutilated bodies or hacked-off limbs. Most estimates give a figure of hundreds of thousands.[1]

Not all those butchered in this way were Communists. Whole families, including children, were wiped out. In some places villages were decimated. Hundreds of thousands more were jailed or herded into concentration camps.

The disaster involved a large proportion of the Party membership. Many of the key figures in the Party, including its general secretary, D. N. Aidit, as well as other prominent leaders such as M. H. Lukman and Njoto (and later, trade union leaders such as Njono) lost their lives, as did thousands of other leaders at all levels.

Yet the Indonesian Communist Party had been a major mass Party. With some three million members and ten million votes it was the largest Communist Party in the non-socialist world. Moreover, it was not an Opposition party, but had close relations with President Sukarno and the ruling circles and exercised considerable influence at State and government level. How, then, was it possible for such a mass Party, with so much weight in the political life of Indonesia, to suffer such a sudden, overwhelming disaster?

In some respects the events in Indonesia in 1965 were similar to those that took place in Sudan in 1971. In both cases radical officers initiated military measures in which the Communist Party became involved. In both cases the radical officers justified their action by reference to the dangers of a coup being prepared from the right, thus explaining what they had done as a pre-emptive measure, in part, so as to foil a putsch being prepared by counter-revolutionary officers. In both cases the radical officers' action was immediately met by a brutal counter-coup from the right which made the maximum use of the initial attack by the radical officers to provide the necessary excuse for their barbarous onslaught on the whole revolutionary and democratic movement. In both cases, the counter-coup of the right was successful and the movement suffered heavily.

Yet beyond these partial similarities between the two situations there were immense differences which are apparent once one begins to examine the Indonesian events of 1965 and before in some detail.[2]

One striking difference was the reaction of the people. In Khartoum, following the action of 19 July, the working people rallied in their thousands upon thousands to demonstrate their support of the new regime, in response to the call of the trade unions. In Djakarta the people of Indonesia did not know what to do; they were not called out to demonstrate; they were told nothing, or were left at the mercy of conflicting advice, with the Communist Party paper *Harian Rakjat*, asserting the Party's support for the September 30th Movement's action on 1 October, while a part of the Party leadership were backing Colonel Untung and his colleagues, and members of the Party's youth section were reportedly involved in the fighting in Jogjakarta, and were present at the Halim Base where the six leading right-wing generals were killed in the first hours of Untung's coup. There was, in fact, the most incredible confusion. There was apparently no unified position among the Party leadership, and the members must have been bewildered and utterly at a loss. Even after Untung's coup was defeated there was no clear lead from the Party. It is no wonder that hundreds of thousands of members, their families and supporters went like lambs to the slaughter.

An analysis of the 1965 events in Indonesia, contained in a document entitled 'For a Sound Indonesian Revolution', and issued by a group calling itself 'The Marxist-Leninist Group of the Indonesian Communist Party', reached London in the latter half of 1967.[3] Apparently issued originally at the end of 1966, this was one of the first – perhaps the first – attempt to make a comprehensive analysis of the 1965 crisis. A good deal of what it said stands the test of time and subsequent study remarkably well.

The essential points of the 1965 analysis are that the coup attempt of Colonel Untung and his colleagues was 'purely adventuristic'; that a section of the Communist Party leadership became involved and backed the action (the document calls it a counter-coup, since its declared purpose was to block an impending right-wing coup) because it had become dogmatically wedded to the theory that armed struggle was the only way forward; and that this concept was combined with serious errors of 'both right-wing opportunism and leftism' which left the Party membership and the working people as a whole immobilised and confused at the moment of greatest crisis.

The military and political action that took place in Indonesia's capital, Djakarta, on 1 October 1965, and which became known as the September 30th Movement was said to be directed against the Generals' Council, a group of right-wing officers allegedly sponsored by the CIA and believed to be preparing a right-wing coup against President Sukarno and the Indonesian Government. The action was undertaken by Colonel Untung and other radical officers, together with 'several units of the Indonesian Republic's Armed Forces, the Army in particular, and consisting of the most progressive servicemen. The Movement concentrated in Djakarta. In other words, it was an action started in the centre, in the hope that it would extend to all regions of the Motherland.'[4]

Part of the problem undoubtedly stems from confusion as to what the September 30th Movement was meant to achieve. In grappling with this the Document poses three very pertinent questions. Was the action considered by its organisers as a revolution or simply as a limited military operation to remove the dangerous right-wing generals and foil their plot? If it was regarded as a revolution, can one say that the objective and subjective conditions in Indonesia at the time were such as to warrant the estimation that Indonesia was in the midst of a revolutionary situation? But if it was not intended as a revolutionary movement, but solely as 'an adventuristic counter-coup', how did the leaders of the Communist Party, a Party of 45 years of struggle and experience, become involved in such a movement? Finally, when the struggle was joined and the counter-revolution struck, why was the Party, for all its three million members, its ten million votes, and the mass organisations which it led, unable to resist the terror in any meaningful way whatsoever?

First of all, there is no doubt that various right-wing manoeuvres and plots were being prepared against the Sukarno regime, taking advantage of Sukarno's illness and of the instability of the Government arising, in part, from its failure to cope with the country's economic ills and consequent inability to relieve the hardship and deprivation suffered by a large part of the population. A political plot, organised by a right-wing trio of political intriguers, Sukarni, Hatta and Chairul, was aimed at seizing political state power. This attempt failed, the right-wing Murba party was banned, and Sukarni, its leader, arrested.

Meanwhile, a military-political plot was also being prepared. This involved the conspirators of the Generals' Council, together with political figures, including once again Hatta. Subandrio, Indonesia's Foreign Minister and Sukarno's right-hand man, apparently learnt of the plot and informed both the President and the Communist Party leadership. The Party leaders met and theoretically took the necessary action to 'prepare the Party for any emergency in case the Generals' Council dared to carry out their dastardly plan'.[5] (The word 'theoretically' is used here since subsequent events in no way indicated that the Party had been prepared as the Document asserts. In fact, they rather showed the inadequacy and confused fashion in which preparations had been made.). The Communist leaders, apprised of the plot of the General's Council, evidently held consultations with the President and with 'left-wing nationalist leaders'. The right-wing generals were pushing ahead with their conspiracy since they feared that President Sukarno was preparing to give his full backing to the formation of a Gotong Rojong Cabinet,[6] to which they were opposed.

The Document believes that if agreement had been reached between Communists and other progressive forces in presenting a joint front against the General's Council — and it evidently thinks that such a possibility was there — then the right-wing coup could have been avoided or defeated, and a positive perspective opened up for the Indonesian people. In other words, an alliance of the widest progressive and anti-imperialist forces, including the Communist Party, was needed to cope with the right-wing generals' plot.

But such a broad alliance, including the Communists, President Sukarno and the left-wing nationalists, and even certain centre groups and parties (or, at least, the neutrality of these latter forces, among them some religious sections) was not established. Instead, the Party leaders or, more probably, a group of them, decided to cut loose and go for a quick military solution.

Following the return of our leaders from a trip abroad, which also included one of the Asian countries[7] (July–August 1965), it became known that the Party leadership had taken a rash decision to begin preparations for playing the role of a 'saviour', with or without President Sukarno and other democratic forces. And all this happened at a time when there was no revolutionary situation in evidence, no instability was manifest in the position of the ruling quarters, the broad masses were not prepared for armed action. There was but a danger of a counter-revolutionary plot, and there were the diseased kidneys of President Sukarno. Had the revolution occurred it would have been based not on the revolutionary situation or the support of the revolutionary masses, but would have rather hinged on Sukarno's lesioned kidneys. Truly, that was a gamble of the first water which had nothing to do with the Marxist theory of armed uprising.[8]

The Indonesian Document, like that quoted earlier from the Sudanese Communist Party, assesses the situation that confronted the Party in relation to Lenin's well-known definition of what constitutes a revolutionary situation, and considers, too, as does the Sudanese Central Committee statement cited above, Lenin's views on the necessary pre-conditions for a successful uprising. In all respects, the Indonesian Document considers that the decision of the Party leadership to help initiate the September 30th Movement was at odds with Lenin's teaching, as were equally the actions of the Party once the military action of Colonel Untung had been undertaken.

Within the framework of these general mistakes the Indonesian Communist Party committed other serious errors which contributed to the débâcle. In its dogmatic and sectarian pursuit of a voluntarist forcing of the pace of the revolution and its decision to stake all on an armed blow the Party neglected the question of allies. This was particularly dangerous in a situation in which, partly due to a sharpening of the class struggle, and partly arising from incorrect tactics by the Party, a certain polarisation of forces had taken place. Among the centre groups who might have been influenced to take a more sympathetic attitude to the democratic left, the more conservative among them had swung over to the main reactionary forces. Further, the religious parties which were unlikely to act decisively against the national front of progressive forces, took a quite different attitude when it was a matter of making a choice between the right-wing generals on the one hand, and the Communist Party and its close allies on the other. 'The religious parties were more sympathetic towards the Generals' Council which they tended to see as a saviour of religion from atheism.'[9]

The question of allies, however, was not confined to the political parties and the civilian population. As always, political relationships in the country as a whole have their bearing on reactions inside the armed forces. This is not so obvious at times of relative peace and political stability. But when tension arises in the broad political field, and when profound crises occur, heavy pressure bears down on the armed forces and political choices then appear necessary.

The Document poses the question of the armed forces at the time of the 1965 crisis in these terms:

We often say that at least 30 per cent of the Armed Forces are the followers of the Hammer and Sickle. However, we often also mistakenly forget what measure of the 30 per cent are loyal to the Party and President Sukarno. One can say with certainty that when the Party and Bung Karno[10] are united, these 30 per cent of the Armed Forces will pledge their hearts and souls to them. When, however, they have to choose between the Party and President Sukarno, it is a good guess that the majority will demonstrate greater devotion to Sukarno; at best they will occupy an unstable position. That is why the factor of President Sukarno has to be seriously borne in mind.

The obvious question to ask, although strangely the Document does not, is what was the position of the other 70 per cent of the armed forces, in other words, the majority? Clearly they were not on the side of the Party – and if they were not clearly on the side of Sukarno, which appears to have been likely, then obviously any action undertaken by a minority faction of the armed forces would have required immediate massive and active intervention by the popular forces if it was to have any chance of success. But this active popular support was not forthcoming. The tactics of the Party and the military organisers of the September 30th Movement in reality precluded such popular response; and after 1 October no apparent steps were taken to encourage the people to come out in support of the overthrow of the Generals' Council.

The more the events leading up to 1 October are examined, the more one looks at what followed, the more one is taken aback at the muddle-headedness, ineptness, and amateurism with which the whole affair was carried out. Practically every mistake in the revolutionary book was committed, mistakes which have been exposed time and again by revolutionary experience, mistakes which have been trenchantly warned against by Marx and Lenin. Insurrection is a serious business. It is not a game. How often has this been said. But what can one make of the gamble that lay behind 1 October?

The adventurist nature of the whole operation becomes even more clear when one looks at the events of 30 September and 1 October and subsequently. Analysing the subjective factor, namely the readiness of the Party and the working class and its allies for armed struggle, the Document states that despite a number of mass actions in the past by workers and peasants, the popular movement was not yet ready for armed battle. 'We were not sufficiently seasoned in non-peaceful action. . . .'

Was this so? Relatively, perhaps. Yet neither the Indonesian Communist Party nor the democratic movement in general were entirely without experience of armed struggle. Leaving aside the uprising in 1926 (only veterans from that struggle would still be around in 1965), there had been armed resistance to the Japanese between 1941 and 1945, armed struggle against the British army after the defeat of Japan, and then two national liberation armed struggles against the Dutch.[11] This was certainly no less experience than had been accumulated by a number of the European resistance movements prior to 1939 but which, as for example in France, Italy, Yugoslavia and Denmark, led sustained armed actions throughout the period of German occupation right up to the moment of anti-fascist victory. Despite numerically large and heavily-armed modern armies which they faced, these resistance movements did not collapse like a pack of cards as did the Indonesian Communist Party and its supporters. Politics, rather than expertise in the use of arms, lies at the bottom of the Indonesian catastrophe.

Quite apart from the correctness or otherwise of the initial decision to launch the attack on the Generals' Council, blunder after blunder was made in carrying it out. When prominent figures of the Generals' Council were arrested and this became known through Colonel Untung's broadcasts there was, at first, popular enthusiasm. But when it was announced that the Cabinet had resigned and a new body, a Revolutionary Council, had been set up, doubts quickly arose. These doubts rapidly increased when it became known that President Sukarno was not party to these decisions and that he had refused to endorse the Revolutionary Council. Even more serious, those who had been named by Colonel Untung as being members of the Revolutionary Council issued statements asserting that 'they had not the slightest idea that they had been appointed to serve on the Revolutionary Council, saying they were devoted to no one else but President Sukarno'.[12] The units of the Generals' Council naturally exploited this to the utmost and charged the Revolutionary Council with being a counter-revolutionary organisation intending to unseat President Sukarno, since the Council had forced the resignation of the Cabinet of which President Sukarno was Prime Minister.

Two possible interpretations spring to mind. Perhaps the devious Sukarno had originally tipped the wink to Colonel Untung, thinking that the intention was only to remove the right-wing generals and, possibly, reconstruct the Government; but at the last moment he drew back, either because he had doubts as to the outcome, or because he suspected that Colonel Untung and his political supporters, including leaders of the Communist Party, were intending to go beyond a mere army purge and were bent on a revolutionary change of system, in which he feared that he himself, assuming he were retained, would be confined to a mere symbolic role. In the circumstances, those who had indicated their readiness to serve on the Revolutionary Council quickly jumped off the band-waggon when they saw that Sukarno'a absence was rapidly transforming it into a hearse.

The only other explanation could be that Colonel Untung and the September 30th Movement were engaged in a shocking fraud, and that neither President Sukarno nor the named members of the Revolutionary Council had ever been consulted or informed as to what was taking place.[13] Either way, it adds up to an appalling gamble.

But that was not the worst of it. For better or worse, the die had been cast. Battle had been joined. To save itself and the Revolution, the Party, *whatever course it had decided to follow*, should have mobilised the working people in support of the policy the Party deemed necessary. Instead, with that strange combination of leftist adventurism and opportunistic court intrigue, it turned aside from organising the struggle and instead placed its reliance on Sukarno.

During these tense days, the Party, having given its support to Colonel Untung's actions, committed the following political mistakes: The organisers and immediate participants in Untung's actions failed to take into consideration the need to draw the masses to their side in order to secure the support of progressive forces within the country. After the successful seizure of Radio Republik Indonesia (RPI) they did not offer the people a positive socio-economic platform, nor did they call upon peasants and workers to watch for the danger of the conspiracy of the Generals' Council.

Instead of issuing a decree for the creation of people's armed forces, a decision was made to give a fresh boost to the military. Following all this, it was hard to count on the support of the masses for the September 30th Movement.

When all the political leaders denied their participation in the Revolutionary Council, the leadership of the Party made a belated statement to the effect that it was wrong to believe that the Party had taken part in the September 30th Movement. However, the Party leadership did not refute allegations that it had supported the purge carried out by Untung and his followers.[14]

The nature of the confusion is the contrast between the statement of the Political Bureau of 5 October, asserting that the Communist Party 'has nothing whatever' to do with the September 30th Movement, and, on the other hand, the editorial of 2 October in the Party paper, *Harian Rakjat*, giving the movement its backing. After stating that 'The issue is one within the army itself', the editorial nevertheless went on to declare: 'However, we, people with political consciousness who are aware of the tasks of the revolution, are convinced that the action taken by the September 30th Movement to save the revolution and the people is correct.' Describing the movement as 'a patriotic and revolutionary action', it proclaimed:

Without fail, the people will show their sympathy with the September 30th Movement and will support it. We appeal to the entire people to heighten their vigilance and be ready to face all eventualities.

It appears that the statement of 5 October was intended to correct the orientation given in the editorial of 2 October. There is some evidence that between these two dates, the Party leaders, especially Aidit, Lukman, and Sakirman, hurriedly tried to cool things down, to persuade Party members to stay at home, not to provoke the army, not to take any action but give their support to President Sukarno and his call for calm. This reliance on Sukarno and the hope that despite Untung's attempted coup, and despite the anti-communist campaign already under way, it was possible to settle matters quietly by political talk was again a complete misreading of what was happening. It was, tragically, while engaged in rushing around Central Java to quieten things down that Aidit was probably arrested and shot.

In Western Java, where the Party influence was relatively small, not only were no special steps taken to warn and prepare the Party organisations, but nothing about the situation or the plans of the leadership was even known. As a result, mass arrests took place without resistance. Because of the confusion, and due, too, to general disillusionment with the political leadership of the Party, there took place a 'shameful mass surrender' in Western Java, resulting in widespread arrests and mass killings.

In the capital, Djakarta, territorial units composed of young men who had just completed their military training stayed at their posts, together with veterans.

However, a decree to arm the people was not issued. When it was apparent that the situation was changing unfavourably for the Movement, it was necessary not to procrastinate but take up arms and start a mobile guerrilla resistance in the city, as Marx had taught, so as not to play irresponsibly with arms but, once having started an armed struggle, to carry it on to the end. For at that time there were opportunities for such actions, since the chief forces of the enemy were still busy chasing the main detachments of the September 30th Movement, the mass of reactionary youth did not yet know what they had to do to crush us, rent by doubts due to the uncertainty of the situation. However, an armed struggle was not taking place. An order was given that weapons be hidden securely and everyone should seek refuge and wait for a political resolution.[15]

Meanwhile, the President issued a decree calling for the enforcement of law and order, the avoidance of armed clashes, and the convening of a Cabinet meeting in order to find a political solution. 'Heated debates' took place in the Party leadership as to what response to make to the President's appeal. Should they back the President's call, or should they continue the struggle and repulse the counter-revolutionary attack?

It was decided to issue a statement in support of a political solution by the President, to attend the full Cabinet meeting so as to bring pressure to bear upon the President during that meeting, to recognise the Generals' Council and agree to the formation of Nasakom cabinet[16] – if this failed to continue resistance.

This, in the opinion of the Document, was the major mistake committed by the Party: 'The passivity and panic among the Party leadership in an emergency situation, which resulted in surrender of all authority to President Sukarno and his political decisions, but not reliance on the strength of the masses.'

Confirmation of this was provided in January 1966 in discussions I had in Havana with one of the Indonesian Communist leaders, during the Tri-Continental Conference. At that time the massacre of Indonesian Communists and their supporters was still going on, and the shocking reports, with all their gruesome details, were then coming through. When I asked what we could do to help, this Indonesian leader, to my astonishment, said: 'We must avoid all panic. The storm will pass. We are relying on Sukarno.'[17]

The same incredible complacency and illusion was expressed in a statement on Radio Djakarta in November 1965, issued by the Committee Supporting the Commands of President Sukarno: 'It is just a temporary condition that the right-wing forces seem to be strong and the progressive forces seem to be weakened. What seems to be strong as such is actually weak and will be smashed, while the one which seems to be weakened in reality possesses a limitless strength and will win.'

Whether the Indonesian Communist leadership was guilty of panic, as the document charges, or was able to avoid panic, as my friend in Havana was half implying, is a matter of debate. Perhaps, after all, the question of panic was not the key issue. The whole affair was characterised rather by recklessness, irresponsibility, confusion and, in the end, by passivity. In such conditions it was not difficult for the counter-revolution to come out on top. This was the price paid for what the Document calls 'the suicidal leftist policies' of the September 30th Movement. Recalling Lenin's advice on insurrection, the Document comments:

Lenin said that the government and bourgeoisie should not be allowed to drown the Revolution in the blood of a *premature* uprising. He cautioned against falling easy prey to provocations. He said that we should wait for the high tide. . . . If 100–300 people are killed by the bourgeoisie, this will not kill the cause of the Revolution. But if the bourgeoisie succeeds in provoking a massacre and 10,000 to 30,000 workers are killed, this *may check* the revolution *even for several years*. For the sake of everything we hold the sacred the Revolution should be nursed carefully until it is really ready to give birth to a child.

Tragically, the '10,000 to 30,000' killed turned out to be some twenty times that number, and the 'several years' is now a decade with no sign of decisive recovery from the holocaust. It is, of course, dangerous to draw generalised conclusions from experiences which, while they share something in common, arise from a differing set of circumstances. But one cannot completely ignore the fact that, leaving aside those countries where a different outcome arose as a result of the military defeat of fascism in the Second World War and, in particular, as a consequence of the presence of Soviet armies, in practically every other case a counter-revolutionary coup accompanied by the heavy slaughter of the active membership of the revolutionary movement has meant the putting back of the struggle for a generation. Thus, the Portuguese people who went down to defeat in 1926, had to suffer fascism for nearly fifty years before they regained democratic rights; in Spain, Franco's victory in 1939 resulted in nearly forty years of fascist darkness; a number of squalid dictatorships in Latin America have lasted for decades after the overthrow of previous democratic regimes.

The world today is different. The political calendar moves faster. No one expects a long political life for Pinochet and his junta. Yet the experience of Indonesia underlines only too tragically the necessity to nurse the Revolution carefully until it is 'ready to give birth'. It underlines, too, the absolute necessity for the working class to win other classes and social strata as allies, and for the Communist Party to secure the co-operation of other political forces and movements. Without such allies, a revolutionary movement cannot succeed; and this holds true whether an offensive or defensive tactic is being followed, whether the struggle is relatively peaceful or whether it assumes armed form.

The Document makes three basic criticisms of the Party which it considers lay behind the mistakes of the September 30th Movement. The 'adventurism' of 30 September and its fatal outcome were 'the inevitable result of the accumulation of the Party's past mistakes, its confused ideological, political and organisational line, all of which caused the Party to be punished by the objective development of history.'

The Document sets out its views on the mistakes in the following terms:

Theoretically, there was, on the one hand, an upsurge of dogmatism which found expression in easy acceptance of concepts revolutionary in form but failing to take stock of local conditions. On the other hand, there was an emergence of revisionism which tended to upend the monolithic doctrine of Marxism-Leninism and replace it with 'national Marxism within the framework of the so-called Indonesification of Marxism-Leninism'.

Politically, the Party was not consistent in defending its class positions and engaged in class collaboration with the bourgeoisie; it gave prominence to co-operation within the framework of the Nasokom; it lost its freedom of action in strengthening the sacred alliance of the workers and peasants; it demonstrated subjectivism and haste in assessing the situation and in evaluating the balance of forces; it failed to define its tactics, shuttling between adventurism and capitulation; it made absolute its choice of the forms of struggle, tending to take just one aspect of the struggle out of the many forms that a party of the working class must employ. All this led to the Party's inability to play the role of leader of the Revolution.

Organisationally, in its internal activities the Party was further deviating from the principles of democracy and collective leadership, it was increasingly falling into the snare of the personality cult, it was demonstrating an increasing lack of internal democracy in the Party, it was stifling initiatives coming from the rank and file, it was fettering criticisms from below and was not encouraging the development of vigorous self-criticism.

To give proper evaluation to these assessments it is necessary to consider the strategy and tactics pursued by the Indonesian Communist Party in the years leading up to the crisis of 1965, for the seeds of the debacle of October 1965 were undoubtedly sown long before.

Like other Parties engaged in the national liberation struggle, the Indonesian Communist Party had, throughout the years of its existence, been faced with the necessity to contend with two weaknesses, two sets of problems, two tendencies – 'a tendency to surrender and a tendency to adventurism', or, in other words, 'a battle against both right-wing opportunism and leftism'. These tendencies were revealed in the tactics pursued towards the national capitalists, in the attitude taken towards democracy and the independent struggles of the workers and peasants and other progressive classes and strata, in the relation of the Party to President Sukarno, and in the use made of different forms of struggle, peaceful and non-peaceful.

Many of these questions were fought out in the 1950s and were, formally speaking, resolved by the policies adopted by the Fifth National Congress of the Indonesian Party in 1954 and further developed at the Sixth Congress in 1959. By these congresses the Party decided on the character of the revolution – 'a bourgeois-democratic revolution of a new type, or a popular-democratic revolution'; the class forces of the revolution – working class, peasants, other petty-bourgeois elements and democratic forces, plus the national bourgeoisie. This revolutionary alliance was to be led by the working class. The governmental form to emerge from the success of this revolution was to be a 'government of people's democracy', based on a united national front of all anti-imperialist and anti-feudal classes. The task of this government was to carry out democratic changes, with the support of the people – not yet socialist changes. The form of struggle to achieve these democratic changes and establish a 'people's democracy' in Indonesia was to be, if possible, peaceful, while bearing in mind that 'the class of the bourgeoisie will strive to foist upon us a non-peaceful way of attaining this end'.

In pursuing these aims in the period 1954 to 1960 the Party made considerable gains, expressed in part in the eight million votes which it secured in provincial council elections. The Party's membership also rose very considerably, as did the mass organisations in which the Party enjoyed considerable influence. Thus, at the time of the coup the Party had 3 million members, the trade union centre, SOBSI, had $3\frac{1}{2}$ million, the peasant unions, BTI, had 3 million, the youth organisation, Pemuda Rakjat, had 2 million, and the women's organisation, GERWANI, $1\frac{1}{2}$

million. Its mobilising power for demonstrations and meetings was very great and there was much substance to the claim that it was the largest Communist movement outside the socialist countries. But this assessment was, in part, a superficial one. The Party was undoubtedly large numerically, and had considerable influence, but, as events were to prove so fatally, it was a Party and movement with grave weaknesses. The class basis of the Party was ignored. 'This resulted,' according to the Document, 'in the Party becoming oversaturated with petty-bourgeois ideology.'

This tendency was strengthened by the fact that the leaderships of many of the basic units of the Party as well as of the branches of the mass peasant organisation, the BTI, were dominated by rich peasants, or by village folk who were not themselves working peasants – such as headmen or teachers. Coupled with a failure to embrace the overwhelming majority of Party members in any Party educational work, the membership was left largely rudderless when the storm hit them. Thus it was that when the terror of October 1965 struck the Party, the members were completely overwhelmed. In many cases Party committees simply disbanded their organisations. Overall, the Party revealed an appalling incapacity to act decisively at the moment of crisis. October 1965 and the months that followed showed conclusively that despite its mass membership, its considerable political influence among wide sections of people, and its huge voting strength, it was seriously lacking as a revolutionary organisation.

The Document draws attention to another major weakness, and that was the failure of the Party to establish a firm financial basis through financial commitments from the bulk of the members. To provide the necessary funds for its work, the Party leadership came 'to rely more and more on donations from people in high social positions'. It is not unknown, of course, for some better off people to contribute to the funds of Communist Parties. This happens in developed capitalist countries as well as in the Third World. But this is normally a minor factor in the total financial resources of such Parties. In the case of Indonesia, however, this became a principal way of acquiring funds for the Party. This had two negative consequences. The millions of Party members and supporters were never linked closely to the Party by the financial sacrifice and commitment which regular donations would have involved; and, equally dangerous, the leadership, relying as it did so much on contributions from rich people, began to follow a line towards 'class collaboration with the national bourgeoisie'.

A number of leading Party officials held well-paid posts in government institutions and in representative bodies. To a certain extent, some of these leaders began to adapt themselves to a bourgeois way of life and a bourgeois way of looking at political questions. Instead of putting the emphasis on building the alliance of the workers and peasants as the main base for the national liberation movement, and of developing the actions of these two basic classes as the principal form for strengthening the whole movement, the Party leadership began to put all the concentration on unity at the top between themselves and leading forces among the national bourgeoisie.

A revealing indication of the impact of these processes on the thinking of the Indonesian Party leaders was the well-known speech of the Party Chairman, D. N. Aidit, to the Reserve Naval Officers, at Surabaya, in 1964, when he said: 'The Indonesian Communist Party has stressed that all communists should be genuine patriots who place national above class interests, and who should not become chauvinists.'[18]

As a consequence of these developments inside the Indonesian Communist Party, especially in the period leading up to October 1965, two apparently opposed tendencies came to the fore. On the one hand, there was 'an over-indulgence in leftist phraseology', which confused the membership, led to sectarian expectations, alienated possible allies and opened the door to provocations. On the other hand, the Party leadership 'tended to depart still further from stepping up mass revolutionary action, engaged in class collaboration with the bourgeoisie and thus were steadily losing our political freedom.'

In the main, the analysis made by the Document correctly assesses the weaknesses and mistakes of the Indonesian Communist Party. Left, sectarian and adventurist words and gestures, coupled with a number of opportunist practices, is not an unknown combination in revolutionary history, although undoubtedly they were present to an exceptional degree in the case of Indonesia.

In some respects, however, the Document fails to emphasise sufficiently two other factors. First, there is the question of democracy. True, the Document refers to the growing tendency towards bureaucracy inside the Party, but it makes no examination of Sukarno's practice of 'Guided Democracy'. This paternalist idea is a common feature in many Third World countries. Sukarno may have thought up the term, but the concept was to a large extent evident in Egypt under Nasser, in Ghana under Nkrumah, in Uganda under Obote, in Bangla Desh under Sheikh Mujibar, and in a number of other countries. In fact, often where right-wing coups succeed it has been against progressive, anti-imperialist governments following a policy of 'Guided Democracy'. The whole concept is basically one stemming from the national bourgeoisie and petty-bourgeoisie, and is based on a combination of contempt for and fear of the mass of workers and peasants. The consequences are the stifling of the independent initiative of the majority of the people; the State and Government control of the main social organisations; and restrictions on the activity of the Communist Party or whatever other form of revolutionary organisation may exist. As a result, when a coup takes place under these conditions, the people often display a striking indifference or passivity and even the politically conscious forces are not in any easy position to organise mass resistance; a handful of troops seize the reigning president and the radio station, and a new regime is installed with comparative ease.

In Indonesia, 'Guided Democracy' suited the national bourgeoisie since it gave them the prospects of controlling the country's political life, curbing reaction yet, at the same time, keeping a grip on the workers and peasants and their Communist Party. In the circumstances described above, with the leadership of the Communist Party becoming increasingly adapted to petty-bourgeois and even bourgeois concepts, the system of 'Guided Democracy' had a serious negative effect on the people and undoubtedly contributed towards that strange acceptance, fatalism and passivity that followed the coup of October 1965.

A second point that the Document does not sufficiently emphasise is the question of the handling of allies. True enough it correctly lays stress on the alliance between the workers and peasants, and this, of course, is absolutely vital in a country like Indonesia. But the class and social structures of developing countries are very complex. Basic classes are still in a process of formation; the peasants are breaking up into rich, middle and poor; the working class, though growing, is relatively small, and in the main is not connected with large scale modern industry, but tends, to quite a degree, to be casual, unskilled, and even migrant. A very substantial part of the population are not capable of being easily slotted into the ranks of workers or peasants; they comprise a variety of forces — artisans, unemployed and pauperised urban dwellers, small shopkeepers, still smaller street traders, fishermen, intellectuals, private doctors and lawyers working on their own account. This numerically considerable layer of petty-bourgeoisie, of clerical employees of various grades, together with backward or even *lumpen* workers, is a ready prey to demagogy, and can be influenced by both the national bourgeoisie as well as the more reactionary bourgeoisie and landlord sections who lean towards foreign imperialism. It is essential for the revolutionary movement to win decisive sections of these intermediate strata to its side, otherwise it will find them, both in the towns and in the villages, providing active elements for the counter-revolution.

Equally important, a revolutionary movement must be able to judge correctly how to handle the national bourgeoisie, that is to say, that section of the indigenous capitalist class which is interested in furthering the country's independence and therefore can still play an anti-imperialist role, even if only temporarily and erratically. The Document rightly draws attention to the tendency of the Indonesian Communist leaders to capitulate to the national bourgeoisie, yet there was a real problem here. At a time when the national bourgeoisie still exercised enormous influence on the people, and especially on the peasants, and intermediate strata, the Party had to tread a correct path of co-operating with the national bourgeoisie without becoming submerged by it, nor giving up its right to achieve a leading position in the national democratic movement as a whole. For a considerable time after the 1951 repression, the Communist Party pursued its course with great skill, building up its strength and that of the mass organisations, helping to keep counter-revolution at bay, and at the same time maintaining its alliance with the national bourgeoisie and avoiding falling victim to provocation and terror as had happened in 1948 and in 1951.

In the Document's conclusions, it seems to me, this problem is virtually glossed over. Yet it cannot be neglected, since the alliance facilitates the Party's work amongst the masses. Equally important, it has a bearing on the position inside the armed forces. Strangely enough, this latter aspect of the problem receives rather scant attention in the Document. Since a considerable section of the army officers came from the national bourgeoisie and the petty-bourgeoisie, then clearly the way the Party works out its relationship with the national bourgeoisie and intermediate strata in civilian political life will largely determine army attitudes towards the Party and towards the further unfolding of Indonesia's revolutionary process.

Of course, the United States was actively preparing for the anti-Communist and anti-democratic coup.[19] This is now such a 'normal' event that any serious political party has to consider carefully how best to counter such activities. A key part of CIA preparations in such situations is always to produce a favourable balance *inside* the armed forces, favourable that is, to its counter-revolutionary intentions. In conditions in which progressive forces, under the impact of generally progressive developments in the country as a whole, have substantial influence among the officers and soldiers, counter-revolution finds it necessary to carry out a 'coup within a coup'; that is to say, to achieve a clearly dominant position inside the armed forces as a necessary prelude to using its military muscle to destroy the civilian opposition.

US aid to the counter-revolution in Indonesia took three forms – financial aid especially for the armed forces, technical training of officers for their future role as 'managers' of the economy, and political action to sort out, encourage and brainwash the right-wing officers into fulfilling the role of agents of the US grand design for South-East Asia. Long before 1965 the US had been selecting top officers in Indonesia for economic and other training in the United States. In many cases these officers were already playing key economic roles in Indonesia, either through the army's own economic institutions (e.g. the army's own oil company, Permina, headed by Colonel Dr Ibnu Sutowo), or through their links with such firms as the Caltex oil company. The oil monopolies played a particularly key role ('There is perhaps no final answer to the question whether . . . it is the oil companies which further the projects of the CIA or whether it is the other way around. . . . Banks and oil companies got into the international intelligence (and coup management) game long before there was ever a CIA').[20]

The general political and psychological push for a coup against Sukarno was assisted by Guy Pauker, a friend of Sumitro (a right-wing leader of the abortive 1958 revolt who, in 1968, was appointed by Suharto as Minister of Trade and Commerce). Pauker, an official of the Rand Corporation, had links with the Council on Foreign Relations (CFR) in New York, which itself has links with the CIA and the US State Department generally. A blue-print for the coup was drawn up for the CFR by Professor Russell Fifield with the Assistance of Pauker. Pauker apparently helped train the so-called 'Berkeley mafia' who were prepared for managing Indonesia's affairs after the coup. As a result, when the crunch came 'one third of the Indonesian general staff had had some sort of training from Americans and almost half the officer corps'.[21] Ransom[22] suggests that the Berkeley Centre for South and Southeast Asian Studies, in the the United States, trained 'most of the key Indonesians who would seize governement power and *put their pro-American lessons into practice*' (italics added).

It is interesting to note that Hilsman's estimate of the value of this training operation has familiar echoes of the conception outlined by

Bissell when explaining the whole purpose of the CIA's covert operations for the US State Department:[23] 'As a result . . . the American and Indonesian military had come to know each other rather well. Bonds of personal respect and even affection existed, as a matter of fact, that gave the Pentagon an understanding of Indonesian motives and aspirations that was better than any other agency in Washington.'[24] A Ford programme for training Indonesian generals in economic management cost $2·5 million. Ford Foundation's director of international training, John Brigham Howard, is supposed to have commented: 'Ford felt it was training the guys who would be leading the country when Sukarno got out.'[25]

In the three vital years prior to the 1965 coup, despite a general deterioration in relations between the United States and Indonesia, and a steady cutting off of all economic and financial aid to the Indonesian Government, aid to the military in Indonesia was stepped up.[26] Total grants in the four years 1962–5 were $35·8 million, compared with $29·5 million for the thirteen years, 1949–61, and a peak of $16·3 million in 1962. While about 250 Indonesian officers had been trained in the United States by 1958, the figure by 1962 was 500, and by 1965 had soared to 4,000.[27] As a result 'hundreds of visiting officers at Harvard and Syracuse gained the skills for maintaining a huge economic, as well as military, establishment, with training in everything from business administration and personnel management to air photography and shipping'.[28] After the 1965 coup US military aid continued to increase, totalling $124·6 million for the five-year period 1971–5.[29] As Admiral Ray Peet, Director of Military Assistance, explained to the US Congress: 'Military Security Assistance to Indonesia is oriented primarily toward the development of a capability to establish and maintain internal security in this strategically located and important nation.'[30]

Setting out his impressive indictment of US intervention in Indonesia, Peter Dale Scott asserts:

'American policy-makers knew in advance about planning for the military take-over, facilitated it, took credit for it when it occurred, and even publicly exhorted the military to displace Sukarno in semi-official US publications'.[31]

The evidence provided by Peter Dale Scott certainly bears out his contention. At the time the Communist Party produced its Document no doubt much of this evidence was not available, yet enough must have been known for this aspect of the coup to have featured more emphatically in its analysis; and if knowledge of these American preparations and involvements were not known sufficiently, this, too, is a sign of a significant political weakness. What cannot be gainsaid is that US intervention and the activities of the CIA were major factors in bringing about the coup against Sukarno. Whether the CIA was able to instigate and provoke Colonel Untung into his adventurist act, or whether, with all their plans for the coup well prepared, they simply made skilful use of the opportunity presented to them by Colonel Untung's desperate throw is not yet known. What is certain is that the United States was fully involved in the preparations for the overthrow of Sukarno's Government, that this was in pursuance of its overall strategy in South-East Asia, and that it had decided, some time prior to 1965, to place its bets on the army generals and do everything possible to ensure their success.

As far back as July 1962, the United States journal, *Foreign Affairs*, argued that there were two main political forces in Indonesia, the Communist Party and the army, and that Sukarno was able to rule by balancing between the two. In this situation, it suggested, 'the officer corps . . . could be the nation's salvation', provided that it 'appreciated its historic role'.

Throughout 1965 activities were stepped up inside the military formations to prepare the ground for the reactionary coup. General Yani, chief of staff of the High Operational Command, made use of his key position to concentrate the most efficient units from all the arms of the service into a single force under the command of the land troops. Thus units of the marines, air force, police and land troops were brought under right-wing control, and made subordinate to an overall reactionary command. These counter-revolutionary preparations explain, in large part, the relative ease and speed with which Untung's ill-fated putsch was crushed within less than twenty-four hours.

It would be presumptuous to claim, or even to imply, that everything about Indonesia's coup of October 1965 is clear today and that consequently one can draw sweeping and definitive conclusions. All that has been attempted here is to draw attention to some of the main features. Heavy reliance has been placed on the Document of the Indonesian Communists, 'For a Sound Indonesian Revolution', which appears to me, despite some shortcomings referred to above, as the most objective study so far. Other studies, such as that issued by a group of Indonesian Communist political exiles in China, tend to see only the opportunist mistakes and fail to see that these were combined with dangerous sectarianism and leftist adventurism. In fact, this latter study, ignoring the state of disarray in which the Party found itself in the months following the coup, and still clinging to its dogmatic reliance solely on armed struggle, actually called on the Indonesian people, in that desperate situation, to resort to arms. Some unfortunately followed that advice at a time when the movement was in retreat, and when what was required were not empty heroic gestures but patient reorganisation of the scattered forces, and the slow, heavy task of rebuilding what had been destroyed. This misguided attempt to resume the armed struggle after the coup had done its deadly work, and when the Party had been decimated, met its expected and tragic end. These were lives wasted on the altar of leftist dogmatism.

NOTES

1 'Estimates of the total death toll vary between 100,000 and one million, the latter figures having been arrived at by a university investigation team acting under instructions from the Indonesian army. The most widely accepted estimate is half-a-million' (Rex Mortimer, 'The Downfall of Indonesian Communism': *The Socialist Register 1969*, London, 1969). This appalling slaughter was, not unsurprisingly, welcomed in some quarters in the West, especially in the United States. *Time* (15 July 1966), for example, hailed it as 'The West's best news for years in Asia'.

2 Because of the quite different circumstances of the two situations there has been a different outcome. In Indonesia the losses were appalling and it is clearly going to take a very long time for the movement to recover. In Sudan the Party central committee began to function almost immediately after the set-back, the illegal network of Party and mass organisations has been re-established, illegal publications are being produced and distributed, and mass actions have been initiated. There is a quiet confidence among Sudanese Communists which is in sharp contrast to the somewhat shattered situation which still characterises the Indonesian Communist Party. The latter, because of its mistakes, suffered such heavy blows that it might well take a generation to recover. The Indonesian experience stands as a grim warning to all who would carelessly and unthinkingly involve the vanguard in armed confrontation in conditions which are wholly unfavourable, or in a way which throws the majority of the movement's supporters into complete confusion and therefore unable to act in any decisive or meaningful way.

3 Substantial extracts were published in *Marxism Today*, September 1967.

4 'For a Sound Indonesian Revolution', op. cit. Hereinafter referred to as 'the Document'.

5 ibid.

6 A Cabinet of 'Guided Democracy', which would represent an alliance of progressive forces, but with a state system exercising considerable control over the popular movement.

7 This is presumably a reference to China, hinting that discussions there had been a factor in determining the attitude of the Indonesian Communist leaders.

8 The Document, op. cit.

9 ibid.

10 i.e. Sukarno. *Bung* means *brother*; the more familiar prefix, *Su*, means *The Good*.

11 In fact, the Party Chairman, D. N. Aidit, spoke quite confidently on this point a year before the 1965 tragedy: 'I should like to warn those persons who are now busily running to and fro with plans for the launching of a second Madiun provocation to keep their heads cool and think things over carefully. If it was impossible to destroy the CPI 16 years ago, at a time when the CPI leadership was only 10,000, it will be even more impossible today when the CPI has gained numerous experiences, has a membership of more than 2,500,000, has cadres who have been steeled both in theory and in the practice of revolutionary struggle' (23 May 1964).

12 The Document, op. cit.

13 This tends to be borne out by the statement issued by the Political Bureau of the Communist Party of Indonesia, on 5 October 1965, which states categorically: 'As regards the "September 30th movement" the Central Committee of the Indonesian Communist Party considers that this movement is an internal matter of the land forces. The Indonesian Communist Party has nothing whatever to do with it. As a result of questioning the Indonesian Communist Party members included in the list of the "Revolutionary Council of Indonesia", it has become apparent that no one approached them and no one obtained their permission to be included in this list.'

14 The Document, op. cit.

15 ibid.

16 President Sukarno's concept of a national coalition government – NAS representing the National Party; A standing for Agama, the religious parties; KOM for the Communist Party.

17 The imperialists read the situation more correctly. They knew that it was an illusion for the Party to place its hopes on Sukarno being able to save the day. Even if some slender possibilities of such an outcome still existed on the day after the coup, they had certainly well passed by January 1966. 'Sukarno is a virtual captive of the army, which is using him to legitimise its own rule' (*Washington Post*, 11 December 1965).

18 Reported in *Hsinhua* (New China News Bulletin), 22 May 1964.

19 For fuller treatment of the role of the US see *Ten Years' Military Terror in Indonesia*, ed. Malcolm Caldwell, London, 1975, especially Peter Dale Scott's contribution – 'Exporting Military-Economic Development – America and the Overthrow of Sukarno, 1965–67'.

20 See Peter Dale Scott, op. cit.

21 Roger Hilsman, *To Move a Nation*, New York, 1967, p. 377.

22 David Ransom, 'For Country: Building an Elite for Indonesia' (see *The Trojan Horse*, ed. Steve Weissman, San Francisco, 1974).

23 See above, pp. 59–63.

24 Hilsman, op. cit.

25 Ransom, op. cit., p. 99.

26 This was similar to the US behaviour later followed towards Chile's Popular Unity Government under Allende.

27 Scott, op. cit., p. 236.

28 Ransom, op. cit., p. 103.

29 See Michael T. Klare, 'Indonesia and the Nixon Doctrine' in *Ten Years' Military Terror in Indonesia*, op. cit., p. 269.

30 ibid., p. 271.

31 Scott, op. cit., p. 209.

I I

Chile — Why the Coup Succeeded

Considerable attention has been devoted above to the counter-revolutionary coups in Sudan and Indonesia. Both of these coups took place as immediate ripostes to a *military* move from the left. In this sense, these two examples were not typical of right-wing coups which, more often, are mounted against a progressive government which has been in office for some time, rather than against a military move from the left to assume power.

It is doubtful whether any coup in recent years has attracted such world interest, or provoked such discussion and controversy in the international revolutionary movement, as the military coup on 11 September 1973 against Chile's Popular Unity Government, headed by President Salvador Allende. This government was regarded by the US monopolies as the biggest challenge to their position in Latin America since the Cuban victory. It was in no sense a threat to the people of the United States, with whom Chile was only too anxious to maintain normal relations; but since the Popular Unity programme, and the steps to implement it taken by Allende's Government, involved radical changes in Chile's economic structure, involving the nationalisation of key industries owned by US companies, these big firms, including ITT and Kennecott Copper, were determined right from the beginning to prevent Popular Unity from achieving its aims.

Secondly, the major US firms and the US Government itself feared that a success in Chile for Popular Unity would prove contagious, and that similar trends would develop in other Latin American countries. There was, after all, a *Frente Amplio* (Broad Front) gaining ground in Uruguay,[1] and significant changes in Peru, Panama, Ecuador and Venezuela, although in none of these countries had the progressive transformation taken the same form as in Chile, nor had it reached the same relatively advanced stage.

Furthermore, the coup against Allende aroused wide controversy in the international revolutionary movement, in other progressive circles and even beyond, because the Popular Unity period was regarded as a test case of the possibility of a people going over to socialism without an insurrection against the existing Government, State and constitution, and without civil war. In other words, a test for the possibility of a *relatively* peaceful revolution; *relatively*, because at no time, as we shall see, did the leaders of the Chilean Communist Party fail to emphasise that intense struggle was needed, neither did they categorically rule out the possibility that even the taking up of arms might become necessary.

This anxiety about the possibility or otherwise of the 'peaceful road to socialism' was not confined to those favouring socialism. Its opponents, too, and especially the big international firms, were equally concerned. In a number of capitalist countries similar perspectives have been written into the programmes of the respective Communist Parties, and in several cases, as in France, Italy, Spain and Japan, significant progress has been made towards such an objective. A victory for the 'peaceful road' in Chile would encourage those striving for the same road elsewhere. Further, it would represent an important ideological victory for socialism, since its opponents always attempt to claim that socialism can only come to power by the forcible and bloody imposition of such a system on the people and not by popular acclaim, including an electoral victory.

Because such major political and even theoretical questions were at stake, the coup against Chile's Popular Unity Government was followed by a very wide-ranging and intense debate, with sharp polemic not only between left and right, but equally fierce partisanship being displayed between different viewpoints within the left, as well as in debate with ultra-left assessments.

The arguments from the right need not detain us too long. The performance of Pinochet's fascist junta in four years has largely exposed its case. The excuse that the coup was motivated by an intention to 'end economic chaos' (which itself was created largely by the internal and external enemies of Popular Unity), cannot stand a moment's serious examination. Inflation after the coup soared to an annual rate of 400 per cent by mid 1976, with unemployment estimated at 20 per cent.

The pretence that the military had to intervene to 'safeguard freedom', and 'restore law and order' – the traditional excuse of all counter-revolutions – cannot be seriously sustained either. The 'freedom' exercised by the jailers and torturers of the Chilean people has been too well documented by UN agencies and other important bodies for there to be any doubts on that score. The violence on the streets and the violations of law and order in the last days of Allende's Government were the work of the supporters of the coup, and were intended to provide the fascist generals with the 'law and order' excuse which they needed for their treacherous plot.

Criticisms on the left are of a more fundamental character, and raise important questions of revolutionary strategy and tactics, of the validity of the 'peaceful road', of the attitude to take towards the armed forces and the State as a whole, the question of allies for the working class, the role of the mass media, of the CIA, land reform and nationalisation, economic management, the role of Parliament and elections, how to assess the relation of class forces, the mistakes of leftism on the one hand and of reformist illusions on the other.

To fully appreciate the significance of the coup and how it was achieved, it is necessary first to consider the programme of Popular Unity as well as its achievements during its three short years in office. Popular Unity came into being in 1969 as a coalition embracing the Socialist Party, the Communist Party, the Radical Party, the Social-Democratic Party,[2] Independent Popular Action, and MAPU (Movement of United Popular Action)[3] which included sections which had broken away from the Christian Democrats.

The Popular Unity programme was the most comprehensive and the most advanced ever adopted by any democratic coalition in Chile. It was more than a mere electoral pact; it was a far-reaching programme for a government to carry out fundamental economic and social transformations on the basis of decisive political changes in the power structure. The programme declared that 'the basic task which faces the Government of the People is to put an end to the power of the imperialists, the monopolists and the landowning oligarchy and begin the building of socialism in Chile'. The programme made clear that it did not consider it feasible to carry through an immediate change-over to socialism; what it projected was a national democratic revolution which, by carrying through basic democratic transformations in the economy and in the State and political structure, would pave the way for socialist change. The programme emphasised that it was the three million workers, *together with the whole people*, all those not committed to the power of reactionary national and foreign interests who, by their 'unified combative action', would be able to 'break the present structures and advance in the task of their liberation'.

In no sense was the programme envisaged as a reformist proposal, limited to the aim of making reforms *within* the existing system. Instead it was directed to making decisive inroads into the power of the ruling class, both in its economic ownership and in its positions in the political structure.

The revolutionary transformations which the country needs [it declared] can only be carried out if the Chilean people take power into their hands and exercise it in a genuine and effective way. The Chilean people, throughout a long process of struggle, have won certain democratic freedoms and guarantees, and they have to remain alert and fight unceasingly in order to preserve them. But they do not possess the actual power. The popular revolutionary forces have united . . . in order to carry out fundamental changes which the national situation demands, *on the basis of the transfer of power from the old ruling groups to the workers, peasantry and progressive sectors of the middle classes in the towns and countryside* (italics added). The popular victory will thus open the way for the most democratic system in the history of the country.

This, then, was no reformist perspective but one for revolutionary change, for a transfer of political power from a relative handful of rich monopolists and landlords into the hands of the vast majority of the people, involving a extension of democracy in every domain. In furtherance of its democratic aims, the programme outlined a series of initial democratic reforms in the different institutions of the State, including the police and the armed forces, which will be dealt with later. It further specified that the Popular Unity Government, formed on the basis of the programme, would be 'a multi-party one', embracing all revolutionary parties, movements and tendencies, and that it would 'respect the rights of the opposition operating within the legal framework'.

In the economic field, too, the programme envisaged far-reaching changes of a character which meant a real challenge to the dominant economic power of the big landlords and the monopolies, both domestic and foreign.

'The united forces of the people', declared the programme, 'seek as the main objective of their policy to replace the present economic structure by putting an end to the power of national and foreign monopoly capital and the *latifundio* (large landed estates) in order to begin the building of socialism.' To this end it provided for the nationalisation ('with full protection of the interests of the small shareholder') of natural resources, large monopolies, banks and insurance, while still maintaining a substantial private sector in industry, trade and on the land, and projecting, too, a mixed sector comprising both State and private capital. Together with this went proposals for a big extension of land reform, directed particularly at taking over the large estates. There were also comprehensive proposals covering a variety of social questions, education and culture, all designed to provide people with higher material standards as well as a much richer and fuller life. Central to all these changes was the democratic activity of the people at every level of society and through every institution and people's organisation. The full use of their power by the people was a constant theme in the programme.

The most far-seeing of those who worked out the programme had no illusions as to the scale of the task they were projecting, the obstacles they would meet, and the extraordinary effort that would be required in order to carry it out. They therefore regarded it as central to their strategy to gather together the full power of the people to the point where it would be strong enough, numerically, organisationally, in the disposition of its strength in the economy and the State, and in ideological influence and in activity, to impose its will on the ruling class and compel it to retreat from its positions of power or be removed.

As far back as 1956, fourteen years before the electoral victory of Popular Unity, the Tenth National Congress of the Chilean Communist Party put forward the following idea:

The possibility of our revolution being carried through by peaceful means, i.e. without it being necessary to resort to civil war, depends on two essential factors: the power and resistance of the enemy classes, and the ability of the working class to unite around itself the majority of the country and win power for the people, by electoral or some similar means.

The Chilean Communist Party's point of view concerning the possibility of avoiding civil war thus rested on two key propositions. First, the power and resistance of the class enemy. Second, the capacity of the working class to unite the *majority* of the people around itself. These propositions will be examined in more detail later, but it should be noted, at this point, that they were two of the essential conditions for avoiding a coup.[4]

The problem of uniting the majority of the people around the working class faced Popular Unity very acutely before, during, and after the presidential elections in 1970. The success for Popular Unity in these elections provided the Chilean people with an opportunity to start putting their programme into practice and so commence a restructuring of society. This opportunity, however, was fraught with complexities and difficulties. Popular Unity, it should be appreciated, never had an electoral majority, although the use of elections, Parliament and the Constitution was a key component of the strategy which lay behind its programme. This strategy was in no sense only a 'parliamentary' one, since it envisaged the democratic participation and activity of the mass of people in extra-parliamentary actions as the key form of struggle. However, elections were part of the strategy, and acceptance of their verdict a natural consequence.

In the 1970 elections Popular Unity's presidential candidate, Salvador Allende, obtained 36·3 per cent of the votes. The Nationalist Party, the party of extreme reaction, obtained 35 per cent,[5] and the Christian Democrat Party, which had been the previous ruling party and was backed by considerable sections of the bourgeoisie while enjoying the support also of a large part of the urban and rural middle class, and even a section of workers and peasants, received 27·8 per cent of the votes. These latter two parties, holding 62·8 per cent of the votes cast already in combination held a strong majority of seats in the Assembly and in the Senate which had been voted in previously during the period of the presidency of the Christian Democrat leader, Frei.

Thus, from the very start, Popular Unity and Allende faced a big problem. They had emerged as the strongest single electoral coalition, and therefore were entitled, according to Chilean constitutional practice, to present Allende for endorsement as President by the Chilean Parliament. Yet Allende had no majority, neither in the Assembly nor in the Senate. How, then, was he able to secure endorsement? Here lies a partial clue to subsequent events. The Christian Democrat Party, because of its variegated class and social composition and because of its attempts to hew a path for itself between the ultra-right Nationalists on the one hand and Popular Unity on the other, had sought to secure a popular base by being all things to all men and presenting a certain 'liberal' and even 'radical' face to the people. Even under Frei it had attempted to use slogans of 'revolution' and 'freedom'. In 1970, two distinct wings had emerged within it – a conservative wing around Frei, and a more progressive grouping around Tomic, the Christian Democrat presidential candidate in the 1970 elections. Due to the influence of Tomic and that of his supporters, the Christian Democrats decided to endorse Allende as President when the matter was voted on in Parliament. This gave Allende his assured majority and so he became President.

From a political standpoint, as well as from an arithmetical and procedural point of view, Allende and Popular Unity were in a very vulnerable position. Although the President, under Chilean law, had considerable executive power in his own right, Popular Unity's minority position in Parliament and its dependence on the goodwill of the Christian Democrats, meant that President and Government were faced with the prospect of instability and considerable pressures from forces outside Popular Unity and even inimical to it. This gave the right-wing and ultra-right plenty of scope to obstruct the Popular Unity Government whenever it moved to bring forward the necessary legislation to implement its own programme; and as the struggle sharpened in 1972 this obstruction was extended to blocking Government efforts to deal with black-marketeering, hoarding, speculation, corruption and violence.

This came about because the Christian Democrats, quite early on, shifted their position. Although they voted in Parliament for Allende to be President, and subsequently voted in support of the nationalisation of the copper companies (the vote on this was actually unanimous, even the Nationalists backing it, so widespread was the support for this measure), they gradually changed their attitude. The right-wing trend in the Christian Democrat Party became more dominant, and a virtual alliance was formed with the Nationalists, the two parties mobilising their Parliamentary voting majority persistently to oppose the Popular Unity Government and the President.

This complex of relationships is key to an understanding of the unfolding of the coup, and was one of the reasons for its success. It had a direct bearing on the situation in the armed forces; it contributed to the economic difficulties; and it led, in the end, to a situation in which considerable numbers of professional people and technicians (for example, pilots, doctors, administrative workers) and small owners (truck-owners and shop-keepers) were mobilised for struggle against the Government. In these circumstances it was easier for the ultra-right to bring its forces on to the streets and commence its campaign of violence and terror. These points will be considered later, but they are made here because it is against this background that one has to consider what the Popular Unity Government was actually able to achieve.

When Allende began his term as President, Chile's economy was in a most unhealthy state. Between 1955 and 1970, gross national product per capita rose by only 0·7 per cent, while the foreign debt soared from $569 million in 1958 to no less than $3,700 million in 1970. Prices were continually rising and unemployment was going up.

At the end of its first fifteen months in office, the Allende Government was already able to record remarkable progress. A report[6] published in March 1972 and drawn up by the parties of Popular Unity showed statistically and factually what important changes the new government had been able to introduce. The initial key measures, of course, were those taken to break the stranglehold of the big monopolies, including those in foreign hands and especially those of the United States, and to abolish large-scale landlordism. These changes, as was pointed out earlier, were not intended to change the system immediately to a socialist one; they were conceived, rather, as radical democratic steps that would help to bring about an important shift in the balance of economic power in the country, assist the further growth of the economy and make possible a better life for the people, thereby helping to influence the political power balance and so open up possibilities of advance to socialism.

In these first fifteen months a major segment of the economy was nationalised. Apart from copper (formerly in the hands of the US Kennecott Copper Corporation and the US company, Anaconda), industries taken over included coalmining (formerly in the hands of private Chilean owners), steel (previously owned by US Bethlehem Company), nitrates (formerly held by the US firm, Guggenheim), the four main textile manufacturing undertakings, and a substantial share of cement and fishing. The main banks, too, were taken over by the Popular Unity Government.

Land reform was carried through on a considerable scale. Large estates totalling $6\frac{1}{2}$ million acres were taken over in the period ending February 1972. This meant that in little more than a year Allende's Government had distributed as much land to the peasants as the previous Frei Government had done in six years. By the end of 1972, Popular Unity had completed its land reform programme and the latifundio system had been largely broken.

These changes of ownership in industry, finance and land, combined with the economic and social benefits granted to the people and the perspectives which the regime had opened up for them, and helped by the considerable measures of economic planning (in no sense complete, bearing in mind that a substantial sector of the economy was still in private hands) that the Government was able to introduce in this first comparatively short stage, had a stimulating effect on the economy. By the beginning of 1972 national productivity had risen by 9 per cent and industrial productivity by 13 per cent. (In the last year of Frei's government industrial productivity had risen by only $\frac{1}{2}$ per cent.) The rate of unemployment was cut back from 8·3 per cent to 3·8 per cent, and 200,000 new jobs were created – and this in a country with less than ten million people is no mean achievement in such a short space of time.

1971, the year of copper nationalisation, saw copper production rise to 730,000 tons, an increase of 40,000 tons over the previous year.[7] Striking advances were registered in other sectors of the economy, unprecedented levels of output being achieved for steel (615,000 tons), cement (1,300,000 tons), refined petrol (5,600,000 cubic metres), and electricity (5,690 million kWh). Nitrate production went up by 23 per cent, and that of coal by 10 per cent.

In the light of the attempts made prior to the coup and subsequently by sections of the British press to accuse the Allende Government of having 'hopelessly mismanaged the economy', the significant progress made in the first fifteen months should not be ignored. This, it should be remembered, was a period of relative political stability and before the measures of the CIA, the US State Department, and the big US firms to 'destabilise the economy' of Chile really got under way. How this 'destabilisation' operated will be considered later; but in its first period of office the Popular Unity Government was able to cope with the economic pressures, and to secure an upturn in the economy. As a result of economic growth and on the basis of the large degree of State ownership and State control of the key sectors of the economy, it was possible, right from the beginning, to bring substantial benefits to the Chilean people.

While prices still rose the rate of increases was lowered and, furthermore, wage increases more than compensated. Thus, people's purchasing power rose by 30 per cent and actual consumption went up by 20 per cent. The shift in the balance of income distribution was marked, with the share of the national income going to the working class rising from 51 to 60 per cent. At the same time, family allowances went up by 50 to 100 per cent, depending on category; and old age pensions rose by 35 to 67 per cent, again depending on category. Steps were taken to provide every child under twelve with half a litre of free milk – and this coincidentally at a time when the British Tory Government was abolishing such distribution in our schools. At a time when in relatively rich Britain the price of school meals was going up, in Chile, free breakfasts and free lunches were being steadily extended for all children in kindergartens and schools.

In education, too, Chile under her Popular Unity Government quickly began to stride forward. By 1972 educational expenditure was the highest in its history. Technical-professional teaching increased its enrolment by 38 per cent and university enrolment went up by 28 per cent. Plans already prepared for 1972 provided for no less than 250,000 young people to receive education in the universities and technical-professional institutes. An equivalent figure for developed, industrialised Britain would be between $1\frac{1}{4}$ and $1\frac{1}{2}$ million. In housing, 100,000 new houses were begun in 1971, a number without precedent in Chile's history; and again, to make a comparison, that would mean in British terms about 550,000 houses.

There were, of course, acute economic problems. A number of mistakes were also made in the handling of economic questions. These were utilised by the internal and external opponents of Popular Unity who made the maximum use of economic weapons to 'destabilise' the economy in order to spread confusion and discontent, consequently creating the political conditions which opened the way to the final coup. The mistakes of Popular Unity, including those of the Communist Party, are examined in more detail below when we come to analyse the causes for the success of the coup. But first it is necessary to consider the actual course of the coup and its preparations from the very first days of the formation of the Popular Unity, even before Allende's election as President.

In a general study of this nature it is not intended to provide a factual and detailed account of all the events connected with the coup in Chile. That the US monopolies and State Department, the CIA, Kissinger and Nixon were all involved in the plot against Chile, a plot which was denounced by President Allende himself from the rostrum of the United Nations a year before it took place, is now so well documented, especially with the official US Senate report[8] on the activities of the CIA, that I shall only provide a few essential points necessary for analysing the coup and its course.

The US plot against Chile began long before Allende was elected. The US State Department and major companies had been involved in all the moves against the left and democratic movement in Chile for many years, including plots against the Chilean Popular Front of the 1930s and 1940s, against the People's Front and the later Popular Action Front of the 1950s and 1960s (with Allende being the successive but unsuccessful Presidential candidate for both these latter formations), and finally against Popular Unity when it was set up in 1969.

The US ruling class had watched over the years most anxiously as the Chilean working class strengthened its unity and began to attract other classes and strata of the population to its side. As the 1970 elections drew near, moves against Chilean democracy were increased; and, as usually happens in these circumstances, pliable agents for this US-inspired plotting were to be found amongst the extreme right-wing forces in the army hierarchy. On 21 October 1969, a group of officers led by General Roberto Viaux attempted to use the Tacna Regiment to create a situation of chaos arising out of problems connected with army pay. The intention was to utilise the resulting tension in the armed forces to provide the opportunity for a military coup which would thus prevent the 1970 elections being held.

This plot failed, and the reasons for its failure are significant for what happened in later coup attempts, including the one that eventually overthrew the Popular Unity Government. The 'Tacna' coup failed for two reasons. First, the organised workers went into immediate action at the call of the Confederation of United Workers. The country was paralysed by a general strike, accompanied by mass occupations of factories, depots and essential services. Second, there was no readiness on the part of the majority of the armed forces, including the officers, to support the coup. Not only were they deterred by the powerful reaction of the workers. They had the strongest reservations about the whole venture even prior to 21 October. After all, a military coup in 1969 would have been a coup against the Christian Democrat President, Frei, and his Government. The Christian Democrat leadership at that time was not prepared to support such a coup to forestall Popular Unity. This position of the Christian Democrats was not unknown to the armed forces. Many of the officers had family ties and political sympathies with the Christian Democrats. Whatever the officers might have thought about the forthcoming elections and Allende's chances of winning, the thought of acting in those conditions against the political supporters of both the Christian Democrats and Popular Unity, that is against the majority political forces in the country, was a step that must have appealed only to the most extreme right-wing of the officer corps. In these conditions, a narrow civilian-political base for the coup meant a restricted military base, too, confirming once again that how an army acts politically is determined, to a large degree, by the total political situation in the country and by the political balance of civilian forces at the given time.

But the 'Tacna' coup was not to be the last effort of the United States against Allende and Popular Unity. The election year, 1970, saw fresh evidence of US plotting against Chilean democracy. A large-scale anti-communist smear campaign was launched with financial help from the US companies in Chile, especially the Anaconda copper company, whose involvement was proved when three young Communists discovered documentary evidence of it in one of the offices of the anti-communist campaign in Santiago.

US involvement in Chilean elections, as has been noted above, dates back a number of years. The US Senate Select Committee Report itself admits:

Covert US Government involvement in large-scale political action programs in Chile began with the 1964 Presidential elections.[9] As in 1970, this was, in part, in response to the perceived threat of Salvador Allende. Over $3 million was spent by the CIA in the 1964 effort.[10]

As the 1970 elections in Chile loomed closer, the US stepped up its intervention against an Allende victory. On 25 March 1970 the 40 Committee[11] endorsed a joint proposal of the CIA and the US Embassy in Chile 'recommending that "spoiling" operations – propaganda and other activities – be undertaken by the CIA in an effort to prevent an election victory by Allende's Popular Unity (UP) Coalition'.[12] For this activity, a sum of $135,000 was authorised by the 40 Committee. Two months later the sum was increased to $390,000. This was apart from direct sums made available by big US companies, for the same purpose. Proposals submitted by the US Ambassador to Chile, Edward Korry, for $500,000 to be made available for use in the Chilean Congress 'to persuade certain shifts in voting on 24 October 1970' (i.e. the date when the Congress and Senate were due to vote in the new President), were deferred until the results of the 4 September elections were known. As things turned out, this blatant attempt to buy up votes of public representatives came to naught in the immediate post-election period; but in view of the way in which Christian Democrat members of Congress and Senate later switched their position, it is not unreasonable to assume that the half a million dollars were later used to subvert elected deputies and so contributed to the eventual overthrow of Allende's Government.

The success of Popular Unity in the 4 September election led to still more frantic efforts by the US State Department and the CIA. Three days after the election results were known, that is on 7 September 1970, the CIA's Directorate of Intelligence circulated an intelligence assessment of the impact of Allende's election victory on US interests. Interestingly enough, the assessment admits that a Popular Unity Government headed by Allende would not 'significantly alter' the 'world military balance of power'. Nor would there be any resultant 'threat to the peace of the region'. It even states that 'The US has no vital national interests within Chile'.[13]

What, then, motivated the fears and hostility of the US ruling circles towards Chile's democratic aspirations? The assessment talks about 'tangible economic losses' – presumably this refers to anxieties regarding Popular Unity's aims to nationalise major US companies in Chile; trade was not necessarily involved, since Chile was only too ready to continue trading with the United States. The CIA assessment also mentions two other sources of anxiety over Allende's victory. It would, states the report, 'create considerable political and psychological costs'. There would be strains inside the Organisation of American States (OAS). Further, it 'would represent a definite psychological advance for the Marxist idea'.

Within a week of the actual publishing of this CIA Intelligence assessment, President Nixon held a meeting with his Assistant for National Security Affairs, Henry Kissinger, the CIA Director Richard Helms, and Attorney-General John Mitchell,[14] to discuss the situation in Chile. Handwritten notes of CIA director, Richard Helms, taken at that meeting on 15 September 1970, indicate the nature of the discussion and the clear intention of President Nixon to stop Allende at all costs:

One in 10 chance perhaps, but save Chile!
worth spending
not concerned risks involved
no involvement of Embassy
$10,000,000 available, more if necessary
full-time job – best men we have
game plan
make the economy scream
48 hours for plan of action.

No wonder Helms drew the conclusion, as he explained in his testimony to the Select Committee, that Nixon 'wanted something done, and he didn't much care how and that he was prepared to make money available'.[15]

Kissinger's testimony basically admits the same intention on the part of the US President and his colleagues:

The primary thrust of the September 15th meeting was to urge Helms to do whatever he could to prevent Allende from being seated.[16]

A cable sent on 21 September from CIA headquarters to the CIA Chief of Station in Santiago explains:

Purpose of exercise is to prevent Allende assumption of power. Parliamentary legerdemain has been discarded. Military solution is objective.[17]

The Select Committee Report, in its summary, states without equivocation:

On September 15, 1970, President Richard Nixon informed CIA Director Richard Helms that an Allende regime in Chile would not be acceptable to the United States. *The CIA was instructed by President Nixon to play a direct role in organising a military coup d'état in Chile to prevent Allende's accession to the presidency*[18] (italics added).

Internal documents of the big international monopoly, the US International Telephone and Telegraphy Corporation (ITT), first revealed by *Washington Post* journalist, Jack Anderson, on 21 March 1972, provide further evidence of the US plot against Popular Unity, with the significant addition of the obvious direct collaboration of the CIA with the big US monopolies themselves. It is, of course, no coincidence that John McCone, a former Director of the CIA, is one of the members of the directing board of ITT.

Almost immediately after the Presidential elections, Nixon's plan to 'make the economy scream' was put into action. A number of steps were taken by US subsidiaries in Chile and by Chilean companies with US links to shake the economy. Capital began to leave the country, there were closures of enterprises and threats of more. There were a number of bombing attacks by right-wing terrorist groups. Rumours of a coup began to circulate. As the Anderson papers later revealed, and as the Senate Select Committee in substance confirmed, all this was part of a prepared plot to 'destabilise' Chile and so create the conditions and the political atmosphere that would favour the carrying out of a military coup against Allende. Involved were the US State Department, the President, the CIA, major US monopolies such as ITT, and right-wing neo-fascist groupings in Chile, including right-wing ultras in the armed forces.

The ITT documents, as well as the Senate Select Committee Report, reveal only too clearly what was plotted. ITT officials had secret meetings with CIA agents, William Broe and Enno Hobbing. State Department assurances of support were confirmed. The US Ambassador in Chile, Edward Korry, 'received a message from the State Department giving him the green light to move in the name of the President. . . . The message gave him maximum authority to do all possible . . . short of a Dominican type of action (i.e. the sending in of US marines, as was done in 1965 to crush democracy in the Dominican Republic and pre-empt the results of the elections at that time) to keep Allende from taking power'.

The plot involved economic pressure 'aimed at inducing an economic collapse', and the instigation of 'massive internal disorders' with attempts to provoke the left into hasty action, all intended to create a situation which would 'justify an armed forces intervention'. The Chilean army was 'assured full material and financial assistance by the US military establishment'.

In the event the coup at that time did not succeed, although it claimed the life of the Army Commander-in-Chief, General René Schneider. Why this particular attempt failed is not only interesting from the point of view of understanding the role of the military in politics in Chile, but is also instructive for our understanding of the reasons for the success of Pinochet's coup in September 1973.

The steps being prepared at the time[19] by the CIA and the US President for a coup against Allende were most devious. There were, in fact, two main lines of attack. In the run up to the key meeting of Nixon and his co-plotters on 15 September, both the CIA and Ambassador Korry provided assessments of the situation, expressing reservations as to the possibilities of a successful military coup at that time. The CIA's view was categorical: 'Military action is impossible; the military is incapable and unwilling to seize power. We have no capability to motivate or instigate a coup' (Memorandum for Dr Kissinger/Chile – 40 Committee Meeting, Monday – 14 September 1970).[20]

Faced with this extreme difficulty to mount a coup to put the military in power, the US leaders were thrashing about to find a political way to achieve the same goal, with the military providing the necessary physical backing to a 'civilian' solution. One proposal, the so-called 'Rube Goldberg' gambit, was to elect the Nationalist leader, Alessandri, as President on 24 October, by a combination of Nationalist and Christian Democratic votes in the Congress; this to be followed by the immediate resignation of Alessandri, thus leaving the Christian Democrat leader, Frei, free to run for a second term for the presidency.[21] A contingency fund of $250,000 was set up to be offered to Frei for this option.

A variant of this political line of action, known as 'Track I', was to 'bribe Chilean Congressmen' as well as to provide for 'propaganda and economic activities . . . designed to induce the opponents to Allende in Chile to prevent his assumption of power, either through political or military means'.[22] Track I, or the Frei gambit, involved 'a voluntary

turn-over of power to the military by Frei', who would then have been
eligible to run for President in a new election. Extraordinary pressure
was brought to bear on Frei to secure his agreement. Apart from the offer
of funds, he was informed that crippling economic measures would be
taken against Chile if Allende was allowed to take office as President on
24 October. Ambassador Korry, for example, warned Frei that 'not a
nut or bolt will be allowed to reach Chile. . . . Once Allende comes to
power we shall do all within our power to condemn Chile and the
Chileans to utmost deprivation and poverty.' Hence, for Frei to believe
that Chile would be allowed to muddle through was 'strictly illusory'.

As the Select Committee Report makes clear, 'the use of economic
instruments as levers' was applied with both Frei and the military to
persuade them to cooperate with the 'Frei gambit'. A major obstacle to
this gambit (apart from Frei's own reluctance to condone a coup while
he was still the President and made hesitant, too, by his assessment of the
situation at the time in the armed forces as well as in the country at large),
was the attitude of General Schneider. For this reason Korry urged that
the Army Commander-in-Chief 'be neutralised, by displacement if
necessary'.

While the push along Track I was proceeding, and unknown to most
of those participating, a second line of approach, Track II, was being
proceeded with. Track II activities were the follow-up to Nixon's
instructions of 15 September. The objective of Track I and Track II was
the same – the prevention of Allende's assumption of office as President.
Both Tracks involved the military and the preparation of a coup. In
practice, as Kissinger admitted in his testimony before the Senate
Committee, Tracks I and II overlapped in many ways. Yet there was a
certain difference. Track II provided for 'a more direct role for the CIA in
actually organising such a coup' (Kissinger, 8/12/75, p. 13).[23] Further,
Track II provided for the CIA's 'active promotion and support for a coup
without President Frei's involvement'.[24]

The botched-up affair that actually took place on the eve of the 24
October meeting and which resulted in the murder of General Schneider
during an attempted kidnapping was a total failure as a coup. There were
even divided counsels in the CIA as to its feasibility, mainly because of the
situation at the time inside the armed forces. Following the 15 September
meeting, CIA Director Richard Helms, according to his testimony before
the Senate Committee, regarded the possibility of pulling off a coup such
as Nixon was demanding to be at that time 'just as remote as anything
could be'. The 'time frame' was far too short; and the Army was

'constitutionalist'. CIA Deputy Director for Plans, Thomas Karamessines, argued that the Chilean military were 'unwilling to do anything. And without their wanting to do something, there did not seem to be much hope.'[25]

The 'Constitutional Coup', that is the 'Frei gambit', with Frei inviting the military to take over, dissolve the Congress and proclaim a fresh election, could not go ahead. As the CIA Santiago Station explained 'neither Frei nor Schneider will act'. Frei was reluctant to 'tarnish his historical image' (Chile Task Force Log, 8 October 1970). General Schneider, whatever his political views may have been, regarded it as his responsibility to ensure that the armed forces safeguarded the constitutional process in Chile. Even the coup-minded officers were reluctant to act at that time. Thus the way to a direct military coup solution with the backing of some civilian political forces was also blocked. The CIA therefore had to face the fact that the only thing left was 'a straight military coup'. Given the opposition of General Schneider and his second-in-command General Prats, and the reluctance of high-ranking coup-minded officers, it became necessary to make 'overtures to lower echelon officers' and thus to promote an army split.

A three-fold programme was set in motion by the CIA to prepare for such a coup, create the atmosphere and conditions for it, lay the ground for justifying it, and organise the practical military steps to carry it out. Cables sent from CIA headquarters to Santiago in October indicate the nature of the programme, which included collecting intelligence on coup-minded officers; creating a coup climate by propaganda, misinformation, and terrorist activities intended to provoke the left into giving a pretext for a coup; and informing the coup-minded officers that the US Government would give them full support in a coup, short of direct US military intervention. The preparations were also to utilise the economic difficulties, both to provoke discontent and to provide an additional justification for the coup since it could be alleged that 'the economic situation was collapsing'.

In October 1970 a number of factors that would have made a coup bid successful were not present. Despite the provocative terrorist actions organised by terror squads, the workers refused to be provoked. The majority of capitalist interests in Chile were not prepared to back the coup card at that time, as clearly indicated not only by Frei's personal reluctance but also by the general readiness of the Christian Democrat leaders to endorse Allende as President. Neither was there a unanimous rush by the major US monopolies with interests in Chile to put their funds and their influence behind the ITT initiative. Further, as we have seen, in the upper ranks of the armed forces there was no enthusiasm for military intervention. The Commander-in-Chief, General Schneider, made it abundantly clear that he would abide by the Constitution, and other high-ranking officers supported him. Even those who were coup-minded took a long, cool look at realities and decided to wait for a more propitious occasion.

The CIA was therefore reduced to relying on lower-ranking officers, in the hope that their action might trigger off a bigger reaction in the armed forces as a whole. In the event, the attempted kidnapping of General Schneider on 22 October and his being mortally wounded in the attempt, flopped badly. There was an immediate declaration of martial law. General Prats, a strong supporter of the 'Schneider Doctrine' of upholding the Constitution, was appointed Commander-in-Chief. The forces represented by Popular Unity, and even beyond, rallied round Allende. In the circumstances, and apart from their own previously worked out position, the Christian Democrat deputies voted for Allende on 24 October.

It has been necessary to spend some time on the failed coup of October 1970 because many of its features appeared in September 1973 in new forms, and in different circumstances. Moreover, the reasons for the failure of October 1970 help to explain the reasons for the coup success in September 1973. It should be appreciated that although the coup failed in 1970, the basic strategy which lay behind Track II was not abandoned. The CIA continued to work on these lines and eventually put the plans into final operation in September 1973.

This much, in fact, is revealed in the Senate Select Committee Report. The Committee apparently received conflicting testimony on this point. Kissinger appears to have given the Committee the impression that Track II was wound up by President Nixon after the murder of General Schneider, and prior to the 24 October vote of the Chilean Congress. In view of Kissinger's record, readers may have their doubts about the trustworthiness of his testimony on this point, especially as the Committee states that it does not have the President's 'new "marching order" in its possession'.[26]

As against Kissinger's testimony, the Committee was given evidence from CIA officials who 'believed that there had been no such definite end to Track II. It merely tapered off, to be replaced by a longer-term effort to effect a change of government in Chile.' The testimony of leading CIA official Karamessines is most explicit on this point:

Mr Karamessines: I am sure that the seeds that were laid in that effort in 1970 had their impact in 1973. I do not have any question about that in my mind either.

Q: Was Track II ever formally ended? Was there a specific order ending it?

Mr Karamessines: As far as I was concerned, Track II was really never ended. What we were told to do in effect was, well, Allende is now President. So Track II, which sought to prevent him from becoming President, was technically out, it was done. But what we were told to do was to continue our efforts. Stay alert, and to do what we could to contribute to the eventual achievement of the objectives and purposes of Track II. That being the case, I don't think it is proper to say that Track II was ended.

Despite Kissinger's protestations, the subsequent course of events tallies with Karamessines' testimony rather than that of the Secretary of State. The seeds sown in 1970 'had their impact in 1973' and Popular Unity was overthrown.

The full details of how the plot against Allende's Government was carried forward over the three years from the time of his inauguration are not yet known, but it can be assumed on the basis of what has come to light so far that the US pressed ahead with its plans on all fronts. From a study like that of Philip Agee[27] it can be assumed that continuously, daily, even hourly, the CIA carried out its operations in a comprehensive and virtually synchronised fashion, employing economic levers to 'make the economy scream', 'black propaganda' to spread confusion, armed thuggery and terrorist acts to cause chaos, create panic, and provoke the working class and the left generally as well as providing an excuse for the military right-wing to act. An additional aim in all this was to produce the kind of psychological atmosphere that would bring about hesitation and division within the armed forces themselves, thus facilitating the work of the coup-minded officers. Simultaneously, the CIA must have been active in establishing contacts and winning influence in various departments of the State, especially the armed forces and the police, and in penetrating the student bodies and universities, as well as radio, television, newspapers and journals. Comprehensive lists of Popular Unity supporters for eventual arrest and even murder must have been prepared; and, in the light of Agee's disclosures, this must have involved not only close working of the CIA with the Chilean police, but also with the postal, communication and immigration authorities so that phone conversations could be tapped, mail opened, and a watch kept on arrivals and departures especially at Chile's airports.

Central to the attack pressed home against Chile's legally elected Popular Unity Government was economic aggression. The United States was well placed to damage Chile's economy which was heavily dependent on US investments, trade and credits. Previous Governments in Chile had readily accepted this dependent relationship since they regarded it as essential to maintain themselves in power. Prior to 1970 the United States invested heavily in Chile, a total of 1,500 million dollars being so invested over the previous decade. These investments yielded huge profits to US monopolies. It is estimated that in 1969 the net return on US capital in Chile was 23 per cent, almost double what was being earned in other Latin American countries. Practically the whole of this profit went to the United States, and very little was ploughed back into Chilean industry. For Chile the consequences were a distorted economy, a high inflation rate, heavy unemployment and widespread poverty, ill-health and bad housing. Not surprisingly, the foreign debt soared from 569 million dollars in 1958 to 3,700 million in 1970.

Some 40 per cent of all Chile's imports came from the United States; for capital goods the figure was 65 per cent. Machinery, transport equipment, machine tools, as well as manufactured goods, chemicals, food and livestock came mainly from the United States. For servicing and spare parts, too, Chile was dependent on the US. All these purchases were financed largely from US credits provided by such agencies as the Export-Import Bank and American private banks, and from international financial institutions such as the World Bank and the Inter-American Development Bank, both of which were effectively under US control. As Senator Kennedy put it so succinctly: 'The World Bank and the Inter-American Development Bank are our (i.e. US) tools to wield however we wish.'

Chile's utter dependence on US credits – in 1970 no less than 78·4 per cent of all her short-term credits came from the United States – provided the US monopolies, the State Department and the CIA with a powerful weapon to use to 'induce economic collapse'. By an abrupt and brutal cutting off of credits, the US was able to create real economic difficulties for the new Popular Unity Government, already battling with serious economic problems inherited from the previous Frei administration. Nixon made no secret of his intention to use economic weapons to baton the Chile Government into submission. He openly threatened that any move to nationalise US companies would be met both by cutting off bilateral economic 'aid' as well as by using the powerful influence of the US to block loans from 'multilateral banks'.

The Export-Import Bank set the example and refused a request for a $21 million loan for the state airline Lan-Chile to purchase three Boeings. . . . Then in August 1971 the bank told Chile that no further loans of any kind would be given and that all loan guarantees to US commercial banks and businesses dealing with Chile would be ended. . . . Before Allende, the Inter-American Development Bank had given $310 million in loans to Chile. Since 1971, virtually nothing. . . . Since then only two tiny loans have been granted, both to right-wing universities. The previous generosity of the World Bank evaporated equally suddenly in 1971.[28]

The private banks followed suit. Deprived of its main source of former credit, the Chile Government had to fall back on its dwindling reserves. This process became more dangerous when the world price of copper fell. To makes things worse, the US copper companies added their own forms of pressure, following their being nationalised. They refused to provide Chile with spare parts which were vital for the normal operation of the mines; and their copper specialists quit the country altogether. In 1972, the Kennecott Copper Corporation was able to secure a temporary seizure of Chilean copper exports then lying in West European ports.

Inside Chile, opponents of Popular Unity, especially the former ruling oligarchy, organised additional forms of economic sabotage. Thousands of head of cattle were slaughtered and smuggled over the border to Argentina. The hoarding of available goods by both well-off consumers and by shops and other enterprises reached staggering heights. An organised black market began to operate alongside the artificially induced shortages.

There were strikes in the copper mines amongst higher paid sections of production workers and administrative staffs, instigated by the opposition parties in support of extravagant claims which the economy could not easily sustain. There were strikes of lorry owner-drivers, too, whose exaggerated fears about their future because of the creation of a State-owned truck service were played upon by political forces striving to bring the government down. In a country like Chile, which relies very much on long-distance lorries to distribute goods, these strikes, with those of shop-keepers, naturally aggravated the economic crisis — and this in turn increased the political tension and polarisation. Goods started to be in short supply, although large sections of workers and peasants had begun to enjoy a higher standard of living than they had ever had under previous administrations.

One most damaging economic effect was a steep escalation in the already chronic inflation. 'Inflation was the reactionaries' main trump.'[29] When Popular Unity took office in October 1970 inflation was raging, having increased by 22 per cent in the first six months of the year. In the first six months of 1971 the new Government was able to bring down the inflation rate to 11 per cent, while at the same time increasing real wages. But the US economic offensive, the credit squeeze, hoarding, the black-market, the stimulation of panic-buying by spreading rumours about the impending scarcity of particular goods, the lorry-owners' strike of October 1972 – springtime in Chile – which created difficulties for the 1973 harvest through holding up supplies of seeds and fertilisers, all contributed to creating serious shortages and escalating inflation. The second lorry-owners' strike in 1973 made matters even worse.

Speaking on 31 August, virtually on the eve of the coup, to six hundred leading voluntary worker-inspectors, whose task was to organise popular committees to combat the black market, the Minister of the Economy stated: 'Inflation has recently escalated to 114 per cent as a result of the intensification by the right wing of its campaign of speculation and black-marketeering. At the same time, the Government has its hands tied because Parliament refuses to pass the necessary legislation to deal with this.'

This latter point illustrates one of the major dilemmas facing the Government, as was pointed out earlier. Allende had become President and Popular Unity had taken office under conditions in which it did not have a majority in the country's elected bodies, the Assembly and Senate. Thus, although pledged by the nature of its programme and politically committed by its own strategy to work for the carrying through of a change to socialism by utilising the country's institutions in a constitutional fashion, backed by the mass actions of the people, the Popular Unity Government was acting in circumstances in which it did not have control of many of the key levers of the constitution. The President had wide powers accorded him under the existing constitution, but the majority in Parliament, the legislative body, was against Popular Unity. The State apparatus, both in its administrative side, as well as the armed forces, the police, and the judiciary, was largely unchanged, especially in its hierarchy. Yet to make State changes in the face of a hostile Parliament was extremely difficult.

It is well to remember these things, not only in order to understand some of the key factors which made it possible for the US and internal reaction to topple the Allende Government; but also to avoid making over-sombre and pessimistic predictions concerning the strategy of many Communist Parties in Western Europe who also envisage utilising constitutional procedures, including Parliament, in combination with popular extra-parliamentary activities, to bring about fundamental and radical changes opening the road to socialism. The difference in these latter cases in Europe is that they are based on having a progressive majority in Parliament, and so possessing legal authority for introducing the charges envisaged in their programmes. This, in itself, would in no sense sweep aside all the massive problems that such popular governments would face, but at least would mean that they were not encumbered with the unyielding obstacle of a hostile Parliament which in Chile, at every step, blocked the efforts to cope with the crisis and carry through its programme.

Chile's runaway inflation was clearly influenced by factors other than those of 'normal' economic difficulty. It was fanned by the United States and by domestic opponents of Popular Unity for definite political purposes — namely to cause political tension in the country, and to hamper Popular Unity's efforts to win to its side sections of the middle strata — farmers, shopkeepers, truck-owners, professional people — who were affected most by the inflation, since the workers were, to a considerable extent, protected by periodic wage adjustments which made up for the increased cost of living. The real aim of the economic attack on Chile was to create political conditions for the military coup. As William Shawcross noted in the *New Statesman* (21 September 1973), the dollar squeeze (it was, of course, not this alone) achieved what ITT official William Merriam had predicted in 1971 to Peter Peterson, the architect of Nixon's Chile policy. 'It produced "economic chaos", the class polarisation and violence Allende sought to avoid, and finally convinced the armed forces to "step in and restore order".'

In the light of the facts now known, in the light of the evidence laid before the US Senate Select Committee that Nixon, Kissinger and the CIA had decided already in September 1970 to organise a coup against Allende, and that a key element in the preparations for the coup was to 'make the economy scream', the attempts made after the September 1973 coup by a number of national newspapers in Britain to put the blame on the Allende Government for its alleged 'hopeless economic mismanagement' were at best ill-informed judgments, if not downright hypocrisy.

Naturally the question arises, was there, then, no mismanagement? Did not the Allende Government contribute to its own downfall by the way it handled economic questions? There were undoubtedly economic weaknesses, some of which were in a sense inflicted on the Government by the leftist mistakes of forces outside it. There were other weaknesses which arose in part from the Government's own inability to achieve a complete unity of purpose and action behind a coherent economic strategy.

The revolutionary economic policy was opposed by opportunists clinging to the traditions of anarchism and bourgeois politics, advocating concessions to unbridled 'economism' (camouflaged, of course, by revolutionary rhetoric), neglecting efforts to boost production and labour productivity, and underestimating the importance of planning. They preached spontaneous development and voluntarism, dismissed financial problems, remained complacent in the face of runaway inflation, and held sectarian views based on narrow group interests.[30]

Millas considers that 'tolerance towards opportunism' had serious effects on the economy, producing a situation in which consumption rose in the first year of the Popular Unity Government by 13 per cent, and imports of semi-finished and manufactured goods by 22 per cent, while the gross national production (GNP) rose by only 8·5 per cent. And this, it must be remembered, was in the first year which was, in many ways the most successful from an economic point of view. The consequences of this 'opportunism' in the economy were soon seen in a catastrophic balance of trade and in soaring inflation. The amount of money in the hands of the population trebled in the first year; in the following two years it shot up again to six times what it was at the end of 1971.

In Millas's view there were a number of additional economic factors which aggravated the economic situation. These included an excessive expansion of the State sector beyond what had been laid down in the Popular Unity programme, with many small and medium enterprises being taken over by the State, often to be run at a loss, thus hindering the Government's economic strategy. There was a tendency to embrace wage-levelling, combined with a hostility to specialists, who either quit the country or became actively hostile to the regime; either way, their capacities to assist the economy were not won.

Incorrect policies were pursued in agriculture, equal wages being introduced for all rural workers regardless of the nature and results of their work. There was insufficient help and attention given to the lands which had been taken over. Because of these and other weakness, the alliance of the peasants and industrial workers went forward falteringly.

Mistakes were made, too, as regards the involvement of factory workers in managing production.

A major shortcoming of the revolutionary leadership was its acceptance of a system of indirect worker participation in factory management under which workers elected to trade union bodies could not be represented on management bodies. This weakened the trade union movement and hampered working-class participation in the solution of problems.[31]

These errors and weaknesses have to be seen, of course, in a general framework of intense struggle and very considerable achievement, as was noted in the *El Arrayan Report*.[32] But failure to overcome these shortcomings played their part in alienating sections of the population from Popular Unity, deepening the divisions in the country, thus contributing to the conditions which made the coup possible.

Yet the economic aggression by external and domestic reaction, assisted unwittingly by mistakes of the popular forces, was not the only form of attack. Parliament, as has been already noted, was utilised to block progressive and necessary legislation. The parliamentary majority in the hands of the Nationalists and Christian Democrats also enabled these parties to put forward unjustified parliamentary motions to secure the removal of Popular Unity Ministers, thus causing delays in government administration and compelling Allende to seek constant changes in government personnel. As can be readily understood, it was usually the most capable and devoted Ministers who were victims of this ploy.

The courts, too, were brought into play against the Allende Government. The hierarchy in the judiciary were economically, socially and politically very much on the side of the previous system, and throughout the three years of Popular Unity Government made their preference only too clear. A particularly scandalous perversion of justice was their consistent protection of right-wing terrorists.

The mass media, the press, radio and television, were mainly in the hands of those hostile to Popular Unity. Most of the press, much of it sensational and libellous in a way far worse than anything existing in Britain, was owned by big monopolies. This was true also of most radio and television stations which maintained a daily torrent of lies, distortions and rumours, all directed to spreading confusion among the people and enmity towards Popular Unity. Even when President Allende went on the air to expose downright lies against him and his Government, the majority of radio and television stations would retaliate with a fresh flood of lies, exaggerations and distortions.

A major weapon against the Government was violence and terror which, as has already been noted, was employed against Allende even before the 1970 elections. Violence continued against the Popular Unity Government throughout its three years of rule. At the end of 1971, when women from the wealthier parts of the capital, Santiago, took part in the so-called 'march of the empty pots' in protest against an alleged shortage of food, as if by pre-arrangement fascist gangs utilised the situation to roam the streets, armed with lead pipes, clubs and chains in order to spread fear and chaos. Apart from assaulting individuals on that occasion, the gangs also attacked the offices of the Communist and Radical Parties, as well as the Ministry of Health. This was the first open attempt since the advent of the Allende Government to provoke the armed forces into restoring 'law and order', but it failed.

In 1972, taking advantage of the first lorry-owners' strike, violence and terror was used again, primarily by the openly fascist organisation, 'Fatherland and Freedom'; and as the months went by, the violence was stepped up. The situation deteriorated so much that by September Allende was warning the country of an impending threat of civil war, which was being prepared with the aid of 'advisers with a lot of international experience'. He added that 'anyone who reads the documents of the ITT will find laid out the whole plan of provocations'. On 14 September, providing more details of the plot, he referred to the fomenting of street riots, the blowing up of roads and the cutting of railway lines.

The terror activities of 1972 failed like those of 1971, but the right-wing gangs never gave up, and taking advantage of the economic difficulties of 1973, right-wing and fascist forces increased their use of violence against the Popular Unity Government. On 29 June units of the 2nd Tank Regiment in Santiago, under a Colonel Roberto Souper, attacked the Presidential Palace and tried to seize power. They were quickly crushed by the army itself under General Prats. There were some strange aspects to this attempted 'coup'. There is some basis for believing that it was not so much a direct and serious attempt to take power but rather linked to the preparations for the subsequent coup of September, and that its main purpose was in part as a dress-rehearsal, to test out the Government's defences, and in part as a deliberate provocation in order to judge better which soldiers, officers and units were likely to be loyal to the Government and which were more dependable supporters of the putschists themselves. There is evidence that on the day of the September coup a number of officers and soldiers whose loyalty to the Government had been clearly expressed on 29 June were effectively isolated and arrested by the coup organisers. The coup in the country, in fact, was prefaced by a coup in the army as we shall examine below.

Two weeks after the failed coup of 29 June, General Roberto Thieme, the secretary of the fascist 'Fatherland and Freedom' movement, made an open call for an armed offensive against the government, making clear that his supporters had been involved in the 29 June attempt. There is evidence that the CIA was funding and in other ways backing the 'Fatherland and Freedom' movement. The *Observer* correspondent (15 July 1973) commented that 'widely published documents show connections between Patria y Libertad (Fatherland and Freedom), the leading association of industrialists, and two CIA agents, in the organisation of the recently ended El Teniente copper mine strike, which cost Chile nearly 80 million in lost foreign exchange'.

The second lorry owners' strike began in July. This time the accompanying acts of terror were even worse than previously. In a television broadcast on 14 August, which itself was cut short by the blowing up of three high tension cables by terrorists, Allende declared that the wave of terror, which was bringing the country to the verge of civil war, had already cost the country 5 dead, 31 seriously injured, 71 attempts against lorries, 37 against buses, 37 attempts on railway lines, and 110 attacks on bridges. A raid with automatic weapons was made on the home of the general secretary of the Socialist Party, and trade unionists were amongst those killed. Roberto Thieme, openly boasted: 'Our purpose is to accelerate the country's chaos and to provoke a military take-over as soon as possible.'[33]

Later, after the 11 September coup, the *Economist* (15 September 1973) appeared to excuse the conspirators and blame the Popular Unity Government on the grounds that the Government had 'eroded faith in the country's democratic institutions', and led people to feel that 'Parliament had been made irrelevant', a feeling that was 'increased by violence in the streets'. Yet all the evidence shows that the Government was trying to proceed democratically, on the basis of the country's constitution, and that the violence in the streets was not that of the Government nor its supporters but was organised by the Government's opponents, especially the openly fascist bodies. 'Almost all the violence since the election of Salvador Allende has been caused by the far right' (the *Observer*, 15 July 1973). The same verdict was given by Dwight Porter in the *Financial Times*: 'The present wave of violence certainly comes from the right' (9 August 1973). In line with the scenario prepared by Nixon, Kissinger, the Committee of 40, the CIA and the Pentagon, not to mention the ITT and other multi-national firms, the violence was aimed to produce a situation of chaos and economic dislocation, and so provide the right-wing element in the armed forces with the traditional excuse of all counter-revolutionary coups, the need to 'restore law and order'.

This excuse, in fact, was made by *The Times* and the *Daily Telegraph* in justification of the coup in the days immediately following it. Yet every justified step which the Popular Unity Government took, or attempted to take, to maintain order and curb the illegal violence was denounced by its opponents as a breach of the constitution and blocked in Parliament where they had a majority. When, however, the army leaders made the supreme breach in the constitution by launching an armed attack on the legal Government, killing the legally elected President, and illegally seizing power, sections of the British press argued that these draconic, illegal and unconstitutional measures were necessitated by alleged unconstitutional acts of the Allende Government.

Thus far we have examined how leading political, economic and military circles in the United States, under the combined thrust of various departments of the State and under the instructions of no less than the US President himself, joined forces with domestic reaction inside Chile to overthrow Allende's government. Further, we have considered the use these forces made of economic measures, the mass media and open violence and terror in order to create the conditions in which the fascist-minded sections of the military hierarchy would best be able to act.

But a big question still remains to be answered. Why was it that the armed forces which helped to stop the army coup of October 1969, which refused to go along with the attempted coup of October 1970, and which quickly snuffed out the 'coup' of July 1973, were nevertheless decisively on the side of coup of 11 September 1973? Clearly by 11 September 1973 changes had taken place *inside* the armed forces; and since this book is a study of the role of the military in politics it is necessary to probe into the reasons for this internal change.

This internal change was a decisive side of the equation. If, as we noted at the start of this study, political power is the ability to compel by force if necessary, then the situation inside the armed forces, one of the main instruments of force, is obviously a key question. But we have also noted earlier that whether an army acts, or the way in which it acts, including the direction in which it turns its guns, does not depend simply on the desires of military leaders, nor on those of political forces anxious to utilise the services of the military. The army is influenced by a whole complex of wider considerations – economic, social, political and ideological; and, in the last resort, it is these which explain the army's behaviour. In this connection one should not ignore the character of the Chilean armed forces:

... in this century the social composition of the [Chilean] army has changed. The armed forces are now just one more middle class institution, with the same outlook and aspirations as bank clerks, school teachers, and civil servants. If they were allowed to vote, it is likely that their votes would reflect the same divisions as exist in society as a whole.[34]

This characterisation by Gott is perhaps too sweeping and takes too little account of the impact of the army as an institution on its members; but broadly speaking, the point about its social composition and political sympathies is correct. Yet, what conditions the outlook and behaviour of the men in uniform is not their social origin in its direct and 'pure' sense, but the reaction on them of their class and social counterparts in civilian life, the way these latter think and act, and the expectations which they place on the army.

To appreciate why the Chilean army lurched to the right in the period prior to September 1973, why it was possible for the counter-revolution to organise a 'coup within the coup', that is to seize control of the armed forces as a prelude to seizing power in the country, it is important to consider the strategy of the Communist Party of Chile and the stand taken by other political parties, both those within Popular Unity and those outside it, including the ultra-left MIR (Movement of the Revolutionary Left) on the one hand, and the Christian Democrats on the other.

Ever since the 1930s the Communist Party of Chile had striven, in one form or another, to build a broad alliance of forces based on the working class rallying around itself other classes and social strata: peasants, professional people and technicians, small and medium farmers, traders, manufacturers – in fact, all non-monopoly sections of the population. In this way a majority of the people could be won, not necessarily for the immediate changeover to socialism, but in support of a democratic, transitional phase which would have the aim of ending the domination of Chile by foreign, and especially United States, monopolies, breaking the back of the large semi-feudal and capitalist landlord class, ending the economic grip of the major Chilean capitalist enterprises, and extending democratic liberties, especially by involving the working people in directly managing their own affairs and helping to run the economy and the State.

It was envisaged by the Communist Party that this alliance of class and social forces would have its political counterpart in the unity of left and democratic parties. This found expression in the Popular Front victory of 1938, the formation of the People's Front in 1952 which later was enlarged into the Popular Action Front (FRAP), for which Allende was the presidential candidate in 1958 and 1964. By 1969 the coalition of democratic and left forces was able to unite and set up Popular Unity.

It was the view of the Communist Party that a government of such political and social forces would be able to embark on major social transformations. These structural changes, and the shift in the balance of class forces which they would involve, would provide the possibility of the Chilean people passing from the democratic, anti-imperialist phase of their transformation of society to the opening up of the road to socialism without a civil war. The *possibility* of such an advance, not its certainty; for the Chilean Communists, who had been compelled to spend over twenty years of their existence underground, and who remembered only too well the shooting down of miners by the military in the last years of Frei's presidency, never ruled out the danger of a military coup, nor the necessity which might arise for the people to take up arms to prevent or defeat such an attempt.[35]

As early as December 1970, shortly after Allende's election victory, Luis Corvalan, General Secretary of the Communist Party, emphasised in an article that although the Popular Unity parties had formed a new Government and were, as he put it, consequently 'in control of the political-power mechanism', the landlords and big industrialists still held strong positions not only in the economy, but also in the legislature and judiciary, as well as in the important sphere of the mass media. Thus the question of power had not yet been resolved, and significant areas of the State, including the armed forces, were still heavily subject to the influence and control of forces inimical to Popular Unity. Explaining the necessity for the Chilean people to consolidate and enlarge the spheres of power they had won, Corvalan stressed the importance of extending this to the whole machinery of the State so that the entire political power was in the people's hands.

The outlook [he wrote] is therefore for a series of clashes between the people and their government, on the one hand, and imperialism and the oligarchy, on the other. We should not, therefore, preclude the possibility of the people having to resort to one or other form of armed struggle. To ward off any such situation the popular forces must immobilise the enemy, straitjacket him, drive him into a corner and thus spare the country the civil war the opponents of reform would so gleefully welcome.[36]

Such warnings were constantly repeated in the next few years. At the beginning of 1971, Corvalan declared: 'The imperialists and the national oligarchy are preparing for subversion, and if that does not work, for a *coup d'état*. Therefore, we must do everything we can to straitjacket them before they can force armed struggle upon us.' In March 1972 he stated that Chile's effort to advance towards socialism without civil war 'presupposes a class struggle and not class harmony, not amicable coexistence between the exploited and the exploiter, and not a rejection of an armed struggle if required'. As late as 8 July 1973, in a speech made at the Caupolican Theatre, Corvalan called on the people to be prepared to use all possible means to meet the growing menace of civil war, at the same time making it clear that it was not the Communists who were seeking civil war, but on the contrary were still striving 'to complete the anti-imperialist and anti-oligarchical revolution, and march forward to Socialism without civil war, although, naturally, maintaining an intense class struggle'. Reaffirming his Party's desire to save the people from the horrors of civil war – 'We have said and repeat today that we are doing, and will continue to do all that is in our power to avoid it' – Corvalan nevertheless issued this call:

. . . the Chilean proletariat will stand firm in their places of work and, as we have also said, if it is necessary to fight we will leave the factories and do so . . . We must be prepared for any circumstances, ready to fight on all grounds. If the reactionary sedition becomes greater, entering the realms of armed struggle, let nobody have any doubts that the people will promptly rise, as one man, to crush it. In such a situation, that we do not desire, that we do not seek, that we wish to avoid, but could nevertheless take place, nothing will be left, not even a stone, that we will not use as ammunition. In such an instance, the new alternative would be to defeat with the maximum speed and energy those who unleash civil war, and liquidate the event before it begins, to spare Chile the injuries and anguish of a prolonged conflict of this type.[37]

It can of course be argued that words are all very well, even fighting words, but that when it came to the eventual showdown, neither the Communist Party, nor Popular Unity as a whole, nor the Chilean working people were able to respond in the way which Corvalan had envisaged only a few weeks before. There are a number of reasons for this, including the factors that operated inside the armed forces. Any consideration of the causes of the failure to stop the coup, let alone defeat it once it had begun, must take into account the strategy of the Communist Party, and the reactions and behaviour of the other political forces, both those inside and outside Popular Unity, apart from those on the extreme right.

The presidential election success of 1970 was regarded by the

Communist Party as a significant step, but it knew only too well what immense problems Popular Unity and the Chilean people faced in the struggle to implement the profound changes set out in the Popular Unity programme. As the Communist Party saw it, the democratic mobilisation of the people, the consolidation of the people's support, the organisation of the people, and the gradual extension of the basis of Popular Unity through the winning of further strata of the population, and the achievement of understanding and cooperation with political forces outside Popular Unity were of key importance. In brief, the aim was to bring about a decisively favourable relationship of class forces, with a heavy majority for Popular Unity and its programme, and with the right-wing and fascist forces isolated. This favourable relationship of class forces would be expressed in the electoral field.

Three key problems had to be faced. How to raise the political level of the workers and other Popular Unity supporters; how to extend the base of Popular Unity, and open up an area of understanding with other social forces and with other political tendencies; how to ensure that the democratic option remained valid and that reaction was prevented from using the State, and especially the armed forces, to block the democratic road. Solving vital economic problems was intimately connected with all these three issues, which themselves were closely intertwined. In brief, what was at stake was the defence and growth of the democratic process.

The Communist Party and Young Communist League, whose respective memberships soared from 150,000 and 50,000 in 1972 to 250,000 and 100,000 in the summer of 1973, strove to make a major contribution to solving these problems. Recognising that mass extra-Parliamentary activity, the constantly expanding democratic participation of the people in carrying forward the Popular Unity programme, was the decisive sphere through which a favourable balance of class forces could be achieved, the Communist Party, together with other parties of Popular Unity, worked to strengthen the mass organisations and to assist in establishing new bodies in which the people could display their democratic initiative in all aspects of building the new social structure.

An important role was played by the million strong trade union movement – CUT (Confederation of United Workers), which helped to plan and supervise production in both private and state enterprises (although with the weaknesses we have noted earlier), and to help defend factories from hostile attacks at times of crisis.

Equally significant were the new organisations which were created by the people in the course of their struggle, first to win the 1970 elections for Popular Unity and then to implement its programme. Nearly 15,000 Popular Unity Committees were set up for the 1970 elections; and after Allende was elected as President they were retained with the idea that they would assume new functions. In a speech to the Central Committee of the Communist Party early in 1971, Luis Corvalan said of these committees:

In all places and at all levels they must discuss with the mass organisations and with the organs of Government the concrete tasks needed if the movement's programme is to be implemented. They will therefore be the motive force behind the programme's implementation and also the means by which the people can actively cooperate in Government affairs. The committees must also increase their vigilance against the manoeuvres and machinations of the right and imperialism.

These hopes were never fully realised, partly because of differences between some of the parties in Popular Unity. Undoubtedly the failure to consolidate and strengthen these committees was a significant shortcoming of Popular Unity. Nevertheless, other grassroots bodies sprang up which enabled the people, in different spheres, to become organised, to gain experience and confidence, and to advance their political understanding. Special youth brigades were established to help construction works and factories in the urban centres, and to assist to reclaim deserts, plant trees and bushes, sink wells, and so on, in the countryside. It was these brigades which did so much during the lorry strikes to help with the distribution of vital supplies, making use of the state-owned trucks. Councils for Supplies and Prices, aimed at mobilising the working people together with small tradesmen to supervise the availability and distribution of goods, and to combat hoarding, speculation and black-marketing, were also set up. Health Committees were formed, as were Centres for Mothers, Farmers' Councils, Citizens' Committees, and so on.

The *El Arrayan Report* of March 1972, drawn up with the approval of all the Popular Unity Parties, placed great emphasis on the democratic participation of the people, making this, in fact, a major theme:

. . . the most pressing task for Popular Unity is the development of its organising capacity, the mobilisation of the people and their support to the Government. . . . In fact, one of the major weaknesses of the policy up till now is considered to be an inadequate participation of the masses of the people in the tasks that the Popular Unity is carrying out. . . . If social change is to be carried out, a mass participation in the work required for this change is, above all, needed . . . the people must take into their own hands the task of fulfilling the programme of policy. This worker participation must, however, be real and democratically governed, to reach all sectors within Popular Unity, Christian Democrats, or independents. . . . All these measures for political mobilisation should mean an effort to make the presence of the workers felt throughout the whole of the present State apparatus, as a basis for the development of a truly popular power. . . . Many concrete tasks will thus be handed over to the people themselves, under forms of participation that will change the character and nature of the State. . . . We will, therefore, make all possible efforts to apply the methods our principles and historic experience have shown as the most suitable revolutionary weapon; the work of the masses. Consult the people and make all decisions through them. This will be our fundamental line of conduct, to be increasingly more general and strengthened . . . The improvement and the functioning ability of the State and Government institutions will depend in the last instance upon the work and participation of the masses.

Clearly, therefore, the parties of Popular Unity – and that included the Communist Party – in no way conceived of the Chilean road of advance as a purely 'parliamentary road', as some of their detractors on the far left have argued. On the contrary, the whole line of march was predicated on the utmost democratic initiative and activity of the people, and their increasing participation in managing the economy and State affairs at all levels. This process was in no sense completed by the time of the coup; but three years' experience had made it possible for growing numbers of ordinary men and women, young and old, in many walks of life, to become more politically aware, to have gained experience and, in the process, become more confident both in themselves and in the capacity of working people to manage the country.

Summarising the task that faced Popular Unity in turning its electoral support into conscious, democratic activity and participation, President Allende emphasised, in a speech after the 1971 successes for Popular Unity in the municipal elections, that 'if votes are important, the task of creating a revolutionary consciousness out of every voter is much more important. . . . We need to convert these 1,400,000 revolutionary consciences which understand perfectly well the significance of the struggle of the people and Chile. . . . I am concerned about the consciousness, the spinal column, the granite base of workers who are not only class conscious but who possess the strength of conviction obtained through dialogue and above all in ideological discussion.[38] So what we have ahead of us is to make these 1,400,000 votes, which for the defeated count as votes, into 1,400,000 granite consciences for us which will defend the present and the future of our country.'

Some commentators analysing the 1973 September coup have presented matters as if Popular Unity had wide support at the beginning, in 1970, but as a consequence of its own mistakes combined with the mounting attacks of its opponents, steadily lost popular backing and by the time of the coup, had become very much isolated. However, things were not as simple as that. Student elections in November 1970, and trade union elections in 1972, provided indications of the massive support rallying behind Popular Unity. In the student elections for the University of Chile Students' Federation (FECH), the largest student body in the country, Popular Unity pushed its vote up by 40 per cent, defeated the Christian Democrat-ultra right alliance, and re-elected a Communist as President. In the trade union elections, the Communist Party and the Socialist Party obtained 70 per cent of the total votes (33 per cent for the Communist Party and 37 per cent for the Socialist Party), with most of the remaining votes going to the Christian Democrats. Among production workers, the Communist-Socialist vote reached 90 per cent. Luis Figueroa, a Communist, was re-elected as President.

There was no doubt that the Chilean working class overwhelmingly supported Popular Unity, with a decisive section being supporters of the Communist Party. But in the post 1970 presidential election period, neither the working class itself, nor the Popular Unity parties with the support they had won hitherto, were enough to achieve the ambitious goals which the Popular Unity programme had advanced. The strategy contained in the Popular Unity programme was to strive to win over a substantial section of the middle strata in town and countryside in order to change the balance of class forces and political alignments and secure majority support in the country for carrying through the main objectives of the Popular Unity programme.

White-collar and professional workers, as well as the middle strata of small and medium farmers, shopkeepers, manufacturers, artisans and self-employed technicians and professional people (lawyers, doctors, and so forth), are a key question for the working class. If important sections of these strata are not won over to the side of progress, or at least to a position of neutrality, hesitancy, or passivity, they will become a social base for reaction which will be able to throw them against the working class.[39] This, as we shall see, was a key factor in the Chilean coup.

As previously noted, the 1970 presidential elections already demonstrated the scope of the problem. The Popular Unity parties gained 36·3 per cent of the votes – that is a little over one third. To advance under such conditions and implement the programme of Popular Unity was a most complex and difficult task; a task so formidable, in fact, that some political analysts have understandably questioned whether it was correct even to have tried. Not only was there the question of the majority of votes in the country going against Popular Unity; in the two Houses of Congress, elected in earlier elections, the opposition had a built-in majority, comprising the ultra-right Nationalists and the Christian Democrats. The latter party contained substantial sections of middle class and professional people, as well as sections of large capitalists, and relied for its popular voting support on substantial numbers of peasants, small traders and even some sections of workers (over a quarter of votes in the 1972 trade union elections went to the Christian Democrats). Large numbers of women, from all classes, traditionally voted Christian Democrat.

Thus, the Christian Democrat Party, while under a leadership which became predominantly right-wing, drew its support from many classes and strata. Politically it was in no way a monolithic body, but contained elements of differentiation which could have provided the possibility of an eventual fruitful and principled dialogue, at least with significant sections of that party. Allende, with the support of the Communists, sought such a dialogue, but there were some tendencies in Popular Unity, amongst the Socialists and MAPU (apart from the clamour from the MIR from outside the ranks of Popular Unity), which were not favourable to such an approach.

From their side, the Christian Democrats were not at all enthusiastic. Only at the very end, a few weeks before the coup, at the height of the transport crisis caused by the stoppage of lorries, buses and taxis, did their leaders, after some prodding from the Archbishop of Santiago, agree to sit down and talk with President Allende. But by then it was too late. The balance of forces had tipped too far. The country was heading for a coup.

Winning a broader class alliance than that embraced initially by Popular Unity was inevitably a difficult task, but it was essential if the forces of progress were really to succeed. Writing at the end of 1972, Luis Corvalan argued:

Our basic task consists in rallying the overwhelming majority of Chileans behind the Government and its revolutionary programme. This is quite feasible because the programme of Popular Unity accords not only with the interests of the working class but also with the aspirations of the middle social strata, with the country's supreme interests. *In other words, the matter concerns the need to isolate our main enemies, winning to our side those sections of the population that are still under their influence* [italics added]. What is needed is to do away with limitations in the pursuance of our policy in this sphere and to give a vigorous rebuff to the attacks of the 'ultra left' wing forces, which with their adventurist actions have been bringing grist to the mill of reaction.

Elections over the three years of Allende's presidency provide some indication of the shifts taking place in the balance of class forces. The nation-wide municipal elections in April 1971, after five months of Popular Unity Government, gave the Popular Unity Parties a combined 50·8 per cent of the total vote. This was a striking advance over the presidential elections of September 1970 (36·3 per cent for Allende), yet it would be incorrect to think that a 14 per cent increase in the vote in municipal elections necessarily represented a real shift of those dimensions in the political thinking and allegiance of people in general.

In four Parliamentary by-elections following the municipal elections, one was won by Popular Unity and the other three by the combined votes of the National Party and the Christian Democrats together with another opposition party, the Radical Democrats. In a later by-election in July 1972, a woman Communist, Amanda Altamirano, standing as a Popular Unity candidate, won the seat against a coalition of the opposition.[40]

These results only provide a partial picture of what was happening in the country. Of more significance were the Assembly elections in March 1973, a mere six months before the coup. Despite the immense economic problems facing the country, despite the sabotage and disruption, despite the terror organised by the 'Fatherland and Freedom' gangs, Popular Unity support rose to nearly 44 per cent – over 7 per cent up on the 1970 September vote for Allende. This would seem to indicate that Popular Unity had not lost support since it took office, but in fact was gaining support. True, it was still less than a majority, but the growth represented in this 7 per cent increase must have included, apart from working people, some sections from the middle strata. It was precisely because Popular Unity, despite the grave difficulties confronting it, was still assured of popular support at the polls, that the counter-revolutionary forces became more desperate and intensified their violence in order to overthrow the Government.

But of course the balance of strength between the contending social and political forces was not to be sought only in election results. It was, as Allende had declared, a matter of Popular Unity turning votes into hundreds of thousands of 'granite consciences'. This was vital because the opponents of Popular Unity had no intention of leaving matters to be decided only by votes. For them, too, extra-parliamentary activity was the key; despite the fact that Popular Unity had no parliamentary majority, the opposition was determined to prevent the march of Popular Unity towards such an eventual electoral victory. A key force on which Popular Unity's opponents depended for extra-parliamentary activity was the middle strata.

To win such sections for progress is never easy. It requires a combination of measures to meet their economic problems, and patient, consistent explanations and persuasion in order to overcome their real anxieties as well as their imaginary and irrational fears. Economic measures to win over these sections were introduced by the Popular Unity Government in line with its programme;[41] yet, at the same time, the deliberate acts of the US State Department and US monopolies directed to 'make the economy scream', and the supporting actions of domestic reaction, producing as they did mounting inflation and shortages of many goods, constantly upset what the Allende Government was attempting. The Government introduced tax and other concessions for traders and businessmen. The Statute for Small Industries and Handicrafts met many of the long-standing aspirations of these sections. The small and medium farmers, who comprised 40 per cent of the agrarian population, were assured by the Government that their farms would not be taken over; and, in addition, they were assisted with credits and technical assistance.

Despite the Government's steps to provide the small producers, traders and farmers with a secure place in the national economy, it still proved very difficult to change the political thinking of these strata and to win them over to support the Government, or at least take a more tolerant attitude towards it. The task of overcoming the fear of change, which is almost endemic with the small-owner; his innate conservatism, his anxiety about the fate of his small property, his deep-seated reservations and often hostility towards the working class, his deep-grained anti-communism nourished by years of propaganda and distortion, and associated in his mind with everyone left of centre; all this presented a grave and complex task for the parties of Popular Unity.

In a sense, the battle for the minds and political support of the middle strata was the fulcrum around which the political struggle unfolded. Popular Unity – and this was a point which the Communist Party repeatedly emphasised – needed to win a substantial section of the small-owners, professional people, technicians and administrative workers away from the side of the two main opposition parties, especially the Christian Democrats. Economic policy, land reform, constitutional difficulties, the armed forces, the danger of a coup, all were linked with the question of the middle strata.

On its side, the counter-revolution understood that it had to retain these sections within its political orbit in order to have an adequate social base for its attack on the Popular Unity Government. The forces of the right calculated that the way to maintain their influence was to help create economic crisis, produce a situation of tension and violence, and sow fear in the minds of the farmers and urban petty-bourgeoisie. Time was an important factor, for if they were to carry through their military coup they stood a better chance of succeeding while at least half the country still gave their voting allegiance and political support to the anti-Government parties.

In this acute situation the tactics of the ultra-left MIR (Movement of the Revolutionary Left) objectively made the work of reaction easier, however sincere may have been the intentions of many of those participating in MIR-inspired activities. When, in opposition to Popular Unity's policy of limiting land take-overs to the large estates (and this was being implemented), some small or medium-sized farms were seized, the right-wing papers came out with banner headlines intended to stampede small and middle farmers into the arms of reaction by stirring up their fears that their own plots would be taken next. With the machinery of propaganda mainly in the hands of the Government's opponents, and bearing in mind the fears already existent in the minds of the small-owners, these infantile tactics of the MIR, apart from solving no economic problems for Popular Unity but only creating new ones, made no policital sense either. Similarly with the calls for the taking over of factories not on the list of major monopolies scheduled for such action by the State; this again gave the right wing the opportunity to spread panic amongst small producers, shop-keepers and so on, and so throw them back into the lap of the anti-Government forces.

Unfortunately some sections of Popular Unity, including among the Socialist Party and MAPU, were somewhat dazzled by the 'revolutionary' slogans and proddings from the MIR, with the result that Popular Unity was hindered from giving a firm and united rebuff to the dangerous antics of the ultra-left. But winning the middle strata was vital for Popular Unity.

Describing how fascism won in Italy in the 1920s Togliatti explained that the discontent amongst the petty-bourgeoisie becomes a real menace, becomes 'transformed' when 'a new factor intervenes; when the most reactionary forces of the bourgeoisie intervene as an organising factor'.[42]

This is basically what happened in Chile. The electoral support for the opponents of Popular Unity was transformed into an active, extra-parliamentary support by the activities of 'the most reactionary forces of the bourgeoisie' intervening as 'an organising factor'. A significant additional role here was played by the United States. Operating through the CIA, top circles of the US monopolies and the US State also intervened 'as an organising factor'. Starting with the 'pots-and-pans' march of upper and middle class housewives, reaction steadily increased the level of its mobilisation and the violence of its attacks. Thus it utilised the private lorry owners, with devasting effect, to cause heavy losses to the national economy, to produce hardship and shortages of essential goods for the people, and to create conditions of tension and difficulty which facilitated the unleashing of violence and terror. In the same way many Chilean shop-keepers, doctors, civil servants, air pilots, higher-paid workers at some of the copper mines, were provoked into actions which, even where those participating were not always motivated by the same aims as the counter-revolution, caused economic and social dislocation. The fascist terror gangs of 'Fatherland and Freedom' were, as their leader Roberto Thieme boasted, from these same middle strata.

A costly lesson for democrats everywhere is thus provided by the Chilean experience; if the working class does not detach the middle strata from their support for the bankers, industrialists and landlords, then these latter forces will use the middle strata against the workers. In periods of relative political stability and peace, in which the middle strata are more passive and generally confine their activity to that of casting their votes in elections, the working class and its allies, even when a minority, can carry on their work under reasonably democratic conditions and even, by the mobilisation of their strength, ensure substantial economic and social advance. But in periods of sharp class confrontation the capitalist class moves to match the workers' mobilisation by the mobilisation of its own supporters, turning them from that of relatively *passive* voters into *active* opponents of the workers and other democratic forces. It was, as Togliatti noted, the ability of the Italian capitalists to 'mobilise the petty-bourgeoisie' which provided it with its fascist arm to smash the working class and democratic movement. In the dramatic days of May 1968 in France, in reply to the

actions of workers and students, the French ruling class backed up its use
of the State machine with preparations for a more decisive showdown by
starting to 'mobilise the petty-bourgeoisie', as seen in the formation of
reactionary 'committees' all over France and in the massive march in
Paris which was a menacing display of its potential.[43] In Portugal, in
1974–5, after the overthrow of fascism, it was the 'mobilisation of the
petty-bourgeoisie' in the North which provided the first check to the
advance of the democratic revolution.[44]

In his analysis and reflections after the Chilean coup, Enrico
Berlinguer[45] has warned against the dangers of the working class
becoming isolated from its main allies and potential allies; equally he
cautions against the democratic movement, even with a 51 per cent
majority, trying to push forward a progressive programme in conditions
that would mean a 'vertical division of the country', with all its
attendant dangers of tension, conflict, violence and even possible defeat.
The question is not just one of arithmetic. Major class conflicts are not
solved by voting figures, even in conditions where elections may be a
major form of struggle and where the revolutionary movement may
regard electoral choice as a key aspect of their road to socialism. What is
required for victory is a number of initiatives – electoral activity, trade
union action, extra-parliamentary activity in a variety of forms, and a
policy directed to winning a massive majority to the side of the
revolution – *a majority which does not limit its support to casting its vote against
reaction*, but which has been won, partly through the economic and social
benefits it has gained from a progressive government, and partly by
political persuasion and by its own involvement, to an understanding
that *it must be prepared to struggle in order to defend its government and to secure
its objectives*. At all costs, a revolutionary movement must strive to avoid a
confrontation which produces a deep fissure right down the middle of
the nation. Even with a majority of 51 per cent, the revolution must so
work as to cut deep into the remaining 49 per cent with the intention of
winning a substantial part of it over to its side.

Mobilisation of one's own forces, the turning of voters into active
supporters and defenders, and the determined, unrelenting but flexible
pursuit of allies, of an ever bigger majority in order to have the best
possible conditions for success – these are two of the key lessons of the
Chilean tragedy.

Drawing on Chile's experience, Enrico Berlinguer[46] describes the
question of alliances as 'the decisive problem for every revolution and
every revolutionary policy'. Dealing specifically with Italy, but in terms

that give his analysis a wider significance, he stresses that 'Between the proletariat and the big bourgeoisie – the two basic class antagonists in the capitalist system – a network of intermediate categories and strata has grown up in the cities and countryside', often lumped together 'under the generic term "middle class"'. In addition, 'alongside and often interwoven' with these intermediate classes and strata there are other social forces – women, youth, the forces of science, technology, culture and the arts, and so on. Where these different classes, strata and social movements stand, and 'in what direction they tend to turn and move will prove a decisive factor. It is evident, that is, that for the fate of democratic development and the advance of Socialism whether the weight of these social forces is thrown on the side of the working class or against it is decisive. . . . With this in mind we have always thought – and today the Chilean experience strengthens our convictions – that unity among the workers' parties and left-wing forces is not enough to guarantee the defence and progress of democracy in situations where this unity finds itself confronted with a bloc of parties extending from the centre to the extreme right.' In such conditions, argues Berlinguer, the central political problem is 'how to avoid the welding of a solid and organic bond between the centre and the right . . . and instead succeed in drawing the social and political forces in the centre into consistently democratic positions'. In this, of course, the unity and political and electoral strength of the working class and left-wing forces and parties are the key – but on their own, without attracting the forces of the centre, it would be illusory to think that they could guarantee the defence of such a government as the Chilean Government of Popular Unity.

In Chile, it must be borne in mind, decisive sectors of the administration and the State could in no sense be regarded as strongholds of support for Popular Unity. Their attitude to Allende's Government was inconsistent; at all times they were undoubtedly influenced by developments in civilian life, and particularly by the anxieties and reactions of those classes and strata with which they could most closely identify.

Thus, the question of the Chilean armed forces and how they would behave was directly linked to the relation of class forces in the country at large. The problem was how to create the political conditions which would make it most difficult for the oligarchy to use the armed forces against Popular Unity. This required the gathering together of the vast majority of the people in order to isolate the coup-plotters, and so influence the army to remain constitutional. This would facilitate the introduction of democratic reforms in the army, including the removal from their positions of power and authority of those officers who, by class origin, sympathies and outlook were most closely tied to the ruling class, and more likely to support counter-revolution. The more such democratic changes took place inside the army, the more the likelihood would grow that the men in uniform could be persuaded to give loyal support to the legally elected government.

This process was bound up with the problem of winning the middle strata over to the side of Popular Unity. Apart from the overall political impact that the achievement of such a broad alliance would have had, it could have exercised a direct influence within the Chilean armed forces themselves. This possibility arose from the fact that the majority of Chilean officers, as in most Latin American armies today, came not so much from the families of the oligarchy but from the middle strata. They were linked by a thousand strings with the urban petty-bourgeois and medium capitalist families to whom they were related, and were therefore likely to be heavily influenced by the same pressures and political ideas that were moulding the thinking and behaviour of their families and friends outside the army. It was to this that Luis Corvalan was referring when, whilst warning of the dangers of a coup and the consequent need to be prepared to engage in armed struggle, he wrote in December 1970[47] of the impact which world events could have under certain circumstances on the armed forces in Third World countries:

These days no social institution is indifferent to the social storms raging all over the world, and the tragedy of the hundreds of millions of poverty-stricken people. The attitude of the armed forces of the Dominican Republic during the US invasion [1965], and the progressive nature of the military government in Peru show that a dogmatic approach to the army is no longer valid.

That there were divisions and different trends within the Chilean armed forces was clear from the start. One section, headed by General Schneider, was prepared to stand by the Constitution and refuse to allow the army to be used against the legally elected Government. Another section, funded and aided in other ways by the United States, and encouraged by domestic reaction with which it had close ties, was involved in the counter-revolutionary conspiracies. These divisions ran right through the officer corps, although many officers, probably the majority, had no firmly decided view either way but were influenced by the ebb and flow of the political struggle in the country as a whole.

Other ranks were mainly conscripts, but their loyalties were also divided. As is usually the case, they tended to follow the lead of the officers rather than take any independent position of their own; the system of hierarchy and obedience to higher command was accepted as the normal pattern.

General Schneider's assassination in 1970 demonstrated the sharpness of the divisions. He was succeeded as Commander-in-Chief by General Prats, who continued to follow 'the Schneider line'.

The problem facing Popular Unity was how to bring about progressive changes in the armed forces in a situation without a popular majority in Parliament, without an electoral majority in the country, with important sectors of the economy still in the hands of private owners hostile to the Government and its programme, with the mass media dominated by Popular Unity's enemies, and with the state apparatus still largely unchanged since the days of the rule of the oligarchy.

Some people have argued that the Allende Government should have made a swift clean-up of the armed forces right at the start, and purged all the Government's opponents and potential enemies. This apparently simple solution, however, presupposes that the right-wing officers were isolated in the armed forces and had no strong support among the civilian population. But at no time was this the actual position. Any precipitate move by the Government could have provoked a crisis in the army and opened the way to a coup even earlier and under conditions in which, because of the political balance of forces, it was likely to succeed.

The Popular Unity Government, therefore, had to proceed with a great deal of patience and skill. The special anti-riot Mobile Guard of the police force, a most unpopular unit, was disbanded. Some of the most obvious and extreme right-wing officers in the armed forces were retired – although subsequent events were to reveal how limited this mini-purge had been. The September 1973 coup exposed the fact that of the twenty-one army generals, only five or six remained loyal. The retention of the fascist junta leaders, Pinochet (army), Admiral Jose Toribio Merino (navy), General Gustavo Leigh (air force) and General Cesar Mendoza (Carabinieri Corps) in their different services prior to the coup indicates how the main plotters were able to elude the net.

The question of the armed forces, like the State as a whole, presented the Popular Unity Government with some unique problems. Zorina has pointed out that Popular Unity was presented with 'the opportunity of carrying out revolutionary transformations both "from above" and "from below", within the framework of the constitution and with the backing of the masses'. The fact, noted Zorina, that Popular Unity came to power by constitutional means 'to a large extent predetermined the conditions in which the Allende Administration operates: the preservation and gradual transformation of the traditional political and judiciary structure, an opposition in Parliament, government, law courts, press, etc. . . . But the rate of these transformations depends to a great extent on this specific situation and the fact that the broadest masses are being steadily drawn into the revolutionary process. . . . The challenge faced by the left-wing forces in Chile is unprecedented in the history of the working class movement: to gain full power with the support of the masses and by legal means while running the country.'[48]

This process involved a phased, gradual restructuring of all areas of the State, including the armed forces; and, owing to the circumstances in which Popular Unity had assumed government, it was being done within a constitutional framework.

'In such a context', noted Zorina, 'the question of attitude towards the old state apparatus calls for a different approach than in a revolution stemming from armed uprising and civil war.' This new context in Chile required achieving 'a proper balance between smashing and using the old state apparatus; to crush the resistance by reactionaries in administrative bodies; to enlist the support of the medium echelon of the civil service; to have the armed forces play a more positive role in carrying out revolutionary transformations, and to ensure the broad, genuine representation of the working people'.

Analysing the situation in the Chilean armed forces and explaining the necessity for an approach that would take into account the fact that 'the Popular Unity parties came to power not as a result of grappling with the armed forces or any part of them', Luis Corvalan argues that 'the military establishment, too, needs change, but that change should not be imposed on it. It must be initiated by the military and based on their awareness of its imperatives.'[49]

The novelty in the situation, as expressed by Corvalan and to an extent by Zorina, lay in the conception that, arising from the social and political changes taking place in the armed forces, and under the impact of political developments in the country, further changes would occur, leading to a qualitative transformation in the armed forces – but that this process would be the result of the efforts of progressive elements in the armed forces themselves, helped, no doubt, by the Government and the parties of Popular Unity but not imposed by the Government against the wishes of the army.

President Allende worked very energetically for this concept. Measures were taken early on in the life of his government to improve the pay and conditions of the officers and soldiers in order to avoid any grievances which could be exploited by the counter-revolution. Army pay was increased by some 40 per cent, flats were built for army personnel, the children of a number of officers were granted scholarships to university and college. Steps were taken as well to involve the army in tasks of an economic and social character so that they might better understand the purpose of the reconstruction of Chilean society which was being attempted, and thereby become more favourable to these changes and so more inclined to keep to the constitutional path.

It was not possible for the political parties to be the main instrument for directly bringing about changes in the outlook of the armed forces. Not only would this have created acute tension between officers and parties, and presented other difficult tactical questions, but the Constitution itself, to which the Popular Unity was pledged, strictly forbade it.

Thus President Allende, as Commander-in-Chief of the armed forces, took on this responsibility. Even before his endorsement as President in October 1970, he met the commanders of all the armed services, and promised them that if he were endorsed as President by the Congress and Senate he would improve their pay and conditions, refrain from interfering with their internal affairs, would consult them on all new appointments on which they would have the final word. At their request, he promised, too, that he would not abrogate the military agreements signed with the United States. This initial meeting made a big impact on many of the officers, the majority of whom refused to be drawn into the CIA-inspired assassination plot against General Schneider. After he became President Allende continued his purposeful work with the army. Starting with a meeting of 2,000 officers and men, in April 1971, he held frequent such gatherings – fourteen in the first seven months of his administration – as well as numerous other smaller consultations.

The President also strove to strengthen the links between the army and the people by bringing the officers more into public life, including their representatives in all important major receptions, and appointing them in delegations sent abroad on important missions on which they worked together with leading civilian representatives of the Chilean government. At various critical moments of the Popular Government's administration, they were even brought more directly into government responsibility.

It might be argued that all this was a wasted exercise. After all, despite the Chilean army's reputation for constitutionalism, its past was not quite so unblemished, although for forty years it had staged no coup, a rather unique attainment in Latin America. The absence of military coups in Chile's history since the thirties, however, was due to the political situation in Chile, rather than to some peculiar characteristics of the armed forces themselves. For over forty years the ruling oligarchy had been able to contain the opposition within the framework of the existing system, and so the army had not found it necessary to organise an anti-government coup. But this did not prevent the army being involved in politics on the side of reaction, and in a most brutal manner on a number of occasions, including the mass repression under President Gonzalez Videla in 1947 and the army's ruthless suppression of the miners' strike during the period of the Frei administration prior to Popular Unity's 1970 electoral success.

This brutality was in keeping with its earlier practice: 30 killed during the dock strike in Valparaiso in 1903, 200 killed in a strike in Santiago in 1905, over 2,000 machined-gunned in the central square of Iquique in 1907, and 3,000 shot in La Corunna in 1925. It is as well to bear these experiences in mind, since some commentators have tended to present the Chilean army prior to the September 1973 coup as a rather liberal-minded institution which broke violently out of tradition and acted completely out of character when it brutally overthrew the Allende Government.

Nor should one ignore the US connection. Links between the Chilean armed forces and the United States were particularly close. It has been estimated by Professor Roy Allen Hansen of the University of California that as many as 68 per cent of the high-ranking Chilean officers on active service received training in US military colleges or at the special counter-insurgency college in the Panama Canal Zone. The Chilean armed forces were dependent on the US for military equipment, and this continued to arrive even after the US had suspended its economic contacts with Chile, following Allende's election.[50]

Yet, there were divisions in the armed forces, many of the officers being sympathetic to progressive changes. A poll conducted in 1969 among 200 officers, including 38 generals, showed that 83 per cent were in favour of social and economic reforms, 14 per cent were clearly reactionary in viewpoint, and only 3 per cent openly supported the idea of a military coup.[51] Even among those favouring reforms,[52] however, there were undoubtedly many who held anti-communist views which they shared with middle class people in civilian life who were apprehensive that radical changes in society would affect their status and their economic and social privileges.

The fact that there were two tendencies in the Chilean armed forces provided Allende and Popular Unity with both the hope and the possibility that they could prevent the counter-revolution turning the army against the Government and the people. It was in no sense an illusion to think along these lines. The attempt had to be made because, in cold political terms, there was no real alternative. For Popular Unity, in the three years of its administration, to have initiated its own confrontation with the armed forces in the midst of its difficult conflict with the substantial, organised and US aided domestic civilian opposition, would have been a certain road to early disaster. By its tactics Popular Unity was able to keep the army to the constitutional path for three years; and the hope and intention was that, by persuading the armed forces to adhere to this path, sufficient time would be gained to secure a more favourable balance of political forces in the country, and that this, in its turn, would assist further progressive changes within the armed forces themselves. The aim was that, stage by stage, the armed forces would be increasingly democratised and transformed into an institution that would support the new social structure being elaborated. Decisive for such a development, of course, was the continued shift in the balance of class forces in favour of Popular Unity in the population as a whole.

But the counter-revolution threw all its energies into the struggle precisely to prevent Popular Unity winning a more favourable balance of political forces to its side; and at the same time, and in parallel with its actions to 'destabilise' the economy and the Government, the counter-revolution proceeded in what was for it an increasingly favourable situation to bring about a decisive change inside the armed forces as a prelude to the overthrow of Allende's government. The coup of 11 September 1973 was preceded by a coup within the armed forces.

Throughout June, July and August 1973 steps were put in hand to place the control of the armed forces firmly in the hands of the ultra-right officers. A particular target was General Carlos Prats,[53] Commander of the Chilean Land Forces. On 29 June, Colonel Roberto Souper's abortive coup attempt took place. Though the coup was immediately put down, assassination plots went ahead, and on 27 July Captain Arturo Araya, the President's naval aide, was shot dead in his flat. There also seems to have been an attempt to set General Prats up for assassination while he was driving his car to the Moneda Palace. A short time later, on 23 August, following a hostile demonstration of officers' wives outside his flat, General Prats resigned from his position of Commander of the Land Forces and as Minister of Defence, a post to which he had recently been promoted. A number of other army generals who, while not necessarily agreeing with Popular Unity, favoured the army remaining faithful to the Constitution, also resigned. General Prats' replacement was none other than General Pinochet. Other putschist officers took over control of the Navy, the Carabinieri Corps and the Air Force and a purge of progressive officers began even prior to the 11 September coup. When the coup itself took place a number of officers and soldiers refused to join it. Many were arrested and killed – soldiers, non-commissioned officers and officers – according to what a junta spokesman is reported to have told a *New York Times* correspondent on 28 September. This happened, for example, with the Buin Regiment, and with the NCO school, where opposition to the coup met with ruthless suppression.

The existence of conflicting trends within the armed forces shows that it was correct for Popular Unity not to treat the armed forces as a single, homogeneous, reactionary institution, but to encourage the more progressive personnel at all levels and strive to keep the balance in the armed forces against counter-revolution. This, as we have argued, could not be achieved solely in army terms. For this tactic to succeed it was necessary that there should have been an increasingly favourable balance in the country as a whole, and a condition of economic and political stability.

Popular Unity strove to achieve these conditions, but a combination of sustained external pressure and internal violence and sabotage prevented it from rallying the balance of political forces sufficiently behind it, especially those associated with the political centre and expressed in great part in the Christian Democrat Party. The refusal of the Christian Democrats in 1969 and 1970 to back a military coup then was decisive in influencing the majority of officers, and so the road was blocked at that time to the putschists. By September 1973, with the right-wing in the ascendant inside the Christian Democrat Party, neutrality on their part, let alone cooperation with Popular Unity, was ruled out, and last minute agreement to meet and talk produced nothing. The Christian

Democrats' assent to the coup was the last, fatal blow. Popular Unity had failed to widen its system of alliances. The counter-revolution, on the other hand, had extended its base,[54] and the way was at last open for the coup to succeed. It was this which was the basic characteristic of the situation.

An analysis by the Chilean Communist Party emphatically makes the same point, explaining:

There cannot be a favourable balance of forces at the military level, which can guarantee the success of the revolutionary process, if a favourable balance of political forces is not formed [i.e. in the country as a whole – J.W.], that is, *if the revolutionary forces do not manage to unite around them greater social forces than those that the enemies of the people can group*. And it was the consolidation of this prior, necessary condition that was not achieved in the period of the Popular Government – and *that determined, basically, our defeat*[55] (italics added).

An Italian Communist leader, dealing with the role of the middle strata and the policy of alliances, has written:

For all its distinctive character, the experience of Chile, too, confirms the importance and necessity of a correct, non-sectarian and non-extremist policy towards the middle strata. We consider that the Chilean army played the part of an executor, of the last actor in a scene already staged in terms of social class alliances.[56]

In other words, the counter-revolutionary action of the army became possible owing to the failure of Popular Unity to unite a majority of people in support of its aims.

There are those who present the argument as if the success of the coup was mainly due to the mistakes of Popular Unity and especially of the Chilean Communist Party. Mistakes were undoubtedly made, and the Communist Party, as well as other political parties of Popular Unity, has analysed a number of these. But a tendency to ascribe all setbacks of revolutionary movements to the *mistakes* made by the participants is a most unscientific way of analysing historical processes. Examination of objective circumstances as well as of subjective factors must be made. Those who took part in the Paris Commune made a number of mistakes, and Marx and Engels have analysed them at considerable length; but anyone who thinks that the Paris working people, by avoiding those mistakes, could have established a permanent island of socialism in the middle of nineteenth century Europe, does not really understand historic processes. The Bolsheviks made a number of mistakes in the 1905 revolution, and these have been analysed by Lenin; but if anyone thinks that a mere correction of the subjective errors in 1905 could have overcome the objective obstacles at that time, including the fact that the mass of the peasantry, as much as they hated the landlords, still believed in the Tsar and therefore did not understand the need to overthrow his tyrannical regime which was the mainstay of the feudal land system — then he or she does not really understand historic processes.

The basic problem in Chile was to extend the democratic alliance so as to embrace the overwhelming majority of the population. This was clearly understood by the Communist Party, but not so fully accepted by other Popular Unity parties.

In a very penetrating and thought-provoking study of the Chilean coup, Professor Sobelev[57] draws some very pertinent conclusions, some of which understandably have a significance beyond Chile itself, especially for a number of capitalist countries in which the relevant Communist Parties have worked out a strategy for a democratic change to socialism without civil war. There are aspects to his analysis, however, that are open to debate — and to be fair to Professor Sobelev, he makes it clear that the lessons which he draws from the coup are, to a considerable extent, tentative and that in his view further discussion is certainly needed. Yet it seems to me that his analysis tends to ignore the real relationship of class forces that existed in Chile. Further, a number of the measures which he believes could have made it possible to defeat the putschists are drawn to a large degree from the different experience of October 1917. Starting from the dubious premiss that Popular Unity had political power, backed by 'a relative majority'[58] — a concept the meaning of which is unclear — Professor Sobelev indirectly or directly criticises Popular Unity for not being able to hold on to its power. He is not consistent when dealing with the question of power. In one place he refers to there having been 'two centres of power in the country: the popular one that concentrated in its hands mostly the executive power in the person of President Allende and his government, and a reactionary centre that held in its hands legislative power, the judiciary, most of the state apparatus and the mass media'. In another place, drawing general conclusions, he writes that 'it seems that it is easier to take over power than to hold it', apparently ignoring his alternative assessment that political power in Chile was shared between 'two centres'.

Having, however, embraced this idea of 'dual power', Professor Sobelev tends to present matters in terms of October 1917, despite his repeated references to the 'new' experiences and lessons to be learnt from

Chile. Thus he argues that what was missing in Chile were 'all-embracing mass organisations', and here he cites the example of the Soviets in Russia. Certainly it was necessary for Popular Unity to back up its governmental and State activities with various forms of popular action, by political parties, by trade unions, by various forms of people's committees – and this was being attempted, even if inadequately – but the relevance of Soviets, which after all would only have had meaning if they had been armed, as they had been in Russia in 1917, is very doubtful. The Soviets in Russia in 1917 were armed because they arose in the midst of the First World War; and the 'national committees in European countries', also cited by Professor Sobelev, arose in the midst of the Second World War. In both instances the working people had certain practical possibilities, because of war conditions, to acquire arms. Chile in the period 1970 to 1973 was in a totally different situation.

This was a real dilemma for Popular Unity, arising not only from the fact that it did not enjoy majority support but also due to its whole strategy of seeking to influence the armed forces away from the manoeuvres of the counter-revolution. It was very different from the situation in Russia in October 1917 when it was a question of the armed Soviets *overthrowing* the bourgeois government of Kerensky. In Chile Popular Unity was *upholding* its own government. To have tried, in these circumstances, to establish armed mass organisations alongside the effort to produce changes within the armed forces could have hindered the latter task and, more dangerously, provoked army action much earlier, certainly before effective armed mass organisations could have been really established. Should Popular Unity have attempted a secret arming of the working people? To have done this on any worthwhile scale could hardly have been kept secret. The few arms that some workers had clearly been able to acquire, and which were used in an heroic but vain attempt to resist the tanks and planes of Pinochet's forces, only revealed the tragic inadequacies of the people's military preparations that were made under such conditions.

Professor Sobelev really fails to grapple with the question of the need for Popular Unity to win a majority to its side. Having called its initial 36·32 per cent a 'relative majority' (even its 44 per cent won in the 1973 elections was still a *minority*), he subsequently argues that 'an ill-organised majority' is a 'passive majority', and that what was required to break reaction's resistance was 'not simply a majority but a vigorously acting and firmly organised majority'. It is, of course, true, as we have pointed out earlier, that in assessing the relationship of forces mere numbers is not the whole story, and that the degree of organisation and mobilisation of one's forces is vital, but in the conditions of Chile the winning of a majority was essential. Yet Professor Sobelev appears to argue as if Popular Unity already had that majority, and as if the problem was that of organising this majority. His view on the question of a majority brings us back again to the idea of Soviet-type 'mass, all-embracing organisations', which would unite 'the majority of working people'. He even argues that the Popular Unity committees could themselves have been transformed into such bodies, and so become 'an embryo of power'.

Despite the criticisms that may be made of Professor Sobelev's analysis, he has nevertheless made a valuable contribution to the international revolutionary movement and its discussions on Chile by posing two vital questions. First, how is it possible within a strategy based on a constitutional, non-insurrectionary road, to bring about changes in the State, including above all in the armed forces and the police, changes not merely of a partial, transient character, but of a more permanent kind which will provide the possibility for the progressive forces to change society without counter-revolution being able to use these State institutions to block the people's path? Second, how to cope with the real danger point, the point of transition, when full power is not yet in the hands of the people but when they have formed a government and have begun the process of change? What must be done to enable the transition to continue? How can the resistance of the class enemy be prevented, or crushed? How can reaction's turn to illegality and violence be dealt with?

These tasks were not solved in Chile; and given the fact that Popular Unity never enjoyed majority support, their difficulties were of a specific kind. Could the coup, then, have been avoided? Yes, if a majority had been won, if the middle strata or substantial sections of it, had been won, if the Christian Democrats or a majority of them had been won, if not to wholehearted support for Popular Unity, at least to uphold democracy and not back the counter-revolution. But this also required that the support of the working class and other popular forces needed to be mobilised for activity to counter the extra-parliamentary support of reaction. The two tasks were closely linked. If Popular Unity widened its base, but still failed to mobilise its forces for action, it could still have been toppled by a coup. If Popular Unity mobilised its support, but failed to extend its base, it would still have run the risk of being defeated by a coup. The question of the role of the armed forces is directly connected with these problems. By extending its base through winning decisive sections of the middle strata, and by mobilising its forces for activity, Popular Unity would have had the best chance to influence the army not to act; and if, despite Popular Unity's wider support and effective organising of the people, the army had struck, the strength of the divisions that would have then been expressed within it, combined with the majority support that Popular Unity would have won, would have provided the best opportunities for the coup to have been effectively resisted and overcome.[59]

Understandably, and despite his very relevant examination of the various economic and political steps which he considers Popular Unity could have taken to widen its social base, organise its own forces, and bring about democratic changes in the state, including in the armed forces, Professor Sobelev has to admit: 'It is very difficult, if not impossible altogether, for us to give a sufficiently substantial answer to the question of what specific measures could have been taken to prevent the reaction's armed action.' He even goes so far as to say that it is quite possible, given the weaknesses and mistakes of Popular Unity, with the working class unprepared to defend the revolution and the army in a strong position, that an armed clash would 'have resulted in an inevitable defeat'.

Professor Sobelev nevertheless draws the conclusion that 'not only the alignment of forces in favour of democracy in conditions of which reaction will not dare risk a civil war, constitutes an imperative condition of the peaceful development of the revolution, but also the permanent and real preparedness of the revolutionary vanguard and the masses to suppress by means of force the armed resistance of the bourgeoisie'. This brings us back once more to the real relationship of forces that was present in Chile. Popular Unity never enjoyed an alignment in its favour, and this itself was a major barrier to being able to deter or, if necessary, forcibly prevent reaction's armed suppression of the revolution.

In this connection it is interesting to note how Volodya Teitelboim, a leading member of the Chilean Communist Party, has outlined the relationship between the necessary force to stop the enemy and the winning of a majority of the people.

The people of Chile . . . did not have sufficient material strength to neutralise the forces of their armed enemies and make them respect their – the people's moral – strength. . . . The important thing in a situation such as Chile's is that the people must be stronger than their enemy. Only then can democracy and freedom triumph. The people's strength is the best constitutional guarantee of the existence of a legally-constituted state.[60]

But he then goes on to point out that to achieve such strength 'the greatest possible unity of all forces is a vital necessity', a unity of the proletariat, the peasants, and 'broad sections of the middle classes', a unity which embraces 'the greater part of the nation, including the democratic elements in the armed forces'.

In a later analysis[61] Teitelboim makes a sharper criticism of the weaknesses of Popular Unity and of the Communist Party, in particular its tendency, as he sees it, to become too wedded to a single scenario for revolutionary change, namely a path without civil war and through the utilisation of the constitution and the existing institutions. Stressing the need to turn an electoral majority into a political majority, an active majority ready to uphold 'by every possible means' the gains made, he criticises the fact that 'during the revolutionary process in Chile, the forms of struggle were considered as important as its goals. Form was exalted to the rank of substance, as it were, and an absolute was made of one path. This was undoubtedly a mistake, for when the concrete situation changed, the masses found their hands tied.'

Yet, how could the change in the form of struggle be effected? 'Adequate military support' and the backing of 'the section of the army loyal to the revolution' was essential. But, as Teitelboim points out, the 'political factor certainly played the main role in the interconnection of the political and the military factor'.

It was, he said, necessary to be prepared to 'change horses' and adopt different forms of struggle when the situation changed. But, 'this is not a matter that can be settled at the moment of change; it requires advance preparations, which may even take years, and this is what Chile's popular movement failed to do'. Instead, in his view, the movement stuck mistakenly to legality and looked upon preparations for other forms of struggle as unacceptable.

It is not always clear from Teitelboim's argument whether he means that irrespective as to whether it had built up a popular majority or not, the Party and the movement should have prepared for armed struggle. He constantly returns to the vital need to have created an active majority on the side of Popular Unity, a majority ready to adopt 'effective defence measures'. At the same time, he points out that 'the peaceful path' would have been possible 'if the idea of the revolution' had won 'the minds of the majority of the people' and prompted it 'to act'.

All this really begs the question. The argument seems to run as follows: an active majority, ready to act, would have made a 'peaceful path' possible; our weakness was that we had not prepared for alternative forms of struggle, for a 'non-peaceful path'. This is true, up to a point; but it only brings us back again to the problem of the alignment of forces, and, in particular, the winning of a majority. Popular Unity, as Teitelboim has pointed out himself on many occasions, had not won the majority. In these conditions, surely to have embarked on alternative forms of struggle, could have proved to be a dangerous adventure?

The winning of the middle strata to the side of the working class and Popular Unity, the winning of a majority of the people, and the turning of that majority into a politically aware, organised, active majority, ready to defend its gains, would have had a decisive effect on the armed forces. It was this political task that was not achieved; and any presentation that seems to play down this question by the way it emphasises forms of struggle as if one can divorce them from the problem of winning the majority, prevents one learning fully the vital lessons from Chile's tragedy.

Thus we are driven back to the two key elements in the Chilean tragedy; the necessity for the revolutionary movement to enjoy the support of the majority, not only of the working class, but of the nation as a whole, and the necessity for the revolution to organise for active struggle the strongest forces so that it can bring to bear the maximum pressure against the enemy. Weaknesses of the revolution in Chile arising out of the objective conditions, combined with errors committed by Popular Unity, including the Communist Party, hindered the winning of a powerful majority (and to achieve that, winning the middle strata was vital); and this fact, together with other objective difficulties and subjective mistakes, made it impossible to mobilise and organise the necessary strength to stop the coup.

Defeating the coup once it had begun was never a serious possibility in those circumstances. Not only is it always difficult to fight from such a defensive position, with the enemy having the initiative. The point was that the battle had to be won *before* the coup had commenced. Having lost the struggle to secure the most favourable alignment of political forces prior to 11 September 1973, Popular Unity was in no position to snatch victory from the jaws of defeat on 11 September itself nor in the ensuing days and weeks. Resistance there was, and many lost their lives in that heroic attempt to thwart the enemy. But within a few days it was evident that the revolution had been struck a deadly blow, against the consequences of which, the Chilean people are now struggling to repair their forces sufficiently to take the initiative again, remove the junta from power and resume their march towards socialism.

NOTES

1 Since driven underground by Bordaberry's repressive dictatorship.
2 In 1971 the Social Democrat Party merged with the Radical Party.
3 In 1973, after the March Congressional elections, MAPU itself suffered a split, a new organisation being set up called MAPU (Workers and Peasants), which also adhered to the Popular Unity coalition.
4 The two are obviously not always identical. There can be a civil war without a coup, leading to a victory for the revolutionary forces; and there can be a coup without a civil war, with a sudden, powerful military blow temporarily crushing all organised resistance.
5 Allende obtained only 39,000 votes more than the Nationalist candidate in a total vote of some three million.
6 The *El Arrayan Report*.
7 These figures are taken from the *El Arrayan Report*. Different figures are provided by a leading Chilean Communist, Orlando Millas, who writes that production in the large mines rose from 540,000 to 571,000 (in 1971), but that output in the medium and small mines fell from 151,000 to 127,000 (1971). This gives a combined figure for 1971 of 698,000, compared with 691,000 in 1970. (See *World Marxist Review*, November, 1975, p. 33.) The more restrained estimate given by Orlando Millas is generally regarded as more accurate.
8 'Alleged Assassination Plots Involving Foreign Leaders'; 'An Interim Report of the Select Committee to Study Governmental Operations with respect to Intelligence Activities': United States Senate, Washington, 20 November 1975 (Report No. 94–465) (hereafter referred to as 'Select Committee Report').
9 Financial support for Frei's 1964 campaign came also from West Germany.
10 Select Committee Report, op. cit., p. 229.
11 A special US State security committee then headed by the US Secretary of State, Henry Kissinger.
12 Select Committee Report, op. cit., p. 229.
13 ibid.
14 Later exposed in the Watergate scandal.
15 Select Committee Report; op. cit., p. 227.
16 ibid., p. 228.
17 ibid.
18 ibid., p. 225.
19 i.e. prior to Allende's parliamentary endorsement as President on 24 October.
20 Select Committee Report, op. cit., p. 230.
21 Under the Constitution of Chile a President cannot run for two successive terms of office.
22 Select Committee Report; op. cit., p. 231.
23 ibid., p. 231.
24 ibid.
25 ibid., p. 233.

26 ibid., p. 254.

27 *Inside the Company*, op. cit.

28 William Shawcross, *New Statesman*, 21 September 1973.

29 Orlando Millas, 'From Economic Subversion to Fascist Putsch', *World Marxist Review*, November 1975, p. 33.

30 Orlando Millas, op. cit. See also Hugo Fazio, 'Analysing Lessons of the Past in the Interests of the Future', *World Marxist Review*, April 1976.

31 Millas, op. cit.

32 See above, pp. 160–63.

33 *Guardian*, 28 August 1973.

34 Richard Gott, *Guardian*, 9 November 1972.

35 This was understood in international Communist circles, despite the attempts of some commentators to claim that Communists had illusions about the 'peaceful' possibilities of advance in Chile. The present author, for example, envisaged over a year before it happened the possibility of Chilean Popular Unity being defeated by a violent coup (see *New Theories of Revolution*, London, 1972, p. 252).

36 Corvalan, 'Chile: The People Take Over', *World Marxist Review*, December 1970.

37 See English translation in *Marxism Today*, September 1973.

38 The transformation of voters into conscious and active defenders of the Popular Unity Government could not be achieved only by 'dialogue' and 'ideological discussion', nor was the political conviction, which Allende rightly noted existed among the core of the working class, obtained in that way. It needed, in addition to ideological work, experience of political activity and struggle, experience derived from democratic participation in building the new society for which the supporters of Popular Unity were striving. This is why the *El Arrayan Report*, with the full support of the Communist Party, placed so much stress on the need to involve the people in all aspects of implementing the Popular Unity programme.

39 In one of his lectures on fascism Palmiro Togliatti pointed out that the 'mobilisation of the petty bourgeoisie' was a vital element in the installation of the fascist regime in Italy (*Lectures on Fascism*, London, 1976, pp. 7–8).

40 She obtained 53·6 per cent of the vote; the combined opposition vote of 44·9 per cent was 8,000 votes less than the joint votes of the two reactionary parties when they stood separately in 1970. Of special significance, there was a big increase in the Popular Unity vote amongst women, traditional supporters of the two big opposition parties; in seven out of the fifteen communes in the constituency there was actually a majority of women voting for the Popular Unity candidate.

41 Figures provided by Ralph Miliband ('The Coup in Chile', *Socialist Register 1973*, p. 458, London, 1974), compiled from 'United Nations sources' show that while the share of the national income of the poorest 50 per cent of the population increased from 16·1 per cent to 17·6 per cent, and that of the richest 5 per cent dropped from 30 per cent to 24·7 per cent, that of the 45 per cent making up the middle strata went up from 53·9 per cent to 57·7 per cent. In other words, the latter actually came off best under the Popular Unity government. Yet these economic benefits were not sufficient to win them for radical change.

42 Togliatti, op. cit., p. 11.

43 It is true that, to mount this procession of some 400,000, it was necessary to bring forces from outside Paris; but this does not invalidate the argument above.

44 See below for an examination of events in Portugal.

45 Enrico Berlinguer, 'Reflections After the Events in Chile', *Rinascita*, 28 September–12 October 1973 (English version in *Marxism Today*, February 1974).

46 op. cit.

47 Corvalan, 'Chile: The People Take Over', *World Marxist Review*, December 1970.

48 I. Zorina, 'People's Unity and Bourgeois Democracy', *Unity*, No. 8, 1972 (Moscow).

49 Corvalan, op. cit.

50 Similar to the tactics used in Indonesia (see above, pp. 148–9).

51 Obviously, many of those who were coup-minded preferred not to admit it; the percentage must have been much higher than 3.

52 Just as the Chilean army had a reactionary past (noted above), so it has, too, some progressive traditions, especially in the 1930s, arising out of the economic crisis, and to be explained, in part, by the changing social composition of the officer corps. In 1931, young naval officers backed strikers in Valparaiso, some even raising the red flag on their warships. In 1932, General Marmaduke Grove, Commander of the Air Force, seized power and proclaimed Chile a 'socialist republic'. It fell after twelve days, but not before it had enacted a number of progressive decrees, some of which were later to be used by the Popular Unity Government. In 1933, General Grove and Salvador Allende helped found the Socialist Party.

53 As has been mentioned, even after the coup, when General Prats went into exile in Argentina, his enemies pursued him and eventually assassinated him, just as they had killed his predecessor, General Schneider.

54 It is an irony of the situation, expressive of the fascist character of the Pinochet regime, that although Pinochet relied on the Nationalist and Christian Democrat Parties to provide him with a substantial base for proceeding with his coup, once the Allende Government had been overthrown Pinochet made it clear that there would be no role for either Party. Some leading personnel of the Nationalists were found posts in the new regime, and offers were made to – and refused by – Frei, the Christian Democrat leader. But neither of these two parties, notwithstanding their support for the coup, are allowed to carry on political activity, and no political party system exists.

55 'The Trojan Horse', statement of the central committee of the Chilean Communist Party, September 1973.

56 Rodolfo Mechini, 'The Middle Strata and the Policy of Alliances', *World Marxist Review*, No. 10, 1976.

57 Professor Alexander Sobelev, 'Revolution and Counter-revolution: Chile's Experience and Problems of Class Struggle', *Rabochy Klass i Sovremenny Mir*, No. 2, Moscow, 1974.

58 Actually 36·32 per cent of the votes at the 1970 elections.

59 Santiago Carrillo (*Dialogue on Spain*, London, 1976) draws the following three interesting lessons from the experience of Chile: '1. It is essential for the proletariat to remain allied with the middle strata and not to become isolated. 2. If you try to carry out a socialist experiment along the democratic road and if you don't have the support of the majority of the people, you must be able to resign in good time from government, so that tension does not degenerate into civil war, and must submit the question to universal suffrage. And you must retire if necessary, so that you can try to return later, when you are stronger. 3. When you propose to remain in power, you should take all the necessary measures to fight at the right time, if the enemy abandons legality and resorts to force' (p. 187).

60 V. Teitelboim, 'Reflections on the Chilean Developments', *New Times*, No. 42, October 1973.
61 V. Teitelboim, 'Reflections on the 1,000 Days of Popular Unity's Rule', *World Marxist Review*, No. 1, January 1977.

12

Portugal – An Army Won and Lost

On 11 September 1973, the Chilean army overthrew a democratic government and established a fascist-type tyranny. On 25 April 1974, the Portuguese army overthrew a fascist government and opened up the way to the establishment of a democratic system. These two entirely dissimilar events serve to illustrate, in fact, a common truth as to the relationship between the state of political thinking and activity of the civilian population, and the role of the armed forces in politics. This common truth is that the army is not an isolated institution, operating in absolute seclusion, but, on the contrary, is increasingly subject to the tidal waves of political thought and activity that drag ever increasing numbers of people in their wake. Which way the army turns, whose politics and economic interests it serves, is not determined in the last resort by events within the armed forces but by the total relationship of class and political forces in the country as a whole. Those who are inclined to think that all wisdom on this point is contained in Mao Tse-tung's formulation that 'Political power grows out of a barrel of a gun', should remember that Mao himself affirmed:

Weapons are an important factor in war, but not the decisive factor; it is people, not things, that are decisive (*On Protracted War*).

The experience of Portugal is very instructive, for here we have an example of an army, with a radical, organised armed forces movement, playing a key role in toppling fascism, in drawing the people along the democratic road and even in the direction of socialism, only to become enmeshed subsequently in political division, to become itself divided, to lose its popularity among the people, to see part of its forces involved in a foolish leftist adventure, and finally to lurch to the right. The tortuous path followed by the armed forces in Portugal can in no way be explained solely in terms of internal strains, divergences and personality conflicts within the armed forces themselves. The road followed by the armed forces has its origins in the total politics of Portugal, especially in the past three years.

Primarily we are concerned with two questions. Why did the army of Portuguese fascism and colonialism become an army of anti-fascism and anti-colonialism? Why, having succeeded with the active support of the people in achieving its two goals of overthrowing fascism and ending the Portuguese colonial system in Africa, did the army end up, within a comparatively short time, swinging the helm over from 'Direction – socialism' to 'Direction – bourgeois democracy'?

It can, of course, be argued that the helm has not swung that far. After all, the Constitution, officially supported by the armed forces, affirms the gains of the revolution, including nationalisation and land reform, and sets out the aim of socialism, not bourgeois-democracy. This is true, yet the Sixth Provisional Government, after the downfall of the Gonçalves Government, as well as the first Government under the new Constitution, the Government headed by Mario Soares, have been governments striving to halt the march to socialism, undo important gains of the revolution and restrict Portugal to the framework of a bourgeois-democratic system. The armed forces have not, in any meaningful way, opposed this evolution.

To deal adequately with the problem as to why the armed forces moved from their revolutionary position of 25 April 1974 and from their role throughout the period prior to the Sixth Provisional Government over to their subsequent non-revolutionary position, it is necessary to extend one's survey a little more widely, beyond the confines of the armed forces themselves, to examine the total character of the Portuguese revolution of 1974–5, to assess the role played in it by the various social classes and strata, and to consider the attitude, strategy and tactics of different political forces and parties.

What was the character of the 25 April revolution? It was a democratic, anti-fascist revolution, which included anti-colonial aims. Its immediate task was to overthrow the fascist regime of Caetano, enable people to enjoy full democratic rights, end the colonial wars in Africa, and allow the former oppressed peoples to exercise their full rights of independence and liberation. Portuguese fascism was overthrown without loss of life and relatively peacefully. This was due to the wide anti-fascist unity of the people and to the vital role played by the anti-fascists in the army, organised in the Armed Forces Movement (AFM). The revolution was supported by a wide array of social and political forces – workers, peasants, students and intellectuals, small and medium traders, producers and businessmen, technicians and professional people – in fact, the overwhelming majority of the

population. To one degree or another, they all support the action of 25
April and rejoiced in ending the nightmare of fascism. But this wide
spectrum of people also reflected many political tendencies. There were
a number of complexities in the situation. Dissimilar movements,
different class interests, contrary political and social tendencies with
varying aims merged in the single action to end the Caetano fascist
regime. Even the Spinola group of officers played a certain objectively
progressive role on 25 April 1974, narrowing the base for any fascist
generals who might otherwise have tried to organise armed resistance at
that vital hour.

To many people outside Portugal the events of 25 April, and in
particular, the role of the armed forces, came as a considerable surprise.
In fact, it was an understandable climax to a process that had been
gathering strength over the years, a process in which mounting anti-
fascist struggles by the civilian population in Portugal and an advancing
tide of national liberation war in Africa marched in harness with ever-
increasing strain and discontent inside the armed forces. There were
factors within the armed forces that contributed towards the growing
army discontent and to the emergence of the Armed Forces Movement as
an organised and politically oriented movement of officers – captains to
be more precise – who decided to act in order to remove the basic causes
of disquiet amongst their army colleagues and amongst the soldiers. But
the two major causes of the armed forces action of 25 April were the
mounting democratic struggle inside Portugal and the national
liberation wars in Africa, which led to the conviction inside the armed
forces that they must act in order to end fascism and end the colonial
wars.

Explaining the overthrow of fascism, Alvaro Cunhal, in an interview
a few days after the army action, said:

The successful armed forces uprising of 25 April was not a bolt from the blue. It
was the culmination of a lengthy process conditioned by factors such as the crisis
of the fascist regime, the economic, social and political consequences of the
colonial war, the isolation and world public condemnation of Portuguese
fascism and colonialism, and the success of the liberation movements in Guinea-
Bissau, Mozambique and Angola, as well as the wide-scale struggle of the
Portuguese people. . . . The conception prevalent abroad that the Portuguese
people are indifferent to politics is completely false.[1] On the contrary, the
popular struggle against the fascist regime and its unceasing and savage
repression developed into a powerful national movement.

'The broad support enjoyed by the united democratic movement of

Communists, Socialists and Catholics was demonstrated once again during the October campaign last year when over 200 meetings attended by a total of 20,000 people were held. Clear proof of the organised strength of the working class was the wave of strikes which has spread throughout the country during the past few months, the meetings of thousands of working people, and the fact that the trade union movement has been able to wrest from government control dozens of fascist trade unions with a membership of over half a million. The student movement, in which all legal students' associations are involved, has conducted demonstrations, meetings and strikes that at times have paralysed the work of colleges for months. The movements of young workers and women are also important segments of the popular struggle. The struggle against the colonial wars has developed into a powerful mass movement, and throughout the country the call to put an end to the war became more insistent. The number of deserters and draft dodgers has now topped the 100,000 mark, and for some time the revolutionary struggle has directly affected the colonial military administration.

'The dissatisfaction in the armed forces grew more apparent. From 1973 onwards there was hard evidence in more than 50 military units of opposition by soldiers, NCOs and young officers. These units included five infantry regiments, five artillery regiments, four air bases, six naval sub-units, eight military schools, as well as cavalry units, anti-aircraft batteries, military hospitals, arsenals, etc. The armed forces had ceased to be the traditionally stable support of the regime. Considerable success had been achieved in bringing the armed forces over to the cause of freedom.[2]

Undoubtedly the national liberation wars in Africa had a major influence on the Portuguese armed forces. Speaking to the press in the Mozambiquan capital of Maputo (formerly Lourenço Marques) a short time after the overthrow of Caetano, General Costa Gomes, then Portuguese Chief of Staff and later President of Portugal, stated: 'Our armed forces have reached the limits of neuro-psychological exhaustion.'[3] They had had enough, and concluded that the only way out was to end the war – and that to end the war the metropolitan regime had to be removed.

It was only over a period of years that the armed forces had reached this conclusion. There had been, in fact, throughout the fifty years of fascist rule, attempts by groups in the armed forces to take military action against the regime – notably in 1947, 1949 and 1959 and 1962. In the decade prior to 25 April 1974 the mounting wave of discontent in the armed forces took a number of forms. In his important book, *The Path to Victory*, first issued in 1964 (ten years' before the overthrow of fascism), Alvaro Cunhal shows how already then, when the colonial wars had only just begun, there were growing signs of protest and disaffection inside the armed forces which were the product of the struggles of the Portuguese people against fascism.

The great political battles of the Portuguese people against dictatorship during the past few years (the big street demonstrations, the strikes in the countryside, the students' struggles) lie at the root of the political radicalisation of the soldiers and of increasingly large sections of the officers. It is this which explains the fact that in the struggles conducted in the armed forces, an outstanding part has been played both by workers and peasants from industrial centres and rural areas where mighty struggles have been taking place and where the Party's position is particularly strong, and by military officers who obtained their political education in the strong student movement.

Cunhal goes on to point out that the subsequent resistance by the men in the armed forces to the colonial wars added 'a new element' to the fight against the fascist dictatorship, at the same time bearing witness to the growing weakness of Salazar's state machine and to the political radicalisation of the people. The three years up to 1964 had produced, in fact, soldiers' struggles that could be numbered 'in their hundreds'. Cunhal provides a really extraordinary detailed list of incidents involving soldiers in varying forms of resistance, in which he cites the names of the different regiments in which the protest actions took place, the actual location where they occurred, the particular form of protest used, often the number of soldiers involved. Many of these were directly linked with the war in Angola, and took the form of resistance to mobilisation and posting to Africa, expressed in actions on local parades, in barracks, on ships and in military hospitals. Forms of action included refusing to commence training, disobeying orders to disperse, holding up embarkation, openly siding with civilians demonstrating against the departure of troops for the colonial wars, and large scale desertions. Often the desertion was not from the armed forces as such but took the form of large groups of soldiers abandoning their mustering centres for overseas duty and returning to their original barracks. Cases of disobedience by soldiers to officers' orders had grown, sometimes taking mass form, and including sit-downs on parade, the physical prevention of officers taking action against rebel soldiers' leaders, and even resulting at times in soldiers giving officers a thrashing. Other minor acts of insubordination had included the breaking of barrack windows, setting fire to bunks and destroying furniture, and outbursts in the mess in protest against poor food or against arbitrary actions by officers, hunger-strikes, boycotts of amusements organised for the troops, total silence at meal-times, and so on. On top of all these multi-form activities there were, of course, an untold number of individual actions of protest by soldiers and even officers.

A significant aspect of the growth of radical ideas amongst the soldiers to which Cunhal drew attention was their participation in civilian mass movements, notably their stand on May Day 1962 and again on May Day 1963, when they stood side by side with the people of Lisbon demonstrating for political freedom. At the same time there was already, even more than a decade before the overthrow of fascism, signs of soldiers' struggles actually taking place in the Portuguese colonies. Starting with demands protesting against delays in receiving their regular pay, the soldiers soon moved on to expressing their opposition to the colonial war and to their fascist commanders, as shown for example in the actions of the Paratroop Rifle Battalion in Luanda in 1961 and 1962.

The struggle [wrote Cunhal] reached its highest point with a meeting of soldiers on Luanda Island. Profiting from the presence of the Battalion's three companies in April 1962, over 300 men in uniform, with orderlies standing guard, held an assembly which elected a control committee for each company, approved the demands to be submitted and decided that no soldier was to make the jump from his plane from that moment onwards. . . . The soldiers extended their contracts with other units and prepared a revolt which would have covered Luanda.[4]

Unfortunately, the movement was betrayed, the conspiracy uncovered and the leaders arrested.

The remarkable thing about all these actions, which continued to grow in the following years, was that, apart from some 'isolated actions' by officers they were mainly taken by soldiers who, in consequence, were often brought into conflict with the officers. The action of 25 April 1974, however, was led by officers, not the highest ranking, but at the level of captains. The earlier struggles of the soldiers, who themselves were moved into action as a result of the activities of the Portuguese people and later under the impact of the national liberation movements in Africa, were one of the factors which resulted in the radicalisation of the officers themselves.

Without the action of the Communist Party, asserts Cunhal, the soldiers' protest actions would not have taken place.

They are due, to a decisive extent, to the Party's political action against the colonial war, to the correctness of the Party's watchwords. In many cases, it was the Party organisation in the armed forces, or isolated communists, who boldly took the lead in these movements. In other cases it was the agitational work of the Party, it was the millions of Party leaflets and manifestos, which gave direction to the militancy of the sons of the people in uniform. . . . The struggles waged by the soldiers since 1961 are a new element in the Portuguese democratic movement: they are an indication of the crisis of the regime and of the *approach* of a revolutionary crisis.

It was to be another ten years before the 'approach' had matured sufficiently for the regime to be toppled, but clearly the physical blow struck on 25 April 1974 was not just an isolated action by a conspiratorial group of army captains who set up their organisation only a year or so before the actual overthrow. It was the climax to years of struggle – by workers, peasants, students, intellectuals and technicians, and not least, by rank and file soldiers.

If the soldiers had become radicalised as a result of the Portuguese people's democratic struggles and under the impact of the national liberation wars, the process that took place amongst the officers was somewhat more complicated. It would be entirely wrong to think that the motives of those officers who took part in the 25 April action, or who backed it, were uniform, let alone clear and sharp. The army was being put in an impossible position. It was being asked to wage three wars in Africa which, it became increasingly clear, it could not win. The pride and prestige of the officers was under attack. They felt humiliated. Their whole position and future, their reputation and their institution, the armed forces, was at stake. They were finding it more and more difficult to sustain any respect and obedience from their own troops. They were being outfought in the guerrilla war. They were acquiring a new understanding of, and even respect for their opponents, the national liberation movements of Angola, Mozambique and Guinea-Bissau. They felt they had more than met their match in the outstanding leaders of these movements.

There were other causes of resentment, some connected with the changing composition of the officer corps itself. Previously the officer class had come mainly from the aristocracy, buttressed by those who came from the ranks of the upper bourgeoisie together with others associated with these two classes. But Portugal's crisis, and especially the colonial wars in Africa, necessitated a rapid growth of the armed forces which reached no less than 200,000 by April 1974 – and this for a country with a population less than a fifth that of Britain. A consequence of this unprecedented growth was the need for a much larger officer corps. This could no longer be based on the sons of the upper ranks of Portuguese society.

. . . by the mid-1960s with the rapid expansion of the armed forces for the African wars, it was apparent that this group [those linked with the aristocracy and the big bourgeoisie – J.W.] was represented only by some of the most senior officers; the younger officers resented their social pretensions and were men of simpler mould. At the same time they also resented the later attempts, in the summer of 1973, of the Caetano regime to placate the militia or conscript officers by offering them advanced promotion, which seemed to the younger regulars to jeopardise their own chances of promotion. The emergence of the AFM, which only later became a *political* movement, arose from these exclusively *regular* ranks.[5]

At the same time, this 'Conflict Studies' report argues, 'the majority of the regular officers of the armed forces were largely non-political', even though 'a militant minority' had become the dominant group in the AFM.

A somewhat similar analysis of the composition of the armed forces has been provided by the *Sunday Times* 'Insight Team'. Noting that before the African wars the Portuguese army had become 'a highly stratified, class-ridden institution', with poorer peasants and Africans in the colonies supplying most of the ranks, while the officers came from the aristocracy and 'the emerging wealthy bourgeoisie', the 'Insight Team' noted:

The military hierarchy was closely intertwined with the professional and financial establishment – and of necessity since officers were badly paid. In metropolitan Portugal generals sat on the boards of large companies and the expertise gained from military training – in engineering, for example – made it easy for middle-rank officers to boost their pay with consultancy positions in commerce. . . . As the prospect of war service grew, recruitment to the officer academies fell dramatically, and with it the requirements for entry. . . . The men who now came forward for a military career were inevitably a different breed: few came from well-known Lisbon families, most were from the provinces. Many also came from the overseas colonies, where they could already see that their future careers would be insecure. . . . The lowering of the entry qualifications to the Military Academy and the increased pay of young officers in the Sixties also meant that many young people who could not afford a university education but wanted to go on with their studies opted for the Academy . . . much of the radical driving force behind the conspiracies of 1973 came from precisely these young men in their early thirties who had passed through the Military Academy immediately after the outbreak of the African wars in 1961–3. The sons of petit-bourgeois parents who were to be undermined by inflation and threatened by decolonisation, they were the first generation of Portuguese officers to rise to the ranks of lieutenant and captain under war conditions. While politicians and generals directed their fate from Lisbon, it was they who had to take command of men in the swamps, jungles and savannahs of Africa. It was they who came into contact with the guerrillas, who had to assess guerrilla motivation, counter their tactics – frequently be killed by them.[6]

The very repression they meted out to the African villagers and the liberation movements deepened their awareness of what was happening:

Faced also with the practical Marxism of the guerrilla movements, expressed in their interrogation sessions with prisoners and in the villages they were trying to 'subdue', some of them began to see their predicament back in Portugal in a new light.[7]

It should be remembered, too, that many young officers had passed through university where they had already been in contact with radical and even Marxist ideas. Ironically, however, an immediate factor which influenced the setting up of the Armed Forces Movement (AFM) was the resentment felt by the regular officers towards the new, rapidly promoted university graduate conscripts. By the summer of 1973 the Government was really desperate for junior and middle rank officers. Normal recruitment could no longer fill the gaps. University graduate conscripts who had already done their military service were an obvious source to take on duties as officers. In the normal way they would have been obliged, as ex-conscript officers (known as *milicianos*) to have entered the Military Academy and then, only after graduation, been given their seniority. In July the Minister of Defence scrapped this system and introduced in its place a rapid promotion procedure which allowed the *milicianos* to jump over the regular officers in the promotion stakes. Conscript officers returning to a regular corps were now allowed to count their conscript service towards their promotion period; their Military Academy training was to be only two half-year semesters compared with four years for regular entrants.

This decree aroused considerable disquiet and hostility amongst the regular officers. Most of them had entered the army in order to obtain a higher education which their families could not afford. The *milicianos*, on the other hand, came from comparatively wealthy backgrounds. The professional officer corps felt threatened and humiliated by the new proposal; so much so, that there was an immediate flood of protests from them to the Government and to the senior military officials. Letters of protest signed by 151 regular officers referred to the wound inflicted on 'the dignity, prestige and professional *brio*' of the regular officer corps.[8]

The Government refused to respond to the protest in any meaningful way, even though the protest had gained the support of the army Chief of Staff, General Costa Gomes, who had been involved in the abortive coup of 1961. This blunt rejection of their protests by the Government was, in a sense, the last straw. Feeling that their prestige, their careers, their lives were being cynically ignored by the Government, facing a war which they increasingly realised they could not win, and aware of the growing mass discontent inside Portugal itself, they came to the conclusion that armed action to remove the government was the only option now open to them. Politically they were in no sense homogeneous. Many were deeply conservative; but a number, including some who had studied social science, taken courses in Subversive Warfare at the Lisbon Institute for Higher Military Studies, read Marxism or been in touch with others who had done so, played a key role in the AFM and helped it to see that the overthrow of the Caetano fascist regime had to be followed by steps to introduce democracy and even press forward for a radical restructuring of society.

Despite the leadership role this radical grouping played inside the AFM, and despite the undoubted ideological influence they were able to exert over the officer corps and the ranks, too, especially in the first year after Caetano's overthrow, it would be wrong to consider that the majority of officers were soundly won for a socialist objective. They were profoundly disturbed by the wars in Africa and by developments in Portugal. They were anxious about their careers and their future. They realised that there had to be a break with fascism. But, deep down, the majority retained their conservative ideas, ideas that are more 'natural' to the professional officer, ideas of hierarchy and obedience, ideas that often spring from the social and economic and political circles from which they have come.

Dealing with the officer corps and their disposition to think in terms of a military coup, rather than seeing their action in relation to the mass upheaval of the people, Cunhal, while asserting that the Communist Party agreed with the radical officers that 'action by a part of the Armed Forces . . . (was) essential to the destruction of fascism', emphasised:

The officers are themselves of this or that social class. In the conditions so far existing in Portugal the formation of a military caste does not completely break the links between the military and the class of its origin. There are officers from the petty and middle bourgeoisie who are today servants of the monopolists. But there are still many non-fascist officers whose political feelings and dispositions are in sympathy with the feelings and dispositions of the petty and middle bourgeoisie. *Their decision to take part in revolutionary action will appear when these classes become engaged in open political struggle.* To count on their adhesion to and participation in a revolutionary movement unconnected with these circumstances is an illusion[9] (italics added).

This significant observation concerning the class and social origins of the officers, and the way in which their behaviour is largely influenced and even determined by the thoughts and behaviour of the social classes from which they come – an observation made by Cunhal ten years before the overthrow of Caetano – holds good for the entire period right up till today. This notwithstanding that some individual officers may have made such a radical break with their past that class and family ties can no longer influence, to any important degree, their political actions and loyalties. Yet, as we shall see, there developed a tendency after 25 April 1974 to regard the AFM virtually as an independent institution, with an autonomous role as a 'vanguard' of the people's struggle for democracy and socialism. This evaluation of the role of the AFM, this conception that the AFM could somehow hew a path for itself independent of the tug of events taking place in civilian life, of the clash of political parties, of the anxieties and activities of the families and classes with which the officers and soldiers were still linked by tradition, by habit, by common aspirations – this was, without doubt, a major cause of the difficulties in which the Portuguese revolution found itself from the beginning of 1975.

The complex class and social character of the officer corps of the Portuguese armed forces, and of the AFM itself, meant that, from the very beginning there was conflict within the armed forces and within the AFM; and this was so even at times when there seemed to be a high degree of unity and agreement. The conflict was mainly between those who wanted to press ahead for deep-going democratic change and those who wanted to limit the modifications so that, in essence, the capitalist system would remain intact.

But it would be wrong to think that the conflict was simply a right-left struggle. 25 April 1974 unleashed the people's initiative and thoughts after fifty years of dark repression. There was an outburst of ideas, theories, political trends, publications and organisations. The rash of posters and slogans that plastered the walls of Lisbon and other towns after Caetano's fall, the incredible variety of newspapers and journals that suddenly appeared, the never-ending flood of meetings, large and small, and the diverse nature of the speeches made at them – all this testified not only to the remarkable extent to which the people had begun to use the freedom they had won, but also to the turmoil of ideas and confusion which became one of the features of political life in

Portugal in 1974 and 1975. The entire complex of ideas which boiled up to the surface as a result of the overthrow of fascism affected the widest strata of the people and all major institutions, including the armed forces and the AFM. In these conditions, ultra-left trends exerted a not inconsiderable influence, especially in Lisbon and some other urban centres where they had an impact among some sections of workers, among students and intellectuals, journalists, professional people and government employees. Naturally enough, in such circumstances, and with thousands of young and politically inexperienced people flocking into the Communist Party in 1974 and 1975, such ultra-left ideas also found expression inside the Communist Party. On more than one occasion, in fact, Cunhal felt it necessary to warn his members and supporters against this error.

Alongside the emergence of the Socialist Party, the Communist Party, and the People's Democratic Party (PPD) and others to the right, a number of leftist parties appeared, including some openly identifying themselves with Trotskyism or Maoism. Within the armed forces and in the AFM all these political trends made themselves felt and had their supporters. Given the petty-bourgeois class nature of the 'captains' who had established and led the AFM, it is not surprising that petty-bourgeois politics, including varying forms of leftism, were also to find expression there. But there was also an understandable trend of military élitism which found expression sometimes on the left, and sometimes on the right, in both cases taking the form of a striving to establish a military domination over civilian life.

With fascism overthrown on 25 April, the question posed to the people was what should be the shape of the new Portugal. Differences on this big question naturally arose. Some of these differences were of a character which, under more favourable conditions, might have been contained within the framework of democratic unity. There were, however, other differences of a far more fundamental character which reflected the sharpening class struggle and the desire of sections of the people to press ahead towards socialism. These differences, since they involved basic conflict between different social classes, had to be fought out politically not only for the sake of Portugal's future, but also to consolidate the gains of the revolution and defeat those who wanted to freeze it at the stage of a mere change of government without seriously making any change in the system. Within that major clash there were, of course, other differences, often over tactical questions – such as how fast to advance, and how far; although these conflicting tactical views frequently expressed, in a particular form, the varying opinions of the different class forces towards the major problems which the revolution had to tackle.

These differences revolved around decisive economic, social and political questions. They included the nationalisation of major enterprises and the extent to which this should be carried out; land reform, its scope, character and ways of implementing it; the role of the AFM, the specific political functions for which it should be responsible, its relationship to other instruments of power and government, and its relations to political parties and mass organisations; the form of the democratic alliance, and the place of political parties within it; the question of democratic rights and the democratic control of the mass media; the new organs of power at the base and through which the people were beginning to exercise their democratic demands; the institutions in the new State, the Constituent Assembly and its sphere of activity, the role of elections in the revolutionary process; the trade unions, their method of organisation and their relationship to the law; decolonisation, how and when it should proceed; external policy in relation to NATO, the EEC, the major western countries, the socialist countries and the Third World.

The new Portugal also faced a number of acute problems such as unemployment, the balance of payments deficit, inflation, short and longer term questions of the structure of the economy, trading policy, ensuring a good harvest, introducing an effective control of the nationalised enterprises and tackling effectively problems of production and productivity, finding homes and jobs for thousands of settlers returning home from the former colonies in Africa, and so on.

On all these many questions there were big differences of opinion between the political parties as to what should be done; and increasingly, the AFM found itself having to take up an attitude to such matters. As things developed in Portugal after 25 April 1974 the armed forces became deeply involved in politics.

That the action of 25 April by the people and the AFM constituted a democratic, anti-fascist revolution is clear enough. That was its main thrust and purpose. But since Portuguese fascism rested on an economic basis of large estates and big monopolies and banks (which, apart from owning enterprises of many kinds, had a dominant control over the main national newspapers); and since it depended, too, on its exploitation of colonial possessions in Africa and Asia; and since the fascist superstructure, including the entire state and administration, excluded the people entirely from the country's political processes and spheres of decision – the most advanced sections of the Portuguese revolution, including the Communist Party, clearly considered that it was urgently necessary to press ahead and follow up the overthrow of fascism by destroying its roots.

This required nationalisation of the monopolies and far-reaching land reforms; a quick process of complete decolonisation, with the people of the African colonies allowed the full exercise of power; and the establishment of a new political and state structure in Portugal that would give people democratic rights as well as the democratic powers of participating in the management of the country's affairs. Such an advanced form of democracy meant that while the revolution would be basically democratic in character, the extent of nationalisation (60 per cent of all capital became state property, thus breaking the back of the former state monopoly capitalism), the deep-going land reform in the south which destroyed the system of large-scale private landownership, and the creation of new forms of people's power, opened up possibilities for the people to advance towards socialism.

Perhaps in the heady days of 1974 and 1975 such an advance may have appeared to many to be on the immediate order of the day. Certainly it was not uncommon to hear it politically argued that there were only two options for Portugal: either to push the revolution rapidly to socialism, or to fall back once again under fascism. The third option, that of an interim form of bourgeois democracy, even of an advanced kind with monopoly capitalism very much weakened, even if not completely destroyed, was not considered a real option – either for the capitalist class, or for the working people. Any attempt to establish a bourgeois-democratic regime, it was said, would fail, since in a country such as Portugal the bourgeoisie could only prosper (because of the backward state of their economy and their former reliance on colonial exploitation) by the most intense economic exploitation of their own working people. This, ran the argument, was out of the question if the people had the democratic possibilities of organising to resist such exploitation. Consequently any bourgeois-democratic path would rapidly lead back to the most intense repression, to fascism.

It is clearly true that the revolution could not stand still, and that any attempt to freeze it would provide opportunities for reaction to press for steps to rob the people of the gains they had made. But this did and does not necessarily rule out the possibility of there being an interim period during which this political choice – forward or backward – is being fought out; and this interim period, the length of which might be short or long, would be one in which the struggle would proceed in conditions approximating more to those of a bourgeois-democratic system.

One has to exercise some caution here, of course. After all, Portugal, even under the Soares Government, is not a normal bourgeois-democracy. The economy, for a start, is not 'normal', since the back of Portuguese monopoly capitalism has been broken. Further, Portugal is just emerging from a major revolutionary period; and even though the anti-fascist revolution, which dealt heavy blows to the whole system of monopoly capitalism, has suffered setbacks and the revolutionary process has been slowed up, the strength of the Communist Party and other left and democratic forces, and the difficulties facing any attempt by big capital to regain what it has lost, makes possible a new resurgence of the revolution.

But this is not inevitable. With the aid of the major Western powers, fresh injections of capital could help to bolster up a system of mixed-economy and steadily reassert the domination of big capital. Even the state-owned enterprises, including the banks, could be utilised by a government with a pro-capitalist policy to switch Portugal more decisively on to the road of monopoly capital. Portugal, therefore, faces a very complex future which it would be rash to assume can be presented in a clear-cut either-or position; either socialism or back to fascism. The road to socialism may well lie through a quasi-bourgeois democratic phase, albeit short, albeit not a classical form of bourgeois-democracy, albeit a phase in which major revolutionary initiatives and processes are intertwined with procedures and activities of a more constitutional character, more akin to those usually associated with normal bourgeois-democratic systems.

In the upheavals of 1974–5 it is possible that some forces on the left, including the Communist Party, did not fully take into account such possibilities. In the midst of such a sudden political explosion, when vast forces of the people are moving into action, when the very needs of the revolution demand that the process be pushed forward as far and as fast as is politically possible, when, indeed, the very act of pushing ahead is, to some extent, essential in order to estimate the relative strengths of the contending forces, it would be strange if there were no tendencies towards impetuosity or over-optimism. The vital thing is that a revolutionary Party should constantly assess and reassess the relationship of forces, and correctly estimate both its own strength and the understanding and mood of the people. A party can overreach itself. But if it comprehends this in good time, and organises a partial retreat in good order, it can ensure that it suffers no real losses and thus has time and opportunity to regroup its forces and prepare for the next test of strength.

The Portuguese revolution, it should be remembered, took place under unusual circumstances. Although there was a wide measure of anti-fascist unity built up prior to 25 April, there had been no firm agreement between all the anti-fascist forces for an economic, social and political programme to be implemented after the overthrow of fascism.

Further, although the Portuguese Communist Party and other anti-fascist forces played a major role in building up the people's democratic movement prior to the overthrow of Caetano, although the people's democratic movement in Portugal and the national liberation movements in Africa helped to produce the necessary progressive changes inside the armed forces, and although on 25 April itself and subsequently the actions of the people in Portugal, despite calls from the military not to go on the streets, were a vital contribution to the democratic victory, it was the AFM which struck the actual physical blow which finally toppled the regime.

The overthrow of Portuguese fascism involved both the armed forces and wide strata of the civilian population. It enjoyed the support of the vast majority of the people. Thus 25 April was not a coup, but a revolution.

Nevertheless, the AFM played a key role and consequently after 25 April it held decisive positions of power, with popular backing. This set its stamp on the character of the next phase of the revolution and on its course. The alliance of the people's movement and the AFM had defeated fascism. The alliance was the basis and best guarantee of safeguarding the revolution, carrying through major changes in the economic, social and political structure and opening up the road to socialism.

But because the AFM held the key levers of power, and because the civilian anti-fascist movement had not been able to hammer out a united programme prior to the overthrow of the old regime, the AFM programme became the basic programme for the progressive forces, rather than the AFM and the civilian movement joining together to work out a common programme around which the entire democratic movement could unite. It is irrelevant to discuss whether this should or should not have been the way to proceed. Things evolved in this way, and accordingly this was the reality that had to be faced by the Communist Party and other democratic forces.

It is hypocritical and senseless to argue, as some people do, that the army should play 'a non-political' role. The army is dragged into politics, as it were. But experiences from many countries tend to confirm – and the Portuguese experience underlines this – that there are complications, and even dangers, attached to the political role of the armed forces. An army is not a political party. Nor is an organisation set up within the armed forces, such as the AFM, a substitute for a political party, especially not for a working-class party, even though it be as progressive as the AFM. An army (and this goes for the AFM, too) reflects different social classes and political trends. Its leading circles have their own interests and connections which influence them; they also have their own ambitions, ambitions which are sometimes dangerous.

The working class should certainly seek to influence the armed forces in a progressive direction and seek forms of unity with them for specific democratic aims, and especially with its more politically advanced personnel. But neither the armed forces as a whole, nor a progressive body within the armed forces such as the AFM, can act as a vanguard of the revolution in conditions where the civilian population already has its own organisations, political parties and traditions of struggle. In such circumstances any attempt by the armed forces, or a section of it, to take on the role of political vanguard can create difficulties for the revolutionary movement, apart from the future dangers that such a precedent could provide. The working class can never subordinate itself to the armed forces, nor abandon its right to work for and win its own position as the leadership of the working people as a whole. It is not a question of the working class claiming an exclusive monopoly in advance, but of having the right and the possibilities of earning its leading position, and not having this usurped in exclusive fashion by the armed forces.

The necessity to avoid such a danger in no way lessens the positive significance of the role played by the AFM in overthrowing fascism. Further, the fact that after 25 April the majority of the AFM and indeed of the armed forces as a whole refused to take the Spinola road of counter-revolution but instead showed themselves willing to support those pressing forward for radical changes, including large-scale nationalisation of the monopolies and the taking over of the large estates, was a factor in the situation which the revolutionary forces could not but acclaim. Even after the lurch to the right in August 1975 following the fall of the Gonçalves Government, and even after the leftist adventure of November 1975, the armed forces were still ready to back the new Constitution with its declared aims of safeguarding the nationalisation measures and the land reform, and of pressing ahead to the goal of socialism.

Thus, while the AFM, because of its heterogeneous class and social character, was unable to fulfil the role of vanguard of the revolution, it undoubtedly had a key role to play in the revolutionary process. This is due not only to the fact that it was an *armed* institution whose reactions could not be ignored, but also because it demonstrated, despite the differences within its ranks, its support for progressive objectives, and its political capacity to make an important contribution to that end, even though its role was not consistent for reasons which we need to examine.

Throughout 1974 and 1975, on 25 April 1974 itself, during the Government crisis of July 1974, through the coup attempt of the 'silent march' of September 1974, and in the defeat of the Spinola-backed coup of March 1975, through the big struggles to take over the large estates and to nationalise the major monopolies, it was the unity between the AFM and the people's movement which was the main driving force of the revolution. Yet, in the last resort, it was – and still is – the activity, organisation and political perspective of the working class and its allies that is decisive. The unity of the working class with other progressive classes is vital. If the unity of the working class is seriously broken, then its ability to rally other class forces to its side is gravely impaired and this, in its turn, will weaken the links between the people's movement and the armed forces, with the consequent eruption of divisions within the armed forces themselves. This is what happened with the AFM.

The divisions that arose within the AFM and led to its decline were partly a reflection of the sharpened class struggle in the country; but they also reflected the division in the ranks of the working class and its allies, including the divisions between the Communist Party and the Socialist Party on the one hand (and divisions between the Communists and political forces further to the right of the Socialist Party), and, on the other hand, divisions created on the other flank by the activities of the ultra-left organisations.

As we have noted earlier, it would be wrong to regard the armed forces in a capitalist country as a uniform, monolithic institution which is always inevitably on the side of reaction and therefore always to be regarded as an enemy. It is true that under capitalism, and more emphatically under the fascist form of capitalist rule, the armed forces are part of the state power of the big monopolies and landowners, with the specific role of maintaining that power, if necessary by repressing the people. This was so in Portugal throughout the fifty years of fascist rule.

But an army is composed of people. Even though it is organised as a separate institution which, to a considerable extent, carries on its functions divorced from the people, it does not exist in a vacuum. It is part of society which itself is under a process of constant change. The impact of political events has its influence on different strata of people, in one direction or another. The army is not immune from this process, especially in periods of political crisis, and of rapid and tumultuous change. An army, it should be remembered, comprises people from different social classes, which have differing political aims and diverse opinions.

Under the impact of a political upheaval, such as has taken place in Portugal over the last few years since the overthrow of fascism, all the political tendencies to be found amongst the people, from ultra-right to extreme left, have found their expression in the Portuguese armed forces. Right-wing, traditionalist, liberal, social-democratic, Socialist and Communist – all have their supporters among the men in uniform. Ultra-leftism has also been expressed there, in many ways – sometimes in elementary forms of anarchism, indiscipline, impatience and lack of political experience. At times ultra-left trends have been more distinctly political, inspired by specific organisations in civilian life. there have been different trends at the top, as well as different trends at the bottom, among the rank and file soldiers, sailors and airmen.

Political variety in the armed forces and within the AFM itself was only to be expected, since there is political variety in society as a whole. The differences of political view within the AFM may not have become so sharp nor assumed the proportions of a major critical problem if unity of the democratic forces were maintained among the civilian population and its parties and organisations. Such latter unity is the key. A vital precondition for unity of the AFM in the vital days of 1975 was the unity of the civlian democratic movement – and central to that unity was the unity of Communists and Socialists. The experience of Portugal simply confirms the lesson of all Western European experience of the past fifty years and more, namely that disunity between Communists and Socialists opens the way to reaction.

The year 1975 was a highly critical one for the fate of the revolution, and also an extremely complex year with the main course of the revolution swinging forward and back between contradictory and contending tendencies. Up to March 1975 (the defeat of the Spinola coup) the revolution continued its great forward sweep. April to August 1975 constituted five months of tense struggle which ended in a victory for the Right tendency, with the forcing out of the Gonçalves Government. From August to November the struggle was still tense; and it ended with the ill-fated leftist action of part of the armed forces, and a consequent further drift to the right. Since then, both in the armed forces and in the State as a whole, as well as in government and civilian politics generally, the shift to the right has continued.

This summary should not be taken to mean that 1975 was a straightforward retreat by the revolution. Even within the setbacks there were gains – the building of the Communist Party and of mass organisations, including the trade unions, went ahead; the gains of land reform and nationalisation were maintained; there were a number of powerful actions by the working class in the towns and countryside; and the progressive movement continued to gain experience and increase its political understanding. Nevertheless, one can detect after the April 1975 elections a quite definite shift of balance in the total political situation, a shift to the right.

Yet, so complex and contradictory was the whole process of the revolution that even prior to the crushing of the Spinola coup of March 1975 there were indications of the emergence of more conservative tendencies. The 'Economic and Social Programme' issued by the AFM-dominated Government in February 1975 had not envisaged a decisive change in economic ownership of the major enterprises. It provided for 51 per cent state ownership of all the major mines, as well as oil and natural gas exploitation. Other nationalisation measures were included, but not the banks and insurance companies, which were the mainstay of the big conglomerates (horizontal monopolies that covered a comprehensive sweep of different manufactures and services), as well as being owners of the big national daily papers and financial sponsors of the PPD and the Centre Social Democrats (not to be confused with the Socialist Party).[10] With economic changes restricted to the above proposals, Portugal would have remained decisively capitalist, although with a considerable state sector. The programme also provided for the expropriation of large land holdings, but this measure, important as it was, would not have changed the character of the economy as a whole.

Spinola's attempted coup of March 1975 precipitated a sharp turn to the left. The eve of this coup revealed not only political tension in the country, but tension and division in the armed forces, with some officers finding it increasingly difficult to control their own troops. Elections at the end of February to the army and air force councils indicated the contradictions in the situation. Well-known participants in the events of 25 April 1974, such as Melo Antunes, Vasco Lourenço and the more leftist Otelo de Carvalho failed to get elected; but amongst those who were successful were two friends of Spinola. The failure of Spinola's coup on 11–12 March was quickly followed by economic and political changes which appeared to set Portugal on a left course. Under the pressure of the bank employees, and of the people generally, the banks were nationalised – and that meant that the big conglomerates and the national daily papers also came under the State.

At the same time, leading forces in the AFM moved to increase military control over the State and the Government. A new Supreme Revolutionary Council was established, replacing the former Council of State. The latter had included civilian representatives, but the former was a purely military body, and was made responsible solely to the general assembly of the AFM. The Supreme Revolutionary Council promised to proceed with the elections for April 1975, but it also assumed the right to veto any decision of the civilian government.

Thus March 1975 found Portugal in the midst of a most contradictory situation. Major democratic gains had been won by the people; mass organisations and political parties had been set up; far-reaching economic measures had been introduced, which broke the back of the former monopolists and big landowners. On the other hand, differences in the country as a whole as to what kind of new Portugal should be constructed were finding their expression inside the armed forces and the AFM. Intertwined with such political differences, there were also tensions inside the AFM, and between it, the civilian population and the political parties as to the extent to which the military should be involved in government and the State, and the form which such involvement should take.

There was a strong view within the AFM – at least, it appeared strong at the time, although subsequent events throw some doubt on the extent to which it was a firmly backed position – that the military were 'here to stay' as far as the political life of Portugal was concerned. This tendency was expressed partly in the 'pact with the Parties' which was agreed between them and the AFM on the eve of the election. Some officers gave the impression that they desired to go back on the promises of 25 April 1974, and intended to open up the way to a military domination of the Government and the State and of political life as a whole; the return to civilian rule, it would appear, was to be under the paternal but firm control of the military itself. Leading elements of the AFM, in the course of the 1975 election campaign, began to project ideas about forming a new party or 'new political force' which would be midway between the Communists and Socialists. Commander Jesuino, the then Minister of Information, went so far as to say that it had been 'an error' for the AFM to have allowed the formation of political parties which, in his view, were hampering the AFM's work through their constant conflicts with one another. So lacking in confidence in the political parties were sections of the AFM that they appealed to voters to leave their voting papers blank if they could not decide which party to vote for. This may have been an innocuous suggestion, but in the prevailing conditions, on top of statements by military leaders denigrating the political parties, it was widely interpreted as an attempt by the AFM to secure a powerful endorsement for itself; and this, it was argued, might then encourage the AFM to enter the political field still more directly, and independent from the political parties.

Whether these fears were exaggerated or not is now to some extent academic. But the tendencies were there; and the consequent anxieties among the people were there, too. These were weighty factors during and after the election. The campaign, the results, and the events which swiftly followed, produced an entirely new situation which, within sixteen months, was to change the balance of power inside the armed forces, in the Government, and in the country as a whole, over to the right.

There is no doubt that events following the elections to the Constituent Assembly in April 1975 helped to deepen the divisions among the civilian movement and this steadily accentuated divisions inside the AFM and the armed forces in general. It is arguable whether the elections should have been held so relatively early in view of the fact that the democratic revolution had scarcely touched the northern half of Portugal where the majority lived, or Madeira and the Azores. In these regions reaction is heavily entrenched, backed by a Church hierarchy which is amongst the most backward, conservative and obscurantist in the whole of Europe, and which had been a mainstay of fascism throughout its fifty years of tyranny. One has only to read the reports of journalists who have visited the North to realise the ignorant, super-stitious and almost medieval outlook of many of its inhabitants, especially in the countryside.

From the point of view of political progress, it would have been preferable if the Socialist and Communist Parties had, prior to the elections, agreed on a joint strategy. In a sense they did not need an agreement on policy so much, since they had both agreed to back the programme put forward by the AFM. But an agreement providing, for example, for joint lists, could have been beneficial to both Parties, and strengthened the position of the left as a whole.

Nevertheless, despite these shortcomings and the knowledge that intimidation of voters was likely in the backward North, the elections went ahead, even though they were for a Constituent Assembly with a specific function of preparing a Constitution, and were not for a Parliament. A massive 92 per cent of the electorate voted.

Elections, as we noticed in relation to the crisis in Chile, are never a sole index of the relationship of class forces. Class structure, the capacity of the different classes to unite and organise their forces, and the degree to which they are engaged in actual movement and struggle for their respective political goals, are key factors which a revolutionary party must take into account when weighing up the relative strengths of the contending class forces and, in consequence, deciding on its strategy and tactics. The position of the State and its institutions, including the armed forces, must also be included in each assessment. In a situation in which the majority of the people are not concerned about the results of a particular election – either because the conditions in which it has been held are so impossible (under severe repression, or in conditions which allow the results to be faked), or because the circumstances in the country are such that the people have found another revolutionary path more appropriate, as did the Russian workers when they 'by-passed' the elected Constituent Assembly and took power through their own elected organs, the Soviets – in such a situation a revolutionary party would accord such election results a limited weight in its total assessment.

How, then, is one to judge the results of the April 1975 Constituent Assembly elections in Portugal, and the events that ensued? A breakdown of the results reveals the nature of the problem. Overall, the Communist Party which had been the main party of the anti-fascist resistance, received some 700,000 votes, 12·53 per cent of the total.[11] In the South, in the key industrial centres and areas of agricultural labour, Communist votes were considerably higher than their national average, reaching close to 40 per cent in some constituencies. In the backward North, however, Communist votes were, in some constituencies, as low as two or three per cent. The modest total vote for the Communist Party – itself a highly creditable achievement after fifty years of fascism – was a measure of the support the Party had won so far. The wide variations between the votes for the Party in the North and the South complicated the problems still further.

The relatively high votes secured by the Socialist Party (37·87 per cent) and the Popular Democrat Party (PPD)[12] (26·38 per cent) – giving a combined total of over 64 per cent for these two parties then in the Government alongside the Communist Party and the military – encouraged them to press for a greater weight in the Government. Subsequent events have shown that, despite their claim that they were merely seeking a strength in government proportionate to their following in the country, they were, in fact, seeking to dominate the Government in order to change the course of the revolution.

The Communist Party, from the very moment of the overthrow of Caetano, had placed at the centre of its strategy the unity of the people's movement and the Armed Forces Movement. But how to maintain this unity, how to keep the civilian movement itself united, how to prevent division breaking out within the AFM, how to keep a political balance between the civilian and armed wings of this alliance, a balance that would also safeguard against a dominance of the political forces by the military? These were the big questions that had to be tackled.

The Communist Party saw the people's movement primarily in terms of the various mass organisations of the working people – the trade unions organised in their united body, the Intersyndical, the workers' committees in factories, the neighbourhood committees which sprang up all over the country, the popular assemblies, the peasants associations in the countryside, the agricultural labourers' union, the movements of students and women. All these are democratic non-Party bodies, based on the principle of the unity of people for specific tasks, irrespective of their political affiliation. These mass organisations, with the Communist Party and other left parties supporting them, were regarded by the Communist Party as the essential core of the people's movement which, together with the AFM, provided the motor of the revolution. In addition to these mass organisations of the working people, the Communist Party was also working to influence different sections of the middle strata, including small farmers, traders, and manufacturers whom it aimed to win over as allies of the working class.

In many of the mass organisations the Communist Party had – and still enjoys – considerable influence, included in their leading bodies. But this, of course, does not signify that the majority of their members, even where these organisations have Communist leaderships, give their *political* allegiance to the Communist Party. In fact, as the elections of April 1975 showed, their votes went mainly elsewhere. Even if one were to assume that every Communist vote was a trade union vote, 700,000 votes when the Intersyndical had about 2 million members means that at least 60 per cent of the trade union votes went to other parties. Considering that the Communist votes must have included many who were not trade union members – housewives, retired workers, self-employed and technical and professional personnel, etc. – the percentage of non-Communist voters in the trade unions (and the same general point goes for the other mass organisations, too) must have been considerably higher than 60 per cent.

Therefore of key importance after the elections was how to carry forward, in the new conditions, the democratic unity of the people. Democratic unity of the civilian movement could not be achieved solely through an alliance of the Communist Party with the mass organisations. Political parties, with their varying voting strengths, had to be taken into account. Secondly, neither could unity within the AFM be maintained if the democratic unity of the people was badly fractured; and key to uniting the democratic and left forces of the people was the unity of the Socialist and Communist Parties. Thus unity of Communists and Socialists was vital for maintaining a high degree of unity within the AFM itself.

Backed by their 64 per cent vote, the Socialist Party and the PPD immediately followed up the election campaign with the demand for the reconstruction of the Government. It is true that the elections had been for a Constituent Assembly and not for Parliament; therefore, strictly speaking, these two Parties had no legal right to call for changes in the Government. But it was widely understood, nevertheless, that the April 1975 elections had revealed a pattern of voting allegiances which could not be lightly brushed aside. Admittedly the voting in the North took place under abnormal conditions, especially in the countryside where people felt a great deal of intimidation and pressure from the reactionary Church hierarchy, the landowners and elements of the old bureaucracy. But the main problem in the North was the political backwardness of the people, an innate conservatism that reaction was soon to mobilise for the attacks on the premises of the Communist Party and other left and democratic organisations. Following the elections of April 1975, the Socialist Party leaders, in pursuit of their aim of greater weight in the

Government, launched an increasingly strident campaign against the Communist Party, the AFM, and subsequently, when they left office later in the year, against the Government, especially its Premier, Vasco Gonçalves, the highest-ranking officer in the AFM prior to 25 April 1974.

Whatever may have been the ultimate motives of the Socialist Party leaders, their anti-Communist campaign quickly opened the doors to counter-revolutionary activity and a reassertion of the right-wing tendencies in Portuguese politics. From the opening of the anti-Communist campaign by the leaders of the Socialist Party in 1975 to today there has been a steady comeback of the right-wing political parties in Portugal and a swing of the pendulum in political life. This trend continued after the downfall of the Gonçalves Government in August 1975, became more pronounced after the leftist armed fiasco of November 1975, and found expression in the general parliamentary elections of April 1976 when the Socialist Party lost ground compared with the Constituent Assembly elections of April 1975, while the right-wing Centre Social Democrats gained.[13]

Voting patterns have been very unstable in Portugal in this period. While in the 1976 parliamentary elections the right-wing CSD gained compared with its vote in the 1975 Constituent Assembly elections (an advance from 433,153 to 858,783, representing an increase from 7·6 per cent to 15·9 per cent), the PPD votes declined by 200,000 and by 2·4 per cent; on the other hand, the Communist vote went up by 75,000, i.e. by over 2 per cent. Yet, shortly afterwards, in the Presidential elections in June, the Communist candidate secured only 7·5 per cent, while Major Otelo Saraiva de Carvalho, with left and ultra-left backing, won 17 per cent. General Eanes, with the support of the CDS, PPD and SP leadership, won the election with 61 per cent. By December 1976, however, the municipal elections showed a different trend again, the Communist Party and its allies (standing together in the 'Povo Unido' – United People's electoral front) gaining 17·69 per cent for the Camaras (roughly equivalent to town councils), and 18·3 per cent for the Municipal Assemblies.

These are indications of a very complex and unstable situation. Thus, after the events of November 1975 and the turn to the right both in the armed forces and in the general political balance, the new Constitution adopted was a very progressive one, setting out a goal of socialism and proclaiming guarantees for the safeguarding of the land reform and the nationalisation measures. Constitutions, of course, do not in themselves guarantee anything; nevertheless, a progressive constitution, such as that adopted by the Portuguese Constituent Assembly, provides an important political and legal framework in which the working people can struggle to secure its full implementation. The fact that the armed forces supported this Constitution is also significant and a further indication of the contradictions in the situation.

An important contributory factor to the difficulties of the progressive wing has been the role of the ultra-left. It is difficult to quantify its overall influence at different stages over the past three years, but a number of ultra-left organisations have been set up, have been very active, carried out a great deal of propaganda work and have initiated some actions involving people beyond their own organised ranks. It is natural in the midst of a revolutionary upheaval when people have been stirred as never before and when millions are experiencing open politics for the first time in their lives that some revolutionary-sounding slogans and demands, and sometimes militant actions, should receive support from some sections of the population. In this situation ultra-left influences also made themselves felt in the armed forces, both among officers as well as among the rank and file.

As often happens with ultra-leftism, extreme positions went hand in hand with a certain élitism and, to a degree, impatience with the people and with 'politicians'. The impression was created in 1975 that some officers, in combination with left political forces in the country, were prepared to push Portugal into socialism whether the majority favoured it or not. What was particularly dangerous about this tendency was that it apparently conceived of such a change being brought about *under the paternalistic control* of the AFM, which would have a position of dominance over the civilian side of the popular movement. This concept found expression in the 'Strategic Programme of the AFM' which its General Assembly adopted on 8 July 1975. Many of the sentiments in this important document would win the approval of socialists, but its provisions for establishing organs of political power indicated that the AFM leaders believed that such bodies should be established under the supervision of the AFM which would act as the dominant partner in the AFM-people's alliance, with the Revolutionary Council as 'the supreme organ of national sovereignty', with political parties reduced to a supporting role and with Parliamentary forms set aside.

The leftists in the AFM played into the hands of the right-wing. When the helm swung to the right, following the ousting of Gonçalves, a purge of the left began in the armed forces. Understandable anger against the removal of left officers was exploited by leftists; justified protests by soldiers and the setting up of a rank and file soldiers' movement – 'Soldiers United Will Win' – led to more and more extreme actions, ending in the fiasco of 25 November 1975.

A number of commentators have presented the events of 25 November as a left-wing plot to seize power, a plot in which the Communist Party was originally involved but which it betrayed at the last moment, by dissuading its members and supporters from rallying behind the action of the mutinous paratroops. In fact, seeing the dangerous adventure into which the left military forces were being enticed, the Communist Party, four days before 25 November, held a central committee meeting which issued a statement declaring 'firmly in favour of a political solution and not in favour of unconsidered actions which may create propitious conditions for a forceful blow from the right'. This solemn warning, fully justified in the light of what subsequently took place, was ignored by leftist forces in the army.

Not that there was, in any real sense of the term, evidence of any left-wing coup. The immediate causes of the army crisis were tension inside the Tancos paratroop regiment, and the struggle for control of the Lisbon Military Region. The Tancos regiment had a previous record as a *right-wing* regiment, having been used, possibly unwittingly, by Spinola in the abortive counter-revolutionary coup of 11 March 1975; and being deceived into blowing up the installations of the radio station, Radio Renascenca on 8 November when the station was under a form of workers' control. Anger at the way they were being duped resulted in a turn of the paratroops to the left and a conflict with the Air Force Chief, General Morais e Silva, whom they wanted removed from his post when he demanded the disbandment of the regiment. The conflict over the Lisbon Military Region arose because the right-wing officers were pressing for the removal of General Otelo Saraiva de Carvalho who had the firm backing of the artillery regiment (RALIS) and of the Military Police, from his post as Commander of the Region. When the Revolutionary Council decreed Otelo's replacement, these forces openly opposed the Council and virtually placed themselves in open mutiny. This action, together with the occupation of a number of air bases by the paratroops, were certainly mutinous actions but they were really acts of protest, intended to compel the military authorities to stop the turn to the right. In no sense did they add up to a coup, to an attempt to take power, despite the accompanying heady rhetoric by various ultra-left civilian organisations at the time, and since.

In fact, if there were preparations for a coup, there is some evidence that it was a coup *from the right* that was being prepared, and that the foolish and impetuous adventure of military left forces on 25 November gave the right-wing the excuse it wanted to carry through its purge of the left in the armed forces and place the left civilian political forces in a difficult situation.[14] It is to the credit of the Communist Party that its leadership enabled the working class and democratic movement to avoid being enticed into a trap which would have resulted in heavy losses.

Throughout the second half of 1975, following on the ousting of the Gonçalves Government, the left were in partial retreat, especially inside the armed forces. At any time leftist adventures are a danger to the struggle of the working people; and at a time of retreat they are doubly so. November 1975 was certainly no time for ill-thought sallies. As the theses of the 8th Congress of the Portuguese Communist Party[15] pointed out, the removal of Gonçalves was accompanied by the 'virtual dissolution of the AFM', while the 25 November rebellion 'consummated the defeat of the military left and the formal dissolution of the AFM structures'. The whole period from July to November 1975 was one of advance by the right in the political life of the country, with its consequent blows against the left inside the armed forces. The divided structures of the AFM became paralysed and were dissolved without much resistance. Despite the great struggles still mounted by the working people in this period, and, despite, in the view of the Communist Party Theses, 'the enormous revolutionary strength shown by the conflicts in the armed forces', reaction and the right wing were able finally to inflict 'a severe defeat on the military left'. There followed 'mass dismissals of left-wing officers, sergeants and soldiers. Units were reorganised. Substitutions in organs of command took place. There was an important change in the correlation of forces which was favourable to the right.'

The Theses are highly critical of the ultra-left, both for their activities among the civilian population as well as for their adventurist influence within the armed forces which resulted in a violent confrontation in conditions that were favourable to the reactionary forces. In addition to their traditional role of bringing confusion and disruption into the movement, and prodding it into futile adventures, the ultra-left, according to the Theses, by giving a 'deformed image of the left', facilitated and promoted reaction's influence over important social strata.

The Portuguese Communist Party firmly refused to be part of these ultra-left adventures, and, by its influence, was able to prevent the working class and popular movement 'from being carried away in the defeat of the military left and the "left-radicals" '. Acting in this way, the Communist Party was able to save itself from a 'bloody disaster that would have paved the way to fascism; it preserved its revolutionary strength and allowed the struggle for the defence and consolidation of the liberties and other conquests of the Revolution to be resumed in the new conditions'.

Despite all the difficulties it has had to face the Communist Party has emerged as the strongest revolutionary force, the most highly organised Party on the left, a Party with deep roots among the workers and peasants, with 115,000 members and a considerable mass influence. By March 1975, following the defeat of the Spinola coup, its prestige was high and the democratic left was in a strong political position. From March to November 1975 the revolution plunged into a deep crisis and suffered serious though not disastrous setbacks.

Whatever their aims and strategies, the spearheads of the revolution – by their attitude to the April 1975 elections, to the Constituent Assembly, to left and democratic *political* unity as distinct from the unity of non-party mass organisations, to the predominance of military-political forms of government, to Parliament and 'popular power' – gave the impression that the country was being swept along in a forced march to socialism, to an imposed type of popular power but with the military holding the main levers of decision and control. It rather looked, at the time, as if the intention were to press ahead whatever the views of the other main political parties, even though they enjoyed a majority of the votes in the April 1975 elections. Such an impression could only lead to a considerable political isolation of the Communist Party, not from its own supporters and voters, but from the other main political forces; and since the Communist Party and its supporters were still a minority, they could not advance. Leadership of mass organisations which have been set up for specific economic and social purposes, even though they contain millions of members, does not mean that those same millions have embraced socialism or support the policies of the Communist Party.

The revolutionary advanced forces had to halt in 1975 because they had not won the consent of the majority of the people to make the leap from democracy, from an advanced democracy, to socialism. The country was split down the middle; and those who were convinced of the need to go over to socialism and understood what had to be done were a minority. Such a minority was strong enough to win wider support for establishing democratic liberties, nationalising key monopolies, and carrying through land reform – but it had not won a similarly wide constituency for the still greater changes that socialism would involve. Attempts to do so from a minority base could only end in setbacks. The existence of the AFM, radical though it might declare itself to be, could be no substitute for the majority of the people. Any belief that the mass organisations, together with the Communist Party and the AFM, could sweep Portugal into socialism in opposition to all the other main political forces which then commanded the overwhelming majority of votes, was an illusion. It was illusory, too, to think that a push in this direction – or, actions which gave the impression that such a push was being made – could be carried through, in the face of the inevitable and fierce opposition of the other parties, without causing a crisis within the AFM and so defeating the entire strategy of rapid advance. As we have seen in the case of Chile, a danger point for the left arises when the right counters the mass actions of the democratic movement by organising its own mass actions, by bringing its supporters out on the streets, even involving others who have become confused by the way events have unfolded with such rapidity and complexity. This happened in Portugal, too; not only in the anti-Communist campaign in the North, but even more serious in the more massive anti-Gonçalves demonstrations in Lisbon and other centres.

Ted Slade has made these pertinent remarks:

Large sections of the population felt by-passed, eventually threatened by what was happening. . . . Three generations of propaganda cannot be washed away in a few months. Soon these groups, the potential and necessary allies of the working class, began to show their bewilderment and disillusion. Their deeply lodged conservatism provided a fertile soil for the right, who have found growing numbers of shock-troops for the counter-revolution.'[16]

Yet setback did not add up to defeat. Democratic rights, land reform, nationalisation, and decolonisation stand as four great symbols of the achievements of the great struggles of the Portuguese people over the past three years. One can add to those gains the creation of the people's organisations and the emergence of millions of new people with new horizons, a new political awareness, new organisational abilities, new capacities of many kinds, and a new determination.

Now the revolutionary movement and the Communist Party face a new phase of their battle. No longer the quick march, but rather the long haul – the further strengthening of the Communist Party, the creation of Socialist-Communist unity on which 'depends the future of democracy in Portugal',[17] the expansion of the mass organisations and the mass movement, the winning of the middle strata and of other political forces, both above and below, the winning of a majority for socialism, a majority prepared to *struggle* for that goal. Progress on these fronts will once again find its expression in the armed forces, not in the precise form that it took in 1974–5, but nevertheless with both troops and officers being won in substantial numbers to support the democratic aspirations of a people striving to advance to socialism. This will require both a considerable growth in the people's movement, as well as initiatives undertaken by the advanced revolutionary forces on the basis of a clear-cut military policy.

It was not intended here to analyse in detail the whole course of the Portuguese revolution, nor to predict how it will evolve in the period ahead. What has been attempted is an examination of the interaction of Portuguese politics on the armed forces. Portuguese experience tends to confirm conclusions that have emerged from our examination of the role of the military in a number of other countries. First, that the way the armed forces react is determined by the total politics of the given country. Second, that in the last resort, whether the army acts on the side of reaction or progress depends on the relations of strength between the different classes; the army is not an institution that the ruling class can simply use whenever it so desires. Third, that in conditions where the working class, the Communist Party and the left in general are, or have become, isolated to a degree from other class forces and possible allies, or are confronted with divisions between themselves and other political forces with influence among the workers, the armed forces will tend to move to the right and even become a directly repressive force. Fourth, to avoid such a danger the working class must combat and defeat the influence of ultra-leftism which divides the forces of progress, pushes them into adventures and premature confrontations, isolates the left and the working class in general, and provides the excuse as well as the apparent reality of a 'coup from the left' or a breakdown of 'law and order', which reaction then uses to justify a right-wing coup. Fifth, that the working class and the Communist Party cannot afford to await a spontaneous evolution of progressive trends in the armed forces as a natural result of political progress in the country as a whole, but must have a military policy and consciously work to influence and win a decisive section of the armed forces over to its side. Sixth, that the building of a wide alliance of democratic forces around the working class is of crucial importance for bringing about such a progressive transformation within the armed forces.

The lessons of Portugal are extremely important for other countries of Western Europe. How an army can be won for revolutionary change, and how it can be largely lost again, is obviously of great significance for the major capitalist countries, both for those with mass Communist Parties, such as Italy, France, Portugal, and Spain, as well as for countries such as Britain and West Germany with a more traditional, mass Social-Democratic movement. Solving the army question is vital for the fate of revolutionary change in these countries.

NOTES

1 This was confirmed strikingly by the events that followed in Portugal after 25 April.
2 Alvaro Cunhal, interview: 'After Half a Century of Oppression, Our People Can Now Be Free', L'Humanité, 29 April 1974.
3 11 May 1974. See Basil Davidson, Jo Slovo and Anthony Wilkinson, Southern Africa: The New Politics of Revolution, London 1976, p. 19.
4 Cunhal, The Path to Victory, 1964.
5 Portugal and Spain: Transition Politics, Institute for the Study of Conflict, London, May 1976, p. 8.
6 Insight on Portugal: The Year of the Captains, Insight Team of the Sunday Times, London 1975, pp. 16–17.
7 ibid., p. 29.
8 ibid., p. 33.
9 Cunhal, op. cit.
10 The PPD has since changed its name. It is now called the Social Democrat Party (PSD).
11 In addition, the Portuguese Democratic Movement (MDP), with whom the Communist Party was in alliance, received 4·12 per cent, giving this block 16·65 per cent.
12 Now Social Democrat Party.
13 Actual votes were:

	Votes	%	Deputies
Socialist Party (PS)	1,887,180	34·9	105
PPD	1,296,432	24·0	71
Centre Social Democrats	858,783	15·9	41
Communist Party (PCP)	785,620	14·7	40

Party names are somewhat misleading. The Socialist Party is dominated by its right-wing, although it has a left core. To the right of the PS is the former PPD (now called Social Democrat Party), and still further to the right are the Centre Social Democrats (CDS).

14 See, for example, *Portugal, The Revolution in the Labyrinth*, ed. Jean-Pierre Faye, Nottingham, 1976; especially pp. 53–100, and 196–200.

15 These were issued some weeks prior to the Congress, held in Lisbon, 11–14 November 1976.

16 Ted Slade, 'Portugal Probe – Questions Remain', *Morning Star*, 23 December 1976.

17 Alvaro Cunhal, 'Results and Prospects of the Portuguese Revolution', *World Marxist Review*, January 1977.

13

Western Europe – Aligning the Army with the People

Throughout Western Europe, experience in this century has brought home to revolutionaries the need to assess carefully the position of the armed forces in their respective countries and to work out and apply realistic policies which will, on the one hand, minimise and, if possible, avoid, the possibilities of the capitalist class being able to utilise the military to suppress the action of civilians for democratic change, and, on the other hand, positively influence those in uniform so that they act benignly towards or even actively assist revolutionary transformations.

The closing stages of the First World War and its aftermath saw the top military brass playing a leading counter-revolutionary role – in Russia, Finland, Germany, Hungary, Italy and Poland – to crush the struggles of its own people. While soldiers were expressing their opposition to continuing the war, taking the road of revolution in Russia, Germany and Hungary, deserting the army en masse in Italy, helping to set up Workers' and Soldiers' Councils in Britain, and carrying through the Black Sea Revolt in the French navy in solidarity with the Russian revolution, the military establishment played its traditional role of siding with reaction in order to uphold the existing capitalist system. In the subsequent period general staffs in Italy, Portugal and Germany actively participated in preparing the way for the fascists to assume power in their respective countries. In Spain, too, the fascist generals were a main instrument of the counter-revolution.

It would, on the basis of this experience, be clearly unwise for revolutionaries to ignore the danger posed by the leaders of the military establishment. The latter's class and social position, their training, their political and philosophical beliefs, their economic privileges, their links with big capital, their key position in the entire power system – all this predisposes the generals to act as loyal defenders of the capitalist system and, if they deem it necessary and possible, to resort to the most extreme measures for that purpose. But, because of this, to draw the conclusion that the entire army is, of itself, 'the enemy', that it will always, under all circumstances, act as the defender of the capitalist system and as the oppressor of the people – an ultra-left viewpoint that has in no sense been completely expunged from the minds of the left, including the Communists – is a line of thinking that can, in the end, contribute towards the army acting in such a reactionary fashion. It is not really revolutionary to be fatalistic about any institutions. The question is: what should be done?

One should, of course, avoid giving generalised answers that are intended to be appropriate for all times and under all circumstances. Yet developments in Western Europe in the past decade, influenced to a degree by the advance of socialism and national liberation on a global scale, have led Communist Parties to give considerable thought to this vital question. As a result, the remnants of past sectarian attitudes have been greatly diminished, futile rhetorical 'anti-militarism' has been abandoned, and in their place policies are being elaborated and serious attention paid to the problem of depriving the big capitalists of their hitherto largely unchallenged power to utilise the State's coercive institutions for their own narrow interests.

Of particular significance is the changed and changing position of the officers. Experience of the 1930s already showed, as for example in the Popular Front periods in France and Spain, that a section of the officers were ready to side with the people in defending democracy and opposing fascism. The Second World War provided other examples of this same evolution, with deep divisions taking place in some armies between those officers who sided with fascism and those who threw in their lot with the democratic forces. Symbolic of this division were the contrasting roles in France of De Gaulle and the quisling Marshal Pétain. Admittedly the actions of patriotic officers in this period could not be considered as evidence that they had embraced socialism as the cause to which they would offer their loyalty. Nevertheless, this refusal by substantial numbers of officers to maintain their 'traditional' role of upholding the most reactionary interests in society confirms, once again, that the behaviour of army personnel all the way up the hierarchy from the bottom to the top is not mechanically predetermined by the nature of the institution to which they belong nor by the function which it is designed to carry out; in the last resort, it is the total politics of the given country, influenced, too, by world events, which explains how the army personnel act as at times of crisis.

A significant factor has been the changes in the class and social composition of the officer corps. We have already noticed how this had considerable influence on the officer corps of the Portuguese army in the 1960s and 1970s. The enormous technological advances in military equipment and methods have rendered obsolete not only army techniques but also, to a large degree, the social forces from which officers tend to be drawn. The aristocratic son of an aristocrat, skilled at hunting, shooting, and fishing, and capable of leading a cavalry charge, is not necessarily the most adept at using the fast-changing, sophisticated equipment with which armies are equipped today, nor of giving leadership to men who are handling such equipment with precision and expertise. A new professional, technical and managerial stratum is what today's armies require for their officer corps; consequently officers are increasingly drawn from the families of the more intermediate ranks of the capitalist class and from professional and technical circles. These strata, in civilian life, are becoming greatly affected by the deep-going political crises of our time and, in one form or another, are tending to be drawn into political activity − some of it associated with right-wing movements, while others are taking a more radical path. These involvements have a 'feedback' into the army among the officers who are their relatives or friends or kindred spirits − and even though the impact may be muted and not find immediate expression, the long-term effects of this process cannot be denied.

The attitude of a number of West European Communist Parties towards the armed forces today takes full account of these changed circumstances in working out their strategies for bringing about revolutionary change. The strategies of these parties are based on an analysis that the great concentration of economic and political power in the hands of the big monopoly firms operating in each capitalist country bears heavily against the interests of the non-monopoly sections of the population who constitute the vast majority. This provides an objective basis for building a broad, democratic, anti-monopoly alliance of these forces, led by the working class, whose organisations constitute the main base of this alliance. Such an alliance will be able to combine extra-parliamentary mass action with a parliamentary majority, thus making possible the carrying through of profound economic, social and political changes, step by step, and on the basis of the consent of the majority. This will open up the possibility of bringing about a change from capitalism to socialism, without armed insurrection and civil war.

To carry through such a revolutionary transformation it will be necessary to transfer political power from the hands of the very wealthy minority into the hands of the working class and its allies. This revolutionary change will not be carried through by a single, violent 'seizure of power', but will be a protracted process in which the majority of the people will exert their will and use their democratic power to enact the transformations they require. It will be a democratic process at every stage, and will set itself the democratic task of ending the dictatorial domination of society by big business and its political organisations. It will be democratic in its methods, since it will strive to bring about revolutionary change by the democratic assertion of the will of the millions of working people who comprise the overwhelming majority of the population. It will be democratic in its deepest sense, since its ultimate aim and purpose is to construct a society in which people have full power to exercise their democratic rights and to take all major decisions concerning their own lives and the shape of society as a whole. To help ensure that such changes are brought about democratically, all democratic rights won by the people will be safeguarded, and political parties, including those opposed to socialism, will be allowed to exist and carry on normal political activity. It is fully understood that to carry out a revolution under such conditions, even though it is predicated on the intention to avoid a civil war, in no sense assumes that it can be done without struggle, even the most bitter and intense struggle, involving millions of people.

Clearly of key importance to this whole strategy is the question of the state institutions, including those of coercion. To summarise briefly the intentions towards these institutions envisaged by Communist Parties pursuing such strategies, the aim is not to 'smash the state machine', but to transform it. The goal is the same – namely, to provide the working class and its allies with state institutions that will assist the carrying through of the democratic transition from capitalism to socialism; but the method intended is very different.

The Communist Party of Spain envisages a positive role being played by the army towards the establishment of the people's democratic rights. The development of the mass movement and the extension of its scope and its system of alliances will 'create conditions in which a part of the state apparatus could lean towards democracy, in which the Army would not oppose the will of the vast majority of Spanish society but would accept and even assist the democratic change which will restore to the people the exercise of sovereignty.'[1] Spelling out this possibility in greater detail, the Communist Party of Spain presents the outline of a process which could, under favourable conditions, accompany the change-over to socialism.

The development of the modern state apparatus has made revolution more difficult than it was in the past. The era of revolutions carried out by small, highly conscious minorities who defeated small bodies of troops and seized power is past, at any rate in the developed countries.[2]

Today, revolution can only triumph with the support and participation of the great mass of the people, *winning over one part of the state apparatus to its side and neutralising the other part* (italics added).

In this sense, the very vastness of the modern state apparatus which makes it appear invincible can also, in some circumstances, be the cause of its weakness. . . . (The) fact that authority, the State, is at the service of the monopolistic groups and the ruling class, does not mean that the mass of officials in all the services are politically fascist.

It is precisely the growing size and technical nature of the state apparatus that obliges it to recruit a large part of its functionaries not from the ruling classes but from the middle strata of the population and often from the forces of culture. And when these social strata start facing up to the regime, their attitude also influences the functionaries (of the State) and creates conditions for attracting or neutralising some of them[3] [a point which we noted above in relation to developments in Portugal].

The strength of this argument of the Communist Party of Spain was borne out in December 1976 by the results of a confidential poll carried out by the Spanish Government to test the views of army officers regarding the question of legalising the Communist Party. The poll showed that the number of senior officers in favour of Communist Party participation in the process of reestablishing democracy had increased from 5 to 30 per cent over the past year, with a clear majority of younger officers supporting such rights for the Communist Party.[4]

Explaining why the Communist Party in Spain was no longer thinking in terms of '*destroying* the State apparatus', but rather of removing from the State institutions sectors such as the political police, the higher ranks of the administration, reactionary personnel in the finance bodies and in the armed forces, and 'neutralising, and even winning over a part of the State apparatus for democratic, even socialist transformation', Manuel Azcarate has drawn special attention to the military policy of the Spanish Communist Party in this connection.[5]

Stressing that the new conditions and the new tasks require 'a new kind of work by the revolutionary forces at the heart of the army – and not only among the soldiers, but also within the officers' ranks', Azcarate noted:

Officer education is currently more scientific than ever before; this opens up a contradiction, experienced by many, between scientific rationality and the age-old myths which are also being inculcated. In fact, studies at military academies are more similar to university studies. Student circles, and others, can influence the terrain of young officers.

More progressive officers publish bulletins in which they criticise shortcomings and put forward their own progressive solutions. This happened in the last few years of the Franco regime, and was an indication of the way in which the widespread people's movement for an end to Francoism and the establishment of a democratic regime was affecting the officers. Similar signs were noticed amongst the soldiers, who had their own independent publications.

We use all possible methods [explained Azcarate] in the effort to break the army's isolation; to make it susceptible to the influence of other progressive currents, such as the left-wing Catholics; to open up a dialogue between the people and the army and to make it aware of social realities. The efforts we are making in this direction are producing results.

When there was a massacre of workers at El Ferrol, a delegation of strikers went to the General Staff headquarters and asked to be received by the admiral in command of the naval base and the locality. He agreed to meet them, and the strikers asked him not to send armed forces against the workers. The admiral invited other ranks to take part in the discussion which proceeded in an atmosphere of mutual understanding. The upshot was that the troops were not used against the strikers.

Citing this example, Azcarate comments that it illustrates the possibilities 'of getting the army to adopt an approach which is not one of confrontation with the people'.

While the Spanish army has not been involved in heavy colonial wars, as the Portuguese has been, it has also passed through a testing and in some ways agonising experience in the past few years in connection with the decline of Francoism and the growth of the Spanish people's democratic movement. The lack of a debilitating colonial war has saved Spain from the necessity to draw on conscripts to fill the ranks of junior officers, as was the case in Portugal; yet changes in the class composition of the officer corps have come about from other causes, accompanied by a different reaction to political and ideological matters.

In a book entitled *The Career Officer in Spain* (its appearance is, in itself, a significant commentary on what is happening in the Spanish Army), Major Julion Busquets Braglut[6] spotlights many of the problems facing the officers. While many who come from traditional strata in society suffer from their declining prestige, and seek to send their children to university rather than into the army, their own activities being carried on very much in isolation from the outside world, the new officer intake is very different. The social class of the army, in Major Busquets' opinion, is moving downwards, with considerable recruitment from among the sons of the lower ranks of the middle class. These new, young officers are taking up university courses, changing from law to economics and political science, acquiring a more scientific and rational view of society and how it works. More than 60 per cent of them have civilian jobs in addition to their military duties, and this takes them out of the barracks and into the community where they come up against other influences, including Marxism.

The formation of the Military Democratic Union, which by 1976 was believed to have the support of about one thousand officers, 'most of them obviously young officers with university backgrounds or university wives'[7] is a significant expression of these new trends among the officer corps of the Spanish army. The arrest of Major Busquets, together with that of Captain José Julvez who took a similar stand against the punishment meted out to Captain Jesus Molina for refusing to inform on railway workers, led to the revelation that a group of twenty-five officers in Catalonia had issued a letter demanding changes in the regime, and democratic reforms in the army, and declaring that the army should not be used as 'a force of repression'. The formation of the Military Democratic Union among the officers was followed by the setting up of a democratic organisation of soldiers, though in recent months neither organisation has apparently found an appropriate way to exert its influence in a more open form. It is noticeable, however, that the main ideas for which the Military Democratic Union, and individual progressive officers have been campaigning, and in particular the concept that the army should belong to no faction, should not be used for repression, and should act in the service of the people as a whole, are being expressed even at the highest level.

We military want to dedicate ourselves to our job of arms and we want the country to resolve all its problems, including the political ones, with the machinery and means of State it possesses. The best cooperation the armed forces can render in resolving these problems is to respect whatever valid option emerges without interfering in activities which are not their concern ... [Spaniards must learn to view their armed forces as] belonging to all Spain and not to a group or a tendency no matter how big that might be.[8]

There is no doubt that the evolution of such opinions among serving officers in the Spanish army has taken place not as a result of any independent maturing of processes inside the armed forces isolated from civilian life, but as a consequence of the total political crisis of the post-Franco system and the widespread people's movement for the restoration of democracy, embracing among others the social strata from which have come so many of the officers. In other words, it has been demonstrated once again that the armed forces, including the officers, are not afflicted by original sin and fated to be permanently used against the people; the political cyclones of our time sweep through their ranks with great force and, in the last resort, help to determine in which direction they turn.

The French Communist Party has given a great deal of thought and attention to this problem, especially in the last few years. The French army faces a number of acute problems which are dragging it into the maelstrom of French politics. Experiences over the past thirty years – defeats in colonial wars, especially in Indochina and Algeria, later employment in repressive operations in Gabon and Chad, the preparations for its use against the French workers during the great strike of 1968, its occasional employment since in several minor strike situations – together with unsatisfactory material conditions, made more difficult of solution because of the huge sums required for France's 'independent nuclear strike force', have produced growing internal strains affecting officers no less than the mass of conscript soldiers. There is widespread discontent, open protest and constant calls for army reform. More significant, in a sense, are the questions being posed as to the whole role of the army in modern society; and this has a special importance in France, given the great likelihood that within a year or two France could be governed by the parties of Popular Union – Socialists, Communists and Left Radicals.

In working out an approach to these problems French Communists start from the standpoint that the struggle of the French people for socialism will meet with the fiercest resistance by the monopoly capitalists who 'will try to resort to illegal means, subversion and violence'.[9] In acting thus, they will, 'as far as possible, use the state apparatus, of which the army is an essential element.' Reactionary French ministers, in fact, have made no secret of their intentions, one of them declaring that the army is 'the last resort of liberal society'; for 'liberal' read capitalist.

French Communists, however, do not regard this possibility as a foregone conclusion. On the contrary, they see the army as an arena of struggle between progress and reaction, an arena in which the advancing strength of the popular forces can win the ascendancy.

The army is not a political entity cut off from the nation. It is an institution steeped in society and is therefore subject to all its contradictions. It is affected by the deep, all-embracing crisis which is shaking and undermining capitalist society as a whole. It is made up of men who, including senior officers, are influenced by the class struggle as well as by the various political currents running through the country. So, in a country like ours, the army's behaviour depends to an important degree on the balance of political forces. This is a lesson to be drawn from the experiences of Chile and Portugal.[10]

But change inside the armed forces will not come about solely as a result of changes in society in general. There must be a conscious effort by those who want to change society in a progressive direction to facilitate changes in the armed forces and to bring the army over decisively on the side of democracy.

It is inconceivable that we should be able to progress along the road of political and economic democracy without removing the state from the influence of the monopolies, and without taking the measures necessary for its democratisation, that is, without fundamentally changing its content so that it may serve the people, those of the whole nation.[11]

In assessing what must be done to democratise the armed forces and change its content, French communists consider that the bulk of officers will come to support such a transformation.

Many officers in fact hold a responsible view of the acession of the left to power. These officers, who are in a majority, consider that if the people has made its democratic choice and expressed itself by universal suffrage, it is unthinkable that this choice should be challenged, and certainly not by resorting to the army. They consider that the army's role is to serve the nation by ensuring its defence; in no circumstances should it be used to settle domestic political problems. Undoubtedly there are reactionary and even fascist elements within the army, who think quite differently and dream of being able to oppose, by all means, a government determined to implement the 'Common Programme'.[12] Every effort must be made to isolate these officers politically from the great mass of those who want to abide by the popular will and loyally serve the country's democratically chosen government. The army is necessary to ensure the sovereignty of France and to safeguard its independence. A government of the left, with Communists taking part, will ask nothing else from such an army.[13]

This optimistic view as to the orientation of the officers is by no means illusory. Even the conservative *Figaro* has estimated, on the basis of a survey, that 50 per cent of the officers voted for Mitterand, the common candidate of the left parties, in the last presidential election. This, incidentally, reflected almost exactly the extent of support at that time for the left candidate in the country as a whole, indicating how the factors influencing political thinking and behaviour among the civilian population have their impact inside the armed forces.

In working out its approach to the armed forces, the French Communist Party has also had to take account of the serious discontent affecting both officers and conscripts. This discontent arises on all sides, and from many causes.

The army appears increasingly unimportant to the country's security,[14] and the result is an identity crisis almost as grave as that caused by decolonisation.

Young soldiers are no longer content to be paid in patriotic speeches and packets of cigarettes, relying on parents to top up their pockets. . . . French officers, increasingly recruited from families of inflation-hit soldiers and minor civil servants, rather than from the well-heeled middle class, also may have a few axes to grind . . . veteran groups . . . complain that the moral and material position of officers and NCOs is being eroded.[15]

While huge sums are allocated for the nuclear strike force, 270,000 young conscripts are housed in barracks, 86 per cent of which are at least 75 years old. Pay for conscripts is abysmally low. 'Pay scales for regulars are comparatively low by European standards. . . . Non-commissioned officers complain increasingly . . . that they are literally unable to make ends meet. Because of changing social attitudes, a military career no longer carries prestige. . . . In 1970 there were mass resignations by junior officers over unsatisfactory conditions. . . . '[16]

The 270,000 young men who are called to the colours every year to do their obligatory twelve months' service are increasingly expressing their protests against their plight.

With an average age of 20, they no longer resemble the conscripts of former times who in the majority came from the countryside. Now 90 per cent of them come from the towns. They are better informed and are no longer satisfied by just learning by heart the pages of the 'Manual of the perfect soldier'. They want to know the why and wherefore of things. What is more, since 1974 they go into barracks with the right to vote at 18 and do not accept being treated as second-class citizens. Without questioning the need for military service and of national defence they are demanding decisive changes. They are no longer prepared to put up with injustice, insults, attacks on their dignity, repression of those who do not hide their views.

These are the reasons for the rising discontent in the army.[17]

In addition to being the worst paid soldiers in Europe, French armymen receive inadequate and antiquated military training, and spend much of their time on menial tasks such as cleaning the barrack square. Democratic and political freedoms are denied, and although the ban on reading *L'Humanité* in the barracks was lifted in 1974, after years of struggle, in many garrisons it is still dangerous to do so.

The crisis of the French army is being further aggravated by the way it is being used for tasks which have nothing to do with national defence, as for example its employment as a strike-breaking force in 1974 against striking postmen and dustmen. When, in September 1974, Vice-Admiral Sanguinetti argued that the 'maintenance of order' was not the job of the army, but that of the police, he was removed from his post of navy chief of staff.

The French Communist Party has displayed great seriousness in working out its policy on the army, and in the way it has presented it. This is in striking contrast to some ultra-left groups who, during the French army unrest at the end of 1975, issued leaflets of an extremely sectarian and provocative character. One of these tracts, distributed to French soldiers in Western Germany, advised them to 'learn to use your weapons well, because one day, perhaps, you will turn them against your officers — your bosses, and the society they protect'. Another one, given out at an air base in January 1975, declared: 'What we want, in the end, is the destruction of the army.'

At the risk of taking the reader through lengthy extracts, I will quote directly from several French Communist Party documents, since the original presentation is at least as important as the main propositions which could otherwise be summarised in my own words. Explaining the reasons for the Party publishing its 'New Democratic Code for Army Personnel',[18] Victor Étienne writes:

The defence of the nation is not the business of regular soldiers alone, but every system of defence has need of them. Reflecting the country as a whole, our army will have amongst its ranks men of all shades of opinion. That is essential.

If we want this army to be truly integrated with the nation and not become the tool of attacks on our people's right to decide its own future, it is of the utmost importance that its officers and NCOs should not be thrust back into the camp of those who still harbour nostalgia for a bygone era. It is vital that the professional soldiers won over to the idea of widened, genuine democracy should be loyal to the new democratic regime. Democratic changes in France do not depend, admittedly, on the army alone, but they must not take place in opposition to it. Professional soldiers have their place in the union of the French people around the Common Programme.

The strategy laid down at the 22nd Congress[19] allows us to work out more clearly the problems of the State in the phase of democratic transformation. It is not a question of smashing and disrupting the State, but of extirpating all its technocratic and anti-democratic mechanisms, in order to make it serve the nation and not the capitalist monopolies. This is all the more realistic in that the administrative services of the State are staffed essentially by competent and devoted men whose opinions are no different from those of the country as a whole. These considerations are entirely applicable to the army.

From all of this, we may conclude that the solution to all these problems, which are at one and the same time political and military, lies in *the democratisation of the military establishment*. Therein lies the deep motivation of the democratic code for officers and regular soldiers. It has nothing to do with any sort of demagogy, in which it would be easy, but dishonest and adventurist to indulge. Any extravagant demagogic promises aimed towards the military could only promote a clannishness in the army and encourage officers and regular soldiers to depart from their duty, which is to organise the country's defences in the sole service of the legally constituted democratic government.[20]

In a special 'Message to Officers and Non-Commissioned Officers of the French Army', issued in August 1973, the French Communist Party emphasised: 'Like other citizens, Army officers and NCOs are conscious of the need for a change reflecting the country's interests. However, they cannot express themselves freely and publicly without breaking the regulations. They are placed in an anti-democratic position. And it is this position that the powers-that-be seek to perpetuate for their own ends.' Expressing its confidence in the majority of officers and NCOs as 'men of integrity', the 'Message' appeals to them on the basis of their aspirations both as patriots and as serving officers:

It is not so long since the representatives of selfish interests were pushing the Army into hopeless adventures, flouting their own pledges in doing so, and condemning officers and NCOs to sully themselves by acts quite out of keeping with French military tradition. Today, you are witnessing the breakdown of many values dear to you. Honour is smirched by a whole series of scandals, patriotism is made a mockery of in order to bolster the interests of transnational and cosmopolitan financial and industrial groupings. This breakdown stems from the same causes as the difficulties you are experiencing in your material and social position, and in your professional and family life.

Writing in *Le Figaro*,[21] Georges Marchais, general secretary of the French Communist Party, declared that 'France must have a real national defence and an army'. He gave two basic reasons for this viewpoint of

French Communists: their unshakeable attachment to the maintenance
of national independence and sovereignty, and their determination to be
'able to construct socialism in France democratically, without foreign
interference, pressures or reprisals'. While not considering that the army,
by itself, and as at present directed and constructed, could be the sole
guarantee of France's security and independence, French Communists
certainly do not ignore the important role that the army is bound to play.
The question is whether the army is to be used by monopoly powers to
serve their own interests, or whether it will defend the interests and
democratic liberties of the majority of the people, of the nation.

Answering the rhetorical question, 'Do we need an army?', Robert
Bouvier[22] replies:

Yes, France does need an army to assure its security and independence, an army
independent of any military bloc, not involved in any collision with imperialist
manœuvres and without any allegiance to the interests of monopoly capitalism.
Militarism and nationalism, as well as the idea of 'smashing' the army, have
nothing in common with this need. [Nor do we agree with] those aiming at the
wrong target and who attack the instrument (the army) instead of the user (the
Government), or those who only think of defence in technical terms, or those
for whom the nation is merely the tool of monopoly state capitalism.

Avoiding any mystique about the army, and at the same time refusing to
be ensnared in any leftist romanticism, Bouvier asserts 'the great
majority of the people are well aware of the need, not for ever, but for a
long time to come, for a real army of national defence'. This requires,
however, important democratic changes in the French army. In a
number of documents[23] and articles in their press, the French
Communists have indicated what they consider these changes should be.
Under these proposals, soldiers' pay would be 20 per cent of the
minimum industrial wage index, there would be provision for free
transport, reduced prices at cultural and sports events, all barrack services
to be free, a speed-up in the modernisation of living quarters, mess and
sanitary services, the development of social, cultural and sports facilities,
real possibilities for conscripts to work for school and higher educational
certificates and to receive further training, uniform leave arrangements
for all conscripts, increase in ration allowance and in other soldiers'
allowances, guaranteed employment on completion of military service.

In addition to advocating policies to meet the material and practical
needs of the men in uniform, French Communist documents lay great
stress on the role of the army and on democratic rights for all serving
men. The Draft Declaration of Liberties[24] (Article 73) declares in part:

The army is at the service of the whole nation. As an instrument for the national defence the duty of the army is to ensure the protection of the national territory against all aggression from outside. It is not to be used against the liberty of any people nor against the liberties of the French people.

The control of the nation over its military apparatus is ensured from the economic point of view by the nationalisation of the armament industries.

The determination of military policy by Parliament and parliamentary control ensures the subordination of military power to political power. An organic law defines the general organisation of national defence.

The basis of recruitment to the army is conscription. Military service is universal and equal for all.

All members of the military forces enjoy the rights of citizens. Democratic statutes guarantee soldiers and officers on active service and in reserve the right to information and freedom of expression and association. Members of the armed forces have the right to join the political party of their choice and to carry out duties and responsibilities therein.

All harassment and corporal punishment is a crime. Every member of the military forces has the right, if he considers himself the victim of such treatment, to immediate communication with his family, an elected representative or a lawyer.

These main ideas are carried forward in the various programmatic and policy documents and articles produced by the French Communist Party in recent years, especially the two bills presented to Parliament, one for conscript soldiers in 1974 and one for officers, NCOs and regular soldiers in 1976. In these two bills sensible account is taken of the need to combine democratic practices with the maintenance of discipline which the nature of army service requires. Thus Clause 1, Section 5, of the draft bill for servicemen states:

Whereas military training and all military activities proper come under the exclusive authority of the commanding officers, the exercise of the democratic rights and responsibilities of the citizen soldiers in the barrack room rests with the latter.

To that end, the conscripts' representatives shall participate in decisions concerning servicemen and shall be members of the various appeals and enquiries commissions and of the Supreme Council for military training, in particular.

Together with the officers and NCO's representatives, the conscripts' representatives shall be responsible for the management of the soldiers' clubs.

Quite clearly, the French Communist Party has no intention of fuelling any anti-officers' campaign nor of creating a form of military 'rank-and-filism' which is frequently indulged in by ultra-left groups. As all the

above references and quotations indicate, French Communists consider
that the overwhelming majority of officers can play a positive role in
carrying through profound democratic changes in French society, and
that serious activity must be undertaken in order to win the officer corps
for this task.

The French Communist Party does not underestimate the difficulty:

The army is steeped in society. Sociological and political divisions cut across it,
and the relations of political forces existing in the country have an obvious
influence on the behaviour of officers. Although many of them wish for a
victory of the Left, others support the present government,[25] and there is a
significant number of officers with a reactionary and even fascist frame of mind,
who would not be displeased to see the army given 'political tasks'. The
experience of the Generals of the 1961 putsch[26] and the OAS officers[27] is there to
remind us that in this area as elsewhere, generalisations are always dangerous.
But it remains true that the democratic tendency, in the broadest sense, is
undoubtedly the dominant tendency in the army.[28]

Baillot cites an interesting opinion poll taken among junior officers –
second lieutenants, lieutenants, and captains – and published in the
magazine Le Point (22 September 1975). Asked whether they thought
junior officers agreed with the course being followed by the
Government, 32 per cent said 'Yes', 9 per cent wanted the Government
to pursue a more right wing path, 27 per cent thought it should adopt a
more left position, and 32 per cent answered 'Don't know'.

This complex and, to an extent, unstable and unresolved balance,
reflects, to a large degree, the state of opinion in France as a whole. It
certainly underlines both the problem facing the French left as well as the
potentialities for democratic change and advance.

Many of the considerations about the army that are occupying the
minds of French progressives are also very much to the fore in Italian
politics. In a number of respects the attitude taken by the Italian
Communist Party towards the armed forces parallels that taken by
French Communists, although Italy has its own specific problems in the
military field.

The starting point for the Italian Communists, as on so many
problems, is the experience of the anti-fascist resistance. During this
period there was created not only a broad political and social alliance of
democratic forces, embracing Communists, Socialists, Catholics and
others who rallied to the patriotic, anti-fascist cause, but also a new
alignment involving the official armed forces alongside the armed
partisans.

At that time a new political and military unity was established between the fighting front representing the armed State units which had been reorganised after the crisis of 8th September 1943[29] with the intake of volunteers, and the partisan groups and civilian society and its political bodies in the government and the National Liberation Committees.

This is a fact of great historical importance for our country, considering what had happened in the past. It has to be recognised – as Luigi Longo recognised in his book, *The People Take to the Maquis* – that despite the fact that the fascist weevil had profoundly penetrated into the army and the other armed forces, with all the ensuing confusion, mistrust, treachery and capitulation of the high command, in general there was an attitude of pride in many sections of the armed forces which vigorously upheld military honour, weapons in hand. The armed forces' break with fascism was the decisive fact and, from every point of view, their subsequent participation in the partisan struggle opened a new chapter in military history.[30]

Making this same point, the joint opening report at the above conference, presented by Ugo Pecchioli and Arrigo Boldrini, pointed out that 'immediately after 8 September 1943, it was certain divisions of the Army and Navy that first grasped where the duty of Italians lay, and threw themselves into the first acts of armed resistance. It is enough to recall Porta S. Paolo in Rome, Cefalonia, the battles in the Aegean Islands, in the Balkans and, in Italy, at Cueno, Ancona and other cities, not to mention the courageous civil and moral example given by thousands and thousands of Italian soldiers in Nazi concentration camps. Then came the patriotic partisan war, characterised by mass volunteer participation and a new relationship between the fighting formations and the populations of the cities, countryside and mountains. Indeed, this relationship was one of the most important factors in giving a democratic stamp to the rebirth of the Italian armed forces'.

Anglo-American intervention at the end of the war prevented the coming to fruition of the democratic tendencies that were then expressing themselves in Italian society; and this intervention stifled, too, the possibilities of the Italian people obtaining a really democratic army. The Communist Party repeatedly called for the setting up of a new Italian army based on mass enlistment in the zones liberated in 1944. 'Our Party was well aware of the political, as well as military need for the Italian armed forces to take part in the great popular upsurge for independence and freedom.'[31] In December 1944 the Government and the National Liberation Committee launched a call to arms to the young people and partisans of the liberated zones of Tuscany, Umbria, the Marche, Emilia and other regions. Thousands answered the call, and the rejuvenated Italian Army was able to take its place alongside the Allied armies and the partisan formations in the battles that led to the liberation of Northern Italy and the final defeat of the Nazi invaders and the Italian fascist remnants.

But this historic process was interrupted by Anglo-American pressure. Although units of the partisans and the military cadres from the Volunteer Liberation Corps were integrated into the regular Army after the Liberation, in the ensuing years many of the military cadres who emerged during the Resistance were forced out of the armed forces, while the British and Americans vetoed the purging of large numbers of high-ranking officers who had been seriously implicated with fascism and the Nazis. Some progressive reforms, however, were introduced. The Office of the Chiefs of Staff was dissolved owing to it having been up to its neck in the disastrous conduct of the war; and the Military Intelligence Service, the most reactionary of departments, closely connected with the fascist regime and with a long record of political spying and provocation and of persecution of anti-fascists, was abolished. Further, new relationships were established in the army ranks, with soldiers being allowed to participate in managing some aspects of barrack life.

Thus, despite Anglo-American intervention, and despite the continuing power of Italian monopoly capitalism, a new army was struggling to be born, an army that would be more expressive of the new democratic Italy emerging from the ruins of fascism.

But such a transformation could not be carried out by the armed forces alone. As we have noted so often, the evolution of changes in armed institutions is governed by the pace and character of the changes taking place in the politics of the country as a whole. The great hopes of the Resistance, partly expressed in the Italian Constitution drawn up in the early post-war period, were dashed. The political forces of Italian monopoly capitalism and reaction, represented in the upper circles of the Christian Democrat Party, and backed by foreign, especially United States, imperialism, came out on top and dominated Italian governments and so, to a large degree, Italian political life, for the next thirty years. This determined developments inside the armed forces. Progressive democratic reform never really got under way. The army remained, in large part, as an institution cut off from the people and compelled to serve the interests not of the majority, of the nation, but of the wealthy and privileged.

This phase, however, is coming to an end — and with its demise is emerging the shape of a transformed army.

Bearing in mind Italy's historical experiences in the twentieth century, and taking very much to heart the lessons of the fascist coup in Chile on 11 September 1973, the Italian Communist Party has striven to re-create the unity of the people with the armed forces that was such a marked feature of the Italian anti-fascist resistance in the last two years of the Second World War. Not sterile anti-militarism, but consistent, intelligent work and activity to re-build links between the people and the armed forces and to deprive the monopolist groups of their possibility of using the military institutions against the democratic strivings of the people – such is the strategic aim of the Italian Communists.

To achieve this, the Italian Communist Party is working to win a wide consent among all the democratic political forces in the country to introduce democratic reforms within the armed forces, to ensure democratic control via Parliament over the general direction of military policy and activity, and to build close links between the armed forces and the public as a whole. In short, to enable the armed forces to play a positive and progressive role within the general framework of a renewed, democratic Italian society.

We want to bring all aspects of military activity in this country into line with constitutional principles, restoring to Parliament and the other constitutional organs their primary right of political leadership and control over everything concerning the organisation of national defense. We want to see a living, constructive relationship established between the armed forces and the various democratic institutions of the State, between the armed forces and the popular organisations.

Only in this way can we overcome the barrier the reactionary forces would like to create between the armed forces and social and civil reality, isolating the military as a 'separate body'. This is why we do not feel that the problem of a democratic reform of the armed forces can be seen as a purely technical or sectional problem. It is instead an integral part of a general vision of renewal of Italian society.[32]

Like the French Communist Party, Italian Communists firmly reject the sterile anti-militarism of the ultra-left.

What sense do 'anti-militarist marches', generalised denigration, firebrand appeals to the 'proletarians in uniform', absurd slogans about 'destroying' the military system, the superficial identification of military service with class oppression, and so forth, really make today?[33]

Such romantic and futile gestures, it is argued, evade the real issues and express a lack of confidence in the power and capacity of the people to defend and promote democratic progress in every field and institution.

Moreover, these ultra-left attitudes display a real impotence and irresponsibility on the part of those indulging in them, leading in consequence to adventurist initatives which provide a pretext for the establishment to take repressive actions against the people's democratic rights and democratic organisations. Leftism, therefore, hinders the real movement for radical reforms in the country, including in the military sphere.

What is really needed on this 'delicate issue', argue Italian Communists, is 'a dialogue and convergence of initiative and action among all the popular and anti-fascist forces for a democratic reform of the military institutions – a reform that will enable the armed forces to establish a genuine, fruitful relationship with the country and properly fulfil the function assigned to them by the Constitution'.[34]

What makes this task doubly urgent is that there exist 'dangerous tendencies to cut off our military organisations from the general democratic development of the nation'. Moreover, and this is 'intolerable and offensive to the honour of the Italian armed forces', there are 'clearly-defined reactionary and fascist forces' that are 'attempting to infiltrate the military organisation and seeking solidarity and support among military circles for their anti-democratic intentions'.

To offset this danger, and to assist the democratic renewal of Italian society, all the 'archaic and distorted aspects of (Italy's) judicial, political and State system' need to be eliminated. As for the Italian armed forces, they 'must not be left out of this process'. The Italian Communist Party does not consider that such a transformation of the armed forces can be carried through by the democratic civilian movement on its own. The members of the armed forces must also be involved in bringing about the necessary reforms; moreover, there is a growing awareness among soldiers and officers that such changes are needed.

For too many years now they have been conditioned and humiliated, through the fault of successive Governments, by backward laws and regulations, political prejudices and reactionary practices inherited from past times and unfortunate regimes. It is no accident today that the need for a democratic reform of the military system is increasingly felt not only by the thousands of young people called up for military service, but also by many career servicemen and even some sectors of the top military leadership.[35]

Among the reforms emphasised by the Italian Communist Party is that of promotion. The present 'absurd promotion system' apart from being open to favourtism and other inequalities, has also produced a fantastic surplus of officers at the higher levels. The ceiling on top-ranking personnel is set at 3,196, comprising 61 army generals, 151 divisional generals, 365 brigade generals, and 2,619 colonels. The number of commissioned officers is set at 31,000. Thus there are about 10 officers for every top military leader. Reforms are also needed in respect of NCOs and conscript officers, who number about 10,000, but who suffer discrimination in pay and promotion prospects compared with the career personnel, even when they have the same responsibilities.

Central to the military policy of the Italian Communist Party is the restoration to Parliament of 'its inalienable role of assiduous and systematic control over military policy and defense administration'. The practice that has grown up over the years of military policy being treated as a kind of private reserve of the executive is 'a flagrant violation of the Constitution' which specifically laid down that the direction of military policy is the prerogative of Parliament. With Parliament largely excluded from playing its assigned role in respect of the armed forces, Italy's military policy has become subordinate to NATO decisions and has led to 'a distorted and improper concentration of decision-making power in the hands of top-ranking military leadership'. The Italian Communist Party is pressing for Parliament to be given back, in practice, its right to control both military policy and the administration of the armed forces. This, it declares, is not to establish any kind of censorship over the military, but rather to allow the democratic working out of the necessary policy measures and to establish 'the necessary living relationship between the armed forces and the country's representative institutions'.

A second principle of Italian Communist Party military policy is that of a conscript army as opposed to a professional one. Italian Communists recognise that conscription, of itself, is no guarantee of democracy. After all, there was conscription in fascist Italy as there is today in fascist Chile, as well as in a number of other countries with reactionary regimes. But in conditions of a democratic Italy, it is considered that a conscript army operating within the framework of, and greatly influenced by and involved in the far-reaching changes envisaged on the Italian democratic road to socialism, would be a safeguard for the new democratic system. If, in place of a conscript army, there was a volunteer system of military service then Italy 'would no longer have an entire army ready to take arms and defend the country, but a category of armed professionals, who could become the ruin of society and the ruin of the State'.[36]

The Italian Communist Party therefore insists that 'only a conscript army can ensure that living relationship between the armed forces and the people which is an essential guarantee for the constitutional system, for the democratic development of the country, and for efficient national defense'.[37]

This stand is shared by the French Communist Party, too, which has come out strongly against the moves in France to replace the present conscript army by an élitist volunteer army, an idea incidentally that was first put forward by De Gaulle more than thirty years ago. Writing at the time of the openly manifested unrest among young conscripts in the French army at the end of 1973, Jean-Claude Le Meur,[38] although showing sympathy for their discontent, argues strongly for the maintenance of conscription while demanding a changed role for the armed forces as a whole:

We stress that the definition of the army's sole mission – to ensure the defence and security of the national territory, in liaison with the population – has a very vital significance. The soldiers – conscripts and professionals – should not be employed for policing civilians; this is an inherent element of respect for the democratic principles of the alternation of power once the majority of our people has freely so decided. This sole mission connotes a new organisation of defence designed to ensure maximum efficacy. It is linked with the setting up of an army (including a larger or smaller proportion of professionals) whose backbone should be the conscripts from whom well-trained reserves would be constituted. *Any move towards a professional army – i.e. an apparatus cut off by its very nature from the living forces of the nation – weakens France's defence capacity.*

With an army whose recruitment is based on the principle of universal military service, the country and the democratic State provide themselves with the means of preparing an authentic popular defence. Not to be overlooked either is the democratic guarantee provided by strong conscript forces opposed to intervention of any kind against the will of the people[39] (italics added).

These views are of considerable significance for Britain where we no longer have conscription and where our professional volunteer army is receiving heavy indoctrination both in the techniques of 'counter-insurgency' and in the anti-democratic and anti-working class views that are an inevitable accompaniment of such training. It would be wrong, however, to think in terms of a simple, clear-cut counterposing of conscript versus professional, or of a simple formula of conscript equals democratic, professional equals reactionary. Boldrini has some interesting comments on this point.

In my humble view we shall get nowhere if we define the problem as an equation, with conscription guaranteeing constitutional institutions and with the professional army, combined with voluntary service, as simply an instrument that can be used for anti-democratic political purposes. We could think of striking historical examples which contradict this counterposing of views. . . . Everything goes to show, invariably and in every case, that the deciding factor is policy, the general context in which the military structure is placed. In the Italian situation then, compulsory conscription, by reason of the text of the Constitution, the country's traditions and the statutory tasks of the armed forces, is a democratic conquest.[40]

Of interest, too, are the views of the Italian Communist Party as regards the forms through which the serving men themselves can exercise democratic rights. It rejects the idea of 'a soldiers' trade union' as being neither 'appropriate today or compatible with the specific and peculiar requirements of military discipline'. It further believes that to accept such a proposition under present circumstances could result in the setting up of 'a number of organisations on the basis of rank', which would 'tend to aggravate existing inequities'. While recognising that the demand for a military trade union expresses, 'albeit in a mistaken form, a real and widespread state of discontent and malaise', it believes that this very real demand for democratic change must be met in some other form. It therefore suggests the establishment of joint military and civilian commissions under the Defence Ministry to examine all questions concerning pay, indemnities, housing, seniority, promotion and other such matters.[41] The line of argument here also leads the Italian Communist Party to be opposed to the setting up of 'party organisations within the barracks', although, naturally enough, it works openly to win Italian soldiers and officers to support the Communist Party. Its success can be judged from the high percentage of soldiers' votes which are cast for the Party.[42]

The French Communist Party also has doubts about setting up trade union organisations in the armed forces. Instead, as indicated in the draft Bill it presented to Parliament at the end of 1974, it proposes the setting up of committees, comprising an equal number of officers (both commissioned and non-commissioned) and of rank and file soldiers, elected by their units. Elected delegates, under these proposals, would have the right to present a collective complaint on behalf of their unit.

Whether or not a trade union form of organisation is the most suitable for military institutions is a matter worth discussing. Certainly, the experience of other West European countries does not lead to any definite or uniform answer.

The same factors that have influenced developments in the armed forces in France, Italy and Spain are at work in other West European countries – the same changes in the social composition of the officer corps, in the education and technological instruction given to officers and other ranks, in the mounting pressures from civilian society bearing down on the army. But whereas in the first three named countries the stage of the struggle, the mass influence of the Communist Party, the growth of left and democratic unity, are all advanced and therefore producing very profound changes in the outlook and behaviour of officers and troops, in most other European countries, where there is more political stability, where the Communist Party and the left generally are less influential, and where the political crisis is less acutely felt, the signs of change in the armed forces are less obvious.

Nevertheless, the Communist Parties in these countries, too, are working out their military policies, striving to secure democratic changes in the army and, either independently or in association with other progressive individuals and organisations, are helping to publish and distribute special material for soldiers and to win support for the introduction of democratic changes. In Holland, for example, where there is a broad mass organisation for conscript soldiers, the VVDM (Vereniging Van Dienstplichtige Militairen), claiming some 30,000 members, and carrying on its activity rather in the nature of a students' union and with a certain degree of recognition from the military authorities, the more radical element has set up a 'Broad Left' caucus, BVD (Bond Voor Diensplichtigen) operating within the VVDM. The Communist Party works with these organisations, but also carries on its own activity, pressing in particular for democratic changes in the army and for political rights for soldiers.

In the Federal Republic of Germany, which has some 500,000 in the armed forces, about half of them conscripts and half professional, there is an organisation for professional soldiers, with about 100,000 members, which tends to be reactionary. There is also a union of State employees, which is affiliated to the trade union centre, the DGB. This union has a branch for professional soldiers, as well as one for Intelligence representatives, but it is not a very progressive organisation.

Consequently, democratic youth organisations carry on their own independent activity to secure better conditions for conscript soldiers and to win them more democratic freedom. During the last few years soldiers in many garrison towns in the Federal Republic have established groups of the Arbeitskreise Demokratische Soldaten (ADS – Working Groups of Democratic Soldiers). These organisations issue their own journals and leaflets and, in a number of places, have linked up with progressive youth bodies in the neighbouring cities. Progressive youth leaders emphasise that it is impossible to obtain more political and social rights for soldiers without the full power of the working class, and especially without the backing of the trade unions. Consequently, popular publications for soldiers also carry information about developments in the working class movement, while progressive papers for the general movement carry news about what is happening in the armed forces.

It should be recalled that the Constitution adopted in West Germany after the Second World War does not deny democratic rights to soldiers, but the army paper issued by democratic soldiers can only be sold outside barracks; it cannot be published by any named soldier, meetings are not allowed in barracks, and soldiers cannot take part in political meetings or activities when wearing uniform.

A programme for soldiers – 'Soldiers for Peace: Soldier 74' – published in Bonn, in the journal *Elan* on 20 April 1974, contains a most comprehensive series of demands, worked out by 'young factory and office workers, secondary school and university students, doing our military service'. Among the demands raised in this programme are higher pay for soldiers, more social and political rights, a cut in the period of conscription, and opposition to the army being trained for civil war. Apart from the proposals covering pay, leave, free travel, canteens, recreation-room equipment, medical facilities and so on, most significant in the programme are the democratic demands:

Our elected delegates must not be replaced or removed. They should only be voted out of their position by those who voted them in.
Soldiers' representatives shall have the right to call meetings of soldiers. Voting for representatives shall take place at Battalion, Brigade and Divisional level.
Delegates have the right to present complaints on behalf of their comrades.
Participation of the delegates in the working out of the duty programmes.
Participation of the delegates in discussions relating to personnel at Company level.
Participation in decision-making regarding general leave and freedom from duty at week-ends in order to eliminate blackmailing pressure by officers on individual soldiers.

The programme also demands freedom for soldiers to engage in political and trade union activity inside and outside barracks 'as provided for in the Basic Law', the right for 'all democratic organisations to operate freely in the Bundeswehr', without penalties or discrimination in promotion for engaging in such activities, and the 'removal of reactionary officers'.

These developments in Western Germany and Holland, and similar developments in other West European countries, apart from the more advanced experiences in Italy, France, Spain and Portugal, all express the desire of the democratic and revolutionary movements in these developed capitalist countries, to grapple with the problem of the armed forces, to elaborate a military policy for the movement, and to carry on consistent activity to bring about democratic changes in this key State institution in order to influence the thinking and behaviour of its personnel in a progressive and democratic direction.

NOTES

1 *Manifesto – Programme of the Communist Party of Spain,* adopted at its Second National Conference in September 1975 (see *Marxism Today,* September 1976).
2 This is an important qualification, since many different factors operate in the developing countries.
3 This is in fact what happened after Franco's death; and the army stayed neutral.
4 *Morning Star,* 13 December 1976.
5 Manuel Azcarate, 'Certain Experiences in the Mass Struggle in Spain', Seminar in Tokyo, 1972.
6 He is also a sociology professor in Barcelona. In 1975 he was sentenced to six months' imprisonment for protesting against the punishment given to another officer.
7 Christopher Hitchens, 'The State of Spain', *New Statesmen,* 9 January 1976.
8 General Manuel Gutierrez Mellado, First Deputy Prime Minister, interview with EFE news agency, Madrid (see *Guardian,* 25 October 1976).
9 Louis Baillot, 'The Democratic Road: What of the Army?', *France Nouvelle* (French Communist weekly journal), 15 March 1976.
10 ibid.
11 ibid.
12 The Joint Governmental Programme drawn up by the Socialist Party, Communist Party and Left Radicals, and the basis of their unity; it was adopted on 27 June 1972.
13 Louis Baillot, op. cit.
14 This is a consequence of the nuclear policy.
15 Douglas Porch, 'An Army Marching on Its Bellyaches', *Guardian,* 15 November 1974.
16 Giles Merritt, 'French Army Discontent – Soldiering on the Cheap', *Financial Times,* 22 January 1975.
17 Fernand Chatal, 'Crisis in the French Army – Grievances in the Garrisons', *Morning Star,* 29 January 1975.
18 i.e. for officers, NCOs and regular soldiers (not conscripts).
19 Of the French Communist Party, held on 4–8 February 1976.
20 Victor Étienne: 'Why a New Democratic Code for Military Personnel?', *France Nouvelle,* 5 July 1976.

21 7 November 1973.

22 *L'Humanité*, 10 December 1973.

23 'Message to Officers and NCOs' (August 1973); 'Immediate Demands of the French Communist Youth Movement' (*Avant Garde* Supplement, March 1974); 'Press Conference of Communist Youth Movement' (July 1974); 'Democratic Statute for Servicemen', issued by Communist Youth Movement (September 1974); 'Democratic Statute for Servicemen', presented to Parliament by French Communist Deputies (December 1974); 'Draft Declaration of Liberties', issued by the Communist Party, May 1975 (see especially Article 73).

24 Issued by the French Communist Party in May 1975.

25 i.e. under the presidency of Giscard D'Estaing.

26 A reference to the attempt to organise a coup in France in order to stop the moves by the French Government to make peace with Algeria.

27 After De Gaulle reached a peace settlement with Algeria, reactionary officers and other right-wing forces set up the OAS to organise terror in France and Algeria in an attempt to thwart the peace agreement.

28 Louis Baillot: 'The Army and the Crisis of Society', *Cahiers du Communisme*, October 1975.

29 This refers to the ignominious collapse of the General Badoglio Government, which virtually 'vanished' from Rome, in a wake of chaos and confusion, thus making it possible for the Nazis to occupy the whole country.

30 Arrigo Boldrini, Concluding remarks at the Italian Communist Party conference on 'The Military Institutions and the Constitutional System', 20–21 February 1974.

31 Pecchiloi and Boldrini, op. cit.

32 ibid.

33 ibid.

34 ibid.

35 ibid.

36 Palmiro Togliatti, speech in Constituent Assembly, November 1946.

37 Peccioli and Boldrini, op. cit.

38 *L'Humanité*, 15 December 1973.

39 A significant example here is the action undertaken by young conscripts of the French army to prevent the right-wing officers carrying through their planned coup in 1960 and again in 1961.

40 Boldrini, Concluding remarks, op. cit.

41 Pecchioli and Boldrini, op. cit. At unit level the CPI believes there should be an elected Committee for each of the main aspects of barrack life, e.g. for health, culture, study, leave, duties, etc. (see Pietro Ingrao – speech at the Conference on Military Institutions and the Constitutional system, February 1974).

42 'Electoral statistics suggest that about one third of Italy's mainly conscript army of 306,000 men supports the Communist Party. (An unofficial Communist estimate . . . puts the proportion at 60 per cent.) *Guardian*, 26 November 1974. (Note, this was before the big electoral advance for the Communists in the 1976 general election.) It is indicative of the way all state institutions are being affected by changes in political life and are being influenced by the constructive policies being pursued by the revolutionary movements in Western Europe that the judiciary and the police are beginning to express the same critical attitude towards the establishment that has been demonstrated by voting patterns and public opinion polls amongst officers and

soldiers in France, Spain and Italy. Thus, in the 1976 general elections in Italy, 31 per cent of the police voted Communist, making the Communist Party the most favoured of all parties among the police. In France, the Police Federation has recently been to the fore in trade union processions demanding higher pay. Many magistrates in France are displaying a quite radical position, and in Spain, during 1976, a number of judges expressed their support for those pressing for a complete break with Francoism. These developments, alongside the processes which we have noted at work in the armed forces, help to demonstrate the extent to which the strategy of a number of West European Communist Parties for bringing about a democratic transformation of the State in place of an attempt to 'smash it', are achieving positive results.

14

Lessons for Britain – and Warnings from Northern Ireland

The army question is coming increasingly to the fore in Britain. The critical situations which the establishment has had to face in the past few years, the growing confrontations between the authorities and impressive popular movements – industrial actions and sit-ins, student demonstrations and occupations, protests against racialism and activities for women's liberation, manifestations of solidarity with national liberation struggles in many parts of the world (Vietnam, Chile, South Africa, Ireland and others) – and the perspective of further conflicts between the people and the ruling class has resulted in a new emphasis being given to the role of the armed forces.

This has been expressed in theory as well as in practice, in the new functions for which the army is being trained. The results of that training have, to a large and painful degree, been witnessed now for several years in Northern Ireland. This army engagement and experience in 'counter-insurgency' operations is providing British troops with technical expertise in coping with urban guerrillas; but that is only part of the job which the army is doing in Northern Ireland. It is also being used for anti-democratic purposes directed at controlling and curbing the activities of the people.

As a result the British army is being terribly brainwashed and acquiring the harsh outlook of a repressive, counter-revolutionary, anti-working class and anti-democratic institution which looks on those who are demanding democratic and national rights as the enemy. This represents an extreme danger to the democratic aspirations of the British people as well.

In many ways the problem of the armed forces in Britain today differs substantially from that in most West European countries. Compared with France or Italy, for example, we have a smaller, more élite army, with no conscription. In consequence, our armed forces are more cut off from civilian life, under a less direct impact and slower to be influenced positively by the growth of democratic and socialist ideas and activities stemming from the civilian population. Furthermore, the democratic and socialist movement in Britain lags somewhat behind that in France and Italy; there is no national crisis related to defeat in colonial wars and to the death of fascism such as that which overtook the army in Portugal; nor are we faced with a situation similar to that in Spain where the collapse of Francoism has produced grave tensions and political differentiation among the officers.

In brief, the growth of class and social conflict in Britain and the spread of democratic and socialist ideas among the people as a whole has not yet reached massive enough dimensions for this to have a decisively profound impact on the thinking, sympathies, and voting inclinations of the officers, NCOs and soldiers.[1]

Yet, these differences not withstanding, and even taking into account some of the specific features of Britain and its armed forces which we shall consider, the basic considerations which lie behind the military policies of other West European Communist Parties, such as those of France, Italy and Spain, and, also, although facing somewhat different problems, that of Portugal, have also a significant relevance for Britain.

Those in Britain who want to see a change from capitalism to socialism need to evolve a military policy as well as a policy covering economics, social questions and political institutions. Further, even with an élite, non-conscript army, there still remains a basic task for the progressive movement to influence the men in uniform, from rank-and-file soldiers up to the officers, so that they respect the democratic wishes of the majority of the people and refuse to allow themselves to be used as a praetorian guard of big business on whose behalf they stand ready to use their armed force to stifle the people's aspirations.

For Britain, too, even with a non-conscript army, rhetorical anti-militarism is no solution; in fact, it only compounds the problem by deepening the divide between the people and the army when what is required is to end the army's isolation and to make itself feel that it is part of the people and not their enemy. It is pessimistic to argue that such a change in the army's outlook cannot be made. Of course, no military policy can operate in a vacuum. Any attempt to influence the army must be related to changes in civilian life. It is idle, in a situation where the majority of the people are not yet won for fundamental democratic change opening up a prospect of socialism, to expect an army to become transformed and display a political tendency that so far only a minority of the people themselves have taken up. To win the heart of the army it is necessary to win the heart of the people.

But winning the heart of the people alone is not enough, either. There will be no spontaneous progressive change among the armed forces merely as a result of the progressive movement winning a decisive majority among the civilian population. The additional ingredients needed are a military policy for winning the army for democratic progress, and, combined with such a policy, persistent and responsible activity to win support for it both in the armed forces and among the general population.

When one looks at the activities of the ultra-right political forces in the country one has to admit that they are far more conscious of the key role of the army in politics and display far more initiative to influence it in a rightward direction. It is, of course, true that they start with an initial advantage, for not only has the army been traditionally isolated from democratic political trends in Britain but the officer corps, especially its upper ranks, has class and strata ties which incline it more to conservative and even ultra-right politics than they do towards the popular movement. But equally of importance is the fact that government policy – and this remains true of Labour Governments as well as Tory ones – is directed towards maintaining the army as an arm of its imperialist goals. This involves repressing the people's struggle for democratic demands in Northern Ireland as well as relying on our links with NATO.

The involvement of Britain's armed forces with NATO remains an acute danger for British democracy. The Government *Statement on the Defence Estimates 1977* (Cmnd 6735) once again asserts that the Government's military policy 'remains firmly based on the North Atlantic Alliance'. Quite apart from the heavy economic burden this entails,[2] the political character and purpose of the alliance contributes towards maintaining our armed forces as an instrument for reaction.

NATO performs a three-fold aim. First, it is regarded as a counter-force to that of the Soviet Union and its socialist allies. Consequently, the whole training, equipment, manoeuvres and deployment of the NATO forces is given an anti-Soviet, anti-socialist and anti-communist thrust which is reinforced by the cold-war character of the political briefing and brain-washing which is an inevitable accompaniment of these military aims and preparations.

Secondly, NATO has a counter-revolutionary purpose in Western Europe. Ostensibly set up to defend 'democracy', its actual function is to maintain capitalism as a system in Western Europe; consequently it has been involved in backing reactionary coups, such as the 1967 colonels' coup in Greece, and was entangled, too, with plans of some top military circles in Italy for similar military intervention against the democratic strivings of the Italian people. It is well-known that 'contingency plans' have been prepared by NATO for other West European countries. It can readily be assumed that the CIA also has a hand in these preparations. These anti-popular purposes of NATO cannot be pursued without, once again, a heavy dose of propaganda intended to render the army more ready to hold down the people in the belief that it is combating what is termed 'subversion'.

A third purpose of NATO, and one that is not so apparent, is that of maintaining the 'overseas' interests of NATO partners. Thus, throughout its war against the liberation movements in Guinea-Bissau, Mozambique and Angola, Portuguese fascism could rely on NATO backing, including military equipment from other NATO countries which knew only too well where this equipment would be used. In the same way, there have been indications that there are forms of military collaboration (not official, of course) between NATO and the apartheid regime in South Africa.

Thus Britain's involvement with NATO strengthens in every way the reactionary and anti-democratic trends in the British army. Important, therefore, to the aim of transforming the British army into a real shield of the democratic aspirations of the British people is the withdrawal of Britain from NATO and the dissolution of all military blocs in Europe.

Quite apart from its links with NATO, the British army plays its own independent reactionary role in many parts of the world. Despite its decline as a world power, Britain remains as one of the main imperialist states, and over the last thirty years has used its armed forces continually throughout the world to maintain its economic and strategic interests and to suppress struggles for democratic advance and national and social liberation. As fascism collapsed in Europe and Asia, the British armed forces moved into action to ensure that popular regimes did not take over power in the wake of the defeated German, Italian and Japanese armies and in place of the discredited and politically isolated puppet regimes. These frankly anti-democratic purposes were pursued by the British army in Italy, France, Greece, Vietnam, Indonesia, Burma and Malaya. Major campaigns against national liberation movements were later launched against Malaya (1948–60), Kenya (1952–5), Aden (1963–8), Oman (1957–9), Cyprus (1954–8), Malaysia (1963–6). There was a major campaign in Palestine (1946–8), lesser involvements in Togoland (1957), Brunei (1962), and Aden (1947), the war in Suez in 1956 and action in Kuwait in 1961. British troops were also used in the war against the Korean people (1950–5). 'Police operations' took place in British Honduras (1948), Singapore (1950), Akaba (1951), British Guiana (1953), Buraimi (1955), Hong Kong (1956), British Honduras (1957), Aden, Jordan and Nassau (1958), Cameroons and Jamaica (1960), Zanzibar (1961), British Guiana (1962–6), British Honduras (1962), Cyprus (from 1963), Zanzibar (1963), East Africa (1964), Mauritius (1966) and Anguilla (1969).[3] In addition to the military actions listed here and taken from official sources, British troops over the past thirty years have been employed on numerous occasions to break strikes, notably in the Gold Coast and British Guiana in 1948, in Nigeria in 1949, Kenya and Tanganyika in 1950.

There have also been undoubtedly a number of actions by British military forces of a strictly 'unofficial' and covert nature. The formation of the Special Air Service (SAS), and its use, together with that of seconded British officers, in Oman, is particularly ominous. So is the growing use of mercenaries, first in Congo (now Zaire) in 1960, subsequently in Biafra, more recently in Angola and now very obviously in Rhodesia.

The constant employment of the British army in this way, always on the side of reaction, always against working people, always against national liberation movements, cannot but run the risk of turning the forces into a compliant and willing tool of the most nefarious and anti-popular purposes of Britain's ruling class. This undoubtedly is one of the most serious effects of the use of the British army in Northern Ireland.

There are two consequences of these developments. On the one hand, the army is more and more being groomed to play an official role as a more directly interventionist and political instrument at the behest of the Government. On the other hand, tendencies have been strengthened and processes set into motion that could lead to the army, or a section of it, cutting loose and playing a role as an apparently independent arbiter by indulging in its own coup politics and compelling the government of the day to capitulate to its demands for strong action against the popular movement, or even to force the government out of office altogether.

Both of these dangers exist, but the first, as things stand at the moment, is the gravest threat to British democracy. In fact, we are already part-way down that road. Over the past thirty years the British ruling class has pursued an aim of producing an army more readily suited to playing a political role. This has involved not only the elaboration of theories concerning 'subversion' and 'urban protest' but also practical measures designed to produce a smaller, more élite and highly trained army, provided with advanced techniques and modern equipment for its new role and politically instructed for the same purposes.

A decisive step in this direction was the abolition of conscription. The war-time experience of a conscript army had caused no little anxiety both among the military top-brass and in ruling circles generally. The nature of the war itself, a war against fascism, had a profound effect at the time on the British people as a whole, including those in uniform. But the presence in the army of workers with trade union experience, of representatives of the British labour movement, of members of the Labour and Communist Parties and non-party socialists, was influential, too. The role of such politicised soldiers, NCOs and even officers, their participation in the army's educational work and their general behaviour, worked as a great democratic leavening, bringing a new spirit and a new outlook to hundreds of thousands of uniformed men and women, who voted overwhelmingly anti-Tory when their chance came in 1945.

The emergence of the Soldiers' Parliaments, in Cairo and elsewhere, the remarkable debates they organised, the radical tendencies which they revealed – all this greatly alarmed the military establishment. Sir James Grigg, then War Minister, described the Cairo Parliament as 'an attempt to subvert discipline'. Goebbels raved that the troops had set up Soviets in Cairo.[4] Parliaments were also set up by troops in Burma and India. The top brass, as well as the Government, were most apprehensive about these developments, and soon moved to suppress the Soldiers' Parliaments. The one in Cairo – which had begun at the end of 1943 and held an 'election' in 1944 resulting in Labour winning 119 votes, the Commonwealth party (formed by Sir Richard Acland) 55, the Liberals 38, and the Conservatives 17 – was the first to go, followed by that in Burma in 1945, and the Indian one in Deolai in 1946.

The authorities were equally apprehensive when soldiers moved from complaints at the end of the war over the delays in their being demobilised to the organisation of strikes and other protest actions.[5] The abandonment of conscription and a return to a non-conscript, volunteer, 'professional' army became the goal of the military leaders and government alike.

With the abolition of conscription the way was open to the new type of army. Today, Britain's Regular Armed Forces (all three services) number 343,000 highly trained volunteer professionals. They are backed up by some 250,000 Reserves (over 170,000 of them former Regular personnel, and about 70,000 of them part-time Volunteers). In addition, there are near to 140,000 Cadets. The armed forces further employs at home and abroad close to 280,000 civilians. The army itself accounts for about 170,000 professionals, 109,000 Regular Reserves and 57,000 Volunteer Reserves, as well as 70,000 Cadets.

Apart from the moulding of the army into a smaller, more efficient and more mobile force 'held ready to deal with localised military action overseas',[6] steps have also been taken to enable it to operate internally, in Britain, in the new conditions of the 1970s. The best known exponent of the new ideas which form much of the basis of the British army's training is Brigadier Frank Kitson, who has set out his theses in his book, *Low Intensity Operations*.[7] This study has attracted much comment, chiefly because it has been regarded as virtually a new military manual offering advice to the army on the way to cope with an internal armed insurrection. Brigadier Kitson appears to be well-placed to offer such advice, having had experience in 'counter-insurgency' in Malaya, Kenya and Cyprus, as well as having significantly commanded the 39th Airportable brigade in Belfast for at least two years subsequent to the crisis that began in 1969. His qualifications as an expert in 'operations and intelligence against terrorists' are praised by General Sir Michael Carver[8] in his foreword to the Kitson book.

There are a number of outstanding and quite frankly alarming features of this study; particularly alarming when one realises Kitson's place in the army hierarchy, and taking into account that part of his army responsibilities have been to give lectures on his thesis to army personnel on a quite considerable scale. Despite a muted reference to possible right-wing insurgents, the whole book is predicated on the assumption that the enemy is the left, the protesters, the organisers of strikes and demonstrations, the communists or, in Third Word countries, 'the down-trodden peoples', the movements for national liberation. Thus, apart from the type of technical training that is a consequence of such an approach, it undoubtedly has deep ideological significance, too. Further, the thesis is built on an assumption that all forms of political protest by the left, the 'subversives', are but a preparation for *armed* action. Hence today's 'subversive' (striker, demonstrator, protester) is tomorrow's military target and opponent. This reinforces the idea already planted in the mind of the serving man that the radical elements in society should be dealt with by force, by military methods.

In a revealing passage Kitson defines subversion as 'all illegal measures short of the use of armed force taken by one section of the people of a country to overthrow those governing the country at the time, or to force them to do things which they do not want to do.'[9] Elaborating this point, and presumably spelling out the kind of 'illegal [sic] measures' he has in mind, Kitson lists 'the use of political and economic pressure, strikes, protest marches, and propaganda'. Thus, with a curious indifference towards the democratic rights won by the British people over years of struggle, (or is it a rather more sinister psychological sleight-of-hand?), he plants the idea that the exercise of their democratic rights by the people constitutes an act of subversion; and since, in his thesis, such activities are but the prelude to armed insurrection, clearly the armed forces would be justified in taking action to repress them.

In pursuit of these aims, according to the Kitson thesis, the military must be prepared, trained and equipped for a role in society as a whole, involving all forms of intelligence, collecting information, compiling dossiers, engaging in psychological warfare to influence civilians to side with the army against the 'subversives', conducting mass surveillance of the population assisted by the use of computers, and so forth. These conceptions, dangerous and disturbing as they are, are all related to actions intended to back up the legitimate civilian government. Although many of his examples are drawn from Third World countries, Brigadier Kitson clearly has Britain very much in mind all the time. In this context, however, of a Britain in the future facing dangers from 'political extremists', he comes very near to an outright advocacy of the army being prepared to 'go it alone'.

If a genuine and serious grievance arose, such as might result from a significant drop in the standard of living, all those who now dissipate their protest over a wide variety of causes might concentrate their efforts and produce a situation which was beyond the power of the police to handle. Should this happen the army would be required to restore the position rapidly. Fumbling at this juncture might have grave consequences even to the extent of undermining confidence in the whole system of government.[10]

What is of particular significance here is the circumstances in which the Brigadier believes it would be necessary for the army 'to restore the position' — namely, the establishment of a broad, popular, democratic alliance combining all the streams of protest into one united flood in the face of which the Establishment would be compelled to yield ground.

As a qualified military man who obviously thinks politically about his job, Kitson perceives that the nature of the task facing the ruling class today is of somewhat different dimensions to that which it confronted previously. The growth of state monopoly capitalism, the concentration of economic power in the hands of a relatively few industrial and financial giants, the ruthless drive of big business for ever bigger profits, the concentration of political power in the hands of the State and a few top politicians acting on behalf of and in concert with the big monopolies and banks – all this is creating an ever wider basis for opposition to the ruling class on a broad front. Workers' actions for higher wages in no sense set the limits of the struggle. A host of social questions – housing, health, education, pensions, social security – are pressing for solution. Problems of transport, environment, pollution, civil rights, racialism, are increasingly the subjects of today's union agendas. The women's mass movement for liberation, the struggle of immigrant people, the demands of students, protest activities on behalf of national liberation movements, actions for peace and disarmament – these and a host of other issues are drawing wide strata of people into conflict, in one form or another, with the establishment.

Thus there exist objective conditions for the creation of a broad, democratic alliance of different social classes and strata, and of various social movements, establishing a united coalition which would direct its combined strength against the ruling power. It is these considerations that lie behind one of the basic conceptions in the Communist Party's programme, *The British Road to Socialism*. It would be an exaggeration to argue that it is to block this aim of the Communists that Kitson has evolved his military tactics. Yet it is no doubt in anticipation of the British people's success in opening up such a road that Kitson wants the army to be prepared to act in defence of the status quo. In other words, whether he is familiar with the Communist Party programme or not, the spectre that haunts him is a broad democratic alliance of the British people, pressing for emphatic social change, for a revolutionary transformation of British society.

Yet, if we were to think that Kitson is pioneering some new approach for the army we would be making a big mistake. To a large degree, he is only spelling out what has been British military theory and practice over a number of years.

Extracts from the Army's training manual, *Land Operations, Volume III – Counter-Revolutionary Operations*, published in *Time Out* magazine (10–16 January 1975), provide a most sinister and disturbing picture of the extent to which the army has already been trained and employed as an armed political wing of the Government directed against radical, labour and popular movements. This is no recent development, although the repression in Northern Ireland and its spill-over into Britain have

brought new refinements. The preface to the manual states quite baldly
that between the end of the Second World War and 1 January 1969,
Britain's armed forces were engaged in no less than 53 'counter-
revolutionary actions' in different parts of the world. These military
interventions were mainly to repress social unrest, workers' strikes or
national independence movements and struggles, but the manual treats
them in the distorted spirit of the cold war, with 'the communists' cast as
the enemy and the principal instigators and inspirers of these various
popular movements. On the basis of this experience of 53 counter-
revolutionary interventions, the manual sets out its approach not only
for handling similar situations in other overseas territories but quite
obviously – and this should occasion special alarm to the British people –
to act in the same way in Britain if the need arose.

The main purpose of the manual is not to analyse the past but to
provide guidance for the future. Central to this guidance is the concept
that a 'triumvirate' consisting of the civil authorities, the military and the
police should work in unison 'as a joint and integrated organisation from
the highest to the lowest level of policy making, planning and
administration.' To make this 'triumvirate' operative a 'National Plan' is
envisaged, along with a Military 'Director of Operations'. A series of six
measures are defined as the basis of the counter-revolutionary operations
in which the army, together with its other two partners in the holy
trinity, will be engaged. It is worth considering these six proposed
measures as set out in the manual:

(a) the passing of emergency regulations to facilitate the conduct of a
    national campaign;
(b) various political, social and economic measures designed to gain popular
    support and counter or surpass anything offered by the insurgents;
(c) the setting up of an effective organisation for joint civil and military
    control at all levels;
(d) the forming of an effective, integrated and nationwide intelligence
    organisation without which military operations can never be successful;
(e) the strengthening of indigenous police and armed forces so that their
    loyalty is beyond question and their work effective. This is often easier
    said than done;
(f) control measures designed to isolate the insurgents from popular
    control.[11]

It will be noted that, although these measures are linked with action to
check 'insurgents', it provides a dangerous pattern for military
intervention in the field of civilian politics. This danger is underlined by

the way the manual slips quite easily from what could be regarded as more correctly military functions into direct intervention against people exercising their democratic rights.[12] Thus among the range of activities which the army would be called upon to undertake as part of its responsibilities in maintaining internal security are

(1) dealing with civil disturbances resulting from labour disputes, racial and religious antagonism and tension or social unrest;
(2) dealing with riots and civil disobedience, with or without the political undertones which savour of revolt or even rebellion.

Given that the army is trained into accepting a scenario which, in the manual, depicts a gradual escalation of normal political activity via 'political agitation and manoeuvring propaganda activities, formation of cells and cadres (political, intelligence and military) and civil and industrial unrest. . . . Civil disobedience, disturbances, riots, strikes, lawlessness. . . . Use of propaganda and psychological means to discredit the government' into open revolutionary warfare, it is quite easy to see the calamitous effects such propaganda could have on the mind of the troops. Indoctrinated in this way, it is inevitable that many of them will tend to consider *any* strike, *any* protest march, *any* sit-in or factory occupation, *any* anti-Government speech or publication, and especially those coming from the left and the labour movement, as being caused by 'communists' and as mere preliminaries for a subsequent armed insurrection.

Since the programme of the Communist Party of Great Britain, *The British Road to Socialism*, sets out a prospect of an advance to socialism in Britain *without* an armed insurrection but on the basis of the democratic verdict of the majority of the British people, a verdict that will find its expression in an electoral majority, too, it is clearly in the interests of the British people, and of the armed forces, as well, that the men in uniform should be aware of that perspective, and of the programmes of other sections of the labour and democratic movement. The demand for democratic rights for military personnel is therefore not a mere question of fairness for the troops. It is vitally in the interests of the civilian population that there should be possibilities for ensuring that the armed forces support the people's democratic aspirations. Otherwise the troops will be left to be brainwashed by the instruction and indoctrination indicated above, with the most dire consequences.

The army manual cited above has been in use for a number of years. Between November 1971 and January 1973 a number of amendments were made to it, embracing new techniques and new technology, much of it based on the experience of the British army in Northern Ireland. These include new methods for controlling and dispersing crowds, including the use of unbreakable plastic riot shields, rubber bullets and guns, CS and CR gas, and water cannon. It will be noticed that such equipment has been much in use in Northern Ireland. As from the end of 1971, the army has also introduced in its manual the employment of photographers to help identify leaders of people's activities, as a preliminary to arresting them. Thus it talks of 'photographing the ringleaders, agitators and others so that they can be identified later as disturbers of the peace. . . . This must be done with discretion, however, as the appearance of a photographer often infuriates the crowd. . . . At night lights will be essential. The arrest of ringleaders could be a major factor in dispersing large crowds.'

In addition to these new techniques for handling crowds, the manual has also added new methods for the general surveillance of civilians, including computerised dossiers[13] and car registration numbers. These are currently in use in Northern Ireland on a really mass scale.

The above is in no sense a complete list of the new technology at the disposal of the army.[14] Apart from new equipment, which is a natural result of scientific and technological developments, 'counter-insurgency' operations of the British army have made use of two tactics in Northern Ireland based on previous experience in colonial repression. One is the use of what Kitson terms 'counter-gangs', a method used against the Kenyan people during the Emergency of the 1950s and being currently employed through the employment of British officers and mercenaries against the Popular Front for the Liberation of Oman.[15] In Northern Ireland the SAS (Special Air Service)[16] fulfils this role, operating sometimes in plain clothes. The *Daily Telegraph* described the SAS as an 'anonymous army . . . based in Belfast and . . . supplied with a constantly changing fleet of vehicles ranging from tradesmen's vans to taxis and mini-cars, all with specially 'souped-up' engines. . . . [The soldiers] look more like labourers and layabouts than soldiers.' The activities of such 'counter-gangs' are normally accompanied by 'black propaganda' to confuse the people and discredit the opponents of the government.

Another method taken over from past experience in the colonies is that of 'mixing up' the army with the police, using them in joint operations, making the public accustomed to seeing military vehicles and uniformed troops on the streets, where they act in normal civilian situations as if it were quite natural for the army to be playing such a role. The joint police/army exercise at Heathrow in 1974 had this as one of its purposes. As one British Brigadier has explained:

Those of us with colonial experience know that it was politically acceptable to hold joint exercises *before* disorder broke out. We had exercises, joint ad hoc headquarters were formed, we even had professional 'rioters'. . . . Unless you can carry out exercises of that nature, no amount of talking about it or continuous dialogue across the police/military interface is of any use.[17]

But it is Northern Ireland, above all, which has become the dangerous training ground for all the techniques now associated with the 'counter-insurgency' role of the British armed forces; and just as the former British colonies were schools of reaction, chauvinism, contempt for democracy and for the organised labour movement and the left as far as the serving men were concerned, so Northern Ireland, in addition to providing the technical experience for the British troops, has proved to be a baneful political and ideological influence, producing an army which could become a serious menace to the British people. 'Every regiment of the British Army has now had tours of duty there.'[18]

Among the worst influences at work is not just the involvement of the troops in crowd control, surveillance, military operations, and a general harassment of the civilian population, but their complicity in torture, as alleged for a long time by the progressive movement in Britain and Ireland, now confirmed by the European Court of Human Rights at Strasbourg, and belatedly and unavoidably admitted by the British Government. Yet, despite this, there are indications that torture is still being employed. All experience from fascist countries confirms that the practice of torture is not only a barbarous outrage to its victims. It is a source of terrible corruption and degeneration for those who carry it out. What should give the British people extra cause for the most serious concern is that the terror and repression carried out against the people of Northern Ireland and which, as a moral duty, they should condemn from the housetops, is equally a rod for their own backs. For the British people to stop the criminal behaviour of the British troops in Northern Ireland is vital if democracy is to be defended here.

Like a foul flood, the authoritarian and anti-democratic indignities meted out to the people in Northern Ireland are washing over Britain. The repressive emergency laws in Northern Ireland are matched by the Prevention of Terrorism Act in Britain under which no less than 2,433 people have been detained, although 95 per cent of them have been subsequently released without charge. The armoured cars that roam the streets in Belfast are beginning to be emulated by Heathrow-type exercises in Britain; military cars have even been seen in London tailing demonstrations. It is significant that at the time of the Heathrow operation the then Home Secretary, Robert Carr, refused to give an undertaking in Parliament that troops and police in Britain would not be employed jointly to break strikes.[19] Computerised information on citizens is now standard practice in Northern Ireland; what is happening in Britain we do not know, but according to the 1972 Computer Survey the United Kingdom Defence Department had 500 computers. It is difficult to credit that they are required solely for strictly internal, military purposes.

All this raises very sharply the need to end the employment of British troops in Northern Ireland as a repressive anti-people's force. This is as much as in the interests of the British people as it is in the interests of the sorely tried people in Northern Ireland. Solving the crisis in Northern Ireland poses the question of the total withdrawal of British troops. It is understandable that some progressive people, seeing that the army is used for repressive purposes in Northern Ireland, should demand its immediate withdrawal. But the army is no isolated institution, nor does it act according to its own judgments. It is part of politics, but it does not direct British political life. It is linked to other political factors, and is only one of the institutions through which British policy is pursued in Northern Ireland.

Analysing this problem, and setting out its views on the way to solve the question of the army in Northern Ireland, the Communist Party of Great Britain has stated:

The question of the withdrawal of British troops cannot be dealt with on its own apart from other factors. The troops are not employed in Northern Ireland for an isolated military purpose. The army is the instrument of an overall repressive policy which is pursued by political, economic, judicial and other means as well. The use of the troops is determined by the total policy the armed forces are directed to pursue by the British Government. This policy is aimed at defeating the movement for democratic demands and maintaining the grip of British imperialism in Northern Ireland. The question of the British troops and their withdrawal is therefore connected with the struggle to compel a change in British Government policy and to secure the adoption of a democratic political solution, which includes the withdrawal of the troops.

That the troops should go is clear. The issue is how to create the political conditions to secure their withdrawal in consultation with the Irish people and their representative bodies and organisations, and under conditions which assist democratic and national progress and do not create new obstacles in the way of those struggling for democracy and against imperialism.

As long as the British Labour Government pursues its present bi-partisan policy of backing reaction in Northern Ireland and maintaining the system of repression, the British troops will continue to be used to implement this reactionary policy. That is why it is decisive to press the government to end its repression, and introduce the necessary democratic reforms, and withdraw the British troops. It is this total policy which is needed.[20]

Exposure of the behaviour of the British troops in Northern Ireland and of the policy they have been instructed to carry out is part of the effort needed to create the political conditions in which democratic procedures can operate in civilian life, thus making it possible to withdraw the troops.

Northern Ireland is not the only dangerous political influence on the British army.[21] British Government policy towards South Africa and Rhodesia, and the aims towards these two countries being pursued by the major British monopolies, also has its effects in the army. Political and military personnel in Britain with sympathies towards the racially-inspired Smith and Vorster regimes in southern Africa in no sense maintain these sympathies as their private personal viewpoint. In one way or another they find an active outlet for their opinions, and the South African Secret Service (BOSS) operators in Britain, as well as their controllers back in Pretoria or Johannesburg, are ever ready to take initiatives which can involve former British army officers or ultra-right political forces with whom they are often linked.

Photocopies of more than a thousand letters and documents from the files of the Institute for the Study of Conflict reveal a network of contacts that extends through the Foreign Office and Ministry of Defence, the Cabinet Office, Bramshill Police Training College, several of the main army staff colleges, and the chemical warfare research centre at Porton Down, the Rhodesian and South African secret services plus a smattering of Conservative politicians.[22]

If the Institute for the Study of Conflict were simply a crackpot outfit of discredited Colonel Blimps it could easily be ignored. (It is, of course, noticeable that extreme right-wing organisations attract psychopaths and paranoics, and this is often true of the military leaders who are drawn to such bodies. Hitler's early associate, Ludendorf, and Franco's Queipo de Llano,[23] are among those who immediately spring to mind.) But putting aside the anti-communist and anti-working class obsessions of those who help to run it, the Institute's political and State connections cannot be ignored. Its council members include such well-known counter-insurgency 'experts' as Brigadier W. F. K. Thompson[24] and Major General Clutterbuck, and its full-time fund raiser is retired Major-General F. A. H. Ling, who was apparently recruited for the Institute with assistance from Sir Peter Wilkinson,[25] former head of administration at the Foreign Office, and Lieutenant-General Sir Thomas Pearson of the Ministry of Defence. Clearly the Institute was established with the cooperation of some very leading personnel in the British establishment.

Mullin also provides information on the Institute's contacts with BOSS and with Colonel Claud Greathead of the Rhodesian Secret Service. In the light of such interconnections between ultra-right political forces, British army personnel, State departments, and secret services of South Africa and Rhodesia, it is really not surprising, shocking though it may be, that British mercenaries, many of them contacted via army lists, should encounter so few obstacles to being recruited and enabled to leave Britain for military service in Smith's armed forces or to help the South African forces in their invasion of Angola.[26]

But for the British people, and especially the labour and progressive movement, there is an additional danger represented by the activities of this Institute and arising from its connections with highly-placed people in the State. This is the provision by the Institute of lecturers for army and police training colleges, where it is able to put forward its theories about 'subversion' and the way to combat it. Significantly, among the subjects on which lectures have been delivered has been 'The Political Aspects of Industrial Conflict'. This has been the theme of lectures at the Royal Military College of Science, at the army staff college at Camberley, and for the 23rd SAS (Territorials) based in Birmingham. One of the 'special reports' prepared by the Institute is entitled 'Sources of Conflict in British Industry'. In this way, future leaders of Britain's army and police are being politically influenced about workers and industrial actions by right-wing conceptions which depict the labour movement as 'the enemy'. This is borne out by a report of one of the Institute's researchers, Peter Janke, who maintains close relations with BOSS and the Rhodesian Secret Service. After visiting the police college at Bramshill in July 1972 to discuss preparations for a course on 'terrorism', Janke reported ominously:

This would be the first time that policemen in this country were introduced to the idea that political terrorism grew out of the early stages of subversion and it was the responsibility of the police to detect these phases. . . .[27]

So once again we have the sinister thesis of Brigadier Kitson and the army training manual that normal democratic activities, especially those by industrial workers, are but the prelude to 'terrorism', thus justifying police and military action not just against 'terrorism' or 'insurgency' when it takes place, but against industrial action, strikes, pickets, demonstrations, processions, since these are assumed to be preparations for illegal violence. That the police are being trained in the same philosophy as the army has been over the last thirty years is particularly dangerous. It gives added point to the concept in the army manual of the need for the close integration of the army, police and the civil power, an integration which has found one expression in the joint exercise at Heathrow. It is more than a little disquieting to learn that the SAS 'did a joint army-police exercise at Stansted' in 1973.[28]

Although there is no intention here to study in detail the role of the police in the general framework of state measures checking the democratic rights of the people, it is important to appreciate – and both Kitson's book and the army manual bear this out – that military plans for coping with civilian unrest depend on joint operations with the police. In fact, 'the country's 800 police stations are . . . linked into the emergency communications system linking every regional district HQ, regional centre, air force base, and naval base'.[29]

Britain is no exception to this increasing use of the police for reactionary political purposes. In the United States, of course, this is common practice; but US methods are not confined to the US itself. Through the US 'Public Safety' programme over one million foreign policemen had received training or supplies by 1970.[30] The International Police Academy in Washington, which has trained several thousand carefully-screened police officers, provides them not only with technical training in 'counter-insurgency', but ensures that they receive a variety of courses containing 'a high dosage of "Marxism" as interpreted by the FBI'.[31] The course usually includes as well a short spell at the Fort Bragg School of Special Warfare, once again indicating the military-police link-up which is such a marked feature of our time. One report to a US Senate Committee in 1965, justifying the aid given to police in repressive regimes, explained: ' . . . the police are a strongly anti-Communist force right now. For that reason it is a very important force for us.'[32]

From information given earlier in this chapter, it is clear that ruling circles in Britain are preparing well in advance for any massive challenge to the system which may come from the democratic movement. In addition to the military and police forces, there are other additional instruments being built up. Private commercial security organisations have mushroomed considerably in the past few years. They now employ a total staff of over 100,000[33] and are no longer confined to their original roles on behalf of private firms.[34]

Through their work at the airports as part of the security system they are being involved in State functions and are becoming part of the apparatus controlling civilians. They have been used in industrial disputes and, perhaps most significant of all, have been employed by the Immigration authorities to take part in the arrest and detention of suspected illegal immigrants.

In addition to this new institution of potential coercion against citizens, there has also been an outcrop of 'private armies'. General Sir Walter Walker's Civil Assistance vigilante organisation,[35] said to have 15,000 members, is among the best known of these. It is often regarded as being part of the ultra-right lunatic fringe; but it would be foolish to ignore that General Sir Walter Walker was the former NATO commander in Northern Europe, and that another member of its Council, Major-General Humphrey Bredin, is former chief of the British Commander-in-Chief's Mission to the Soviet Forces in Germany. One can assume that such former high-ranking officers still have connections and influence in military circles. Even the openly fascist organisations are not without some links with army personnel. It is known that the National Front has members working as immigration officers as well as among prison staff, so it would not be surprising to find that they are also trying to organise in the army. The recent revelations of the training of 'Column 88', an extreme right-wing organisation, with the collaboration of an officer in the Territorials, may be only the tip of a medium size iceberg.[36]

In the light of all these activities, the neglect and lack of attention paid to the army[37] by the labour and democratic movement in Britain is a serious blindness. Fortunately the coup in Chile came as a rude awakening to the British labour movement as to the role of the armed forces in destroying the democratic and socialist hopes of the Chilean people. But the initial shock has, to an extent, worn off – and although the danger of a potential threat from the army to the endeavours of the democratic movement in Britain is well enough understood, there has been very little conscious effort to work out a policy for the armed forces and to campaign to win support for it in the labour movement and among the general public, as well as in the armed forces itself.

A welcome and to some extent isolated sign that more attention is now being paid to this was the debate in Parliament on 16 June 1976, on the Armed Forces (Re-Committed) Bill. A number of Labour MPs used the occasion to argue in favour of trade union and other democratic rights for service personnel, including an improved and more democratic procedure for handling complaints and for dealing with problems of discipline. Those who spoke up in this way were not unaware of the wider implications of what they were proposing. Writing subsequently, Mr Ron Thomas, MP, one of those who spoke up in the debate, pointed out:

To many of us the whole question of trade union rights (for service personnel) is inexorably linked with the democratisation of the armed forces which we believe is an urgent and demanding challenge for the whole labour movement. To sustain the demand for the democratisation of the armed forces it is sufficient simply to recall the events in Chile and other countries where the armed forces were or became remote from the aspirations of the workers, and indeed became the instruments of bloody repression against the democratic rights and aspirations of the working people. The free and effective exercise of trade union rights at all levels is of course a prerequisite, indeed, the only driving force, to bring about the democratisation which is urgently needed.[38]

Trade union rights alone are not enough to ensure democratisation of the armed forces. The soldiers need political rights, too.

The full elaboration of a military policy for winning the army to adopt a firm democratic stand remains a pressing task for the British labour and progressive movement. A democratic military policy must, first of all, direct itself to establishing the role and function of the armed forces. The army's role should be the patriotic one of defending the people and their democratic achievements, and making it possible for them to carry out further democratic changes without foreign aggression or intervention. It should have no internal functions which result in it being employed to suppress the people's democratic activities or the struggles of workers and their trade unions. Nor should it intervene in industrial disputes by carrying out jobs normally performed by the workers involved in the dispute.

Secondly, a progressive military policy should also concern itself with the specific problems of soldiers and officers as regards pay, promotion, training, leave, discipline, leisure facilities, accommodation, health and so on.

Thirdly, there needs to be a two-fold democratic campaign in support of democratic procedures and rights *within* the armed forces, along with democratic supervision from *outside*. Democratic rights for serving men and women include the democratic political rights enjoyed by the civilian population (the right to belong to political parties, attend political meetings, read political literature and newspapers, etc.), subject only to the exigencies of the service and actual service operations and discipline. Democratic rights for the forces also involves there being a democratic procedure governing their channels for complaints and redress of grievances, and a democratic method for dealing with cases of alleged indiscipline which allows the person charged full rights, with legal counsel of his or her own choice, including civilian counsel, in order to ensure a proper defence.

One way in which many of these matters could be handled is by allowing soldiers to elect delegates of their choice. This could be either to soldiers' committees, on a unit or other basis; or, as has been suggested and as is practised in some West European countries, by allowing trade unions to function in the army. Experiences of trade unions in the army in different countries has been rather mixed and inconclusive; and, as we have noted, finds little favour in progressive circles in France and Italy. It may well be that in Britain, with our very long and powerful trade union tradition, and given the fact that today more and more sections are being attracted towards unions (such as the police, high-ranking civil servants, top managerial personnel, churchmen, etc.), trade unions in the British army may be more successful than has been the case with other armies in Western Europe.

The trade union movement may well be one of the instruments through which the civilian population could maintain its democratic links with the army as a whole, and play a part, too, in supervision so as to ensure that democratic procedures *within* the army were being satisfactorily adhered to and that grievances were being properly dealt with. Democratic supervision of the armed forces would also, and above all, require parliamentary supervision. This would need to be no mere formality, but a real, living supervision exercised through committees of MPs who would make frequent visits, receive documentation, hear individual as well as collective complaints through the agreed representatives of the soldiers, sergeants, NCOs and officers. Possibly other public bodies and social organisations could also be drawn into the work of supervision.

In addition to the above steps, a progressive military policy would also need to pursue consistently the aim of winning the army for a progressive standpoint, to side with the people's democratic aspirations. The winning of democratic and political rights for the army should give full legal rights to the progressive movement and provide possibilities to it as well as to explain its policies to soldiers and officers, not only on military matters but on the whole field of politics and ideology. This conscious effort to win the army for democracy would be a decisive element in a progressive military policy.

Of special significance would be the role of the officers. The repressive use of the army either as a coercive instrument of a reactionary government or as the organiser of a coup *against* the government is not likely to be initiated by soldiers. It is the officers who take the lead and give the instructions, and the soldiers who normally obey. The struggle to win the army for democracy must therefore also set itself the aim of influencing the officers. The success of this struggle is, as we have noted with respect to Chile and Portugal, for example, very much influenced by what is happening in civil society.[39] The officers are increasingly from the upper and lower middle strata. What these same strata think and do in civilian life has a great influence on the thinking and behaviour of the officers. In its turn, the conduct and opinions of the officers can also have a feedback amongst the middle strata in civilian life.

The class and social origin of the officers in the British army is of significance here. In the early 1960s it was estimated that nearly 50 per cent of the army's intake into the officer corps came from the existing officer class, nearly half came from public schools, and 77 per cent came from the A–B socio-economic group, that is, the top 12 per cent in our society. This balance has now been emphatically altered. Only about 35 per cent now come from military families, and about 36 per cent from public schools.

Analysing these changes, Caird comments:

The evidence suggests that the higher up the chain of command you go, the more likely you are to encounter the old stereotype; but for obvious reasons that position can't last much longer. The officer corps has begun to represent more closely the composition of the population as a whole. More officers than before come from a middle-class rather than upper class background . . . about one in every four army officers has now had a university education. The modern officers' mess is nowadays more likely to be a forum for strategic debate than an overgrown public schoolboys' playroom.[40]

At the top of the military hierarchy, however, other considerations come into play. Family and class ties and interests incline them to the status quo, and often to a more conservative outlook altogether. There is another aspect, too, which should not be overlooked; that is the tie-up between those at the top of the military hierarchy, the Ministry of Defence and the big arms firms.[41] On 27 April 1976, in reply to a question in Parliament put by Mr Frank Allaun, Labour MP for Salford East, the Defence Minister, Roy Mason, revealed that in the five years 1971–6 no less than 97 serving officers and 86 Defence Ministry civil servants joined firms which had contracts to supply arms to the Ministry of Defence. In this way those at the top of the military hierarchy become part of the military-industrial complex; and given that this avenue of promotion, as it might be called, beckons attractively while officers are pursuing their army career, it can be understood that for those influential enough to enjoy this as a realistic perspective, the maintenance of the present social and economic system is very much related to their own stake in the system.

The question of a progressive military policy also involves the problem of military expenditure. A substantial cut in arms expenditure, and the bringing home of all troops overseas would not only make a contribution to solving Britain's economic difficulties; it would have an important impact, too, on questions of state political power. The bringing of the troops home would cut off a major source of political infection in that it would end the counter-revolutionary and anti-national liberation role of our forces overseas. Both the experience and the ideological moulding in such reactionary purposes would be lessened appreciably. Further, the size of the armed forces and its structure would undergo changes once the forces' role was limited to that of national defence and no longer extended to cover external aggression, oppression or intervention on the side of counter-revolution. Such changes would need to be combined with steps in Britain itself to end all training in anti-democratic and anti-working class measures which at present go under the name of 'counter-insurgency' programmes. Special counter-revolutionary units and structures such as the SAS would need to be abolished, and officers who have been connected with these special departments would need to be re-allocated to duties which limit their possibilities of putting into practice the reactionary policies in which they have been instructing the forces under their command. The work of military intelligence, too, would need a drastic overhaul; a new direction would have to be given to its work, and consequent changes made in personnel.

A strategy such as that contained in the British Communist Party's programme, *The British Road to Socialism*, which envisages winning over the middle strata as part of its aim of building a broad, democratic alliance, would find it essential to win at least part of the officers to the side of democracy, both to help strengthen the alliance and to help solve the army problem. Winning the officers is also important with respect to influencing the soldiers. A concept of 'rank-and-file soldiers versus officers' could produce unwanted divisions and tensions in the army and make it more difficult to influence either soldiers or officers in a progressive direction. If there are to be any differentiations in the army – and in real life these will occur – the needs of democratic change in Britain demand that these should centre around the major *political* contradiction, that of the majority versus the big monopolies and their system of political power, and not be diverted to secondary contradictions of officers against soldiers since, in the main, the officers are not the direct representatives of big capital (apart from the top brass), but are, on the contrary, potential allies of the democratic front. The army, including its officers, must be won to see that in a new, more democratic Britain laying the basis for a process towards socialism, there is a place for the army, including its officer corps.

It would be fatal for the democratic movement to allow any narrowness, or leftist indulgence, to dissuade it from its task of winning the army.

In Britain the task of transforming the army presents particular problems. As we have noted, for years the armed forces have been trained as a counter-revolutionary force and heavily indoctrinated with anti-democratic ideas.[42] It does not at all follow that such views will remain the permanent outlook of the troops. After all, in Portugal an army that was trained as an instrument of fascism eventually changed right round, overthrew the fascist government and opened the doors to democracy. There is, however, one important difference and that is the question of conscription. In Portugal large scale conscription, including for officer duties, meant that ideas from civilian life found a direct entry into the armed forces. In Britain we have an élite, professional, non-conscript army. This makes the task of democratisation more complicated.[43] It is not political realism to advocate ending British non-conscript practice, which has long been the tradition except in war periods and in the post-1945 situation. The problem, therefore, is that of democratising a professional, volunteer force. Although this may present its own special difficulties, in essence the problem is the same as that of the armies in France or Italy, where conscription is the norm.

Given that there is a possibility to carry through a change-over from capitalism to socialism without armed insurrection, but by reliance on a

massive democratic majority, struggle against the army is not the aim in
such a perspective. Instead of 'smashing the State', which involves
'smashing' the army which is a main institution of the State, the aim
would be to transform the army, democratising it and making it an
institution for the defence of democracy and the democratic changes
which the majority would be working to carry through.

If there were a solid majority for such changes, the army would be in an
unprecedented situation. To go against that majority, that united bloc of
various class and social forces, would be a hazardous throw for the
military hierarchy and produce grave strains and tensions within the
armed forces. To be right on the periphery of society, to feel completely
isolated and alienated from the nation can have a profound impact on
those who have been placed in such a situation.

No political realist would deny that in the face of great impending
change there would be forces in our society that would try to utilise the
armed forces against the people, either in support of a government which
the majority no longer wanted, or in a direct coup to pre-empt a radical
governmental change, or even to overthrow a progressive government
which was implementing a programme of far-reaching economic and
social change. The power of the people, fully exercised, would be a
massive check to such dangers. If the organised working-class movement
displayed its full strength and took industrial action, including a general
strike, factory occupations and so forth; and if such moves were
accompanied by action by printers, journalists, radio and television
personnel, thus depriving the opponents of democratic change of their
opportunity to spread confusion and chaos (as their mass media were
able to do in Chile against the Allende Government); and if local
government employees and workers in public services and government
departments also acted to back up those striving for democratic change —
if, in fact, right across the nation individuals and organisations
representing different class and social forces comprising a broad
democratic alliance were to go into action, then even a professional army
would not remain unaffected.

The important thing, however, is not to wait for that decisive moment
before acting but to work now, as part of the process of building a broad
democratic alliance, to democratise the armed forces so that the chances
of reaction using the army, or part of it, are progressively lessened.

While it is true, as we have stressed more than once, that the army is
effected all the way to the top by the big social and political upheavals
taking place in civilian life, it would be an illusion to think that these

events outside the armed forces are influencing soldiers and officers only in one direction. They are subject to *all* the influences that wash over them from civilian life – the most backward-looking and conservative as well as the most progressive. Further, this is taking place at a time when the ruling circles are only too aware of the significant role that the army plays in politics today, and are taking very conscious and deliberate steps to win the army for the most anti-democratic positions.

It is sometimes argued that the most that can be expected is to 'neutralise' the army, and that it is foolish to believe it can be won for a more definite commitment to democracy, let alone to socialism. There are two things to be said in reply to such an argument. First, that the extent to which the army stays neutral and accepts the democratic wishes of the majority depends on the necessary political work being carried out beforehand by the progressive movement, including winning democratic rights for the troops and ensuring that they have a reasoned understanding of what it is the progressive movement is striving to achieve. Second, what is most likely to make the coup-minded officers hesitate to sweep aside the people's democratic verdict is a massive response by the organised workers, as indicated above. Third, even the most rabid ultra-right officers would be deterred from attempting to use the army to thwart the wishes of the civilian majority by the knowledge that a substantial part of the soldiers and the officers would not agree to play this game because they had already been won to support the standpoint of the democratic majority in favour of socialist change.

In any case, how far to the left the army can be won, whether to be only neutral or to be more politically committed, the task of those working for socialism remains the same; namely, to work out a military policy and to pursue it energetically both among the general public and within the army itself.

If the labour and progressive movement does not win the army for democracy, others have a better chance to win it for counter-revolution. As the class struggle intensifies, and as more people become organised and take up activity for profound democratic change and renewal of our society, two opposing tendencies become more accentuated in the army, in line with what is taking place in civilian life. The big monopolies and the political circles on their side become more desperate and also begin to mobilise their forces for action, as distinct from periods of relative political calm when they tend to rely on their propaganda and the relative passivity and acquiescence of the majority. A sharpening of the class struggle, as the term indicates, means that *both* sides become more active. This finds its reflection inside the armed forces where the most reactionary officers begin to take a more direct political role and become not only more active, but dangerously so, to the point of considering all manner of wild and reactionary adventures. This is a law of all political crises, and, whatever may be the degree to which this becomes manifest in Britain in the coming period, and whatever the form in which it is expressed, it would be entirely wrong to think that Britain will be an exception in this matter. Experience elsewhere shows only too clearly that the battle for the soul of the army is a necessary part of the struggle for a radical transformation of society.

NOTES

1 In this context, however, we should not ignore the significance of the new stirrings among the police whose growing demands for the right to have a trade union, to affiliate to the TUC and take industrial action are motivated not solely by dissatisfaction over wages. They are influenced, too, by the general growth of trade union organisation in Britain which now embraces over 11 million working people in all walks of life; and they are not unaware that industrial muscle has proved in recent years a potent force for winning successes for organised workers.

2 It is interesting to note that Britain's defence expenditure (officially estimated for 1977–8 at £6,329 million) as a percentage of Gross National Product (5·5 per cent) is greater than that of all other NATO countries with the exception of the United States (6·4 per cent) and Greece (7·1 per cent). (See the Defence Estimates 1977.)

3 List taken from a compilation by Rod Caird, *Morning Star*, 10 October 1975.

4 See R. J. Spector, *Freedom for the Forces* (undated pamphlet of the National Council for Civil Liberties) for a unique account of the democratic movement in the British army at the end of the Second World War.

5 Collective actions by airmen against their grievances in Karachi and Kallang (Singapore), were treated as mutiny, and their leaders arrested. L.A.C. Attwood (Karachi) was court-martialled and found guilty, but had his sentence quashed following widespread protests in Britain. Aircraftsman Norris Cymbalist, Kallang, was sentenced to 10 years' penal servitude (later reduced to 5). Strikes by soldiers in Egypt protesting against the slowing down of demobilisation were also treated as mutinies, and again the leaders were arrested.

6 *The British Army in the Nuclear Age* (Army League pamphlet, 1959).

7 Frank Kitson, *Low Intensity Operations*, London, 1971.

8 At the time he wrote the foreword he was Chief of General Staff. Brigadier Kitson is no unorthodox maverick; his book represents very much the official army view. After all, he is the Commandant of the Army's School of Infantry at Warminster.

9 Kitson, op. cit., p. 3.

10 op. cit., p. 25.

11 As quoted in *Time Out*, op. cit.

12 Kitson does the same. See above.

13 'Military intelligence has now acquired a comprehensive file on almost everbody' in Northern Ireland, according to Charles Douglas-Home, *The Times*, 16 August 1974.

14 See, for example, *The New Technology of Repression – Lessons from Ireland*, British Society for Social Responsibility in Science, 1974.

15 A similar force is the Selous Scouts employed by the Smith regime in Rhodesia against the national liberation movement.

16 SAS and direct mercenaries sometimes merge. SAS personnel have been reported to have taken part in military actions in Malaysia and Thailand, and there is some suspicion that some may be operating in southern Africa, including in Smith's army in Rhodesia (see article by Chris Mullin, *Tribune*, 16 February 1976).

17 Brigadier Bidwell, Editor of the Royal United Services Institute journal, in a report of an RUSI seminar on 'The Role of the Armed Forces in Peacekeeping in the 1970s', held in April 1973.

18 *The New Technology of Repression*, op. cit., p. 40.

19 See *Hansard*, 24 January 1974.

20 Resolution on 'Britain and Northern Ireland', adopted by the 34th National Congress of the Communist Party of Great Britain, 15–18 November 1975.

21 It is also worrying that, according to Army Minister Robert Brown, a number of British officers, including some serving in Northern Ireland, have received special training in the United States special warfare school at Fort Bragg (*Morning Star*, 28 October 1976).

22 Chris Mullin, special feature, 'How to Win Friends', *Guardian*, 16 July 1976.

23 'Half buffoon, half executioner' – see Ramon Sender, *The War in Spain*, London, 1937, p. 19.

24 Not to be confused with Sir Robert Thompson who 'pioneered' the 'stategic hamlets' in Malaya, and advised the United States on similar tactics in South Vietnam.

25 Until recently, according to Mullin, Sir Peter was the Co-ordinator of Intelligence in the Cabinet Office.

26 Sir Harold Wilson, when he was Prime Minister, warned that these mercenaries 'presented a potential threat to democracy in Britain which could not be ignored' (*The Times*, 11 February 1976). Despite these brave words, and the Prime Minister's statement that 'lists of former soldiers' were being used by those recruiting mercenaries, nothing really effective has been done to stop this sordid trade.

27 Mullin, op. cit.

28 Martin Woollacott, 'The Troops' New Role', *Guardian*, 1 July 1974.

29 Tony Bunyan, *The Political Police in Britain*, pp. 278–9, London, 1976. This study provides a remarkable amount of information, showing conclusively the way in which the police have been used for anti-working class and anti-democratic political purposes; and, more alarming, the extent to which their future participation in such activities is being prepared on a still more substantial scale, and in association with the military.

30 See *Police on the Homefront*, National/Action Research on the Military-Industrial Complex; Philadelphia, 1971.

31 ibid.

32 ibid.

33 See *Observer*, 6 February 1977. This is approaching the size of the police force itself.

34 A newspaper column has alleged that 'the British Army has been training Securicor people in handling arms' (Open File, *Guardian*, 13 July 1974).

35 It is important to note that it was formed mainly to provide a force to man industries and services in the event of strikes.

36 'Column 88' is in reality a para-military organisation of fascist sympathisers. 'It has strong international links and its members are said to include several Army officers' (*Guardian*, 20 April 1976).

37 And to the police, for that matter; as well as the need to press for the banning of private armies, and the severe restriction and control of commercial security organisations.

38 Ron Thomas, 'Soldiers' Rights', *Labour Monthly*, August 1976.

39 Analysing the defeat of Popular Unity in Chile, Millas has noted that failure to win the middle strata to the side of the democratic movement enabled imperialism and reaction to make 'the middle strata the social basis for the fascist rising'. Given the 'family ties and social origin (middle strata) of most officers of the armed forces', this failure to win these strata in civilian life meant that the battle to win the support of the officers, and thus of the army, was lost even before the actual coup took place (see Orlando Millas, 'Stages of the Struggle', *World Marxist Review*, February 1977, p. 40).

40 Rod Caird, 'Smaller, More Highly Trained', *Morning Star*, 7 October 1975. N.B. In the Navy, by 1970 only 39 per cent of boys entering as officers came from public or direct grant schools. By 1975 it had dropped to 29 per cent (see *Guardian*, 25 February 1976).

41 A memorandum submitted to the Royal Commission on the Private Manufacture of Trade in Arms on behalf of the Communist Party of Great Britain on 4 May 1935 stated that the Board of Directors of Vickers-Armstrong in 1932 included the former Chief of Staff of the British Army Headquarters in France, a former Master-General of the Ordnance and a member of the Army Council, former top civil servants at the Ministry of Munitions, the War Office and the Ordnance Committee.

42 It was very noticeable that in 1974, coming in the wake of major class confrontations and to the accompaniment of violent anti-trade union propaganda by most sections of the national press, articles began to appear speculating as to whether there could be an army coup in Britain. Even more ominous, there were reports of talk among officers of the need for them to be ready to intervene. It is noticeable, too, that this same period saw a certain emergence of 'vigilante' type bodies, indicating their willingness to help 'maintain law and order', especially in a strike situation.

43 We should not ignore Professor E. J. Hobsbawm's warning: 'The more the army becomes a series of specialised and well-paid élite groups – parachutists are a good example – the less "civilian" their reactions are likely to be' ('The Labour Movement and Military Coups', *Marxism Today*, October 1974).

Index

Abbas, Khalid Hassan, 118
Abboud, General, 26, 67, 100–2
Acland, Sir Richard, 280
Aden, 278–9
Adoula, Cyril, 58
Agee, Philip, 59, 64, 65, 172
Ahmed, Ahmed Taha, 73
Aidit, D. N., 131, 139, 145, 152
Alessandri, Jorge, 168
Alexander, General, 128
Algeria, 14, 53, 67, 68, 255, 273;
   Communist Party, 98
Allaun, Frank (MP), 296
Allende, Salvador, 9, 56, 67, 152,
   154ff.
Altamirano, Amanda, 190
Amin, Idi, 8, 129
Anaconda Copper Company, 161,
   164
Anderson, Jack, 167
Andreski, Stanislav, 45, 47
Angola, 23, 129, 216, 218–20, 278–9,
   290; MPLA, 97
Antunes, Melo, 234
Araya, Captain Arturo, 202
Arbenz, General, 56, 58, 67
Argentina, 9, 82, 85, 212
Attwood, L.A.C., 300
Azcarate, Manuel, 252–3, 272

Babiker El Nur, Lieut.-Col., 108,118
Babiker, Tigani, 81, 97
Badoglio, Marshal, 273
Baillot, Louis, 262, 272–3
Bakir, Ahmed, 76

Bakry, Mohammed, 73
Bangla-Desh, 9, 145
Barre, Mohammed Siyad, 79, 90–3,
   95, 98–9
Batista, Fulgencio, 45, 84, 88
Be'eri, Eliezer, 7, 15, 53ff., 64, 76, 80,
   86, 97–8
Ben Bella, Ahmed, 67
Berlinguer, Enrico, 16, 35, 194–5, 212
Bethlehem Company, 161
Bidwell, Brigadier Richard, 301
Bismarck, 39, 42
Bissell, Richard, 59, 60, 61, 63–4, 149
Boldrini, Arrigo, 263, 268, 273
Bolivia, 9, 25, 60, 67, 84; Communist
   Party of, 84, 98
Bordaberry, Juan Mana, 49, 85, 210
Bosch, Juan, 56
Bouvier, Robert, 260
Brazil, 9, 48, 67, 82, 85
Bredin, Major-General Humphrey,
   292
Brinton, Crane, 22, 36
British Honduras, 279
Broe, William, 167
Brüning, Heinrich, 13
Bundy, McGeorge, 58
Burchett, Wilfred, 64–5
Burma, 9, 60, 67, 278
Busia, Dr Kofi, 8, 43
Busquets, Major Julion, 253–4

Caamano, Francisco, 84
Caetano, Marcello, 69, 121, 216–17,
   221, 223–4, 229, 237

Caird, Rod, 295
Caldwell, Malcolm, 152
Caltex Oil Company, 148
Cambodia (Kampuchea), 49, 56, 129
Carr, Robert, 288
Carrillo, Santiago, 212
Carvalho, Otelo de, 234, 239, 241
Carver, General Sir Michael, 281
Castro, Fidel, 97, 115
Chairul, 134
Chiang Kai-shek, 131
Chile, 9, 48, 74, 85, 123, 131, 152, 154–214, 256, 267, 275, 292ff.; Christian Democrat Party, 156, 159–60, 164, 168, 170–1, 178, 182, 187–9, 190ff.; Communist Party, 154–213; Confederation of United Workers (CUT), 164, 185; *El Arrayan Report*, 178, 186, 210–11; Fatherland and Freedom, 179–80, 193; Independent Popular Action, 156; MAPU (Movement of United Popular Action), 156, 189, 210; MAPU (Workers and Peasants), 210; MIR (Movement of the Revolutionary Left), 182, 189, 192; Nationalist Party, 159, 160, 168, 178, 189, 190, 212; People's Front, 163; Popular Action Front, 163; Popular Front, 163; Popular Unity Committees, 186; Popular Unity Government, 9, 16, 49, 56, 67, 85, 154–213; Radical Democrats, 190; Radical Party, 156, 179, 210; Social Democratic Party, 156, 210; Socialist Party, 156, 180, 188–9, 192, 212; Tacna Regiment, 164; University of Chile Students' Federation, 188; Young Communist League, 185
China, 15, 60, 129, 131, 150–1
Clutterbuck, Major-General Richard, 290

Cohen, Aharon, 66, 67, 74, 76
Communist International, 32
Communist Manifesto, 70
Conein, Lieut.-Col. Lucien, 58
Congo, Belgian, *see* Zaire
Connolly, James, 79, 115–16
Corvalan, Luis, 183–6, 189, 196, 198, 211–12
Cox, Idris, 76
Cronje, S., Ling, M., and Cronje, G., 121
Cuba, 45, 49, 58, 60, 84, 97, 129, 154; Bay of Pigs, 60, 64
Cunhal, Alvaro, 216–19, 223, 225, 246–7
Cymbalist, Norris, 300
Cyprus, 14, 278–9, 281

Davidson, Basil, 90, 96, 98, 246
Decraene, Phillipe, 8
De Gaulle, General Charles, 249, 268, 273
D'Estaing, Giscard, 173
Diem, President, 58–9
Dominican Republic, 49, 56, 84, 167–8, 196
Don, General, 58
Douglas-Home, Charles, 301
Dulles, Allen, 64
Dutt, R. Palme, 15

Eanes, General Ramalho, 239
Ebert, Friedrich, 12
Ecuador, 10, 84, 154
Egypt, 43, 51, 66, 67, 70ff., 88–9, 116, 118–19, 129, 145, 300; Arab Socialist Union, 104; Communist Party, 72–3, 89, 98; Confederation of Trade Unions, 73; Free Officers' Movement, 72–3; Middle East Defence Pact, 72; National Committee of Workers and Students, 72–3; Trade Union Congress, 73; Wafd, 73; Workers'

Committee of National Liberation, 73

El Atta, Major Hashim Mohammed, 108, 111–12ff.

El-Sheikh, Shafie Ahmed, 103, 111–12, 121

Engels, Frederick, 21, 26, 36, 38–40, 42–3, 46–7, 91, 123, 203

European Court of Human Rights, 287

European Economic Community, 226

Export-Import Bank, 173

Farouk, King, 43, 52, 66, 72–3

Fifield, Professor Russell, 148

Figueroa, Luis, 188

Finland, 10–11, 131, 248

First, Ruth, 57, 64–7, 74, 76, 101, 120

France, 7, 11, 14, 27, 29, 35, 39ff., 50, 53, 63, 80, 123, 137, 155, 193–4, 211, 248–9, 255–62, 268–70, 272–8, 297; Common Programme, 256, 259, 272; Communist Party, 246, 255–62, 265, 268; Communist Youth Movement, 273; Left Radicals, 255, 272; OAS, 262, 273; Police Federation, 274; Popular Union, 255; St Cyr, 81; Socialist Party, 255, 272

Franco, General, 11, 123, 131, 141, 253, 255, 272ff., 289

Frei, Eduardo, 159, 161, 164, 168–70, 173, 200, 210, 212

Gabon, 8, 255

Garang, Joseph, 104

Germany, 11–13, 32, 39, 41–2, 50–1, 53, 63, 123, 137, 248, 263–4, 273, 278; Freikorps, 13; Horsing terror, Saxony, 12; Kapp Putsch, 12, 13; National Socialist Party, 13–14; Zeigner Government (Saxony), 12

Germany, Federal Republic of, 210, 258, 270–72; ADS (Working Groups of Democratic Soldiers), 270; DGB (German Trade Union Centre), 270; Social Democrats, 246

Ghana, 8, 43, 48, 67, 127, 145, 279

Gomes, General Costa, 217, 223

Gonçalves, Vasco, 215, 231, 233, 239

Gott, Richard, 98, 182, 211

Goulart, João, 67

Gowon, General Yakubu, 67, 74

Gramsci, Antonio, 12, 16, 19, 32, 36

Great Britain, 7, 11, 17–21, 24, 28–9, 33–6, 40, 50ff., 63–4, 72, 116, 118–19, 123, 162–3, 246, 248, 263–4, 268, 275–302; Bramshill Police Training College, 289–90; British Road to Socialism, 283, 285, 296; Camberley College, 290; 'Column 88', 292, 302; Communist Party, 280, 283, 285, 288, 296, 301–2; Conservative Party, 280; Heathrow (police/army exercise), 287–8, 291; Industrial Relations Act, 24; Institute for the Study of Conflict, 246, 289–90; Labour Government, 70; Labour Party, 19, 280; Liberal Party, 280; NALGO (National Association of Local Government Workers), 34; National Front, 292; NUPE (National Union of Public Employees), 34; Pentonville Five, 24; Porton Down Chemical Warfare Research Centre, 289; Prevention of Terrorism Act, 287; Royal Military College of Science, 290; Sandhurst, 81, 125; SAS (Special Air Service), 279, 286, 290–1, 296, 301; Securicor, 301; Soldiers' Parliaments, 280; TUC, 24, 34, 300; UCS (Upper Clyde Shipbuilders), 24; Warminster School of Infantry, 300

Greathead, Col. Claud, 290

Greece, 7, 11, 14, 46, 53, 56, 75, 277–8, 300

Grigg, Sir James, 280

Groener, General Wilhelm, 12

Grove, General Marmaduke, 212

Guatemala, 56, 58, 60, 67

Guevara, Che, 25

Guggenheim Company, 161

Guinea-Bissau, 23, 129, 216, 220, 278

Gutierrez, General Manuel, 272

Guyana, 56, 279

Halpern, Manfred, 85–6, 98

Hamadalla, Major Farouk Osman, 108, 118

Hansen, Roy Allen, 200

Hatta, 134

Helms, Richard, 64, 166, 167, 169

Hilsman, Roger, 148, 152

Hitler, Adolf, 13–14, 131, 289

Hobbing, Enno, 167

Horthy, Admiral, 10

Howard, John Brigham, 149

Hungary, 10–11, 50, 248

Indonesia, 9, 48, 60, 67, 131–54, 212, 278; BTI (Peasant's Union), 143–4; Communist Party, 131–53; Generals' Council, 133ff.; Murba Party, 134; Pemuda Rakjat, 143; Revolutionary Council, 137–8, 152; September 30th Movement, 131–53; SOBSI (Trade Union Centre), 143

Inter-American Development Bank, 173–4

International Telephone and Telegraph (ITT), 154, 167, 171, 179, 180

Iran, 56, 60, 67

Iraq, 49, 66ff., 89, 129; Ba'ath Socialist Party, 71, 90; Communist Party, 70–1, 89, 98; Itihad Al-Shab, 71;

National Congress Party, 71; Portsmouth Treaty, 70

Ireland, 50, 53, 79, 275, 287; Easter Rising, 112, 115–16; Northern Ireland, 14, 275, 277ff.

Ironsi, General Aguiyi, 67, 74

Italy, 7, 11, 14, 19, 27, 35, 50–1, 53, 123, 137, 155, 192–4, 211, 248, 263ff., 297; Catholics, 262; Christian Democratic Party, 264; Communist Party, 11–12, 20, 36, 94, 99, 246, 262ff.; National Liberation Committees, 263; Social Democrat Party, 20, 36; Socialist Party, 20, 36, 262

Jagan, Cheddi, 56

Janke, Peter, 290

Janowicz, Morris, 80, 97

Japan, 63, 137, 155, 278; Communist Party, 36

Jesuino, Commander, 235

Julvez, Captain José, 254

Karamanlis, Constantine, 46

Karamessines, Thomas, 170–2

Karume, Sheikh Abeid, 8

Kassem, General, 70, 71, 89, 95

Keita, Modibo, 8, 67

Kemal Atatürk, 68

Kennecott Copper Company, 154, 161, 174

Kennedy, Senator Edward, 173

Kennedy, Gavin, 9, 15, 125, 130

Kenya, 278–9, 281, 286

Kerensky, Alexander, 50, 205

Khamis, Mustapha, 73

Khan, Ayub, 9, 67

Khan, Yayha, 9, 67

Kissinger, Henry, 65, 163, 166ff., 180, 210

Kitson, Brigadier Frank, 281ff., 291, 300

Korea, 60, 278

Kornilov, General, 75, 123, 130
Korry, Edward, 165, 167–9

Laos, 49, 60, 129
Le Bon, Gustave, 22, 36
Leigh, General Gustavo, 197
Lenin, V. I., 16, 21–2, 26, 28–33, 35ff., 75–9, 90–1, 96–7, 99, 102, 106, 112, 116, 119ff., 135–6, 141, 204
Libya, 8, 74, 78, 116, 118–19
Liebknecht, Karl, 12
Lieuwen, Edwin, 82, 84, 98
Ling, Major-General F. A. H., 290
Llano, Queipo de, 289
Lodge, Cabot Henry, 58, 59
Longo, Luigi, 263
Lonrho (Company), 121
Lourenço, Vasco, 234
Ludendorff, Field-Marshal Erich, 289
Lukman, M. H., 131, 139
Luxemburg, Rosa, 12

McCone, John, 167
Machel, Samora, 97
Machiavelli, Niccoló, 16, 35
Mahgoub, Abdel Khalig, 109–11, 121
Makarios, President, 14, 56
Malaya, 278, 281, 301
Malaysia, 278, 301
Mali, 8, 67
Mannerheim, Marshal, 10, 131
Mansfield, Peter, 73, 76
Mao Tse-Tung, 214
Marchais, Georges, 259
Marchetti, Victor, and Marks, John D., 58–62, 64–5
Martin, Kingsley, 70
Marx, Karl, 26, 28, 36ff., 90–1, 115, 119, 124, 136, 140, 203
Mason, Roy, M.P., 296
Mendoza, General Cesar, 197
Merino, Admiral Jose Toribio, 197
Merriam, William, 176
Miliband, Ralph, 55, 211

Millas, Orlando, 177, 210–11, 302
Mirsky, Dr G., 40–1, 43, 47, 66–7, 76, 80, 97
Mitchell, John, 166
Mitterand, François, 257
Mobutu, Lieut.-Gen. Joseph, 7, 58, 67
Molena, Captain Jesus, 254
Mossadeq, Mohammed, 56, 67
Mowrer, Edgar, 11, 15
Mozambique, 23, 97, 129, 216–17, 220, 278; Frelimo, 97
Muhiaddin, Khalid, 72
Mujibar, Sheikh, 145
Mussolini, Benito, 11

Nasser, Gamal Abdul, 69, 71–3, 76, 79, 88, 95, 145
Nato, 46, 53, 226, 267, 277–8, 292, 300
Neguib, Mohammed, 72–3
Netherlands, 137, 270, 272; BVD (Broad Left), 270; Communist Party, 270; VVDM (Conscripts Organization), 270
Neto, Agostinho, 97
Nigeria, 67, 74–5, 279; Biafra, 67, 279
Nimeiry, General Jaffar, 75, 90, 103ff.
Nixon, Richard, 163ff.
Njono (Indonesian trade unionist), 131
Njoto (Indonesian trade unionist), 131
Nkrumah, Kwame, 67, 68, 127–8, 145
Nuri Said, 70–1, 76

Obote, Milton, 8, 67, 145
O'Brien, William, 115
Organisation of American States (OAS), 166

Pakistan, 9, 67
Panama, 10, 84, 154, 200
Papandreou, George, 46
Papadopoulos, Konstantinos, 46
Pearse, Padraic, 116

Pearson, Lieut.-Gen. Sir Thomas, 290

Pecchioli, Ugo, 263, 273

Peet, Admiral Ray, 149

Peron, Juan, 9

Peru, 10, 25, 28, 60, 67, 79, 83–4, 98, 154, 196

Pestalozza, Luigi, 91ff.

Pétain, Marshal, 249

Peterson, Peter, 176

Philippines, 60

Pilsudski, Marshal, 10

Pinochet, General, 49, 98, 131, 141, 155, 168, 197, 202, 212

Poland, 10–11, 248

Porter, Dwight, 180

Portugal, 7, 10, 22ff., 36, 68, 121, 129, 141, 194, 211, 214–47, 250, 253, 256, 272, 276, 278, 295, 297; AFM (Armed Forces Movement), 14, 22–3, 35, 68–9, 215–16, 221–6, 229–40, 242, 244; Centre Social Democrats, 233, 239, 246; Communist Party, 68, 217, 219ff. 276; Constituent Assembly, 226, 235–6ff., 238–9, 240, 243; Constitution, 215, 239–40; Council of State, 234; Intersyndical, 237–8; Parliament (elections), 238–9; People's Democratic Party (PPD), 225, 233, 237–39, 246; Portuguese Democratic Movement (MDP), 246; Povo Unido, 239; Sixth Provisional Government, 215; Socialist Party, 217, 225, 231–2, 235–9, 245–6; 'Soldiers United Will Win', 241; Supreme Revolutionary Council, 234, 240–1

Prats, General Carlos, 85, 98, 170–1, 179, 201–2, 212

Puerefoy, John, 58

Radek, Karl, 32

Rahman, Hag Abdel, 111

Ramanantsoa, Major-General Gabriel, 8

Rand Corporation, 148

Ransom, David, 148, 152

Rhodesia, 279, 289, 290, 301; Secret Service, 290; Selous Scouts, 301

Rudé, George, 22–3, 36

Russia, 19, 29ff., 52, 248, see also Soviet Union; Bolsheviks, 28, 36, 203; October Revolution, 10, 29, 32, 46, 50, 75, 204–5; 1905 Revolution, 115, 203–4

Sadat, Anwar, 73, 118, 125

Sakirman, 139

Sanguinetti, Vice-Admiral, 258

Santos, Eduardo, 89, 98

Schneider, General René, 168, 169, 170–1, 196–7, 199, 212

Scott, Peter Dale, 149, 152, 153

Shawcross, William, 176, 211

Sihanouk, Norodom, 56, 64–5

Silva, General Morais e, 241

Slade, Ted, 244, 247

Smith, Hedrick, 58, 64

Sobelev, Alexander, 204–7, 212

Somalia, 8, 43, 67–8, 74, 79, 90–6, 98–9, 122; Revolutionary Socialist Party, 90ff.; Supreme Revolutionary Council, 90, 98; Youth League, 91

Souper, Col. Roberto, 179, 201

South Africa, 275, 278, 289, 290; BOSS (South African Secret Service), 289, 290

Soviet Union, 14, 51, 80, 91, 94, 128, 141, 277, see also Russia

Spain, 7, 11, 14, 27, 35, 40–1, 50–3, 131, 141, 155, 248ff., 270ff.; Communist Party, 246, 251–2, 270–2, 276; Military Democratic Union, 254; Popular Front Government, 123

Spinola, General Antonio, 216, 231, 233-4, 241
Suarez, Mario, 215, 228
Subandrio, Dr, 134
Sudan, 8, 25, 48-9, 67, 74-5, 78, 90, 100-22, 129, 132, 151, 154; Communist Party, 75, 79, 98, 100-22, 151; Federation of Workers' Trade Unions, 103, 111-12; Free Officers' Organisation, 100ff., Movement of Democratic Soldiers, 113, 118-19; National Democratic Front, 105, 107, 113; Women's Association, 109; Youth Federation, 109
Suez (1956 war), 278
Suharto, Lieut.-Gen. T. N. J., 148
Sukarni, 134
Sukarno, 67-8, 131ff.
Sumitro, 148
Sutowo, Col. Dr Ibun, 148
Syria, 28, 49; Communist Party, 98

Tanzania, 129, 279
Teitelboim, Volodya, 207-9, 213
Thailand, 9, 301
Thieme, General Roberto, 179-80, 193
Thomas, Ron (MP), 293, 302
Thompson, Sir Robert, 301
Thompson, Brigadier W. F. K., 290
Togliatti, Palmiro, 12, 192-3, 211, 273
Tomic, Romiro, 159
Torres, General Ivan, 9, 67, 84-5
Torrijos, General Omar, 84
Tri-Continental Conference, 140
Truman, David, 65
Tshombe, Moishe, 67
Turkey, 67-8, 76

Uganda, 7-8, 48, 67, 129, 145

United States, 10, 45-6, 51ff., 83, 85, 88, 98, 128, 147ff., 199ff., 210, 263-4, 291, 300-1; CIA, 56-65, 87, 147-50, 156, 162ff., 180, 193, 199, 278; FBI, 62, 291; Ford Foundation, 149; Fort Bragg School of Special Warfare, 81, 125, 291, 301, Fort Gulick, 81; International Police Academy, 291; OSS, 58 64; Pentagon, 14, 53, 58, 62, 180; State Department, 148-9, 162-3, 167; Watergate, 210; 40 Committee, 65, 165, 168, 180
Untung, Colonel, 132, 133, 135, 137-9, 150
Uruguay, 9, 25, 48-9, 65, 85, 154; Frente Amplio, 9, 154

Vega, Luis Mercier, 82-3, 98
Velasco, General Alvarado, 79, 84, 98
Viaux, General Roberto, 164
Vickers Armstrong, 302
Videla, Gonzalez, 200
Vietnam, 49, 51-2, 58-60, 129, 275, 278, 301
Von Papen, Franz, 13

Walker, General Sir Walter, 292
Wilkinson, Sir Peter, 290, 301
Wood, Dennis B., 45, 47
World Bank, 173-4

Yani, General, 150
Yemen, Democratic Republic of, 49, 66, 129

Zaire, 7, 58, 60, 67, 279
Zanzibar, 8, 279
Zinoviev, Grigori, 32
Zorina, I., 197-8, 212